P9-AGA-125

DATE DUE

DEMCO 38-296

Handbook of Subacute Health Care

Kathleen M. Griffin, PhD
President and Chief Executive Officer
Griffin Management, Inc.
Scottsdale, Arizona

An Aspen Publication®
Aspen Publishers, Inc.
Gaithersburg, Maryland
1995

Riverside Community College
Library
AUG '97 4800 Magnolia Avenue
Riverside, California 92506

RA 394 .G74 1995

Griffin, Kathleen M.

Handbook of subacute health
  care

Library of Congress Cataloging-in-Publication Data

Griffin, Kathleen M.
Handbook of subacute health care / Kathleen M. Griffin
p.   cm.
Includes bibliographical references and index.
ISBN 0-8342-0661-7
1. Health services administration—Handbooks, manuals, etc.
I. Title.
[DNLM: 1. Long-Term Care—handbooks. 2. Health Policy—United
States—handbooks. 3. Nursing Homes—United States—handbooks.
4. Hospitals, Convalescent—United States—handbooks. 5. Insurance,
Health—United States—handbooks. WX 39 G851h 1995]
RA394.G74   1995
362.1′068—dc20
DNLM/DLC
for Library of Congress
95-15485
CIP

Copyright © 1995 by Aspen Publishers, Inc.
All rights reserved.

Aspen Publishers, Inc., grants permission for photocopying for limited personal or internal use.
This consent does not extend to other kinds of copying, such as copying for
general distribution, for advertising or promotional purposes, for creating new collective
works, or for resale. For information, address Aspen Publishers, Inc.,
Permissions Department, 200 Orchard Ridge Drive, Suite 200,
Gaithersburg, Maryland 20878.

Editorial Resources: Amy Myers-Payne

Library of Congress Catalog Number:
ISBN: 0-8342-0661-7

Printed in the United States of America

1 2 3 4 5

Table of Contents

Contributors

Author/Editor

Kathleen M. Griffin, PhD
President and Chief Executive Officer
Griffin Management, Inc.
Scottsdale, Arizona

Coordinating Editor

Carol Frattali, PhD
Associate
Griffin Management, Inc.
Scottsdale, Arizona

Allwyn J. Baptist
Partner
National Director of Hospital Services
BDO Seidman
Chicago, Illinois

Harvey Brown, Jr., MSN, NHA
Executive Vice President
Presbyterian SeniorCare
Washington, Pennsylvania

Michael H. Cook, JD
Partner
Katten Muchin & Zavis
Washington, DC

Laurel L. Fleming, JD
Associate
Katten Muchin & Zavis
Chicago, Illinois

John F. Heller, MPA, MHA
Senior Vice President
Medical Specialty Unit Operations

Integrated Health Services, Inc.
Owings Mill, Maryland

Patricia Larkins Hicks, PhD
President
Outcomes Management Group
Columbus, Ohio

Christine M. MacDonell
National Director
Medical Rehabilitation Division
Commission on Accreditation of
Rehabilitation Facilities
Tucson, Arizona

Phyllis A. Madigan
Senior Vice President of
Business Development
Mariner Health Care
Mystic, Connecticut

Mary M. Marshall, PhD
President
Management and Planning Services, Inc.
Atlanta, Georgia

Theodore N. McDowell, Jr., JD
Partner
Parker, Hudson, Rainer & Dobbs
Atlanta, Georgia

Murry Mercier, CPA
Vice President
Information Systems
Integrated Health Services, Inc.
Owings Mill, Maryland

Peg Pashkow, MEd, PT
Vice President, Rehabilitation Services
Rehabilitation Hospital at Heather Hill, Inc.
Chardon, Ohio

Ellen P. Pesch, JD, LLM
Associate
Katten Muchin & Zavis
Chicago, Illinois

Jonathan L. Rue, JD
Partner
Parker, Hudson, Rainer & Dobbs
Atlanta, Georgia

Jerome R. Serwa
Senior Manager
Healthcare Consulting Services
BDO Seidman
Chicago, Illinois

Mary Tellis-Nayak, MSN, MPH
Director
Long-Term Care Accreditation Service
Joint Commission on Accreditation of
Healthcare Organizations
Oakbrook Terrace, Illinois

Cristie Upshaw Travis
Chief Executive Officer
Memphis Business Group on Health
Memphis, Tennessee

Mark W. Vaughan, MA
Medical Planner
Watkins Carter Hamilton Architects
Bellaire, Texas

Valerie S. Wilbur
Director of Government Affairs
Katten Muchin & Zavis
Washington, DC

Preface

During the past several years, subacute providers have demonstrated that there is a cost-effective alternative to acute hospital care. As health care providers and payers consolidate and integrate, subacute levels of care tend to be critical factors to the successful management of health care costs. Minimizing costs without compromising quality, however, requires the presence of certain fundamental structures as well as subacute care operating systems.

This book is intended to serve as a basic resource for subacute providers. Each contributing author has had a significant amount of experience in managing or consulting with successful subacute care programs. As a result, the information reflects actual operations rather than hypothetical solutions to operational problems.

Individuals involved with, but not providing subacute care, also will find this book of value. For example, payers, employers, legislators, regulators and investors might evaluate subacute providers in light of benchmark information about subacute care contained in this book.

Although the health care system is expected to continue to undergo dramatic changes in the future, the subacute industry appears to be a firmly rooted niche in the continuum of patient care, and one that will continue to grow and develop. This book should serve as a point of reference for subacute care as it evolves.

I wish to express my gratitude to each one of the contributing authors who have shared valuable expertise in their chapters. I also want to thank Carol Frattali, PhD, for managing the multitude of tasks related to coordinating and editing the manuscripts. Thanks is due also to Jane Garwood and Amy Myers-Payne of Aspen Publishers for their continued support. Finally, I want to express my appreciation to my staff, especially Florence Esdon and Nancy Gosewisch, for their untiring dedication and assistance in completing this book.

—Kathleen M. Griffin, PhD

Part I

Introduction

The Subacute Care Industry

Kathleen M. Griffin

The subacute care industry, which began to emerge in the mid 1980s, is a response to at least five factors:

1. *New technologies:* New medical technologies are increasing survival rates of infants born with severe anomalies and sustain life in patients of all ages with disease and trauma. Many of these patients require long periods of hospitalization. Some never recover fully and require intensive nursing and therapies for the rest of their lives.

2. *The increased number of elderly Americans:* Although Americans are living longer than ever before, often their last years of life are filled with chronic medical problems that require prolonged, intensive, and extensive health care. Life styles of today's elderly Americans were not influenced by the wellness orientation prevalent in those born after 1960. Many older adults have chronic conditions that require inpatient care at some point in their lives.

3. *The rise in managed care in the United States:* As health maintenance organization (HMO) penetration continues to in-

crease, and as other forms of managed care are implemented by insurers, there seems to be more utilization of alternative health care delivery sites for patients who previously stayed hospitalized. Although home health has been a predominant alternative health care delivery site for these types of patients, the level of intensity of services required by the patient may preclude discharge to home, or the cost of home health services at the intensity level required may exceed the cost of a subacute health care unit. Moreover, given today's changing family constellation, the presence of a caretaker in the home is rare, and the at-risk patient may require inpatient care.

4. *Acceptance of alternative health care delivery sites:* Americans now have grown accustomed to receiving the care that they formerly received in the acute hospital in a variety of other settings: as hospital outpatients, in physician's offices, in surgicenters, in mobile vans, in subacute care facilities, and at home.

5. *Medicare reimbursement:* The demographics of aging in the United States have caused a general swelling of the popula-

tion of Medicare beneficiaries and a disproportionate number of Medicare patients in acute hospitals. Concurrently, the Medicare prospective payment system (PPS) for acute hospitals has spawned aggressive utilization review in acute hospitals and active programs to seek appropriate discharge placement for Medicare patients as soon as medically possible. Although there is no federal category for reimbursement of subacute care, there are strategies that allow favorable reimbursement for subacute care level Medicare patients in skilled nursing beds.

During the past 5 years, there has been a gradual change in the nature of subacute care. Initially, the focus of subacute providers was patients with chronic care needs, patients who probably would not improve their health status to a functionally independent level. Chronic care patients would live out their lives in the subacute care facility or would be transferred at some point to a less expensive level of care, such as a skilled nursing facility. Four events, however, have prompted a movement away from the chronic care patient in favor of the transitional patient, that is to say the patient who requires a hospital level of care but who has the potential for making significant improvement in his or her health care status in the short term with the probability of returning home.

First, hospitalized patients are now advised at admission about their do not resuscitate rights. Patients who may have remained hospitalized on life support systems for years now may be allowed to die with dignity. Second, advancements in technology have made it possible for some chronic care patients on life support systems to be cared for at home, thus reducing the population of chronic care patients who remain as inpatients. Third, special Medicaid rates for chronic care patients and case-mix Medicaid reimbursement systems for residents in nursing facilities in certain states have induced skilled nursing facilities in those states to upgrade staffing levels and expertise to attract chronic care patients to their general skilled nursing beds. Finally, the increase

in the availability of hospital-like subacute care facilities combined with favorable experiences of managed care patients and case managers with the care programs provided in these types of facilities has persuaded case managers and discharge planners that subacute care facilities often are the best choice of placement for certain patients.

SUBACUTE CARE DEFINED

Definitions of subacute care have been prepared by several organizations. The definitions developed by two organizations, the International Subacute Healthcare Association (ISHA) and the Joint Commission on Accreditation of Healthcare Organizations, appear to contain the key components reflected in most other definitions.

ISHA defines subacute care as follows: Subacute care is a comprehensive and cost-effective inpatient program for patients who have had an acute event as a result of an illness, injury, or exacerbation of a disease process; have a determined course of treatment; and do not require intensive diagnostic and/or invasive procedures. The severity of the patient's condition requires physician direction, intensive nursing care and significant utilization of ancillaries, and an outcomes-focused interdisciplinary approach utilizing a professional team to deliver complex clinical interventions (medical and/or rehabilitation). Typically short term, the subacute level of care is utilized as an inpatient alternative to an acute care hospital admission or as an alternative to continued hospitalization.[1]

- *Comprehensive:* Subacute care programs are designed to provide the full range of necessary medical, rehabilitation, and professional services required to provide efficient and effective care for the specific medical conditions treated within a program.
- *Cost effective:* Subacute programs are designed to maximize value to patients and payer sources through the delivery of necessary, appropriate care with optimal outcomes in the lowest-cost setting.

• *Outcomes orientation:* Subacute programs are designed to achieve quantifiable, measurable outcomes such as, but not necessarily limited to, functional restoration, clinical stabilization, avoidance of medical complications or exacerbation of a disease process, and discharge to the patient's least restrictive living environment.

• *Professional staffing:* Subacute interventions, because of their duration, complexity, and intensity, are provided under the direction of a physician. An interdisciplinary team provides a coordinated program of care. The team may include a physician, nurses, therapists, social workers, psychologists, pharmacists, dietitians, case managers, discharge planners, and other professionals.

• *Program description:* Programs are organized around patient populations with related treatment or service needs that result in common goals, measures of outcomes, treatment plans, and resources delivered at similar levels of intensity. Subacute programs may include medical rehabilitation and respiratory nutrition, cardiac, oncologic, and wound care programs. Levels of intensity for specific disciplines will vary from program to program but will generally range from 3.5 to 8.0 nursing hours per patient day, up to 5 hours per patient day for therapy, as well as appropriate use of nutrition, laboratory, pharmacy, radiology, and other ancillary services.

• *Site of care:* The site of care is not a distinguishing characteristic of subacute care. Subacute programs can be delivered in a variety of settings, including acute hospitals, specialty hospitals, freestanding skilled nursing facilities, hospital-based skilled nursing units, outpatient ambulatory centers, residential living facilities, and home health settings. Most existing subacute programs are inpatient programs serving as an alternative to prolonged acute hospitalization. Given the existence of a broad range of treatment and cost alternatives to acute hospitalization, however, the site of care should not be a limiting factor in the delivery of subacute services. Distinctions among subacute services should be focused on program differences, not settings.

• *Continuum of care:* Subacute care is essential to the development of a complete continuum of care. Subacute programs are necessary components of vertically integrated health care systems.

The definition favored by the Joint Commission is as follows: Subacute care is comprehensive inpatient care designed for someone who has an acute illness, injury, or exacerbation of a disease process. It is goal-oriented treatment rendered immediately after, or instead of, acute hospitalization to treat one or more specific, active complex medical conditions or to administer one or more technically complex treatments in the context of a person's underlying long-term conditions and overall situation. Generally, the individual's condition is such that the care does not depend heavily on high-technology monitoring or complex diagnostic procedures. Subacute care requires the coordinated services of an interdisciplinary team, including physicians, nurses, and other relevant professional disciplines, who are trained and knowledgeable in assessing and managing these specific conditions and in performing the necessary procedures. Subacute care is given as part of a specifically defined program, regardless of the site. Subacute care is generally more intensive than traditional nursing facility care and less intensive than acute care. It requires frequent (daily to weekly), recurrent patient assessment and review of the clinical course and treatment plan for a limited (several days to several months) time period, until the condition is stabilized or a predetermined treatment course is completed.[2]

SUBACUTE PATIENTS

Subacute patients vary in acuity levels and exhibit a variety of problems. Subacute services generally fall into one of these categories, however:

- medically complex patients who are chronically ill or have multiple medical problems or disorders; these patients need medical monitoring and specialized care but can be managed in a subacute setting
- respiratory care patients who require ventilator weaning or ventilator care programs as a result of a respiratory disease, injury, or impairment or who require medical and nursing care as well as therapies to recover from an acute respiratory episode
- recuperating surgery patients who need rehabilitative therapy but no longer need intensive care services
- patients who require rehabilitation for a variety of reasons, most frequently after orthopedic surgery or a stroke
- patients with head injury who have brain injuries as a result of ischemic or hemorrhagic stroke, blunt trauma, or penetrating trauma
- cardiovascular patients who require a cardiac recovery or rehabilitation program, often related to congestive heart failure or a major cardiac infarct
- patients with such medical conditions as septicemia or osteomyelitis who require short-term intravenous therapy
- oncology patients who require chemotherapy, pain management, and rehabilitation
- wound management patients with chronic wounds (eg, pressure ulcers, necrotic wounds, or peripheral vascular disease ulcerations) related to diseases that need management before the wounds will heal

Although patients of all ages may have one or more of these disorders, the vast majority of subacute patients are geriatric.

SUBACUTE CARE CATEGORIES

Despite the attempts of ISHA and the Joint Commission to define subacute care, there remains a great deal of perplexity about exactly what subacute care is. A major reason for the confusion about the definition of subacute care is that there really are four different categories of subacute care. Various providers tend to focus on one or two of the categories of subacute care.

Transitional Subacute Care

Transitional subacute care can be described as a short stay (5 to 30 days) with high nursing acuity (5.5 to 8.0 hours per patient day). Transitional subacute facilities and units are utilized by payers, providers, and physicians for patients who require regular medical care and monitoring; highly skilled and intensive nursing care; an integrated program of therapies, both rehabilitative and respiratory; and heavy utilization of pharmaceutical and laboratory services. This type of subacute care unit or facility serves as a hospital stepdown entity and results in a significant reduction of acute hospital days. A transitional subacute facility actually serves as a substitute for continued hospital stays, not as an alternative hospital discharge placement. For example, stroke patients may be transferred to a transitional subacute unit on day 5 of hospitalization in the acute hospital, and coronary bypass patients who are not off the ventilator within 4 or 5 days may be transferred for a weaning program. Transitional subacute facilities and units will have a variety of physician program directors or consultants, a dedicated staff of acute or critical care nurses, 24-hour respiratory therapy, and 7 day per week rehabilitation therapies.

Hospital-based subacute units and staff model HMO-owned subacute units typically are in this category. Because HMOs, particularly staff and group models, tend to be the most aggressive of the managed care organizations in managing acute hospital days, this is the type of subacute care entity that is prevalent in areas with high managed care and is the type that will draw the largest volume of managed care patients. Clinically, patients in transitional subacute units may require cardiac recovery from heart attacks or cardiac surgical procedures, pulmonary management for tracheostomies or ventilator weaning programs, multiple stage III and IV decubiti or vascular or other surgeries, or oncology procedures, including chemotherapy and radiation therapy. They may require rehabilitation for cerebral vascular accidents or for complications of orthopedic surgery; care for medically complex conditions combined with diabetes, digestive disorders, or renal disorders/failure; or wound management for burns.

General Subacute Care

General subacute units are most often utilized for patients who require medical care and monitoring at least weekly, short-term nursing care at a level of approximately 3.5 to 5.0 hours per patient day, and rehabilitative therapies that may extend from 1 to 3 hours per patient day. Short stay in nature (10 to 40 days), general subacute care facilities see a significant number of Medicare patients who may require subacute rehabilitation or certain subacute nursing services, such as intravenous therapies for septic conditions, but have no other significant medical complications. Although there is some overlap in the clinical programs between the transitional subacute units and general subacute care facilities, the key difference is the acuity level of the patients. A sizable number of patients in the general subacute units are Medicare beneficiaries because younger patients at these acuity levels tend to be cared for by home health services.

Although most of the nursing facility companies that have committed to a subacute product line are creating separate general subacute units, some nursing facilities simply have dedicated certain beds in skilled units for these general subacute services. These latter facilities sacrifice the opportunity for higher managed care per diems and exceptions to the Medicare routine cost limitation; their capital investment to enter the subacute industry is minimal, however.

The goal of both transitional subacute units and general subacute units is to manage the patient's recovery or rehabilitation in a cost-effective manner and to discharge the patient home or, in some cases, to a less expensive level of care, such as long-term care or assisted living.

Chronic Subacute Care

Chronic subacute units manage patients with little hope of ultimate recovery and functional independence, such as ventilator-dependent patients, long-term comatose patients, and patients with progressive neurologic disease. Typically, these patients require nursing staffing at the level of the general subacute unit (3 to 5 hours per patient day), medical monitoring biweekly to monthly, and restorative therapies, usually provided by nursing staff with guidance from rehabilitation therapists. These patients either will eventually be stabilized so that they can be discharged home or be cared for in a long-term care facility or they may die. Their average length of stay is 60 to 90 days.

Long-Term Transitional Subacute Care

Long-term transitional subacute facilities most often are licensed as hospitals rather than as nursing facilities; they are PPS exempt as long-term care hospitals and have average lengths of stay of 25 days or more. Typically, these facilities provide care for acute ventilator-dependent or medically complex patients. Because they are hospitals, attending physicians may visit the patients daily. Nursing staff tend to be primarily registered nurses, and nursing hours per patient day may range between 6.5 and 9.0 depending on the types and acuity levels of patients.

SUBACUTE PROVIDERS

Subacute care is provided in a variety of settings, including hospital beds, hospital-based skilled nursing beds, diagnosis-related group (DRG)–exempt long-term hospitals, DRG-exempt rehabilitation hospitals, and skilled nursing beds in freestanding nursing facilities. Providers may be independent or a component of an integrated health care system. The health care industry appears to be aggressively reorganizing itself.

Alliances and partnerships are emerging to form high-quality, cost-effective, integrated delivery systems or care that provide a comprehensive array of services in a highly competitive environment. Freestanding, unaffiliated subacute providers are now approaching hospitals and capitated physician groups to affiliate with systems. Conversely, integrated health care delivery systems that are spearheaded by acute hospitals are now seeking partners that will provide subacute care to the capitated lives in their system.

As subacute providers become essential components of integrated health care delivery systems, their role within the health care system actually becomes clarified. The specific role of the provider type, however, depends largely on the other provider components of an integrated health care delivery system.

Hospital Swing Beds

The swing bed program authorizes rural hospitals with fewer than 100 beds to use beds interchangeably as either hospital or skilled nursing beds.[3] The Medicare patient who no longer requires acute hospitalization can be well served by the swing bed program, particularly in rural areas, where nursing facilities often do not admit high-acuity patients. In the swing bed program, the patient who no longer meets criteria for acute hospitalization may be "transferred" to a skilled nursing facility without leaving the bed. Rather than the patient being transferred, the bed status is transferred from a hospital bed to a skilled nursing bed.

In an integrated delivery system, the hospital swing bed program is utilized in two ways. First, the swing bed extends the continuum of care for the rural hospital with limited ability to discharge patients to skilled nursing facilities due to a lack of skilled nursing beds or the inability of the skilled nursing facility to accept higher-acuity patients. Second, the swing bed program serves as a skilled nursing facility for the integrated system for patients who receive their care at one of the system's tertiary care hospitals. Patients residing in the community surrounding the system's rural hospital with the swing bed program simply are transferred to the rural hospital, where they are placed in a bed that has "swung" to a skilled nursing facility bed.

Long-Term Care Hospitals

Also known as long-term acute hospitals, the long-term care hospital may qualify for an exemption from the hospital PPS if it has an average length of stay for its patients of 25 days or more.[4] The long-term care hospital must be a separately licensed entity. There is no distinct part unit for long-term care DRG-exempt hospitals within acute hospitals.

Integrated health care delivery systems that include more than 1000 acute beds may be able to maintain an appropriate census in the long-term care acute hospital within its system. Most integrated health care delivery systems that include a long-term care DRG-exempt hospital provider, however, learn that the referral base must extend beyond the acute hospitals within the integrated health care delivery system. The primary reasons relate to the requirement that the patients in the long-term care hospital must need a hospital level of care (as opposed to a subacute skilled nursing level) and that the average length of stay for the patients in the long-term care DRG-exempt hospital must be 25 days or more. As alternative health delivery sites such as home health, nursing facility–based subacute units, and outpatient centers become more prevalent, and as their capabilities allow them to admit higher-acuity patients, the number of potential patient referrals to long-term care DRG-exempt hospitals tends to decline. Nevertheless, for integrated delivery systems that include tertiary care and teaching hospitals with large numbers of beds, the long-term care DRG-exempt hospital may serve an important role within the continuum of care of the integrated health care delivery system.

Rehabilitation Hospitals

Rehabilitation hospitals also are eligible for exemption from Medicare's PPS. Regulations, however, tend to limit their ability to provide subacute care within the rehabilitation hospital beds.

First, rehabilitation hospitals are required to ensure that 75% of their admissions include patients with 10 rehabilitation diagnoses. In addition, Medicare patients in rehabilitation hospitals must be able to tolerate and benefit from 3 hours of daily rehabilitation.[5]

As a result of these limiting regulations on Medicare admissions to rehabilitation hospitals and the declining census in many rehabilitation hospitals, a number of these providers are converting rehabilitation hospital beds to skilled nursing beds within their hospitals. This allows the rehabilitation hospital to provide the continuum of rehabilitation services, both acute and subacute.

Within an integrated health care delivery system, the rehabilitation hospital or the rehabilitation unit within an acute hospital often tends to change its role, particularly as the patients requiring orthopedic rehabilitation are transferred directly from the acute hospital to a subacute setting. The acute rehabilitation hospital, then, tends to focus on patients with neurologic rehabilitation diagnoses such as stroke and head injury. Moreover, rehabilitation hospitals may develop programs for medically complex patients whose diagnoses do not fall within the typical rehabilitation diagnostic categories. For example, the rehabilitation hospital or unit may develop a specialized ventilator weaning program that includes physical and occupational therapies for strengthening and conditioning and speech-language pathology services for dysphagia.

The regulatory requirements for long-term care hospitals and rehabilitation hospitals to qualify for the exemption from PPS can be challenging to providers. As a result, most subacute care today is provided in beds licensed as skilled nursing beds. There is, however, no federal category for subacute care different from the hospital or skilled nursing designation.

Hospital-Based Subacute Skilled Nursing Units

Nearly 2000 acute hospitals today are believed to have skilled nursing units. Most of these skilled nursing units within acute hospitals are transitional subacute units. The *Federal Register* of September 4, 1980, defines hospital-based skilled nursing facilities as follows:

> An SNF [skilled nursing facility] is determined to be hospital based when it is an integral and subordinate part of a hospital and is operated with the other departments of the hospital under common licensure, governance and professional supervision (all services of the hospital and the SNF are fully integrated).[6(p292)]

The sponsoring hospital and the hospital-based subacute skilled nursing facility must submit a combined Medicare cost report. The hospital-based subacute skilled nursing facility must be licensed under the laws of the state as a skilled nursing facility. Most states require a certificate of need for new construction of skilled nursing facility beds.

If a hospital has not owned or operated skilled nursing facility beds within the past 3 years, then new provider status can be obtained for a newly established hospital-based subacute skilled nursing facility. New provider status exempts the hospital-based subacute skilled nursing facility from the routine cost limits and reimburses the facility for reasonable costs for a period of 3 years. In addition to the 3 years of cost-based reimbursement, hospital-based skilled nursing facilities may be cost based for the start-up year if the start-up year does not comprise a full 12 months. After the cost-based reimbursement period, the routine cost limits apply unless the hospital requests, and is approved for, an exception to the routine cost limits. Ancillary services are reimbursed on the basis of cost and are not subject to routine cost limits. Capital cost reimbursement also is available and separate from the reimbursement for routine costs and ancillary services.

The benefits of a hospital-based subacute skilled nursing facility to the sponsoring hospital include the following:

- It serves as an effective way of increasing the margins on Medicare and other fixed payment patients. The hospital-based subacute skilled nursing facility provides the opportunity for reducing the average length of stay of Medicare beneficiaries and other fixed payment patients, such as those reimbursed by managed care organizations. As a result, the direct costs related to these fixed payment patients are reduced.

- There is a favorable reimbursement structure. The sponsoring hospital's direct costs are covered under the Medicare reimbursement regulations. In addition, the hospital is able to reallocate existing indirect costs. Finally, there is an attractive ancillary and capital cost reimbursement available for the hospital-based subacute skilled nursing facility.

- There is modest risk. Given an appropriate demand analysis, the certainty and stability of the demand are controlled by the hospital. In addition, the new provider exemption allows the sponsoring hospital to recuperate the start-up costs.

- Other hospital programs are enhanced. Certain hospital programs, such as rehabilitation units, can be enhanced by a close working relationship with the hospital-based subacute skilled nursing facility.

- Patients remain within the hospital-based health care system. Patients who are now transferred to external nursing facilities for subacute or skilled nursing care can be transferred directly to the hospital-based subacute skilled nursing facility for part or all of the postacute care needed. Typically, because the Medicare beneficiary is required to provide a copayment amount after day 20 in a skilled nursing facility, hospital-based subacute skilled nursing facilities attempt to maintain an average length of stay of less than 20 days. Should the patient require continued subacute or skilled nursing services, he or she can be transferred to another skilled nursing facility if there is an adequate number of skilled nursing days remaining. (Medicare beneficiaries have as a benefit up to 100 skilled nursing days after a hospital stay of at least 3 days.)

Because of the favorable Medicare reimbursement combined with typically unfavorable Medicaid reimbursement for patients in skilled nursing beds, hospital-based subacute skilled nursing facilities usually are certified only for Medicare and not for Medicaid. So long as the patient's length of stay remains less than 20 days and the patient is eligible for Medicare Part A benefits, Medicaid as a secondary payer is not relevant. Should a patient require more than 20 days of subacute care in the skilled nursing bed and be a Medicaid recipient, however, he or she may be transferred to an area skilled nursing facility for appropriate care.

Even beyond the period that the hospital is exempt from the routine cost limitations of Medicare, most hospital-based subacute skilled nursing units continue to serve the Medicare beneficiary. The exception to the routine cost limits that is available to subacute providers can be utilized by the hospital-based subacute skilled nursing units to recoup the additional costs for caring for the higher-acuity transitional subacute patient. For example, many hospital-based subacute skilled nursing units provide 5.5 to 6.0 hours of nursing care per patient day. The licensed to unlicensed nursing mix tends to be different from that in the freestanding nursing facility, with more licensed nurses, particularly registered nurses, providing services in hospital-based subacute skilled nursing units. As a result, hospital-based subacute skilled nursing units frequently find that the routine costs for providing care to this group of subacute patients exceed the routine cost limit imposed by Medicare, and an exception to the routine cost limit must be requested. Chapter 4 provides information about Medicare exception requests.

In most integrated health care delivery systems, the vast majority of the transfers to the hospital-based subacute skilled nursing unit come directly from the host hospital rather than from other hospitals in the system. Physicians are just as reluctant to follow their patients in a subacute skilled nursing unit located in another acute hospital as they are to follow that patient to a subacute unit within a freestanding skilled nursing facility. Moreover, patients and families typically prefer to remain within a single facility for all their inpatient care.

Managed care organizations tend to avoid using hospital-based subacute skilled nursing units, however, primarily because the costs tend to be higher than those for the subacute units in freestanding skilled nursing facilities. Fully capitated physician groups also tend to seek out freestanding nursing facility subacute units as contracted providers because of the typically lower cost. As integrated delivery systems enter into fully capitated agreements with managed care organizations or directly with large employers, the freestanding nursing facility–based subacute unit may emerge as an increasingly important component of the integrated system.

Subacute Units in Freestanding Nursing Facilities

Subacute units in freestanding nursing facilities typically provide one or two of the categories of subacute care, usually transitional, general, or chronic. New facilities constructed after 1993 frequently include in-wall oxygen and suction as well as physical dimensions suitable for providing care to transitional subacute patients. Most nursing facility–based subacute providers, however, are nursing facilities that have been renovated to create a separate subacute unit without the in-wall oxygen and suction systems. Therefore, freestanding nursing facility–based subacute units typically provide general subacute care and focus on three programs: rehabilitation, wound management, and intravenous therapy programs. Few nursing facility subacute providers can be persuaded to provide chronic subacute care unless special arrangements can be made for Medicaid payment in their state because chronic subacute patients have a high conversion rate to Medicaid.

Within an integrated delivery system, the freestanding nursing facility–based subacute provider allows the system to package its services along a continuum for managed care organizations, regardless of whether the system is fully capitated. The integrated system may de-velop a case management procedure, wherein a patient's care is managed by an individual case manager throughout the entire continuum: acute hospital, subacute hospital-based or nursing facility–based unit, home health or outpatient care, and long-term care. Integrated systems that are not fully capitated find that the system's nursing facility–based subacute provider is an especially attractive component when large numbers of traditional Medicare patients who enter the health care system have transferred their benefits to a full-risk Medicare HMO. In such cases, the system will encourage direct admissions to the nursing facility-based subacute unit from the hospital emergency department or physician clinic, particularly when the patient exhibits a medical condition that can be treated in an inpatient setting other than the acute hospital. For example, geriatric patients may come to the emergency department because of pneumonia, urinary tract infections, respiratory distress related to chronic obstructive pulmonary disorders, or respiratory distress related to congestive heart failure. The transitional subacute unit in a nursing facility that has appropriately qualified staff, an ancillary infrastructure, and medical direction often can provide care that is comparable to the care that would have been provided in an acute hospital, but at a lower cost than an acute hospital admission would have been.

Summary

The subacute provider appears to be taking on an important role as integrated delivery systems become the next generation of managed care. Some experts predict that national integrated health care delivery systems will control the majority of the market by the turn of the century. It is likely that each integrated delivery system will include a variety of subacute care levels and providers and that the role of each provider will depend on the types and roles of other providers—acute, subacute, home health, and outpatient—within the integrated health care delivery system.

KEYS TO SUCCESS FOR SUBACUTE PROVIDERS

Regardless of where subacute care is delivered, certain components of the subacute setting are found to correlate with profitability and success. The three keys to profitability (Table 1–1) are as follows:

1. The subacute setting serves as an alternative to acute hospitals. As relative newcomers in the health care continuum of care, subacute units and facilities must be able to prove that the care provided is comparable to the quality of care in acute hospitals. Patients, families, physicians, and referral sources must perceive it as a positive alternative to either an admission or a continued stay in an acute or rehabilitation hospital.

2. The subacute provider must target patients with the right payer mix. Depending on the primary motive for the development of the subacute care unit or facility, the provider must ensure that procedures are in place to target patients for whom reimbursement meets the subacute provider's financial objectives. The subacute provider must clearly define the program and types of patients to be admitted to the subacute unit or facility.

3. The subacute care must encompass a high-quality, integrated, interdisciplinary, and cost-effective program that focuses on patient outcomes. Referral sources must believe that the subacute provider is focused on quality as well as cost.

The seven keys to success (Table 1–2) are as follows:

1. The subacute unit or facility must radiate the characteristics that referral sources, patients, families, and physicians seek: the quality care of the acute hospital environment; an interdisciplinary, programmatic approach to care; and the warmth and comfort of a facility in which patients will stay for periods extending from 2 weeks to 3 months or longer. Subacute units within

Table 1–1 Keys to Profitability for Subacute Providers

Key	Explanation
Alternative to hospitals	Patients, families, physicians, and referral sources must perceive that the subacute unit is a positive alternative to an admission or continued stay in an acute or rehabilitation hospital.
Payer mix	The payer mix (Medicare and/or managed care) must be able to provide favorable profitability. Admission criteria must focus on the right payer mix.
Efficiency/quality	Referral sources must believe that a high-quality integrated program is provided in a cost-effective way.

hospitals or nursing facilities should be established in separate wings that clearly convey a different orientation from that of the acute hospital or the nursing facility.

2. The subacute program should have clearly defined protocols or care paths for the two to four programs in which the provider specializes. The programs should be designed to meet the health care needs of specific, targeted patient populations, which are defined based on patient diagnosis, medical acuity, and functional dependency relative to intensity of service requirements and expected outcomes. The admission criteria, continuing stay criteria, and discharge criteria should be clearly delineated for each program.

3. Clinical direction of a subacute program should be provided by a physician who is qualified by virtue of training and experience in the area(s) related to the program being offered. In addition to an overall medical director and medical program directors, a medical staff of credentialed and privileged physicians should be created so

Table 1–2 Keys to Success for Subacute Providers

Key	Explanation
Attractive facility	No one wants to go to a nursing home or a unit in the "old part of the hospital."
Programs of care	The subacute programs should have specific protocols or care paths for the two to four programs in which the provider specializes. Admission criteria are clear for each program.
Medical staff	In addition to a medical director, a medical staff of credentialed and privileged physicians are attending or consulting.
Dedicated clinical staff	Under the direction of a program director, nursing and social services staff along with rehabilitation, dietary, and respiratory therapy staff provide care in the subacute unit or facility.
Admissions	Procedures are user friendly to all referral sources and allow for an expedited admissions process.
Outcomes	Patient outcomes are measured and reported by means of a quantitative instrument.
Financial reports	Management information systems are adequate to provide frequent and detailed reports on costs and profitability by patient.

that physicians may serve as either attending or consulting staff in the subacute unit or facility.

4. A dedicated clinical staff for the subacute unit or facility should be developed. A program director should be identified as the person responsible for the overall management of the subacute program. Typically, the program director has a nursing therapy background and has accumulated experience and expertise in health care finances and marketing. In addition to the program director, an interdisciplinary team comprising nursing, medical staff, social services, rehabilitation therapists, dietitians, and respiratory therapists should provide care to patients in the subacute unit or facility.

5. Admissions procedures must provide for timely admissions that are user friendly to all referral sources. Procedures may involve pre-admission assessments of hospitalized patients, which should be performed within two hours of the receipt of the referral by the subacute provider. The referral source should be notified immediately following the preadmission assessment regarding the acceptance or denial of admission. If admission is denied, the referral source should be provided alternative recommendations for placement of the patient. If the patient is accepted for admission, the subacute provider should create procedures that minimize paper work and other delays relating to admissions.

6. Patient outcomes should be measured by means of consistent data collection focused on functional status and discharge placement. The subacute program should incorporate a continuous quality improvement process based on the systematic measurement of both functional and medical patient outcomes. Patient outcomes must demonstrate that the subacute level of care had positive long-term effects.

7. Financial reports must be adequate to provide detailed information about the cost of care and the operating margins by individual patient type and payer source. The subacute provider must thoroughly understand the financial interrelationships among costs, payment rates, and methodologies. Management within the subacute setting must be able to monitor effectively the financial status of the subacute unit or facility.

CONCLUSION

The subacute industry has rapidly evolved into a recognized niche within health care. Its continued growth will be dependent on two factors:

clear demonstration of the cost-saving potential of moving patients out of high-cost acute care hospitals and into lower-cost subacute care units and facilities, and patient outcomes that demonstrate that subacute program treatment interventions have positive long-term effects. As health care providers move from competitors to collaborators within integrated health care delivery systems, it seems clear that cost-effective, quality subacute levels of care will be important components in the continuum of care provided by the integrated health care systems of the future.

REFERENCES

1. International Subacute Healthcare Association (ISHA). *Definition of Subacute Care.* Minneapolis, Minn: ISHA; 1994.
2. Joint Commission on Accreditation of Healthcare Organizations. *Digest: Subacute Care Protocol.* Oakbrook Terrace, Ill: Joint Commission; 1994.
3. 42 CFR §482.64.
4. 42 CFR §412.23(e).
5. 42 CFR §412.23(b).
6. Quoted in McDowell TN. The subacute care patient. Hospital responses to the challenge. *J Health Hosp Law.* 1990;23:292.

2

Federal and State Policy Initiatives and the Subacute Industry

Theodore N. McDowell, Jr.

Federal and state policy initiatives surrounding subacute care reflect its emergence as an established level of care within the health care industry. During the 1980s, policy issues focused on the development of subacute care as a response to a treatment gap between acute care services and traditional long-term care services. The explosive growth of the subacute care industry in the early 1990s created a second generation of policy issues. Policymakers must now struggle with the reality that a new provider category has developed in the health care industry without clear regulatory or policy oversight.

This chapter reviews the historical policy issues surrounding the development of subacute care. The primary historical issues are quality of care, access to care, and cost considerations. To understand these policy issues and the emergence of subacute care as a specialty niche, it also is necessary to examine the underlying, interrelated incentives within the health care industry that created the issues.

This chapter also discusses the second-generation policy issues that have evolved as the subacute industry has matured. The emerging policy issues focus on the impact of subacute care on the quality, access to, and cost of health care; appropriate regulation of subacute care; appropriate Medicare and Medicaid reimbursement for subacute care; the relationship between the subacute industry and the hospital and nursing facility industries; and the role of subacute care in health care reform. The chapter identifies federal and state policy initiatives addressing the emerging issues. These initiatives will shape the future of the industry.

HISTORICAL POLICY ISSUES

After the implementation of Medicare's Prospective Payment System (PPS) for hospitals in 1983, policymakers and health care providers identified a treatment gap between acute care services and traditional long-term care services. Policymakers expressed concern that patients falling into this gap were receiving inadequate or inappropriate health care services. Numerous government and industry reports explored the quality, access, and cost issues associated with the treatment gap (Exhibit 2–1).[1] Simultaneously, many providers attempted to fill the gap by developing subacute strategies and services.

Exhibit 2–1 Historical Policy Issues

Quality of care
- PPS quicker-and-sicker discharge phenomenon
- Subacute phase of recovery eliminated from the hospital stay
- Inadequate postacute care services

Access to care
- Hospital discharge delays
- Inadequate postacute care services
- Unavailability of nursing facility beds
- Refusal of postacute facilities to accept subacute discharges

Cost of care
- Hospital costs associated with placement delays
- Nursing facility costs associated with treating sicker residents
- Overall effect of subacute care on health care costs

Quality of Care

During the 1980s, government reports identified the quicker-and-sicker discharge phenomenon resulting from the incentives of PPS.[2,3] The cost-containment pressures of PPS and other regulatory initiatives created incentives for hospitals to discharge patients as quickly as possible and with greater need for subacute care. In essence, the subacute and transitional phases of recovery were eliminated from the hospital stay.

The government reports concerning the impact of PPS expressed concern that the health care system had not developed sufficient postacute care treatment alternatives to meet the increased subacute need. The reports concluded that appropriate postacute services may be unavailable for patients being discharged from hospitals at an earlier point in their recovery.

Access to Care

The lack of adequate postacute care services to treat subacute patients also was evidenced by access problems. Despite the incentives for hospitals to discharge patients quicker and sicker, hospitals in many states documented severe problems in placing subacute hospital patients in

postacute care settings.[4-7] Access problems were created by inadequate postacute care services, the unavailability of nursing facility beds, or the refusal of facilities to accept certain types of subacute patients.

Cost Considerations

The access problems and placement delays created cost concerns for hospitals, and the discharge of sicker patients created cost concerns for nursing facilities and other postacute care providers. Hospitals attempted to document that they were absorbing a large portion of the costs associated with placement delays.[4-7] Nursing facilities asserted that Medicare and Medicaid reimbursement rates no longer adequately covered the increased operational costs associated with residents needing more intensive medical care.[8] Nursing facilities argued that subacute residents threatened the financial viability of nursing facilities already operating on paper-thin profit margins.

In contrast to the claims by the hospital and nursing facility industries, historically the Health Care Financing Administration (HCFA) and government officials have not viewed the cost considerations associated with placement delays and subacute care as significant enough to warrant modifications to the reimbursement or regulatory schemes within the health care industry. For instance, a 1990 report to Congress by HCFA concluded that, overall, the financial effect of administratively necessary days on hospitals was relatively small and primarily affected a subgroup of hospitals.[9] The reports, however, noted that subacute issues reinforced the troubling observation that cost-containment efforts aimed at one segment of the health care industry were insufficient to contain overall health care costs unless the entire system was reformed to align all incentives toward cost containment.

Underlying Incentives

The factors underlying the historical policy issues involve a number of interrelated incentives, including reimbursement incentives, low nursing facility bed supply combined with high nursing facility occupancy rates, hospital inefficiencies in case management, patient characteristics, and gaps in available services in a community (Exhibit 2–2).

Reimbursement Incentives

The primary incentive underlying the historical policy issues and the development of subacute care was reimbursement. Because there is no separate Medicare or Medicaid reimbursement for subacute care, the facility providing such care must seek reimbursement under Medicare's PPS reimbursement system for hospitals, the Medicaid reimbursement system for hospitals, the Medicare or Medicaid reimbursement system for PPS-excluded hospitals, the Medicare or Medicaid reimbursement system for nursing facilities, or some form of managed care reimbursement. During the 1980s, the treatment gap issue developed largely as a result of the disincentives to provide subacute care found in the various reimbursement systems.

Under PPS, hospitals are paid a predetermined price for inpatient services based on the average cost of treating a patient in a particular diagnosis-related group (DRG).[10] The DRG system creates

a quicker-and-sicker discharge incentive. Furthermore, the PPS outlier provisions for unexpected lengths of stay or extraordinary costs typically are inadequate to cover the cost of treating a subacute patient in the acute hospital setting. As a result of the PPS system, a larger portion of an episode of illness is now considered subacute, and discharged hospital patients require more intensive postacute medical services.

In terms of Medicaid hospital reimbursement, states are required to develop reimbursement methodologies that are reasonable and adequate to meet the costs incurred by efficiently and economically operated facilities. Reimbursement methodologies vary from state to state. Generally, Medicaid reimbursement levels are inadequate to provide an incentive for hospitals to retain Medicaid inpatients during the subacute phase of recovery.

Pushing against the Medicare and Medicaid reimbursement incentives for early hospital discharge are the Medicare and Medicaid reimbursement methodologies for nursing facilities. Medicare skilled nursing facility (SNF) services are reimbursed on a reasonable cost basis with cost limits.[11] The costs required to treat a subacute patient often exceed the SNF's cost limit. Furthermore, Medicaid reimbursement typically is inadequate to cover the costs of treating the heavy care or subacute patient. Consequently, the Medicare and Medicaid reimbursement systems contain a disincentive for most SNFs or nursing facilities to accept subacute patients.

Similarly, Medicare reimbursement for PPS-excluded hospitals also creates a disincentive to treat high-acuity patients. PPS-excluded hospitals, such as long-term care hospitals and rehabilitation hospitals, are reimbursed under Medicare on a reasonable cost basis with target ceiling limitations.[12] The cost of treating the high-acuity subacute patient often will exceed target ceiling limitations.[13]

The one bright spot for subacute providers within the reimbursement system involves managed care reimbursement. During the early and late 1980s, however, managed care was not as significant a reimbursement source for subacute

---

Exhibit 2–2 Incentives Underlying the Historical Policy Issues

Reimbursement
- PPS quicker-and-sicker discharge phenomenon
- Medicare cost limits for skilled nursing facilities
- Inadequate Medicaid reimbursement for nursing facilities
- Medicare target ceiling limitations for PPS-excluded hospitals
- Lack of managed care penetration

Low skilled nursing facility bed supply/high occupancy rates
Restrictive certificate of need policies
Inefficient hospital case management
Patient characteristics
Gaps in community services

providers as during the early 1990s. In sum, the Medicare and Medicaid reimbursement systems in place during the 1980s, combined with a lack of significant managed care penetration into the subacute industry, created a general disincentive to treat subacute patients. The result was a treatment gap.

Other Non-Reimbursement Incentives

In addition to reimbursement incentives, a series of studies by Lewin-ICF during the 1980s suggested that states with a low SNF bed supply combined with high SNF occupancy rates experienced the most hospital placement delays.[4] The studies found that a low number of beds in a state per 1000 elderly may produce placement delays. State variations in nursing facility bed supply were caused primarily by restrictive certificate of need (CON) policies and restrictive Medicaid reimbursement policies for nursing facilities. Low bed supply/high occupancy rates provided nursing facilities with discretion to avoid admitting the high-cost subacute patient. The studies found that hospital placement delays were sensitive to small changes in nursing facility occupancy rates.

Other studies identified as an additional factor hospital inefficiencies in case management of patients and discharge planning because such services may affect the degree of placement delays and inappropriate placements. Studies also attempted to determine patient characteristics that may influence placement delays. Finally, gaps in available services in a community were seen as creating some of the quality, access, and cost issues.[1]

Policy Initiatives During the 1980s

During the late 1980s, federal and state regulatory and government agencies were unwilling to develop policy initiatives specifically addressing subacute care. During this developmental phase of the subacute industry, policy activity emphasized research attempting to identify the scope of subacute care and the issues associated with the new level of care. Policymakers also identified

and analyzed a number of issues such as Medicaid problems concerning patient access to nursing facilities,[14] nursing facility quality of care problems,[15] Medicare and Medicaid reimbursement for nursing facilities,[14,16] problems associated with cost-based reimbursement for PPS-exempt specialty hospitals,[13] discharge delays from hospitals,[4–7] and the impact of PPS on hospital discharge behavior.[2,3,9,17]

Many federal and state policy initiatives aimed at other areas of the health care industry also indirectly affected the development of the subacute industry. For instance, the shift in reimbursement for swing bed hospitals pursuant to the Omnibus Budget Reconciliation Act (OBRA) of 1990 improved the ability of swing bed hospitals to provide subacute care.[18] Similarly, the development of case-mix reimbursement systems for nursing facilities began to encourage facilities to provide services for heavy care or subacute patients.[1]

For the most part, the late 1980s and early 1990s were characterized by industry initiatives to develop subacute services combined with a "wait and see" attitude on the part of policymakers and government officials. The providers taking an active role in the development of the subacute industry included long-term care hospitals, rehabilitation hospitals and units, swing bed hospitals, freestanding SNFs, and hospital-based SNFs.

EMERGING POLICY ISSUES

The historical policy issues discussed above focused on the recognition of a new patient care level and the underlying reasons for the development of the subacute specialty niche. Most of the policy issues were negative in the sense that the analysis identified problems causing the development of a subacute level of care and barriers to the development of adequate subacute services.

During the early and middle 1990s, new policy issues have emerged that reflect the maturation and growth of the subacute industry. The shift is based, to a large extent, on the increasing importance of managed care within the health care industry. The growth of managed care represents the driving force behind the explosion of sub-acute care. Managed care organizations identify subacute providers as a cost-effective alternative to the hospital setting, and the subacute provider obtains more favorable reimbursement from the managed care payer compared with standard Medicare or Medicaid reimbursement rates. Managed care arrangements allow subacute pro-viders to develop quality programs for high-acu-ity patients and still remain financially viable.

The attractiveness of subacute care to man-aged care organizations is further evidenced by the growing interest of investment firms and en-trepreneurial organizations in this level of care. Some analysts predict that over the next 5 years the industry could become a $10 billion to $20 billion per year business.[19-21] The analysts are bullish on subacute care because it is in line with the cost-containment trend in the health care in-dustry and the demographic trend toward an older population.

Additional factors contributing to the expan-sion of subacute care during the 1990s (Exhibit 2–3) include advancements in medical technolo-gies, an increasing elderly population, the policy emphasis on cost containment, the shifting of medical care to nonhospital settings, and the push toward health care reform and managed competi-tion. All these factors suggest that subacute care is now an established industry category that must be acknowledged and addressed from a regula-tory and policy perspective. Furthermore, sec-ond-generation policy issues (Exhibit 2–4) are emerging as the industry matures.

Exhibit 2–3 Factors Driving the Growth of Subacute Care

Managed care
Investment capital
Health care reform
Cost-containment incentives
Advancements in medical technologies
Demographic trends
Shifting of medical care to nonhospital settings

Exhibit 2–4 Emerging Policy Issues

Quality of care
Access to care
Cost of care
Regulatory oversight
Medicare and Medicaid reimbursement
The relationship between the subacute industry and the hospital and nursing facility industries
The role of subacute care in health care reform

Quality, Access, and Cost Issues

The growth of subacute care requires an analy-sis of the impact of such care on the core issues of quality, access, and cost. The present debate on these issues evidences a skepticism on the part of government officials as to the legitimate place of these new providers in the health care industry combined with the recognition that subacute care has become an established industry category de-spite the lack of recognition or oversight by regu-latory and government agencies.

Quality of Care Issues

Subacute providers claim that they have up-graded their facilities, staffing, equipment, and operations to a level above the capabilities of a standard nursing facility. The upgraded facilities have the capability to compete with hospitals by providing quality services in a lower-cost setting. These facilities function as an alternative to con-tinued hospitalization. Critics, however, argue that many subacute providers may not be living up to their quality claims.[22] This debate will re-main unresolved until adequate outcomes mea-sures and data are developed to determine the actual quality of care provided in subacute facili-ties, regulatory standards for the industry are de-veloped to provide guidelines, and an industry definition of subacute care is agreed upon so that policymakers and the industry can distinguish between sham providers and providers that have developed recognized subacute programs (Table 2–1).

Industry providers, rather than policymakers and regulators, are taking the initiative in developing outcome measures and data for subacute programs. Industry groups are attempting to develop systematic procedures for determining the effectiveness and efficiency of subacute programs as well as patient satisfaction with the results of such programs.[23,24] Consumers, providers, managed care payers, and accreditation organizations are all pushing for adequate outcomes measures. One example involves the development by Formations in Healthcare of a preliminary system of measuring outcomes specifically designed for the subacute industry (see Chapter 10 for more information). The rehabilitation industry also has been active in developing outcomes measures for rehabilitation programs, and these measures can be applied to certain rehabilitation-oriented types of subacute programs. As a general matter, however, it must be recognized that outcomes measures for the subacute industry, as for the rest of the health care industry, are in their infancy. It may be many years before accurate and meaningful measures become available.

In terms of regulatory standards for the industry, accreditation organizations are taking the lead in this area in the absence of action by the HCFA and other government entities. The standards developed by the Joint Commission on Accreditation of Healthcare Organizations for subacute providers as well as the standards developed by the Commission on Accreditation of Rehabilitation Facilities (CARF) represent positive initial steps in this area (see Chapter 13 for a detailed discussion of these accreditation standards). Similarly, a limited number of states, including Illinois, California, Maryland, and Virginia, have developed regulatory standards relating to subacute services.

In the absence of government and regulatory definitions of subacute care, industry organizations are developing definitions. These efforts could form the basis for identifying legitimate subacute providers and for initiating discussions with regulators to recognize subacute care as an industry category. Presently, definitions have been developed by organizations such as the American Health Care Association, the International Subacute Healthcare Association, and the Joint Commission. Managed care payers and industry providers also are developing definitions. See Chapter 1 for a discussion of definitions.

Access Issues

Subacute providers assert that they are improving access by filling the historical treatment gap between acute care and long-term services and by providing an appropriate level of care for an underserved patient category. In contrast, critics suggest that subacute providers may be creating new access problems for Medicaid patients, indi-

Table 2–1 The Quality of Care Debate

Proponents	Critics	Future Resolution
Subacute providers offer: • upgraded facilities • upgraded staff • upgraded equipment • specialized programs	Quality claims cannot be substantiated by data	Development of outcomes measures and data to evaluate and substantiate quality claims
	Many subacute facilities are simply providing high-level SNF services	Regulatory standards to provide guidelines
Subacute facilities function as an alternative to continued hospitalization	Compared with hospitals, subacute facilities: • lack sufficient back-up services, equipment, and staff • lack the expertise and intensity of services to treat complex patients	Recognized definition of subacute care to differentiate legitimate from sham providers
Subacute facilities are an essential component of an integrated system		

gent patients, and rural residents.[25] For example, a common strategy for many freestanding, for-profit subacute providers involves developing a payer mix that emphasizes managed care and Medicare patients and reduces Medicaid services. Hospitals suggest that such providers may be skimming off the more profitable managed care patients and leaving the Medicaid and indigent patients to be treated in hospital facilities. Similarly, many of the freestanding subacute providers acknowledge that rural areas do not have a sufficient managed care base or patient population to support the development of facilities.

In response to the criticisms concerning access, it can be argued that the criticisms are based on a narrow analysis of one limited segment of the subacute industry. The criticisms focus on the freestanding, for-profit subacute provider operating as an SNF. As part of the access debate, policymakers also should analyze whether Medicaid subacute patients are receiving adequate care through other subacute providers, such as long-term care hospitals, rehabilitation hospitals and units, or hospital-based SNFs. Arguably, the needs of all subacute patients, including rural and Medicaid patients, may be addressed if the entire continuum of subacute providers is kept in perspective. For instance, it may be most efficient and cost effective from a policy perspective to have rural subacute patients receive services through the swing bed program or through hospital-based SNFs within a rural hospital rather than in a freestanding facility.

In addition, the access difficulties surrounding Medicaid subacute patients may reflect problems with the Medicaid reimbursement system more than problems associated with the subacute industry. Such a conclusion is suggested by the finding that Medicaid access to subacute providers improves in states that have developed negotiated exceptions for high-acuity patients in SNFs and in states that have developed a separate Medicaid reimbursement level for subacute care.[4–7,14]

Cost Issues

Subacute providers claim that they are a low-cost, quality alternative to the hospital setting. Some providers estimate 30% to 60% savings in cost compared with the hospital alternative.[19–21,25] This claim underlies the attractiveness of subacute care to the managed care industry, and it supports the health care reform emphasis on cost containment.

In 1994, Abt Associates conducted a study of the cost benefits of subacute care delivered in SNFs instead of acute care hospitals.[26] A panel of clinicians identified and analyzed 62 DRGs that included patients who potentially could be treated in properly staffed and equipped subacute SNFs. The panel estimated the number of days patients would need to spend in a hospital before they could be transferred to a subacute SNF. The panel developed the following three DRG groupings:

1. 5 DRGs require no prior hospitalization (Table 2–2)
2. 4 DRGs require only 2 days of hospitalization before the patient is moved to a subacute SNF (Table 2–3)
3. 53 DRGs require 3 days or more of prior hospitalization

The report concluded that subacute care in SNFs could save the Medicare program between $7 billion and $9 billion annually. To realize the estimated cost saving, Medicare would have to reduce and rebase hospital payments for specified DRGs to reflect shortened hospital stays and/or eliminate, for selected DRGs, the 3-day prior hospital stay currently required for patients to qualify for Medicare SNF benefits. Such changes would be resisted by the hospital industry. The cost-savings estimates also may be inflated by the study's failure to consider subacute providers other than freestanding SNFs, such as specialty hospitals or hospital-based SNFs.

Despite the industry estimates and the Abt Associates report, some analysts dispute the cost-containment assertion. These analysts argue that subacute care may actually increase health care costs if the financial analysis focuses on overall health care costs.[25,27] Subacute care may be adding a new level of costs and services to the health care system because the government and other

Table 2-2 Subacute DRGs Treatable in Nursing Facilities, No Prior Hospitalization Required

DRG Code	DRG Description	Medicare Discharges	Current Medicare Hospital Payment ($)	Potential SNF Share (%)	Current Hospital Days	Potential Hospital Days	Potential Nonhospital Days	Daily Nonhospital Charge ($)
238	Osteomyelitis	6,381	11,464	80	14.84	0	14.84	350
243	Medical back problems	117,272	4,759	50	7.19	0	7.19	250
254	Fx spm stm & disl of uparm lowleg ex foot age ▶ 17 w/o cc	14,324	3,483	80	5.82	0	5.82	250
271	Skin ulcers	20,018	9,602	80	14.58	0	14.58	250
410	Chemotherapy without acute leukemia as secondary diagnosis	136,216	4,121	50	3.62	0	3.62	350

Source: Data from *Subacute Care in Freestanding Skilled Nursing Facilities: An Estimate of Savings to Medicare*, by Abt Associates, June 1994.

Table 2-3 Subacute DRGs Treatable in Nursing Facilities, Prior Hospital Stay of Two or Fewer Days Required

DRG Code	DRG Description	Medicare Discharges	Current Medicare Hospital Payment ($)	Potential SNF Share (%)	Current Hospital Days	Potential Hospital Days	Potential Nonhospital Days	Daily Nonhospital Charge ($)
96	Bronchitis & asthma ▶ 17 w cc	195,938	6,211	80	7.30	2	5.30	300
239	Pathological fractures & musculoskeletal & conn tiss malignancy	60,693	7,328	80	10.44	2	8.44	300
278	Cellulitis age ▶ 17 w/o cc	26,055	4,281	80	6.56	2	4.56	350
296	Nutritional & misc metabolic disorders age ▶ 17 w cc	204,689	6,672	80	8.62	2	6.62	200

Source: Data from *Subacute Care in Freestanding Skilled Nursing Facilities: An Estimate of Savings to Medicare*, by Abt Associates, June 1994.

payers now must pay for subacute services along with acute care, long-term care, and home care services. Consequently, when an entire episode of care is analyzed, overall health care costs may remain the same or actually increase. These analysts conclude that health care costs will never be fully contained until the entire system is addressed through cost-containment incentives such as managed care or a global budgeting system.

In some ways, both the claims of the subacute providers and the arguments made by critics contain some validity. Within a managed care context, subacute providers clearly are considered a low-cost alternative to more costly hospital services. Thus as the entire health care system moves toward managed care and capitation arrangements, subacute facilities may represent a legitimate cost-containment strategy. Under a capitation arrangement, the subacute facility becomes one choice within a continuum aimed at placing patients in the most appropriate, cost-effective setting. On the other hand, the health care system still contains reimbursement incentives that encourage revenues generated by the amount of services provided. Consequently, when subacute care is viewed from a cost-reimbursement or fee-for-service perspective, the danger does exist that subacute care adds another layer of costs and charges to the system.

In sum, the claims of the subacute provider may be legitimate when viewed from a managed care or capitation perspective, but the claims of the critics may reflect dangers inherent in the present Medicare, Medicaid, and fee-for-service system. The bottom line conclusion may be that health care costs will never be contained from an overall perspective until all incentives within the system are aligned toward cost containment.

Regulatory Oversight

It has become clear to regulators that the development of the subacute care industry has outpaced the implementation of regulatory oversight. Both hospital and nursing facility regulations appear to be inappropriate or ineffective as a means to provide adequate guidance for these new providers. The existing regulatory schemes, such as Medicare and Medicaid certification requirements, CON guidelines, and state licensure requirements, do not provide adequate standards for the subacute industry. In many cases, present regulations create barriers to efficient operations. Examples of current regulatory barriers to the provision of efficient subacute services include inadequate Medicare reimbursement for physician visits to subacute patients in a SNF, the 3-day prior hospital stay requirements for SNF benefits, the Medicare coverage rules concerning respiratory therapy services in a SNF, and various OBRA 1987 requirements for nursing facilities that are inappropriate or inapplicable for subacute programs aimed at short-stay, high-acuity patients.[28]

Efforts to develop regulatory oversight are beginning at the federal, state, and accreditation levels. At the federal level, current initiatives are targeted at specific problem areas. For instance, on October 13, 1993, the HCFA issued a bulletin addressing a specific subacute strategy commonly described as a hospital-within-a-hospital strategy.[29] The bulletin instructs HCFA regional offices to scrutinize closely acute care hospitals attempting to develop a long-term care hospital within the same physical plant or on the same campus as the acute hospital. The bulletin discusses the HCFA's concern that the strategy represents a circumvention of Medicare regulations. Subsequently, on September 1, 1994, the HCFA issued a rule in the *Federal Register* establishing new conditions of participation for long-term care hospitals that significantly restrict the hospital-within-a-hospital strategy.[30] The conditions are intended to ensure that long-term care hospitals actually function and operate as separate, distinct entities. See Chapter 15 for a discussion of these conditions of participation.

The HCFA's response to the hospital-within-a-hospital strategy reflects the agency's present piecemeal approach to subacute care. For the HCFA to become an effective regulator of the subacute industry, the agency must move away from fragmented oversight and develop a comprehensive regulatory scheme for subacute providers. A step in that direction may involve the HCFA's 1994 call for demonstration projects concerning subacute care, which was published in the *Federal Register* on January 13, 1994.[31] In 1994, HCFA commissioned Lewin-VHI to study the subacute care industry with respect to the definition and characteristics of subacute care, the public policy impact of subacute care, and future areas of research.[32]

At the state level, regulatory efforts typically are tied to the development of Medicaid reimbursement categories for subacute providers. Specific licensure requirements or CON criteria are often associated with special reimbursement levels for designated types of subacute programs. For instance, in 1993 Maryland began to develop a subacute reimbursement mechanism for ventilator programs in SNFs, and this initiative was accompanied by the creation of new licensure standards designed specifically for the ventilator programs.[33]

Perhaps the most comprehensive attempts to provide oversight and standards for the subacute industry are being initiated by national accreditation organizations. In the near future, two sets of quality standards should be in place for surveying and accrediting subacute providers. Both the Joint Commission and CARF are working toward quality standards that should be implemented in the near future.

Reimbursement Initiatives

Federal Initiatives

With the exception of possible provisions contained in a comprehensive national health care reform package, it appears unlikely that federal policymakers will implement any specific reimbursement system for subacute care. The hesitancy to implement any broad-based reimbursement reforms specifically targeted at subacute care is seen in a 1990 HCFA report to Congress.[9] The report considered four Medicare policy options to address hospital costs relating to placement delays for subacute patients. Under one option, Medicare would pay a separate per diem rate for administratively necessary days reported by hospitals subject to review by the HCFA and peer review organizations. A second option proposed an adjustment to PPS rates to provide higher payments to hospitals with difficult access to nursing facilities and lower payments to hospitals with easy access to nursing facilities. The adjustment could be made to all DRGs or just those that most commonly lead to postacute care. The third option involves adjusting the Medicare day outlier policy. The day outlier threshold that must be satisfied before a hospital can receive outlier payments could be reduced. The fourth policy option is to pay a PPS add-on payment for postacute care including administratively necessary day costs.

The HCFA report rejected all the considered policy options and recommended continuation of the current Medicare payment policy under PPS for hospitals. The report recognized that each of the alternatives had advantages but concluded that each option also had potentially serious problems for reasons of equity and/or efficiency.

Despite the HCFA's hesitancy to develop a new subacute level of reimbursement, the agency's growing recognition of and interest in subacute care is evidenced by agency statements expressing an intent to gather information about subacute care and by the recent call for demonstration projects relating to subacute care published in the *Federal Register* on January 13, 1994.[32,33] The HCFA notice states that the agency is looking for projects that will demonstrate innovative approaches to the cost-effective delivery of long-term care services. The HCFA desires these studies to create a better understanding of the trends and factors affecting the cost, accessibility, and quality of subacute and long-term care services under Medicare and Medicaid and to explore cost-effective delivery and financing mechanisms. Such studies will examine methods of providing services to special populations with the greatest need for services and will explore whether new types of services or provider organizations should be developed to supplement those now covered under Medicare and Medicaid for subacute and long-term care populations.

Although the development of a new category of Medicare reimbursement is unlikely at this point outside a national health care reform package, many reimbursement reform efforts aimed at other Medicare reimbursement categories could have a significant impact on subacute providers. Reform efforts that should be monitored by subacute providers include the following:

- HCFA's case-mix demonstration project for nursing facilities under Medicare and Medicaid[1]
- possible revisions to the current cost-based Medicare reimbursement system for SNFs, such as elimination of the routine service cost limit differential between freestanding SNFs and hospital-based SNFs[16]
- the development of a Prospective Payment System for PPS-exempt specialty hospitals[13]
- as a more likely alternative to a Prospective Payment System, modifications to the present cost-based reimbursement system for specialty hospitals
- a possible moratorium on future long-term care hospitals[34]
- limited revisions to the PPS system, such as developing a cost-based reimbursement category for ventilator-dependent patients being treated in acute care hospitals[35,36]

State Reform Initiatives

Many states have begun experimenting with specific Medicaid reimbursement rates designated for subacute facilities. Often, these initiatives will be limited to specific facilities that can document the specialized care offered within the facility or for a restricted number of medical conditions, such as ventilator dependent patients and those with acquired immunodeficiency syndrome.[37] Informal reform also is evidenced by states that are willing to negotiate exceptions to standard Medicaid nursing facility reimbursement for providers that can document that they provide high-acuity specialty services.

Subacute providers also should monitor state reimbursement initiatives in the following areas:

the development of managed care Medicaid programs that include long-term care services,[38,39] the development of Medicaid case-mix reimbursement systems for nursing facilities,[1] and Medicaid reform options requiring equalization of Medicaid and private pay rates.[14] Each reform option will have a different impact on subacute providers.

The implementation of a managed care program for long-term care services creates incentives for long-term care services to be provided in noninstitutional settings. Home health care services and other community-oriented programs may take the place of traditional services provided in a SNF. At the same time, subacute care is likely to play a significant role in a managed care system because subacute programs emphasize short-term, outcomes-oriented programs aimed at efficiently transitioning patients back into the community.

A Medicaid case-mix system offers the opportunity to create incentives for nursing facilities to provide subacute levels of care for Medicaid patients. Given the budget constraints in most states, it seems questionable whether a Medicaid case-mix system will incorporate reimbursement levels that are sufficient to cover the costs associated with subacute care.

Finally, rate equalization, which requires Medicaid and private pay rates to be equal, could significantly hinder the provision of subacute care in nursing facilities if the fixed rate is insufficient to cover subacute costs. Rate equalization may increase incentives to admit Medicaid residents because there will no longer be a differential between Medicaid reimbursement and other reimbursement systems. Nursing facilities, however, would lose the ability to negotiate managed care reimbursement levels that are above Medicare and Medicaid reimbursement rates but below hospital reimbursement rates under managed care contracts. Consequently, the subacute provider would be limited in its ability to compete as an alternative to the hospital setting and would lose its ability to utilize managed care as the financial vehicle for upgrading its services.

The Relationship between the Subacute Industry and the Hospital and Nursing Facility Industries

Because subacute care falls between acute care and traditional long-term care, a critical policy issue involves the relationship of subacute care to both the hospital and the nursing facility industries (Table 2–4). At this point, the nature of the relationship is uncertain. On the one hand, subacute care offers opportunities for long-term care providers and hospitals to develop effective joint venture arrangements and integrated delivery systems (see Chapter 15 for a discussion of these opportunities). On the other hand, as subacute care becomes the point of integration between the hospital and nursing facility industries, policy debates arise concerning the appropriate site of subacute care, CON requirements, licensure requirements, and Medicaid reimbursement.

Perhaps the most significant policy debate currently focuses on the appropriate site of subacute care. Policy arguments favoring hospitals as the appropriate site for subacute care include the following:

- The hospital industry has tremendous excess capacity, which will probably increase with health care reform, and it makes sense for that excess capacity to be converted to a subacute level of care.[22]
- Models for hospitals to develop a continuum of care including a subacute level

already exist in the form of hospital-based SNFs, rehabilitation units, and swing bed programs.

- Hospitals, compared with nursing facilities, have access to acute care back-up services and appropriate equipment and staffing pools to provide a higher quality of care for the subacute patient.

On the other hand, nursing facilities can counter with the following arguments:

- OBRA 1987 requires the development of rehabilitation services and a higher level of care in nursing facilities, and these requirements have positioned nursing facilities to provide adequate subacute services.
- Nursing facilities can provide subacute services at a lower cost than acute care hospitals.

As a compromise position, it can be argued that subacute care is appropriately provided in both hospital and nursing facility settings and that the policy goal should be a level playing field for all subacute providers. This policy perspective is supported by at least the following arguments:

- At this point, there are insufficient outcome data to substantiate a claim by either the hospital industry or the nursing facility industry that a hospital or nursing facility site provides better quality subacute care.
- Although freestanding subacute facilities can make the claim that their costs are 30% to 60% less than hospital costs, it remains to be seen whether hospitals could reduce costs if a separate subacute level of care were authorized under Medicare.
- The definition of subacute care covers such a wide variety of medical conditions that it may turn out that some conditions are better treated in a hospital setting with back-up equipment and facilities and that other subacute conditions are more appropriately treated in a nursing facility.
- The definition of subacute care covers a wide variety of acuity levels (eg, between 3

Table 2–4   The Relationship between the Subacute Industry and the Hospital and Nursing Facility Industries

Opportunities	Policy Debates
Subacute care as a bridge between the hospital and nursing facility industries	Appropriate site of care
	CON requirements
	Licensure requirements
	Medicaid reimbursement
Hospital–nursing facility joint venture arrangements	
Integrated delivery systems	

and 8 nursing hours per day and 1 to 6 therapy hours per day), and the range of acuity levels suggests that it may be inappropriate to limit subacute care to one type of setting.

- Both industries have strong policy arguments, with hospitals arguing that excess acute capacity and swing bed programs call for subacute care in a hospital setting and nursing facilities arguing that lower costs and OBRA 1987 policies identify nursing facilities as the more appropriate site.

- Health care reform is likely to change the incentives and levels of care even further in the future; consequently, it may not be appropriate at this point, before the implementation of a comprehensive reform package, to make a policy decision concerning the appropriate site of subacute care.

One project that may shed some light on the appropriate site of care controversy is Illinois' 13-site comprehensive medical rehabilitation demonstration project.[40] The project began in 1994. The project includes hospital- and nursing facility–based programs to determine the most appropriate setting for subacute care. These sites are expected to include seven hospital-based and six nursing facility–based participants. All participating providers are required to obtain a CON and are subject to specific state regulations. Presently, a new level of reimbursement is not contemplated for the demonstration facilities.

A second study concerning the appropriate site of care is an HCFA-funded research project comparing rehabilitation care in rehabilitation hospitals and SNFs. The study is designed to determine whether SNFs or rehabilitation hospitals provide more cost-effective rehabilitation care. The study may be utilized by the HCFA in the future to develop new payment methods for selected types of subacute programs.[41]

In addition to the appropriate site of care issue, conflicts between state hospital and nursing facility associations have focused on CON, licensure, and Medicaid reimbursement provisions. Presently, the CON controversies tend to focus on exemptions to CON review for conver-

sion of acute care beds to long-term care beds and the implementation of CON criteria that may result in an advantage for either hospitals or nursing facilities to obtain CONs for subacute facilities.[37]

North Carolina has experienced two controversies in the CON area. In the late 1980s, the hospital industry and the nursing facility industry negotiated a CON exemption that authorized hospitals to convert acute care beds to SNF beds under certain limited circumstances.[4–7] In 1993, North Carolina's nursing home association opposed a proposal by the state hospital association to impose CON restrictions on nursing facilities planning to provide the increased levels of rehabilitation implicit in the provision of subacute care. The nursing home association asserted that OBRA 1987 rehabilitation requirements already mandated that appropriate rehabilitation services be provided to all nursing facility patients and that additional rehabilitation CON criteria should not be imposed on nursing facilities. The proposed CON modification was defeated in the state legislature.[37]

A second example involves two recent CON issues in Florida. The first issue focuses on 1995 state legislative efforts by the Florida Hospital Association to implement legislation allowing the one-time conversion of up to ten vacant acute care hospital beds to subacute beds without a new CON. This legislative initiative is being vigorously opposed by Florida's nursing home industry. The second controversy involves the assertion by hospitals that their CON applications for hospital-based SNFs should be reviewed by the Florida Agency for Health Care Administration under different CON rules and procedures than freestanding SNFs. In 1995, a Florida administrative law judge found that the types of patients served in hospital-based SNFs were different from those served by community-based SNFs and should be treated as a different type of CON application. This administrative law judge's decision is being appealed to a state court, although an appellate court decision is not expected until 1996.[42]

An example of a licensure conflict between a state hospital association and a state nursing home association involves a 1993 Texas licensure proposal. Under the proposal, state licensure standards for hospitals concerning comprehensive medical rehabilitation would have been imposed on nursing facilities. The hospital industry asserted that the proposal was necessary to ensure quality care in subacute SNFs. The nursing facilities argued that the requirement was an unnecessary barrier to cost-effective subacute programs. The state licensure revision was not implemented, in part because of the opposition of the Texas nursing home association.[37]

Health Care Reform

Health care reform is the overarching concern of all the policy initiatives discussed in this chapter. At this point, the role of subacute care in a managed competition model or other reform models is uncertain. Obviously, subacute providers must closely monitor the reform proposals at both federal and state levels. The reader should refer to Chapters 20 and 21 for thorough discussions of the implications of national and state health reform efforts for subacute care.

CONCLUSION

It is clear that the subacute care industry has moved beyond the historical policy issues surrounding the treatment gap between acute care services and traditional long-term care services. At the same time, most of the second-generation policy issues associated with the maturation of the subacute industry remain unresolved. The key issues have been identified, and initial steps have been taken to accumulate research data on the issues to develop appropriate policy initiatives. In some cases, policy initiatives are being tested. Resolution of the issues and analysis of the policy initiatives over the next few years will determine the legitimacy of the subacute industry and shape its future. Given the attention being paid to subacute care by regulators and policymakers, significant initiatives and changes are likely to occur during the late 1990s.

REFERENCES

1. McDowell TN. Subacute Care Providers: Filling a Treatment Gap. In: Gosfield A, ed. *1992 Health Law Handbook.* New York, NY: Clark Boardman Callaghan; 1992:173–204.

2. *Quicker and Sicker: Substandard Treatment of Medical Patients,* HR Rep 387, 101st Cong, 1st Sess (1989).

3. Kosecoff J, Kahn K, Rogers W, et al. Prospective payment system and impairment at discharge. *JAMA.* 1990;264:1980–1984.

4. Lewin-ICF. *Subacute Care in Hospitals, Synthesis of Findings* (prepared for the Prospective Payment Assessment Commission). Washington, DC: Lewin-ICF; 1988.

5. Michigan Hospital Association. *Patient Placement Delays in Michigan Hospitals.* Lansing, Mich: Michigan Hospital Association; 1989.

6. United Hospital Fund of New York. *Transitional Care: The Problem of Alternate Level of Care in New York City.* New York, NY: United Hospital Fund of New York; 1989.

7. Massachusetts Hospital Association. *Impact of the Nursing Home Bed Shortage on Massachusetts Hospitals: Patients Awaiting Placement Survey Report.* Burlington, Mass: Massachusetts Hospital Association; 1990.

8. Shaughnessy PW, Kramer AM. The increased needs of patients in nursing homes and patients receiving home health care. *N Engl J Med.* 1990;322:21–27.

9. US Department of Health and Human Services, Health Care Financing Administration. *Administratively Necessary Days. Report to Congress.* Washington, DC: US Department of Health and Human Services; 1990. Health Care Financing Administration Publ No 03307.

10. 42 CFR Part 412.

11. 42 USC §1395f(b); 42 USC §1395yy(a).

12. 42 CFR §413.40.

13. Prospective Payment Assessment Commission. *Interim Report on Payment Reform for PPS-Excluded Facilities.* Washington, DC: Prospective Payment Assessment Commission; 1992. Congressional Rep C-92-05.

14. US General Accounting Office. *Nursing Homes: Admission Problems for Medicaid Recipients and Attempts To Solve Them* (report to Howard Metzenbaum, US Senate). Washington, DC: Government Printing Office; 1990. General Accounting Office Publ No GAO/HRD-90-135.

15. Institute of Medicine, National Academy of Sciences. *Improving the Quality of Care in Nursing Homes.* Washington, DC: National Academy Press; 1986.

16. Prospective Payment Assessment Commission. *Medicare's Skilled Nursing Facility Payment Reform.* Washington, DC: Prospective Payment Assessment Commission; 1992. Congressional Rep C-92-01.

17. Neu CR, Harrison SC. *Posthospital Care before and after the Medicare Prospective Payment System.* Santa Monica, Calif: Rand Corporation; 1988.

18. PL 101-508, §4008(j), *amending* 42 USC §1395tt(a)(2)(B)(ii)(II).

19. Burns J. Subacute care feeds need to diversify. *Mod Healthcare.* December 13, 1993; 34–38.

20. Pallarito K. Charting the rapid rise of subacute care. *Mod Healthcare.* February 24, 1992; 52–56.

21. Wall T. Future looks bright for subacute industry. *Subacute Care Manage.* 1994;1:97–102.

22. O'Connor J. Vladeck puts nursing homes in their place. *McKnight's Long-Term Care News.* September 1993; 1: 46.

23. Lellis M. Developing outcome measures for subacute programs. *Natl Rep Subacute Care.* 1994;2:1–4.

24. Cline K. Data collection improving in subacute outcomes measurements. *Subacute Care Manage.* 1994;1:20–23.

25. National Health Policy Forum. *Adding to the Continuum: Emerging New Markets for Subacute Care.* Washington, DC: National Health Policy Forum; 1993. Issue Brief No 66.

26. Abt Associates. *Subacute Care in Freestanding Skilled Nursing Facilities: An Estimate of Savings to Medicare.* Cambridge, Mass: Abt Associates; 1994.

27. Severts S. Subacute care at what cost? *Healthcare Financ Manage.* November 1993;16.

28. Lellis M. Senator Hatch introduces bill to remove government barriers to subacute care. *Natl Rep Subacute Care.* 1994;2:5–6.

29. Department of Health and Human Services, Bureau of Policy Development. *Circumvention of PPS-Exclusion Criteria.* Washington, DC: Department of Health and Human Services; 1993. Ref No FQA-812.

30. 59 *Federal Register* 45330–01.

31. 59 *Federal Register* 1961.

32. Wall T. Government lays groundwork for regulatory, reimbursement changes with study. *Subacute Care Manage.* 1994;1:145–148.

33. Lellis M. Maryland to reimburse nursing homes for vent patients. *Natl Rep Subacute Care.* 1994;2:4.

34. Burns J. Sorting out subacute care. *Mod Healthcare.* April 25, 1994;28–32.

35. Pallarito K. HCFA begins project to evaluate cost-based rates for ventilator units. *Mod Healthcare.* January 20, 1992;21.

36. Lellis M. HCFA urged to study treatment of ventilator-dependent patients in subacute facilities. *Natl Rep Subacute Care.* 1993;1:6.

37. Cline K. States step in to define, regulate subacute care. *Subacute Care Manage.* 1994;1:9–11.

38. Arizona Health Care Cost Containment System. *Overview: Arizona's Health Care Program for the Indigent.* Phoenix, Ariz: Arizona Health Care Cost Containment System; 1993.

39. Cline K. As states implement managed Medicaid programs, reimbursement may improve. *Subacute Care Manage.* 1994;1:61–65.

40. Cline K. Demonstration project: Illinois considers licensing requirements for subacute care. *Subacute Care Manage.* 1994;1:30–32.

41. Lellis M. Who provides more cost-effective care—Rehab hospitals or SNFs? *Natl Rep Subacute Care.* 1994;2:5–6.

42. Lellis M. Florida subacute providers clash over certificate of need. *Natl Rep Subacute Care.* 1995;3:1–3.

3

Subacute Provider Profile

Cristie Upshaw Travis

Providers seeking to respond to pressure from third party payers to provide a less costly alternative treatment setting to hospital-based care have developed subacute care programs. Much of the focus in discussions of how subacute services are developing has been on individual companies and the strategies they are employing to position themselves to take advantage of this new opportunity. Little information is actually available about the subacute industry as a whole.

In the spring 1993, the Moore Group, a national health care consulting and market research firm, conducted a survey of freestanding nursing facilities and hospital-based skilled nursing units to identify the common characteristics of subacute providers and to develop a provider profile of the subacute industry. Because the focus of this survey was institution-specific, the results focus not on individual companies and their chosen strategies but on how the subacute industry is evolving. Survey results have been published in *Contemporary Long Term Care.*[1]

STUDY FINDINGS

Study Methodology

During the 3-month period from March through May 1993, a telephone survey of provid-

ers in 15 markets covering eight states (Arizona, Arkansas, California, Colorado, Idaho, Kansas, Texas, and Utah) was conducted. In total, more than 400 freestanding nursing facilities and nursing facility type units in hospitals were contacted. Figure 3–1 presents the distribution of survey respondents by state.

Survey participants were asked a series of questions designed to capture information about the facility's existing or planned subacute services. Information collected included facility capacity, Medicare certification status, types of patients treated, services provided, discharge disposition, frequency of rehabilitation services, and market position strategies.

Based on the results of the telephone survey, providers were assigned to four distinct categories: providers of medical subacute services, providers of intensive rehabilitation services, providers of both medical subacute and intensive rehabilitation services, and providers that did not offer either medical subacute or intensive rehabilitation services. For the purposes of this study, providers of medical subacute services were defined as those treating medically complex patients requiring specialized treatment services, such as intravenous therapy, tracheotomy aspiration, respiratory or ventilator

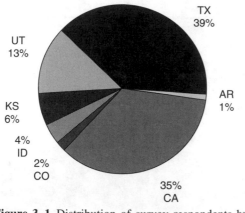

Figure 3–1 Distribution of survey respondents by state.

services, and postsurgical care. Intensive rehabilitation services were defined as including those services that served as an alternative to acute rehabilitation services and/or that were provided for patients in need of rehabilitation (ie, physical therapy, occupational therapy, and speech-language pathology services) but who were unable to tolerate the 3 hours of therapy a day generally required in an acute hospital rehabilitation program. Respondents were not required to operate separate, distinct medical subacute or intensive rehabilitation units to be categorized as providers of these services.

All respondents categorized as providing subacute medical and/or intensive rehabilitation services shared the following characteristics: Patients were discharged primarily to their home, rather than to long-term care, lengths of stay were relatively short, and facilities generally contracted with third party payers.

The distribution of survey respondents into the four categories given above is presented in Figure 3–2. As this figure indicates, a total of 94 respondents (22%) were identified as providing medical subacute (8%), intensive rehabilitation (8%), or both services (7%) at the time of the survey.

Major Findings

The following major findings represent the characteristics shared by the 94 identified providers of medical subacute and/or intensive rehabilitation services.

Provider Type

Fifty-six (60%) of the providers were freestanding nursing facilities, and 38 (40%) were hospital-based subacute providers (Figure 3–3). Four of the hospital-based providers (11%) were certified as long-term care hospitals.

Provider Ownership

Approximately 70% of all identified subacute providers were affiliated with a statewide, regional, or national health care company (Figure

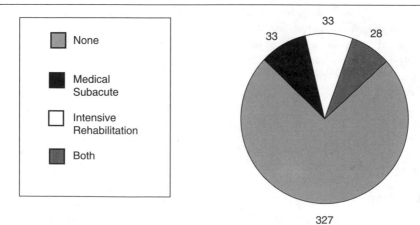

Figure 3–2 Distribution of survey respondents by subacute care category.

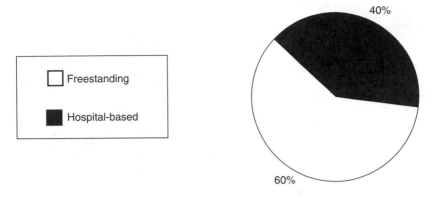

Figure 3–3 Distribution of identified subacute providers by provider type.

3–4). National health care companies accounted for 51% of the identified subacute providers. Providers offering only medical subacute services were less likely to be associated with a health care company (61%) than providers of intensive rehabilitation only or both types of subacute services (79% and 72%, respectively).

Service Mix

An equal number (33) of the subacute providers were identified as providers of medical subacute and intensive rehabilitation services (Figure 3–5). The remaining 28 (30%) provided both types of subacute services. The majority of

medical subacute providers (76%) were hospital based. The majority of intensive rehabilitation providers (88%) were freestanding nursing facilities. Sixty-eight percent (68%) of the respondents providing both types of subacute services were freestanding nursing facilities.

Facility Size

Medical subacute services were primarily provided in freestanding nursing facilities ranging in size from 101 to 149 beds (Figure 3–6). There were no distinct size characteristics found among those nursing facilities offering intensive rehabilitation services.

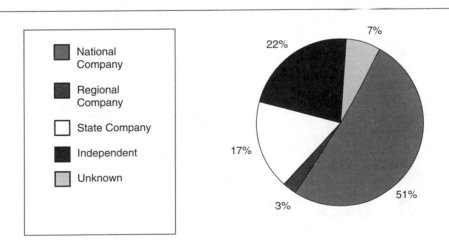

Figure 3–4 Identified subacute providers by type of ownership.

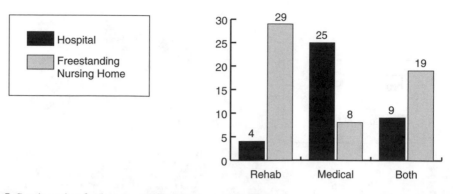

Figure 3–5 Service mix of subacute providers by type of facility.

Managed Care Contracting

Details regarding the subacute provider's contractual agreements with managed care organizations were collected for the facilities surveyed in California. Approximately 88% of the identified providers in California had contracts with managed care organizations that included coverage for subacute services (Figure 3–7).

Therapy Staff

Approximately 73% of the intensive rehabilitation providers and 64% of the providers offering both medical subacute and intensive rehabilitation services directly employed therapy staff. The remaining providers generally contracted out for therapy services. Providers using contract therapy services either used these services in combination with directly employed staff or relied totally on contracted services to provide therapy.

Rehabilitation Market Characteristics

The number of acute, hospital-based rehabilitation beds in a market did not affect the presence of subacute rehabilitation services. Intensive rehabilitation providers were identified in 11 of the 15 markets. The hospital-based rehabilitation bed-to-population ratios in these 11 markets ranged from a low of 6.9 beds per 100,000 population to a high of 65.5 beds per 100,000 population.

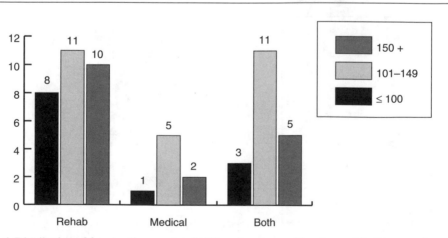

Figure 3–6 Distribution of freestanding nursing facility subacute providers by total facility capacity.

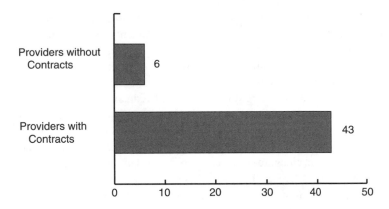

Figure 3–7 Number of identified subacute providers in California with managed care contracts.

DISCUSSION

Several observations about the development of the subacute industry can be made based on the survey results. First, national health care companies are fueling the growth of subacute services. With 51% of the identified providers being affiliated with national health care companies, it is clear that these companies are taking the lead in developing subacute services. The ability of companies to design and implement subacute programs on a national scale is enhanced by their diversified financial base of operations, their corporate-based expertise in new service development, national and regional contracting with third party payers, and their marketing and management expertise. The costs associated with the development of these corporate services can be spread over all the company's facilities and therefore are not the economic burden of any one facility. It is more difficult and costly per unit of service for independent providers to develop similar levels of expertise. Access to capital, either through public offerings or through venture capital investment, also provides an advantage to companies in rapidly developing subacute services on a regional or national scale. During the past 2 years, more than $600 million in initial public offerings has been raised for the expansion of subacute services.[2] In addition, because of their multiple sites, companies have the ability to

establish affiliations with other multisite health care companies, thereby creating integrated service delivery networks in several markets with just one agreement. The interest of long-term care companies offering subacute services in developing affiliations with Columbia/HCA Healthcare Corporation is the latest indication of this national and/or regional networking trend.[3]

Also, the development of market-specific and regional integrated service delivery networks may provide independent subacute providers with some of the advantages previously available only to the national companies. As members of a network, independent subacute providers have access to a solid referral base. Additional management and marketing expertise is available from the other network members, including hospitals, nursing facilities, managed care organizations, and outpatient providers. Capitation-based networks have an economic incentive to develop and provide services in the most cost-efficient setting, a factor that will support the continued growth and investment in subacute services.[4]

Two distinct types of subacute services are evolving: medical subacute services, generally provided by hospitals; and rehabilitation subacute services, generally provided by freestanding nursing facilities. The survey results indicate that the majority of medical subacute providers are hospitals (76%) and that the majority of intensive rehabilitation providers are freestanding nursing facilities (88%). The distinction in the settings in which each type of subacute service is provided may be based in part on reimbursement issues and in part on the traditional role that hospitals and nursing facilities have played in patient care. Subacute rehabilitation patients tend to require more ancillary services, including therapies, and less direct nursing care than medically complex patients. Given that ancillary services are reimbursed at cost and that nursing services are subject to the routine cost limitation (RCL), rehabilitation patients represent a greater potentially unrestricted source of revenue for skilled nursing providers. In addition, hospital-based skilled nursing facilities (SNFs) receive a higher RCL, which therefore allows hospitals better reimbursement for medically complex patients than is available to a freestanding nursing facility.

Medicare payment policies for skilled nursing services are undergoing revision, however. In the Omnibus Budget Reconciliation Act of 1993, the administrative and general add-on for excess overhead previously provided to hospital-based SNFs have been eliminated, and the Department of Health and Human Services has been asked to consider eliminating the differential in the RCL between hospital-based SNFs and freestanding nursing facilities. With the removal of more favorable reimbursement for hospitals and the subsequent creation of a more equitable business environment, the distinction in the types of subacute services being provided by hospitals and freestanding nursing facilities may diminish.

From a patient care perspective, hospitals have traditionally provided services to acutely ill patients. As such, the necessary emergency and support services are readily available should they be required for medical subacute patients. Physician acceptance and convenience are additional factors that support the development of medical subacute services in hospitals as opposed to freestanding nursing facilities. Significant changes in utilization and reimbursement resulting from the initiation of Medicare's prospective payment system and continued pressure from managed care to develop alternative, less costly treatment settings have forced hospitals to develop multi-level systems of care. Hospitals have significant excess capacity and therefore have the physical space to develop new, alternative treatment programs designed to generate revenue to cover fixed costs and to maintain or enhance market share. Medical subacute services provide hospitals with an opportunity to utilize existing space and offer a less costly treatment setting to manage Medicare patients better and to meet the increasing demands of managed care for lower-cost treatment.

In heavily managed care markets, the vast majority of respondents had managed care contracts that covered subacute services. Survey results indicate that in California 88% of the identified subacute providers had managed care contracts that covered subacute services. Because of their capitated fee structure and resulting requirement to provide care in the least costly, most appropriate setting, managed care companies utilize alternatives to hospitals more willingly than traditional indemnity insurance plans. Managed care contracts, including Medicare health maintenance organizations, provide a financial base upon which to build a subacute program and offer an alternative reimbursement source to Medicare.

A comparison of the distribution of survey participants to identified subacute providers by state also points out that the development of subacute services may be somewhat tied to the market penetration of managed care organizations. Figure 3–8 indicates that, although California facilities only represented 35% of the total facilities surveyed, 52% of the identified subacute providers were located in California. As managed care becomes the preferred model in the rest of the United States, the acceptance, and therefore the development, of less costly treatment settings, including subacute, will increase proportionately.

CONCLUSION

Although the profile of subacute providers is still evolving, the 1993 survey of subacute pro-

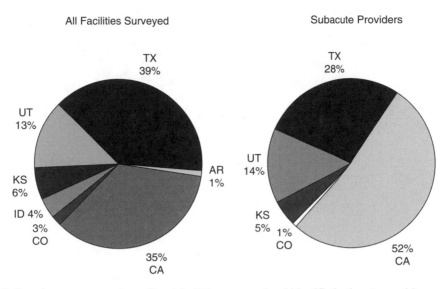

All Facilities Surveyed

TX
39%

UT
13%

KS
6%

ID 4%
3%
CO

35%
CA

AR
1%

Subacute Providers

TX
28%

UT
14%

KS
5% 1%
CO

52%
CA

Figure 3–8 State-by-state comparison of total facilities surveyed and identified subacute providers.

viders indicates that, in general, subacute providers are:

- affiliated with a health care company
- hospitals, if they provide medical subacute services
- freestanding nursing facilities, if they provide intensive rehabilitation services
- able to achieve economies of scale based on a bed capacity appropriate for total nursing facility services, with no unique bed size requirements for the provision of subacute services
- contracting with managed care providers to ensure an adequate base of non-Medicare patients
- directly employing their own therapy staff if they provide intensive rehabilitation services

- located in markets with low and high bed-to-population ratios for acute, hospital-based rehabilitation services

Reimbursement policies appear to have significantly affected the profile of the industry as it has emerged. Medicare policies differentiating freestanding nursing facilities from hospitals and managed care market penetration have helped determine who provides which type of subacute service and where those services are established. The ability of health care companies to develop and implement new products rapidly, including subacute services, on a national scale has resulted in national companies dominating the subacute provider base. As payment policies and mechanisms change under proposed reform and as market-specific networks and affiliations continue to evolve, the profile of subacute providers will probably change.

REFERENCES

1. Travis C, Goldstein S. Subacute provider profile. *Contemporary Long Term Care.* 1993;16:35–38.
2. Burns J. Subacute care feeds need to diversify. *Mod Healthcare.* December 13, 1993;23:34–38.
3. Lutz S, Burns J. Long-term-care firms eye Columbia ties. *Mod Healthcare.* 1994;24:6.
4. Grayson M. Warden speaks out. *Hosp Health Networks.* 1993;67:31–37.

An Overview of Provider Reimbursement: Medicare, Medicaid, and Managed Care

Theodore N. McDowell, Jr.

From a reimbursement perspective, subacute care can be viewed as a response to the idiosyncrasies of the health care reimbursement system; a strategy to manage Medicare patients within the health care system in a cost-effective and financially viable manner; and, within a managed care or managed competition model, a quality, low-cost alternative to the hospital setting. These three perspectives facilitate an understanding of many of the problems, criticisms, opportunities, and benefits associated with reimbursement strategies for subacute providers.

The analysis of the historical development of subacute care in Chapter 2 clearly shows that the conflicting incentives within the Medicare and Medicaid reimbursement system were a primary factor creating this new level of care. The idiosyncrasies of the system resulted in inadequate postacute care services for subacute patients. The Medicare and Medicaid reimbursement systems not only create a treatment gap for subacute patients but also create barriers to adequate reimbursement for subacute care. The lack of a separate Medicare or Medicaid reimbursement category for subacute care forces the facility seeking to provide subacute services to fit its services within a preexisting Medicare/Medicaid category. Medicare and Medicaid provider categories such as long-term care hospitals, rehabilitation hospitals, hospital-based skilled nursing facilities (SNFs), and freestanding SNFs become the vehicles for subacute care providers.

Many of the strategies discussed in this chapter involve obtaining adequate Medicare and Medicaid reimbursement for quality subacute services. These Medicare and Medicaid patient management strategies have led some critics to argue that subacute care is an attempt by providers to "game" the reimbursement system to increase revenues and that subacute providers will no longer play a role in the health care system once the reimbursement incentives are realigned under a managed care or managed competition model.[1] These criticisms, however, fail to recognize that subacute care has grown beyond a Medicare or Medicaid patient management strategy. The driving force behind subacute care is now managed care. Within a managed care system, subacute care is viewed as a low-cost, quality alternative to the hospital setting. In fact, most freestanding subacute facilities would not be financially viable without an emphasis on managed care reimbursement. Consequently, the central role of managed care in the subacute industry suggests that this level of care, rather than becoming obsolete, will grow in importance as financial incentives are altered under a managed care or managed competition approach.

To understand fully reimbursement strategies for subacute providers, it is necessary to analyze and compare the Medicare, Medicaid, and managed care reimbursement systems and strategies for each of the provider types offering subacute services. Thus, this chapter looks at the strategies being utilized by the following providers: swing bed hospitals, prospective payment system (PPS)–exempt specialty hospitals, freestanding SNFs, and hospital-based SNFs.

SWING BED HOSPITALS

Swing Bed Reimbursement

The swing bed program under Medicare, and under Medicaid for states that have adopted the program, offers an opportunity for rural hospitals to address the medical needs of subacute patients, to avoid the costly placement delays associated with such patients in rural areas, and to address both the excess of hospital beds in rural areas and the shortage of rural long-term care providers. The swing bed program authorizes small, rural hospitals that meet the eligibility requirements to use beds interchangeably as hospital, SNF, or nursing facility beds.[2] The hospital can swing its beds among a hospital, an SNF, and a nursing facility level of care on an as-needed basis. Reimbursement is based on the specific type of care provided in the bed.

Before the Omnibus Budget Reconciliation Act (OBRA) of 1990, routine service costs applicable to SNF type services provided in a swing bed were reimbursed under Medicare based on the average statewide Medicaid per diem rate for routine services furnished by SNFs during the previous calendar year. OBRA 1990 requires reimbursement for routine service costs furnished after October 1, 1990 to equal the payments for such costs under the Medicare program for freestanding SNFs in the swing bed facility's area.[3] This modification has improved reimbursement for swing bed services under Medicare.

Medicare reimbursement and Medicare certification requirements distinguish between rural hospitals with 1 to 49 beds and larger rural hospitals with 50 to 99 beds. The larger swing bed hospitals are subject to a 5-day transfer rule, which requires a swing bed patient to be transferred in 5 weekdays to an SNF in the hospital's geographic area if there is an available SNF bed. Medicare will not reimburse for extended care services after the 5-day transfer period unless the patient's physician certifies within the 5-day period that the transfer is not medically appropriate.[4] In addition, SNF patient days in a cost-reporting period may not exceed 15% of the product of the number of days in the period multiplied by the average number of licensed beds in the swing bed hospital for that period.[5] Medicare will not reimburse the larger rural hospitals for SNF services to the extent that they exceed the 15% limitation except with respect to services to patients already receiving extended care services when the 15% limit is reached.[6]

Medicaid reimbursement for extended care services in a swing bed hospital varies from state to state and will be based on each state's reimbursement methodology for nursing facilities or be developed under the Boren Amendment criteria. It should be kept in mind that in many states Medicaid reimbursement schemes place unique limitations on swing bed reimbursement.

In contrast to the other subacute provider categories discussed in this chapter, most swing bed hospitals do not rely on managed care reimbursement. In most cases, managed care penetration will be low in rural areas and will not create sufficient volume to justify a swing bed hospital basing its strategic plan on a managed care approach.

Evaluation of the Swing Bed Program

During the late 1980s, a number of evaluations analyzed the characteristics of the swing bed program; Exhibit 4–1 summarizes these characteristics.[7] The research concerning payer mix and length of stay suggests that swing bed programs focus on short-stay Medicare patients. Table 4–1[7] shows the payer mix and the average length of

Exhibit 4–1 Common Characteristics of Swing Bed
Programs

Patient characteristics
- Short stay
- Medicare beneficiaries

Medicare patient management strategy
- Beds utilized as holding beds until Medicare
  patient can be discharged
- Allows hospital to avoid costly Medicare
  placement delays
- Allows hospital to develop a continuum of care

Services
- Subacute
- Rehabilitation oriented
- High intensity
- 20% more costly than traditional SNFs because
  of subacute orientation

Referral patterns
- Mostly from acute settings
- Predominantly from the swing bed hospital itself

Volume thresholds
- 1500 to 3000 swing bed days per year
- Above threshold, costs begin to exceed revenues
- Above threshold, hospital converted to a SNF

Quality of care
- High-quality subacute services
- Not equipped to provide traditional long-term
  care services

---

stay of swing bed patients. Although this research is based on 1985 data, a more recent analysis suggests that the previous research remains an accurate picture of most swing bed programs. A 1992 study found that the average length of stay in swing beds during 1990 was 16.7 days.[8]

The research on payer mix and length of stay indicates that the swing bed program is utilized mainly as a Medicare patient management strategy.[7] Swing beds often serve as holding beds until patients are sufficiently rehabilitated to return home or until nursing facility beds become available in the community. The program allows rural hospitals to avoid costly placement delays, which can have a more significant financial impact under the Medicare program on small rural hospitals than on other hospitals.[9] The swing bed program also allows rural hospitals to provide a

continuum of care without expending the capital necessary to develop a hospital-based SNF.

A Health Care Financing Administration (HCFA) 1989 evaluation confirms that most swing bed programs concentrate on short-stay subacute patients.[10] The programs tend to treat rehabilitation-oriented medical conditions, such as hip fractures, rather than the chronic medical conditions addressed in the traditional community SNF. Compared with community SNF patients, swing bed patients were found to be 20% more costly because of the emphasis on rehabilitation services and ancillary services.

The HCFA evaluation also pointed out that most swing bed admissions are from the acute care setting and, more particularly, from the swing bed hospital itself. This finding suggests that the swing bed program may be utilized primarily to address access problems for a particular hospital rather than regional subacute needs.

In addition, the HCFA evaluation identified volume thresholds associated with the cost effectiveness of a program. Although the volume threshold varies from facility to facility, as a general matter a facility's volume threshold will fall between 1500 to 3000 swing bed days per year. Once a hospital exceeds the volume threshold, the costs associated with operating a swing bed program begin to exceed revenues, and it no longer remains advantageous to operate the program. In essence, hospitals operating above the volume threshold have converted into SNFs.

In terms of quality of care, the HCFA evaluation concluded that swing bed programs provided higher-quality subacute services than freestanding, rural SNFs. On the other hand, swing

---

Table 4–1 Payer Source and Average Length of Stay
(ALOS), 1985

Payer Source	Percentage of All Swing Bed Days	ALOS (days)
Medicare	49	14
Medicaid	8	48
Other (mostly private pay)	43	30
All sources	100	17–20

bed programs were not as well equipped to provide traditional long-term care services.

Summary

The swing bed program is an important subacute strategy in rural areas. In many rural areas, it may be the only provider of such services given the lack of SNF facilities within a rural area, the inability of many rural SNFs to provide subacute levels of care, and the hesitancy of many freestanding subacute providers to enter into rural areas because of the lack of managed care penetration. Finally, it is possible that the swing bed program could become a model for subacute services in the future under a managed competition model. For instance, if health care reform creates further excess capacity in acute care beds, the swing bed program would offer an opportunity for hospitals to utilize excess beds for alternative purposes and create a smooth transition for patients back into the community.

SPECIALTY HOSPITALS AND DISTINCT PART UNITS

Types of Specialty Hospitals

Many specialty hospitals and distinct part units within a hospital are designed specifically to meet the needs of the subacute patient. The specialty hospital or distinct part unit will be exempt from Medicare's PPS for hospitals and will be reimbursed on a reasonable cost basis subject to an annual target ceiling limitation or target amount.[11]

The Medicare regulations exclude the following five types of hospitals from PPS reimbursement: psychiatric hospitals, rehabilitation hospitals, children's hospitals, long-term care hospitals, and cancer hospitals.[12] In addition, rehabilitation distinct part units within a hospital also are exempt from PPS reimbursement.[13] Presently, the long-term care hospital, the rehabilitation hospital, and the rehabilitation distinct part unit are the providers that tend to be most active in the subacute industry. As more subacute pro-

grams are being developed to address cancer patients and pediatric patients with traumatic injuries or congenital deformities, children's hospitals and cancer hospitals in some cases may be considered legitimate vehicles for developing specialized subacute programs.

Medicare Reimbursement

Although Medicare certification requirements vary among the different types of specialty hospitals, all the PPS-excluded specialty hospitals are reimbursed on a reasonable cost basis subject to target ceiling limitations. The target ceiling limitation is a ceiling on the operating costs per case for which Medicare will reimburse the specialty hospital or unit. Each excluded provider's target amount equals the provider's allowable operating costs per case for the provider's base period increased by a statutorily prescribed inflation factor.[14]

If a specialty hospital's costs fall below its target amount, then it is paid its costs plus an additional bonus equaling the lower of 50% of the difference between its costs and the target amount or 5% of the target amount.[15] In contrast, if a provider's costs are higher than the target amount, then Medicare will pay a provider an additional payment equaling 50% of the amount by which costs exceed the provider's target amount after any exceptions or adjustments.[16] The additional amount, however, may not exceed 10% of the provider's target amount.[17]

Historically, perhaps the primary reimbursement issue for specialty hospitals has involved costs exceeding the provider's target amount. A Prospective Payment Assessment Commission (ProPAC) analysis[18] based on 1989 cost data reveals the extent of the problem (Table 4–2).

As a general matter, the provision of subacute services by specialty hospitals theoretically could result in such hospitals being denied reimbursement by peer review organizations (PROs). For instance, the PROs could decide that a specialty hospital's services are more appropriately SNF level than hospital level.[19] From a practical perspective, such denials rarely occur, although

Table 4–2 ProPAC Analysis of Costs Exceeding Provider's Target Amount

Type of Facility	Percentage over Target Amount
Rehabilitation facilities	53
Hospital	43
Distinct-part units	55
Psychiatric facilities	66
Hospitals	61
Distinct-part units	68
Long-term hospitals	72
Children's hospitals	58
Cancer hospitals	57

Source: Reprinted from ProPAC, *Interim Report on Payment Reform for PPS-Excluded Facilities,* Congressional Report C-92-05, October 1992.

the concern may be one reason why many specialty hospitals are hesitant to identify themselves as subacute providers. The level of care issue also results in most specialty hospitals providing services to more long-term transitional patients or chronic subacute patients compared with general subacute patients.

Reimbursement Strategies

In response to Medicare reimbursement problems, specialty hospitals often rely on a five-pronged strategy (Exhibit 4–2). First, new specialty hospitals usually attempt to establish favorable target ceiling limitations by maximizing costs in the provider's base year. This strategy is one reason why new specialty hospitals tend to have more favorable target ceiling limitations and are performing better financially than many older specialty hospitals operating under restrictive and outdated ceiling limitations.[18] The process of establishing ceiling limitations during a base period has been criticized by the HCFA as inefficient and contributing to the escalation of health care costs.[19]

As a second strategy, these providers closely monitor costs to avoid exceeding their target amounts. Most providers develop comprehensive monitoring programs that examine patient acuity, patient functional status, case-mix information, and labor costs. Such monitoring programs will affect the operational and clinical aspects of a facility. The monitoring programs also increase the importance of case management and discharge planning systems within a specialty hospital or unit.

Third, specialty hospitals may seek relief from target ceiling limitations through exemptions and exceptions to the ceiling limitations. The bases for exemptions and exceptions include new hospital status, extraordinary circumstances, noncomparability to the base year, significant wage increases, and nonrepresentative base period.[20] As a general limitation to all the adjustments, the hospital's operating costs must be reasonable and attributable to circumstances specified by the hospitals and verified by the Medicare intermediary.[21]

New specialty hospitals are exempt from ceiling limitations for a start-up period, which expires at the end of the first cost reporting period beginning at least 2 years after the hospital accepts its first patient.[22] A new hospital is defined as a provider of inpatient hospital services that has operated as the type of hospital for which the HCFA granted it approval to participate in the Medicare program, under present and/or previous ownership, for less than 3 full years.[22] Medicare regulations clarify that a newly established distinct part unit will not qualify for the new pro-

Exhibit 4–2 Specialty Hospital Reimbursement Strategies

Establish favorable Medicare target ceiling limitation
Monitor costs
Obtain Medicare exemptions/exceptions to ceiling limitations
  • New hospital status
  • Extraordinary circumstances
  • Noncomparability to base year
  • Significant wage increases
  • Nonrepresentative base period
Develop managed care strategy
Support favorable reforms to Medicare reimbursement system

vider exemption unless the entire hospital would qualify as a new hospital under the Medicare regulations.[23]

After the new provider exemption expires, the hospital must seek an exception to the target amount. Perhaps the most common exception for specialty hospitals is the noncomparability to base year category. This exception allows an adjustment for significant distortions in operating costs of inpatient hospital services between the provider's base year and the cost reporting period subject to the limits. Adjustments for cost distortions include adjustments to take into account Federal Insurance Contributions Act (FICA) taxes; services billed under Medicare Part B during the provider's base period but paid under Medicare Part A during the subject cost reporting period; malpractice insurance costs; increases in service intensity or length of stay attributable to changes in the type of patient served; a change in the type of services provided by the hospital, such as an addition or discontinuation of services or treatment programs; and, the manipulation of discharges to increase reimbursement.[24] Thus a hospital that develops programs for a higher patient acuity level and shifts its treatment focus to serve a new category of subacute or transitional patient may be able to obtain an adjustment based on increases in service intensity, increases in length of stay, or changes in programs and services.

In addition to the noncomparability to base year exception, other exceptions may be available to a specialty hospital on a more limited basis. The extraordinary circumstances exception is limited to unusual costs due to extraordinary circumstances beyond its control, such as strikes, fires, earthquakes, floods, or other unusual occurrences with substantial cost effects.[25] Providers generally have found it difficult to obtain extraordinary circumstances exceptions, and the exception typically will be inapplicable to increased costs related to patient acuity and subacute programs.

In the early 1990s, the HCFA developed exceptions related to wage increases and nonrepresentative base periods. Effective October 1, 1991, HCFA considers an adjustment to take into account a significant increase in wages occurring between the base period and the cost reporting period subject to a ceiling. The increase in the average hourly wage for the geographic area in which the hospital is located must be above a threshold wage index value.[26]

Effective with cost reporting periods beginning on or after April 1, 1990, the HCFA may assign a new base period for a provider to establish a revised ceiling if the new base period is more representative of the reasonable and necessary costs of furnishing inpatient services.[27] A rebasing may be difficult to obtain because the hospital must document higher costs resulting from substantial and permanent changes in furnishing patient care services since the base period.[28] The regulations require the HCFA to take into account changes in the services provided by the hospital, changes in applicable technologies and medical practice, and differences in the severity of illness among patients or types of patients served. A rebasing will only be made if the cost distortions cannot be addressed adequately through the more restrictive adjustments available under the noncomparability adjustment.[29]

As a fourth strategy, many specialty hospitals are developing managed care strategies to shift the payer mix away from Medicare and Medicaid patients. The specialty hospital can position itself as a low-cost alternative to the traditional acute care hospital or as a component of an integrated delivery system's continuum of care. Specialty hospitals often establish programs for chronic subacute and long-term transitional subacute patients that are managed care oriented.

As a final strategy, many specialty hospitals are pushing for modifications to the present Medicare reimbursement system. For instance, pressure is being exerted on the HCFA to address the disadvantages experienced by many specialty hospitals that have been in existence for a number of years. Such facilities often are subject to extremely low target ceiling limitations compared with newer facilities that have been able to develop more favorable ceiling limitations. Providers assert that the rebasing mechanisms developed in 1990 are too restrictive to alleviate the disadvantage. This reimbursement issue may be addressed in the future by increases in the ability of older facilities to rebase their target ceiling limitations based on more recent cost data.[18,19]

Reform Proposals

In light of the Medicare reimbursement problems experienced by many specialty hospitals and the view that cost-based reimbursement is inefficient in terms of cost containment, policymakers are considering comprehensive modifications to the present cost-based methodology. Policymakers are exploring new payment systems to replace the cost-based methodology. OBRA 1990 called for the US Department of Health and Human Services (DHHS) to recommend by April 1992 a new Prospective Payment System for PPS-excluded hospitals and units or a means of substantially revising the current system.[30] Although DHHS has not issued a report at this time, ProPAC has published an interim report on the issue.[18]

The ProPAC report concludes that development of a Prospective Payment System for specialty hospitals may be extremely difficult and should be viewed as a long-term strategy at best. Most of the progress related to developing such a system has been achieved by the rehabilitation industry. Even Prospective Payment Systems for rehabilitation hospitals remain in the developmental stages, however, and actual implementation of such systems remains a long-term strategy. The ProPAC report, however, did suggest some revisions to the present system to alleviate inequities within the system. Suggested modifications include developing separate updates for each type of specialty hospital, rebasing the target amount for older providers, and improving the exception process.

The future viability of specialty hospitals as subacute providers may be affected by other reform proposals being considered by the HCFA and government agencies. For instance, during congressional hearings on health care reform in 1993, the HCFA proposed a moratorium on long-term care hospitals as a means of reducing Medicare costs.[31] The HCFA estimated that the moratorium would save approximately $530 million over a 5-year period. Such a moratorium obviously would restrict the use of long-term care hospitals as a strategy in the future.

A second example involves the new conditions of participation for long-term care hospitals issued in the *Federal Register* on September 1, 1994.[32] The new requirements address a common subacute strategy called the hospital-within-a-hospital strategy. Because of the HCFA's concern that such arrangements may circumvent the intent of the Medicare statute and regulations, the rule significantly restricts the ability of PPS hospitals to implement the hospital-within-a-hospital strategy. See Chapter 15 for a full discussion of these new conditions of participation.

As a third example, on May 27, 1994, the HCFA issued a proposed rule to modify the definition of a transfer from a PPS hospital to include transfer from a PPS hospital to a specialty hospital, such as a long-term care hospital or rehabilitation hospital.[33] Presently, the movement of a patient from a PPS hospital to a specialty hospital is considered a discharge. The PPS hospital receives full diagnosis-related group (DRG) payment, and the specialty hospital receives its standard cost-based reimbursement for treating the patient. In contrast, the recharacterization of the movement of the patient as a transfer would result in a full DRG payment being made to the specialty hospital as the discharging hospital and the transferring hospital being paid a per diem rate for each day of the patient's stay in the PPS facility. This modification could result in PPS hospitals referring more subacute patients to SNFs as opposed to specialty hospitals because SNFs would not be subject to the new transfer provision. In response to numerous negative comments, the HCFA decided not to implement the proposed rule in 1994.

As a final example, the HCFA has considered developing a cost-based reimbursement category for ventilator-dependent patients within acute care hospitals.[34,35] Such a development could undermine many long-term care hospitals, which rely primarily on ventilator-dependent programs. This possibility may be one reason why many long-term care hospital companies diversified their programs away from ventilator programs during the early 1990s.

FREESTANDING SNFs

The Basic Strategy: Radical Shift in Case Mix

Freestanding SNFs considering the development of subacute units or programs face significant challenges. The freestanding SNF must operate in a highly regulated industry and comply with Medicare certification requirements that are often unrelated to or inappropriate for subacute programs. The freestanding SNF also faces restrictive Medicare and Medicaid reimbursement systems that often are insufficient to cover the costs of treating subacute patients. Finally, higher operating costs for subacute programs may appear to be a barrier to entering the industry in light of the low profit margins experienced by traditional SNFs. The result is an apparent disincentive for the traditional, freestanding SNF to treat subacute patients.

To meet the challenge and overcome the barriers, the basic reimbursement strategy for a freestanding subacute SNF involves a radical change in case mix. The shift in case mix includes an increased emphasis on managed care patients, an increased emphasis on Medicare patients, and the elimination or reduction of Medicaid patients. This shift in case mix necessitates significant modifications to the facilities, equipment, operations, staffing, and programs of the SNF.

The radical change in case mix is seen by comparison of the case mix of the traditional SNF with that of the subacute SNF. As seen in Figure 4–1, the traditional SNF will have a payer mix emphasizing Medicaid and private pay (out-of-pocket) residents, with only a small percentage of the payer mix including managed care residents and Medicare residents.[8] In contrast, Figure 4–2 represents the payer mix objectives of many subacute SNFs. The primary goal is to emphasize

managed care patients and achieve a payer mix with more than 50% managed care patients. In many cases, however, it may be difficult to push the managed care payer mix to 50% given the lack of managed care penetration in most areas. The case-mix goal also includes increased emphasis on Medicare residents, with many subacute facilities having 50% to 70% of the case mix represented by Medicare. Finally, the subacute SNF will typically reduce, or may even eliminate, the Medicaid patients in its facility.

The Managed Care Strategy

Managed care companies view the freestanding subacute SNF as a low-cost alternative to the hospital setting. Many analysts estimate that subacute facilities can provide services at 20% to 60% lower costs than the hospital.[36–38] From the provider perspective, the subacute facility views managed care as beneficial because the reimbursement level will be considerably higher, in most cases, than Medicare or Medicaid reimbursement. Managed care reimbursement for the subacute SNF tends to fall between $250 and $600 per day depending on a variety of factors, such as managed care penetration in the area and the specific programs developed in a facility.[39]

The Medicare Strategy

The increased emphasis on Medicare patients raises important Medicare reimbursement issues

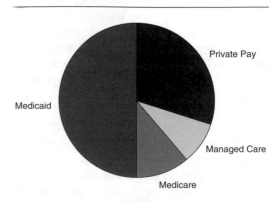

Figure 4–1 Traditional SNF case mix.

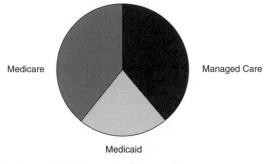

Figure 4–2 Subacute SNF case mix.

that often are not experienced by the traditional SNF. As background, Medicare reimbursement for SNFs involves three components: routine costs, capital costs, and ancillary costs. Reimbursement issues for subacute SNFs will cluster around routine costs and ancillary costs.

Routine Costs

The Medicare regulations establish four routine cost limits (RCLs):[40]

1. *freestanding SNFs in urban areas:* the cost limits are based on 112% of the mean per diem routine service costs for this group

2. *freestanding SNFs in rural areas:* the cost limits are based on 112% of the mean per diem routine service costs for this group

3. *hospital-based SNFs in urban areas:* the cost limits are based on the limit for freestanding SNFs in urban areas plus 50% of the amount by which the mean per diem routine service costs for urban hospital-based SNFs exceed those for urban freestanding SNFs

4. *hospital-based SNFs in rural areas:* the cost limits are based on the limit for freestanding SNFs in rural areas plus 50% of the amount by which the mean per diem routine costs for rural hospital-based SNFs exceed those for rural freestanding SNFs

During the late 1980s, many SNFs experienced financial problems because the RCLs were based on 1982 and 1983 data. To address this issue, OBRA 1990 requires the HCFA to update SNF RCLs for cost reporting periods beginning September 1989 by using cost data from 1988 to 1989.[41] The benefits of the new RCLs, however, may be overshadowed by the OBRA 1993 freeze on cost limits. OBRA 1993 freezes the RCLs for fiscal years 1994 and 1995, and consequently there will be no rebasing or inflationary adjustments for 3 years.[42]

The freeze on cost limits may exacerbate the serious problems experienced by most subacute SNFs in terms of costs exceeding the RCLs because of the high patient acuity level found in subacute SNFs compared with traditional SNFs. The HCFA recently estimated that 62% of hospital-based SNFs and 23% of freestanding SNFs will have costs exceeding their RCL during fiscal years 1994 and 1995.[43] The RCLs force subacute SNFs to rely heavily on the exemptions and exceptions to the RCLs.

The basic exemption/exception strategy depicted in Figure 4–3 involves obtaining a new provider exemption and subsequently applying for an atypical services exception. The new provider exemption applies to providers that have operated as the type of provider for which it is Medicare certified (under present and previous ownership) for less than 3 years. The exemption expires at the end of the provider's first cost reporting period beginning at least 2 years after the provider accepts its first patient.[44] Under the exemption, the SNF is reimbursed for its full routine costs during the start-up phase. The new provider exemption is based on the assumption that a new facility has start-up costs that are not experienced by established providers.

After the new provider exemption expires, most subacute providers will apply for an atypical services exception. This exception most often relates to atypical nursing services in a subacute facility. To obtain the exception, the provider must show that actual costs exceed the applicable RCL because the items or services are atypical in nature and scope compared with the items and services generally furnished by similarly classified providers.[45] During 1994 and 1995, when the

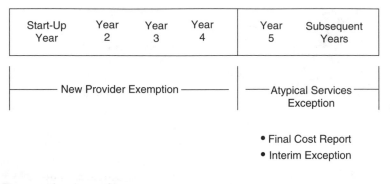

Figure 4–3 RCL exemptions/exceptions.

RCLs are frozen, SNFs cannot calculate excess costs based on the frozen rates. The calculation must be based on what the RCL would have been if unfrozen.[43] The facility also must show that the atypical items or services were furnished because of the special needs of the patients treated and are necessary in the efficient delivery of needed health care.[23]

The prevalence of atypical services exception requests increased dramatically during the early 1990s. HCFA officials suggest that such requests increased by a factor of 20 between 1988 and 1993 and predict that such requests will continue to increase in the future.[19]

During the late 1980s and early 1990s, many providers experienced problems with the procedures for the atypical services exception because the HCFA had not published any manual provisions outlining the procedural steps for exception requests or the documentation necessary to substantiate the request. In an attempt to address the issue, the HCFA published transmittal number 378 in July 1994.[46] The transmittal revises the *Medicare Provider Reimbursement Manual* and implements specific procedures for exception requests.

The transmittal requires exception requests to be filed with the intermediary within 180 days of the date on the intermediary's notice of program reimbursement. Within 90 days of receipt of a complete exception request, the intermediary must make a recommendation to the HCFA. In turn, the HCFA must make a final determination within 90 days after receipt of the intermediary's recommendation. Before the transmittal, the HCFA was afforded 180 days to make a final determination.

As an alternative to an exception request at the end of a cost reporting period, the SNF may apply for an interim exception. Most providers prefer the interim exception to improve cash flow.[47] If a provider has never received an atypical services exception in the past, an interim exception can be obtained by projecting costs in excess of the limit. The projected costs and the actual costs are reconciled at the end of the cost reporting period. If a provider has obtained an atypical services exception for the previous year, it can receive an interim exception based upon the previous year's exception. Again, a reconciliation will take place at the end of the cost reporting period based on actual data.

The HCFA transmittal identifies the documentation to be submitted in support of an atypical exception request. The SNF's request must include information documenting costs and comparing such costs with the facility's peer group cost data. The exception request also must show a higher case mix based upon factors such as discharge data, shorter average length of stay, higher incidence of ancillary services, and higher average Medicare utilization.

It should be noted that additional exceptions may be available in limited circumstances. For instance, a facility may be able to obtain an extraordinary circumstances exception if it can show that it experienced higher costs due to extraordinary circumstances beyond the provider's control.[48] Extraordinary circumstances are narrowly construed to include events such as strikes, fires, earthquakes, and floods. The circumstances generally are inapplicable to subacute programs.

Also, a provider may be able to take advantage of the exception for unusual labor costs. This exception relates to providers that experience a percentage of labor costs that varies more than 10% from that included in the promulgation of the limits.[49] Finally, an exception exists for providers in fluctuating population areas.[50] The provider must show that it has a population that varies significantly during the year, that the appropriate health planning agency has determined that the area does not have a surplus of beds or similar services in the area, that the provider's services are necessary, and that the provider meets the occupancy standards established by DHHS.

Ancillary Services

Medicare makes a distinction between routine services and ancillary services. Routine services are defined as the regular room, dietary, and nursing services; minor medical and surgical supplies; medical social services; psychiatric social services; and the use of equipment and facilities for which a separate charge is not customarily made.[51] Ancillary services, on the other hand, include services for which charges are customarily made in addition to routine services.[52] Examples of ancillary services include physical therapy, occupational therapy, and speech-language pathology services. Ancillary service costs are apportioned to Medicare on the basis of the ratio of Medicare beneficiary charges to all patient charges. The ratio is determined for each ancillary department and is applied to the total cost of that department to determine Medicare's share of overall costs.[53]

The intensive rehabilitation services and other ancillary services required by many subacute patients increase the importance of Medicare reimbursement for such services. Subacute providers must decide whether to provide ancillary services directly or to contract for such services with outside suppliers. This decision should be based on a thorough financial and reimbursement analysis. Subacute providers increasingly are bringing ancillary services in house to maintain quality and reduce costs. This trend is reinforced by the expressed preference of many managed care organizations.

Subacute providers also should monitor modifications to reimbursement for ancillary services, such as the 1995 modifications to Medicare reimbursement for physical therapy, occupational therapy, and speech–language pathology services. Providers also may need to advocate for changes to reimbursement schemes that create barriers to effective services, such as the Medicare rule requiring respiratory therapy to be provided in a SNF pursuant to an arrangement with a hospital.

Medicare Reform Efforts

During the early 1990s, policymakers examined the Medicare SNF reimbursement system and offered proposals for reform. In a 1992 report, ProPAC identified current problems, including rapidly rising expenditures, inequitable distribution of payments, barriers to SNF services, and poor-quality care.[54] The report emphasized that the current payment method does not adequately account for variations in costs relating to patient acuity levels and resource utilization, resulting in substantial payment inequities across providers. The system's failure to take into account important cost variations also affects access for subacute Medicare patients.

The ProPAC report identified the goals of payment reform as including recognition of legitimate differences in factors that affect costs, thereby promoting equitable payment for efficient providers; encouragement of appropriate access to care for Medicare beneficiaries; encouragement of the provision of high-quality care; and provision of incentives for efficient use of resources. With those goals in mind, the report analyzed various payment policy options, including retrospective cost-based payments with limits, retrospective cost-based payments without limits, prospective per diem payments without a case-mix adjustment, prospective per diem payments with a case-mix adjustment, and payments bundled with hospital DRG payments.

The report supported efforts to develop and implement a case-mix adjustment to Medicare SNF payments similar to the demonstration project being developed by the HCFA.[55] The HCFA case-mix demonstration project will be implemented in four states under Medicare and Medicaid. The system will prospectively set payments that will be adjusted to account for the mix and service needs of patients in a facility. The case-mix system classifies nursing facility residents into mutually exclusive categories based upon resident acuity and the amount of resource utilization needed for a resident. Reimbursement for a resident will vary depending on the resident's categorization.[56]

The proposed case-mix system contains a hierarchy of resident categories based upon the relative resource utilization or cost associated with each category. Each resident will be assigned to the highest-cost category for which he or she qualifies. Within each category, additional distinctions are made based upon intensity of service, resident functionality, and additional problems. The Medicare case-mix demonstration project offers an opportunity to create incentives for nursing facilities to treat subacute patients effectively. The future adequacy of a case-mix system, however, requires the upper level under the case-mix system to be high enough to cover actual subacute costs. It is questionable at this point whether the case-mix system will contain a level that is adequate to cover the cost of most subacute programs. Furthermore, the Medicare portion of the demonstration project has experienced a number of delays, and the actual implementation date remains uncertain.

The Medicaid Strategy

Under the Medicaid program, states have some flexibility to develop differing methodolo-gies as long as they adhere to the Boren Amendment criteria. Methodologies vary from case mix, to facility specific, to class rate to managed care methodologies.[57,58] The current policy trend appears to be toward a case-mix system. Regardless of the specific Medicaid reimbursement methodology employed by a state, in most cases Medicaid reimbursement will not cover the full cost of treating subacute residents. This situation creates a barrier for SNFs to accept Medicaid-eligible subacute residents. Consequently, the common strategy for subacute SNFs involves either eliminating or reducing Medicaid-oriented services.

The reduction or elimination strategy creates policy concerns. Many critics argue that the avoidance of Medicaid residents creates a two-tiered system and exacerbates the severe access problem already experienced by many Medicaid long-term care residents. For instance, a 1990 General Accounting Office report concluded that Medicaid recipients have more problems getting into nursing facilities than higher paying private payers.[59] The higher private rates create financial incentives for nursing facilities to select private payers over Medicaid recipients. These incentives may be enhanced for the subacute provider relying on managed care reimbursement levels, which may be even higher than private pay rates.

If Medicaid access problems persist, pressure may increase on policymakers to consider a number of policy reforms. Policy options to increase access include requiring equal Medicaid and private pay reimbursement rates, increasing Medicaid rates, and basing Medicaid payments on care needs of individual residents.

The equalization of nursing facility rates may reduce placement delays for Medicaid recipients because the option removes a nursing facility's financial incentive to prefer private payers over Medicaid recipients. The equal rates option, however, would not alter a nursing facility's incentive to select lighter care patients compared with subacute patients. Furthermore, adoption of such an option could result in many subacute facilities declining to participate in the Medicaid program.

Although an increase in Medicaid reimbursement rates will improve the overall access of Medicaid recipients to nursing facilities, placement delays are likely to continue for subacute patients. In addition, most states may be unable to increase Medicaid rates for nursing facilities because of budget constraints.

The option that may most effectively address subacute placement delays involves basing Medicaid payments on the care needs of the individual. States that have implemented case-mix reimbursement methodologies have shown a reduction in heavy care placement delays.[60] Given Medicaid budget restrictions, however, the upper rate level under a case-mix system may continue to be too low to cover subacute care costs.

In sum, it does not appear that any of the general policy options for overall Medicaid nursing facility reimbursement possess the potential to provide adequate reimbursement for a subacute level of care. Some states, however, are developing a specific subacute level of reimbursement under Medicaid or are authorizing negotiated rates with special care units. These trends may create new incentives for subacute facilities to increase Medicaid-oriented programs.

Industry reports indicate that facilities in Pennsylvania, New Jersey, New Hampshire, Maine, and Florida have negotiated exceptions to Medicaid rates for subacute facilities based upon a showing of the unique level of care provided by the facility.[61] The negotiated exception argument also must include a showing that the subacute specialty facility will actually reduce Medicaid costs overall because the specialty facility will serve as an alternative to more costly hospital care.

Many states have gone beyond negotiated exceptions and have developed specific subacute levels of reimbursement under Medicaid.[61] In most instances, the new reimbursement levels are limited to a high-profile subset of subacute conditions, such as ventilator-dependent patients and patients with acquired immunodeficiency syndrome (AIDS). For instance, Virginia has four special rate categories targeted for different types of adult specialized care populations: ventilator-dependent patients, complex health care, comprehensive rehabilitation, and AIDS. The specialized rate categories include minimum requirements related to physician visits, nursing services, coordinated multidisciplinary teams, and medical or rehabilitation requirements. Although the program grew considerably in the early 1990s, it continues to represent only a small portion of reimbursement for SNFs in Virginia.

A second example involves California's MediCal program, which defines a subacute unit as an identifiable unit of a SNF that is approved by the California Department of Health Services. Subacute care reimbursement is divided into all-inclusive per diem rates for hospital-based, ventilator-dependent patients; hospital-based, non–ventilator-dependent patients; freestanding ventilator-dependent patients; and freestanding non–ventilator-dependent patients.[62]

Other states that have developed special rates that may be applicable to subacute programs include Wisconsin, Arizona, Vermont, New Jersey, New Hampshire, Maine, and Illinois. Although these special Medicaid reimbursement levels may increase incentives for subacute providers to treat Medicaid recipients, it appears that even in the states with special rates the primary focus continues to be Medicare and managed care patients.

HOSPITAL-BASED SNFs

The Basic Strategy

Hospital-based SNFs are a primary subacute strategy for hospitals and hospital systems. The hospital-based SNF allows the hospital to develop a continuum of care and to address placement delays associated with difficult-to-place subacute patients. When the hospital-based SNF strategy is compared with the freestanding subacute SNF strategy, important differences become apparent. The hospital-based SNF should be viewed from the overall hospital system perspective. The success of the facility will depend on the benefits achieved by the overall hospital system as much as on the actual financial performance of the SNF itself. In contrast, the freestanding subacute SNF must stand on its own with respect to financial viability. Historically, systemwide benefits resulting from hospital-based SNFs have related primarily to Medicare reimbursement issues, and consequently these facilities have been limited to a Medicare patient management function. Recently, many hospital-based SNFs have broadened their functions to include a strong managed care component.

Definition of Hospital-Based

The term *hospital-based* refers to a reimbursement category established by the HCFA under the Medicare program, and the category does not depend on geographic location. To obtain hospital-based status, the hospital must show that there will be common governance between the hospital and the SNF, integrated services between the SNF and the hospital, and a common cost report filed each year by the hospital and the SNF.[63]

Benefits of Hospital-Based Status

Figure 4–4 summarizes the various benefits that hospital-based status provides to a SNF.

Higher SNF Medicare/Medicaid Reimbursement

An initial benefit for a hospital-based SNF involves higher Medicare and Medicaid reimbursement rates compared with those for freestanding facilities. Under Medicare, hospital-based SNFs have higher RCLs.[40] Similarly, Medicaid reimbursement rates often are higher for the hospital-based facility than for the freestanding SNF.[64] This rate differential is based upon the assumption that hospital-based SNFs treat a sicker patient requiring more intensive services and resource utilization.

The reimbursement rate differential has been a controversial issue within the nursing facility industry. Although some research studies support the reimbursement rate differential,[65] other studies suggest that reimbursement differences based

solely on facility type are inappropriate and do not reflect actual case-mix patterns.[66] The nursing facility industry continues to criticize the differential as failing to recognize the increased service capabilities being developed by freestanding facilities and as creating an unfair competitive advantage for hospitals. The administrative and general add-on for hospital-based SNFs has already been eliminated by OBRA 1993. OBRA 1993 retains the cost limit differential between freestanding and hospital-based SNFs, but Congress has instructed DHHS to consider eliminating the differential in the future and to make a recommendation by October 1, 1995.[67] Consequently, to retain the RCL differential, hospital-based SNFs will need to document that facility type does correlate with higher costs and higher resource utilization.

Medicare Patient Management

The hospital-based SNF allows hospital systems to develop a continuum of care to manage Medicare patients effectively as they transition from the acute care setting back into the community. The development of the continuum of care allows the hospital to reduce its inpatient lengths of stay, reallocate Medicare expenses, and address access issues.

Hospitals can reduce their inpatient lengths of stay for Medicare patients by utilizing the SNF as a transitional facility for Medicare patients. For instance, inpatient length of stay for hip fracture patients can be reduced to 4 to 5 inpatient days.[64] As a result, the hospital's performance under PPS is improved.

A second overall system benefit involves the reallocation of Medicare expenses from the hospital to the SNF as a new cost center. Costs previously identified with other areas of the hospital can be partially reallocated to the hospital-based SNF. Consequently, a portion of Medicare costs previously allocated to an inpatient PPS reimbursement area can be distributed to a cost-based, extended care reimbursement area. Cost reallocation can benefit the hospital in the ancillary services area and in the support services area.[68]

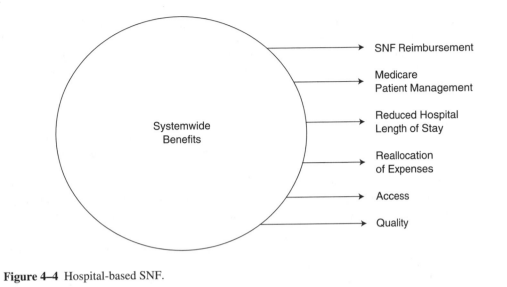

Figure 4–4 Hospital-based SNF.

Furthermore, the hospital-based strategy allows a hospital to address access problems relating to long-term care services. The hospital-based SNF becomes a transitional facility for subacute patients. Consequently, the hospital is able to avoid the placement delays and accessibility problems related to subacute patients.

Quality of Care

In light of the trend toward integrated delivery systems, it can be argued that hospital-based facilities may improve the quality of subacute services offered to patients. The development of a continuum within the same health care system may reduce fragmentation of services and improve the quality of care. The proximity of the facility to the hospital may facilitate patient–physician interaction. Also, the integration of services between the SNF and the hospital offers a complete range of back-up services as well as immediate access to such services. The SNF can take advantage of the hospital's resources, medical equipment, ancillary services, and comprehensive rehabilitation services. The SNF can also benefit from the hospital's quality assurance programs, infection control procedures, and medical record systems. Finally, a study performed in the late 1980s suggests that hospital-based facilities often have superior nurse staffing patterns compared with freestanding facilities and have a ready pool of hospital nurses should a staffing shortage occur.[64]

Common Problems Facing Hospital-Based SNFs

Despite the overall system benefits and Medicare patient management benefits discussed above, hospital-based SNFs also face certain problems. Surveys suggest that two thirds of hospital-based SNFs are losing money or breaking even at best when financial performance is analyzed without regard to overall system benefits.[69] Furthermore, a 1992 ProPAC report indicates that almost twice as many hospital-based facilities as freestanding SNFs received less than 85% of their costs under Medicare reimbursement.[54]

A second disadvantage may involve the inability of the hospital to adjust to the highly regulated nursing facility industry. Hospitals may have difficulty adjusting to OBRA 1987 certification requirements and other regulatory issues facing nursing facilities. Hospitals often experience operational difficulties by attempting to transpose hospital management systems onto the hospital-based SNF. The hospital-based SNF may get lost in the hospital's management hierarchy and become a neglected stepchild in the hospital system.

Responses to the Problems

To address the disadvantages, hospital-based SNFs are developing a number of responses. First, many hospital systems are willing to break even financially on their hospital-based SNF as long as they can document the overall system benefits, such as reduced inpatient lengths of stay for Medicare patients. Consequently, hospitals are developing sophisticated analyses of DRG categories to identify long-stay patients and to develop subacute programs in the hospital-based SNF that are specifically tailored for the long-stay patients.

Second, given the importance of Medicare patients for most hospital-based SNFs, the SNFs are becoming proficient in utilizing the exemptions and exceptions to the Medicare RCLs. The exemptions and exceptions may be even more important for hospital-based facilities compared with freestanding facilities in light of the HCFA's 1994 estimation that 62% of hospital-based SNFs will have costs exceeding the cost limit over the next 2 years compared with 23% of freestanding SNFs having costs exceeding RCLs over the next 2 years.[43]

Third, to address many of the management issues, hospital-based SNFs are beginning to engage subacute providers to manage the hospital-based SNF. The management arrangement allows the hospital to benefit from the management expertise of the subacute provider while still obtaining the hospital system benefits of a hospital-based facility.

Finally, perhaps the most significant development involves the expansion of hospital-based SNFs into the managed care arena. These facilities are moving beyond a Medicare patient management strategy and are learning from freestanding facilities with respect to managed care benefits.[36] This strategy may require the hospital to expand its referral sources beyond the hospital system. The hospital-based SNF will be required to contract with health maintenance organizations and other third party payers as well as other potential referral sources within the community.

Hospitals that are considering such a strategic expansion should be aware of two barriers to expansion. An external barrier involves the hesitancy of many facilities outside the hospital system to refer patients to the hospital-based SNF for fear that, once the patient is referred to the hospital system, the patient will be lost to the referral source. A second barrier within the hospital system itself involves the failure of the hospital to recognize the overall benefits of placing many managed care patients in the subacute facility as an alternative to hospitalization. The hospital often feels that such an approach reduces the hospital's financial performance. This barrier may result in the hospital-based SNF becoming a stepchild within the hospital system rather than a key component of a true system.

Both these barriers may be eliminated in the future as economic, structural, and political reform pushes health care providers toward integrated delivery systems. As providers come together into one system, the concern relating to loss of patients begins to diminish. As integrated delivery systems begin to assume capitation risks, provider incentives shift from increasing volume to providing efficient care at the appropriate level. In such an environment, any potential competition for patients between the hospital-based SNF and the acute care hospital also diminishes. Table 4–3 summarizes the problems faced by hospital-based SNFs and their possible solutions.

MANAGED CARE REIMBURSEMENT MECHANISMS

It is essential for subacute providers to understand the various payment mechanisms under managed care arrangements given the emphasis on managed care as the driving force behind most subacute strategies. The different payment mechanisms under a managed care arrangement

Table 4–3 Hospital-Based SNF Problems and Solutions

Problems	Solutions
Poor financial performance	Emphasize overall hospital system benefits
Difficulty adjusting to SNF regulations	Obtain Medicare exemptions/exceptions to the RCLs
Inefficient management	Engage a subacute management company
Stepchild syndrome	Expand into managed care
Barriers to referrals from non–hospital system sources	Management paradigm shift toward managed care principles

will produce different incentives for subacute providers and will create different financial risks.

A managed care company may approach a subacute provider with any of the following payment arrangements:

- *Discounted charges:* Under this arrangement, the provider agrees to provide medical services at a discount from its standard charges for such services in lieu of requiring full payment. The discount can be a single fixed percentage of the standard charge for all services, or the discount can be different for certain services or categories of services. Many providers establish target discount rates based on the anticipated volume of business under a managed care contract.

- *Per diem payments:* Under a per diem arrangement, the managed care payer pays the provider a fixed rate for each day an enrollee is treated within the provider's facility. Most subacute providers will develop acuity level pricing structures, which include different per diem rates for different patient acuity levels.

- *Per case:* Under a per case method, the payer pays the provider a fixed rate for each case of inpatient treatment. There will generally be a different per case payment based upon service categories and patient categories. A per case method is similar to the DRG reimbursement system for hospitals under Medicare.

- *Capitation:* Under a capitation arrangement, the provider receives from the managed care payer a fixed payment per enrollee per month. For the monthly fee, the provider agrees to provide certain specified medical services to the payer's enrollees. The number of enrollees, rather than the utilization of services, controls the provider's revenues. The provider receives the fixed payment per month regardless of the amount or costs of services provided to enrollees.

- *Percentage of premium:* Under this arrangement, a provider agrees to accept a percentage of the managed care payer's monthly premiums in return for providing all covered medical services to the enrollees during that month.

The different incentives associated with each payment arrangement are summarized in Table 4–4.

The payment arrangements also involve different risks for the provider. As the payment arrangements move toward capitation, the financial risks shift from the payer to the provider. Consequently, the provider will need to structure its managed care contracts carefully to include protective mechanisms. Possible protective provisions are summarized in Table 4–5.

Finally, the relationship between managed care reimbursement and Medicare reimbursement may create some legal, regulatory, and reimbursement issues. Potential issues include reporting of uniform charges on an SNF's cost report despite the fact that the SNF may be utilizing different charges for the same service rendered to different residents, the Medicare prudent buyer concept, and the impact of the Medicare

Table 4–4 Provider Incentives under Managed Care Payment Arrangements

Payment	Admissions	Patient Days	Ancillary Services
Discounted charges	+	+	+
Per diem	+	+	–
Per case	+	–	–
Capitation	–	–	–
Percentage of premium	–	–	–

+, Increase use rate; –, decrease use rate.

lower-of-costs-or-charges principle on managed care discounts.[70]

CONCLUSION

The reimbursement strategies for subacute providers will vary depending on the provider category. Different approaches will be used by swing bed hospitals, specialty hospitals, freestanding SNFs, and hospital-based SNFs. At the same time, with the possible exception of the swing bed program, the reimbursement strategy for most subacute providers will involve the following key components:

- an emphasis on managed care arrangements as the driving force from a financial and operational perspective
- an increased emphasis on Medicare patients, often resulting in reliance on exemp-

Table 4–5 Managed Care Payment Mechanisms: Provider Risks

Payment Arrangement	Risk	Strategies
Discounted charges	Price	Service carve-outs Volume requirements
Per diem	Intensity Severity Price Stringent utilization review	Service carve-outs Acuity pricing Stop-loss threshold
Per case	Intensity Severity Price	Case carve-outs Outlier strategy Stop-loss thresholds
Capitation	Intensity Severity Price Frequency Actuarial/marketing	Investigation of payer Bridge rate Service carve-outs Stop-loss threshold Minimum reimbursement level Outlier strategy
Percentage of premium	Intensity Severity Frequency Actuarial/marketing	Investigation of payer Bridge rate Service carve-outs Stop-loss threshold Minimum reimbursement level Outlier strategy

tions and exceptions to limitations on the applicable cost-based reimbursement system
* a reduction or elimination of services for

Medicaid patients, with the exception of states that are beginning to develop special reimbursement categories or exceptions for subacute levels of care

REFERENCES

1. National Health Policy Forum. *Adding to the Continuum: Emerging New Markets for Subacute Care.* Washington, DC: National Health Policy Forum; 1993. Issue Brief No 66.
2. 47 *Federal Register* 31518 at 31518; 56 *Federal Register* 54539 at 54540.
3. PL 101-508, §4008(j), *amending* 42 USC §1395tt(a)(2)(B)(ii)(II).
4. 42 CFR §413.114(d)(2)(1).
5. 42 CFR §413.114(d)(1)(ii), (d)(2)(ii), (d)(3).
6. 42 CFR §413.114(d)(2)(ii), (d)(3).
7. Heil J. Strategic planning. In: Grim S, ed. *A Swing-Bed Planning Guide for Rural Hospitals.* Chicago, Ill: American Hospital Publishing; 1993;23–35.
8. Helbing C, Cornelius E. Skilled nursing facilities. *Health Care Financ Rev.* 1992;(suppl):97–122.
9. McDowell TN, Rue JL. Survival and success strategies for rural hospitals. In: Gosfield A, ed. *1992 Health Law Handbook.* New York, NY: Clark Boardman Callaghan; 1992:377–419.
10. Shaughnessy PH, Schlenker RE, Silver HA. Evaluation of the national swing-bed program in rural hospitals. *Health Care Financ Rev.* 1988;10:87–94.
11. 42 CFR §413.40.
12. 42 CFR §412.23.
13. 42 CFR §412.25 and 412.29.
14. 42 CFR §413.40(c).
15. 42 CFR §413.40(d)(2).
16. 42 CFR §413.40(d)(3)(iii)(A).
17. 42 CFR §413.40(d)(3)(iii)(B).
18. Prospective Payment Assessment Commission. *Interim Report on Payment Reform for PPS-Excluded Facilities.* Washington, DC: Prospective Payment Assessment Commission; 1992. Congressional Rep C-92-05.
19. Hoyer T. Subacute care: Issues and opportunities. Presented at the 15th Annual Institute on Medicare and Medicaid Payment Issues; March 17, 1994; Baltimore, Maryland.
20. 42 CFR §413.40(f), (g).
21. 42 CFR §413.40(g)(1).
22. 42 CFR §413.40(f)(1)(i).
23. 42 CFR §413.40(f)(1)(ii).
24. 42 CFR §413.40(g)(3)(ii).
25. 42 CFR §413.40(g)(2).
26. 42 CFR §413.40(g)(4).
27. 42 CFR §413.40(g)(i).
28. 42 CFR §413.40(i)(1)(B).
29. 42 CFR §413.40(i)(1)(C).
30. PL 101-508 §4005(b).
31. Lellis M. Medicare cuts in Clinton health plan could hurt subacute providers. *Natl Rep Subacute Care.* 1994;2:4.
32. 59 *Federal Register* 45330–01.
33. 59 *Federal Register* 27708.
34. Pallarito K. HCFA begins project to evaluate cost-based rates for ventilator units. *Mod Healthcare.* January 20, 1992;21.
35. Lellis M. HCFA urged to study treatment of ventilator-dependent patients in subacute facilities. *Natl Rep Subacute Care.* 1993;1:6.
36. Burns J. Subacute care feeds need to diversify. *Mod Healthcare.* December 13, 1993;34–38.
37. Mangano J. Hospitals foresee future in subacute care. *Qual Manage Update.* 1993;3:1–9.
38. Elkins R. Critical standards for selecting a subacute care center. *Med Interface.* October 1993;82–92.
39. Pallarito K. Charting the rapid rise of subacute care. *Mod Healthcare.* February 24, 1992;52–56.
40. 42 USC §1395yy(a).
41. PL 101-508 §4005(e).
42. PL 103-66 §13503.
43. 59 *Federal Register* 762–01.
44. 42 CFR §413.30(e)(2).
45. 42 CFR §413.30(f)(1)(i).
46. *Health Care Financing Administration Transmittal 378* (implementing Chapter 25 of the *Medicare Provider Reimbursement Manual,* Part I). Washington, DC: Health Care Financing Administration; 1994.
47. McDowell TN. How to obtain exemptions/exceptions to Medicare cost limits for skilled nursing facilities. *Natl Rep Subacute Care.* 1994;2:1–2.
48. 42 CFR §413.30(f)(2).
49. 42 CFR §413.30(f)(8).
50. 42 CFR §413.30(f)(3).

51. 42 CFR §413.53(b).

52. Health Care Financing Administration. *Medicare Provider Reimbursement Manual*, Part I, Section 2202.6. Washington, DC: Health Care Financing Administration; 1995.

53. 42 CFR §413.53(a)(1).

54. Prospective Payment Assessment Commission. *Medicare's Skilled Nursing Facility Payment Reform.* Washington, DC: Prospective Payment Assessment Commission; 1992. Congressional Rep C-92-01.

55. PL 101-508 §4008(K).

56. Health Care Financing Administration. *Multistate Nursing Home Case-Mix and Quality Demonstration: Description of the Resource Utilization Group Version III (RUG III) System.* Washington, DC: Health Care Financing Administration; 1991.

57. Schlenker R. Comparison of Medicaid nursing home payment systems. *Health Care Financ Rev.* 1991;13:93–109.

58. Buchanan R, Madel R, Persons D. Medicare payment policies for nursing home care: A national survey. *Health Care Financ Rev.* 1991;13:55–71.

59. US General Accounting Office. *Nursing Homes: Admission Problems for Medicaid Recipients and Attempts To Solve Them* (report to Howard Metzenbaum, US Senate). Washington, DC: Government Printing Office; 1990. General Accounting Office Publ No GAO/HRD-90-135.

60. United Hospital Fund of New York. *Transitional Care: The Problem of Alternate Level of Care in New York City.* New York, NY: United Hospital Fund of New York; 1989.

61. Cline K. States step in to define, regulate subacute care. *Subacute Care Manage.* 1994;1:9–11.

62. Lellis M. California's Medi-Cal subacute program. *Natl Rep Subacute Care.* 1994;2:1–4.

63. McDowell TN. Subacute care providers: Filling a treatment gap. In: Gosfield A, ed. *1992 Health Law Handbook.* New York, NY: Clark Boardman Callaghan; 1992;173–204.

64. Lewin-ICF. *Subacute Care in Hospitals, Synthesis of Findings* (prepared for the Prospective Payment Assessment Commission). Washington, DC: Lewin-ICF; 1988.

65. Shaughnessy P, Kramer A, Schlender R, Polesovsky M. Nursing home case-mix differences between Medicare and non-Medicare and between hospital-based and free-standing patients. *Inquiry.* 1985;22:162–177.

66. Sulvetta H. Cost and case-mix differences between hospital-based and freestanding nursing homes. *Health Care Financ Rev.* 1986;(suppl):75–83.

67. Omnibus Budget Reconciliation Act of 1993, PL 103-66 §13503.

68. Whitman J, DeAngelis P, Knapp M. *Restructuring Hospital Capacity: The Hospital-Based Skilled Nursing Facility.* Chicago, Ill: Hospital Research and Educational Trust; 1986.

69. Sabatino F. Survey: Managed care led '89 diversification improvements. *Hospitals.* January 1990:56–59.

70. Cook M. Contracting with managed care entities. Presented at the National Health Lawyers Association 1993 seminar, Long-Term Care and the Law; January 19–21, 1993; Coronado, California.

Part II

Operations

5

Physical Facilities for Subacute Programs

Mark W. Vaughan and Harvey Brown, Jr.

Subacute health care programs, since their inception, have been based in various facility types. Some programs are found in dedicated units within general acute care hospitals, hospital-based long-term care units, or rehabilitation hospitals. Others are found in smaller freestanding facilities, such as specialty hospitals or skilled nursing facilities.[1] The location of subacute care programs, however, is dependent on several factors, including demographics, access to payment, reimbursement requirements, and licensing and regulatory issues.[2]

Because of the relative newness of subacute care in a dynamic health care market, its specific guidelines and licensure standards are only in the formative stages. As such, definitive and time-tested standards related to the physical facility do not currently exist. Rather, subacute care facilities typically follow the general licensure and accreditation requirements of other health care settings, including those of specialty hospitals, hospital-based skilled nursing facilities, and nursing homes.

To define the parameters of a subacute care environment, one must first understand what is meant by subacute care. Because the industry now recognizes four different categories of sub-acute care, one must fully understand the differences. Transitional subacute care and general subacute care, in their broadest sense, are defined as a system of health delivery whereby a health facility or service provides the most appropriate level of care, while simultaneously preparing a patient and his or her significant other(s) for transitions to other levels of care. These types of patients are experiencing a state of movement between illness and wellness that tends to require longer nursing hours per day but shorter lengths of stay. Chronic subacute care and long-term subacute care, however, are defined as providing patients with the most appropriate level of care over a longer period of time. The common denominator among the four categories of subacute care is provision of care in facilities that fall somewhere between the acute care setting and home or the best alternative environment. Ultimately, subacute care services are meeting an identified health care need while also preventing patients from entering or reentering costly acute care hospitals. Subacute care services also are directed toward reintegrating patients into their community at lower costs and within physical environments matching the level of care required.[1]

This chapter describes a design philosophy, identifies essential human elements, and details the features of the subacute care environment, regardless of whether the program is in a free-standing facility devoted to subacute care only or a component of a skilled nursing facility or hospital that provides other levels of care. The effect of the environment on subacute services also is addressed, as are obtaining the necessary approvals and construction considerations. Finally, case studies of subacute care environments are provided to offer guidance to those providers wishing to institute or enhance a program.

DESIGN PHILOSOPHY

Subacute care facilities must offer patient-centered amenities that psychologically prepare a patient for the next appropriate level of care. For this reason, program developers should seek architectural design solutions that provide nurturing and therapeutic environments. These are not typically discovered by accident but through the implementation of good design principles.[1] In addition to enhancing the overall quality of health care, Roger S. Ulrich[3] describes the clinical benefits of good design. "Good design can reduce anxiety, lower blood pressure, improve the postoperative course, reduce the need for pain medication, and shorten the hospital stay."[3(p20)]

In the design of appropriate physical facilities for subacute care programs, three design considerations are of paramount importance: the human touch, the natural environment, and the building environment.

The Human Touch

Healing is influenced by the human touch. The human touch involves emotional support, physical assistance, encouragement, prayers, visiting time, family security, dining with family members, and preparation for new environments. Specific architectural provisions encouraging the human touch in subacute care facilities may include the following:

- programs offering follow-up and outpatient care
- indoor pet therapy programs

- overnight accommodations for family members, such as private family rooms or built-in furniture in the patient rooms (eg, Murphy beds, couches, or chairs that recline into beds)
- dining space with meal preparation accommodations, such as kitchens and private dining rooms, where families can prepare and enjoy meals together
- activity spaces that promote socialization, such as family/day rooms, entertainment rooms, and wider circulation corridors with areas for furniture
- preparatory training spaces, such as practice rooms or activities of daily living spaces, transitional apartments, group homes, and/or family cottages; these spaces offer a testing ground for both the patient and the family/caregiver before they return home
- policies that allow 24-hour visitation privileges, visitation from family pets, and excursions with family members
- private waiting rooms used to prepare, counsel, and encourage family members and friends who are involved in the care of the patient
- space for multilevel care programs that encourage long-term friendships between two or more patients within the same facility, thus allowing patients to become active participants in the "passive care" of other patient friends[1]
- libraries, reading rooms, and other educational spaces that provide patients and families access to information, allowing them to become active participants in the patient's care

The Natural Environment

Nature is one of the most relaxing and consistently soothing elements that can be integrated into a design. In addition to patients being able to breathe fresh air and observe the outdoors, the natural environment includes such "positive distractions" as the sounds of rain and running water, the scents of flowers, and the sight of seasonal color, ocean waves, and animals. These help orient the patient while stimulating his or her senses, thus leading to improved health.[4]

In subacute care facilities, the natural environment plays an important role in the recovery process for patients transferring from an acute care environment. The natural environment is equally important for long-term care patients because of mobility and activity limitations.

Subacute care facility designs can provide exposure to the natural environment by providing views and spaces that allow encounters with nature and green space and by providing spaces that encourage human activity. Architectural design ideas that will promote nature therapy include the following[1]:

- skylights and windows allowing clear views of the outdoors
- facility locations that promote views of mountains, city skylines, lakes, rivers, ponds, bays, or coastlines
- patios, roof gardens, stair towers, and stargazing decks
- passive landscape barriers for wind, noise, and unsightly views
- greenhouses or outdoor vegetable and flower gardens
- outdoor activity areas with park equipment for visiting families and their children
- outdoor pet therapy areas
- natural amenities within the interior of the facility by means of plants, sunlight, courtyards, aviary cages, fountains or waterscapes, aquariums, outdoor photography, video scenery, and landscape art[1]

The Building Environment

The building environment is often outside the developer's control. Careful consideration must be given to building sites, and their physical features must be weighed against adverse psychological features. Some building features could cause regression in a patient's health or well-being, such as traffic noise, paging systems, odors, poor exterior views, and designs suggesting an institutional or sterile image.[5]

Location

Several desirable features of the building environment can be ensured when one is planning and designing a subacute care facility. Proximity to residential and business areas provides a link between patients and the outside world.[6]

Design Differences

Subacute care facility designs can vary greatly, depending upon licensure classification, number of private/semiprivate beds and their configuration, existing building constraints, staffing ratios, and whether it is located in a freestanding building or a dedicated unit within a hospital.

Entrances

Regardless of the building type, subacute care settings should have a dedicated entry. If the subacute program is contained within another operating facility, it should distinguish itself from an existing nursing unit. Clear wayfinding, a planning concept combining ideal circulation with understandable graphics, helps orient the patient/family and is critical for all types of subacute programs. Although freestanding subacute care facilities typically have their own ground floor entrances with related architectural massing and symbolic entrance identifiers, hospital-based units usually require a route that may lead through many areas of the hospital. For this reason, it is important to post specific signs that lead clearly to the subacute care entry (eg, a name plate affixed to the appropriate elevator call button). Parking accommodations for family members and physicians should be located as close to the dedicated entry as possible, thus minimizing the stress that often accompanies parking at busy hospitals.[7]

Accessibility for Individuals with Disabilities

Subacute care settings should be designed for maximum accessibility for individuals with disabilities. Although this includes staff and visitor accessibility, it is largely needed because subacute care is being provided increasingly to patients who are wheelchair bound and have other disabilities that limit sensory, cognitive, and physical abilities. For this reason, patient bedrooms, bathrooms, activities of daily living areas, and any other area requiring patient transfers should be equipped to manage disability. Currently, many subacute care facilities are constructed to provide much more wheelchair accessibility than the minimum handicap accessibility requirements of local codes and/or the Americans with Disabilities Act.[5] General or specialty hospitals that implement disability-free environments in more than 10% of the patient bedrooms and toilets eliminates unnecessary stressful moves for nondisabled patients. This provision is needed most when a facility is fully occupied. It also creates greater flexibility for subacute programs that have a higher percentage of patients with disabilities. However, if a subacute program is licensed as a skilled nursing facility (eg, hospital-based long-term or freestanding nursing facility), then a minimum of 50% of patient bedrooms and toilets must be designed and constructed to be accessible. If the subacute program is contained within a rehabilitation hospital, then all patient bedrooms and toilets must be designed and constructed to be accessible.[8]

Privacy Issues

Privacy is an important design consideration, particularly for the subacute care patient. For this reason, subacute care facilities should strive for the highest private room mix that can be achieved economically. If semiprivate rooms must be incorporated into a program, then their design should also respect the privacy of each patient. This can be accomplished with more rectilinear rooms that allow beds to be located at each side with their own window, privacy curtain, television, lockable wardrobe closet, and visitor chair/sleeper. The most desirable semiprivate room layout has the bathroom door positioned so that either patient can access it without crossing through the other patient's area. These layouts, like layouts found in intensive care units, can be

effective for the more severely involved patients who require closer nurse observation. In fact, some subacute care programs are incorporating small open wards, with three or four beds grouped together, specifically for patients who require special care and close observation.

Staffing Ratios

Some chronic subacute programs are developed with as few as 9 beds. The typical subacute care program has at least 20 beds, however, of which about 50% are in private rooms. A higher private room mix is ideal but may be prohibitive as a result of staffing, facility size, construction costs, and efficiency considerations. Patient-to-nurse ratios may vary. An example of a staffing pattern is 3:1: three patients to one nurse aide, one licensed practical nurse (LPN) to three nurse aides, and one registered nurse (RN) to three LPNs. Thus there is one RN for every 27 patients.[9] In this example, 27 beds is an economical number to have in the subacute care unit (Figure 5–1).

Isolation Rooms

Because infectious diseases are easily transmitted through microbial contamination of air, a minimum number of isolation rooms is required. Minimum state health requirements usually state that health care facilities must provide at least one isolation room for every 30 beds or fraction thereof. More isolation rooms than the minimum requirement are recommended by the Centers for Disease Control and Prevention because of the increased outbreaks of multidrug-resistant strains of staph disease, tuberculosis, and the rapidly growing prevalence of human immunodeficiency virus.[10]

Patient Rooms

Subacute care is most often classified and reimbursed under the requirements for skilled nursing facilities. Nevertheless, subacute patient rooms are larger than typical nursing facility rooms. In fact, some hospital medical-surgical nursing units may even have rooms that are too small to meet hospital licensure standards for a skilled nursing facility. For instance, the number

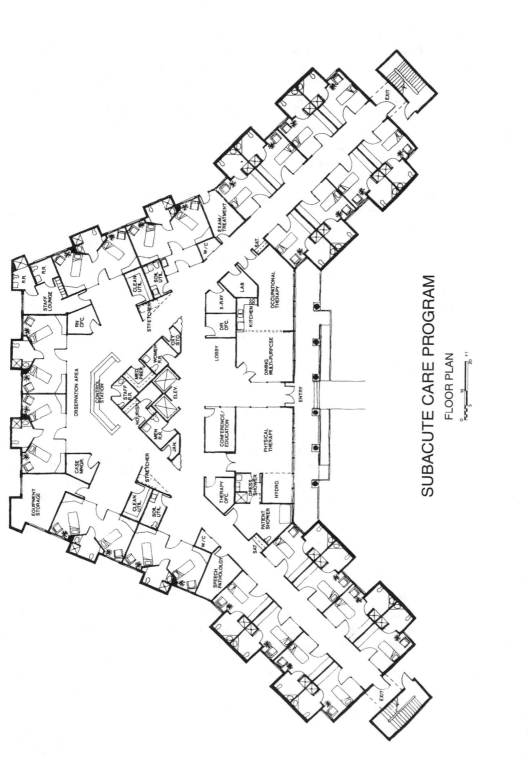

SUBACUTE CARE PROGRAM

FLOOR PLAN

Figure 5–1 Preliminary study of a 27-bed freestanding subacute program floor plan.[8] Courtesy of Mercy Hospital, Pittsburgh, Pennsylvania.

of available beds in an 80-bed hospital could be reduced by as much as half if it was converted to a subacute care facility.[11] Therefore, it is recommended that private rooms have a minimum of 120 ft[2] (minimum dimension in any direction not less than 10 ft) of clear floor space, and semiprivate rooms should have a minimum of 100 ft[2] of clear floor space per bed (recommended maximum of two beds per semiprivate bedroom).[12] Rooms that are larger than the recommended or required minimums will more easily accommodate bedside equipment and nursing personnel and also will provide visitors with room to visit and stay overnight comfortably. This will allow placement of large equipment around the bed, such as ventilators, without obstructing nurse access to the patient. Subacute care programs that emphasize rehabilitation usually require the greatest amount of floor space.[13] Existing facility conversions must also consider the cost and implementation of medical gas headwalls as well as future space requirements of bedside medical technology.

Interior Design

The subacute care setting should have homelike environmental features. Unless medical reasons dictate otherwise, it is essential that the patient be able to see similarities between home and the confinements of the subacute care space. Space for medical equipment may take priority over patient room furniture, but once the equipment is no longer used it should be stored away from patient and visitor view.

Allowing patients to make choices concerning their environment offers them an opportunity to take more control in their own health care. For this reason, patient rooms should be designed to allow personal decor. This amenity provides the patient with a connection to his or her real world. Examples are wall or shelf space for pictures, flowers, books, and get-well cards; tack space or surfaces for pin-ups; and options to paint, wallpaper, or stencil walls, hang curtains, and make door identifiers.[1]

Other interior amenities that contribute to successful first impressions and a recognizable residential image include carpeting in public lounge areas, painted gypsum board ceilings, indirect lighting, recessed incandescent lights and wall sconces, color-coordinated furniture, drapes, and wall coverings. Corridors can also maintain a residential image by incorporating wood for required handrails, flower niches, framed paintings, crown molding, vinyl wall covering with residential patterns, and nurse stations that are open and inviting to visitors. Furniture in both public spaces and patient rooms should resemble pieces traditional to specific locations.[7]

Summary

A subacute care setting should be inviting. It should allow a patient and his or her family and friends to enjoy one another without the sterility associated with traditional institutions. It is no surprise that subacute care developers who realize up front the benefits of good design philosophies are more likely to have happier patients and more referrals.[1]

OBTAINING APPROVAL

Subacute care–related patient illnesses differ in their acuity and number of nursing hours required per day. Subacute patients often receive the same level of care as they would in acute or long-term care hospitals, and in many cases they are located within a dedicated unit within a hospital. For these reasons, it is beneficial to hire health architects with knowledge and experience in the design and construction of both acute and long-term care facilities. Architects and other consultants who are closely familiar with applicable certificate of need requirements as well as state building, life safety, and state health codes should be hired. In addition, they should have good working relationships with state health agencies and inspectors. This may also mean hiring architects, interior designers, and construction contractors from areas within the state or region where the facility is being developed.[7]

The owner or administrator and design team should meet early in the development process with local and state officials to discuss the schematic plans of the project. This allows enough time to explain the project's intent and identify potential problems before the design is finalized. There are certain items that should be brought to preliminary plan review meetings. Vonderheide makes several recommendations regarding preliminary approval meetings:

> . . . What we brought to the meeting was a narrative of the program's clinical issues, construction narrative, preliminary floor plans, cost estimates and the sequencing schedule. Representing us were architects, engineers, in-house construction agents and clinical and development personnel, while the state brought construction personnel, the fire marshal, building officials and healthcare representatives.[7(p17)]

Additionally, these kinds of preliminary project meetings can expedite the approval process because the state and local planners will already be familiar with the project upon final construction plan submissions. Often, plans are submitted to code authorities after the project documents have been issued and construction has begun. This situation can potentially result in significant code-related plan changes, further delays to project approval, and costly change orders.

CONSTRUCTION ISSUES

Subacute care, like many other businesses, is a health care niche that is attracting developers and their desire to achieve a high return on investment.[13] Reimbursement limitations tend to work best with health-related business ventures that require the least amount of capital investment. Although there are a growing number of new subacute care facilities being built from the ground up, most are being operated within buildings previously used for other types of health care.

New Building Construction

There are many benefits to having a newly constructed building designed specifically to meet the needs of subacute care patients and staff. Implementing a new building design would, at a minimum, include the following benefits:

- a one-of-a-kind floor plan and an architectural image specifically tailored to this level of care
- an optimal floor plan designed to enhance patient-centered care
- ideal and efficient layouts that could save long-term staffing costs
- convenient ambulatory access
- more opportunities to design and capture amenities that surround the patient with nurturing and therapeutic environments
- a site location that is ideal for its catchment area

Existing Facility Renovation

If a subacute program can be established within an existing facility and will take substantially less money and time to upgrade compared with constructing a new building, it becomes the better option. Some subacute care programs are opened as separate businesses, leasing space within a hospital; others may occupy an entire building of a smaller freestanding facility that is either leased or purchased. These include such facilities as psychiatric, geriatric nursing care, drug and alcohol rehabilitation, and physical rehabilitation. Minor renovations are typically needed within an existing building to meet the unique needs of the subacute care program.[9]

Physical facility evaluations are recommended before the development of a subacute care program within an existing setting is considered. Many potential settings can be eliminated easily with a quick surface evaluation. The following questions address just a few of the major points to consider in conducting a quick evaluation:

- If the facility is to be housed within an existing hospital, will the hospital be a good "partner" for a separate subacute provider, and will it refer its patients needing subacute services?

- Will the development of subacute care services change the existing facility's licensure classification?
- How much renovation to the existing facility is needed or required, and what will it cost?
- Are the current bed configurations and sizes conducive to a successful subacute care program?
- Is the facility or wing too small? Will additions be needed?
- Is the facility too large? Will there be wasted space?
- Are there dining facilities (eg, kitchens) on site, or will outside dietary services be used?
- What is the remaining life of the facility? Will major repairs be needed in a relatively short time?
- Does the facility have in-wall oxygen and suction system capabilities?
- Are exterior window sills no higher than 30 inches above the bedroom floor?
- Are corridors at least 8 ft in width?
- Does the renovated area contain asbestos abatement?
- Are existing heating, ventilation, and air conditioning systems sized appropriately to meet required minimum air changes for the facility and particularly for patient isolation room requirements?

Some renovations may seem small but may require the entire facility to be upgraded to comply with the most recent local and state building and life safety codes. For instance, subacute care settings operating within designated units of a hospital are typically regulated under long-term care licenses. For this reason, health regulations and construction guidelines can be more stringent than requirements being met by normal acute care hospitals. These include such items as hand rails on both sides of the corridor, exiting criteria, maximum corridor lengths, nurse call annunciators and dome light systems, non-locking doors, activities of daily living toilets and

rooms for transitional training, bathrooms and toilets with grab bars, required physical therapy and occupational therapy rooms, patient dining and recreation areas, and fire detection and sprinkler systems. Many issues surrounding the value and usability of an existing building can best be examined by a qualified health architect or consultant who specializes in health facilities.[13]

Many construction situations may be waived by the governing authority approving the construction project. This is particularly important for subacute care settings being developed within existing hospitals. For instance, some or all existing bathrooms may not be accessible for individuals with disabilities, but complete enlargements would create noncomplying patient room sizes. In these situations, the developer or architect must prove that an undue hardship would occur if such construction upgrades were made. The final decision, however, is ultimately left to the discretion of local and state code authorities. With these conditions, small renovation projects can quickly turn into complete gut-and-redo projects, and in some situations costs per square foot begin to approach those of new facility construction.

Construction Practices

Once a building has been selected or designed for the subacute program and has been approved by local and state code authorities, then owners must ensure that contractors follow appropriate construction practices. There are specific requirements that should be practiced to maintain a safe working environment. In addition to complying with the National Fire Protection Association's Life Safety Code and other local codes, owners and developers of subacute programs, who are members of the Joint Commission on Accreditation of Healthcare Organizations, must also comply with the requirements of their accreditation. There are also some guidelines to follow if the subacute care program is being constructed within an existing health facility that continues to operate its patient care business adjacent to construction renovation areas. Particular concerns include the following:

- Phasing and sequencing of construction should be coordinated with existing facility nursing supervisors for optimal construction hours, access to patient bedrooms on/above/below the unit, and in-wall oxygen and suction system and other mechanical/electrical/plumbing system downtime associated with the existing facilities.

- Hospital-based settings that are being constructed or renovated to include a subacute care unit should be completely sealed off so that noise and dust cannot penetrate to other parts of the facility that are actively utilized by personnel and/or patients.

- Construction personnel should have access to other parts of the hospital and must follow policies regarding the use of radios, smoking, and dining privileges.

EFFECT ON SERVICES

Subacute programs that are established within existing hospitals and intend to share basic support services may be disadvantaged. That is, those subacute care facilities operating as separate businesses within a hospital will many times take second priority over the hospital's own departmental needs. The effect is a situation where services such as physical therapy, pharmacy, diagnostic radiology, respiratory and cardiopulmonary, dietary, laundry, and clinical transport suddenly become overloaded, undersized, and understaffed. Further evaluations of existing facility capabilities compared with the subacute care patient and product line should be undertaken. This will help determine whether the venture is feasible or whether upgrades to the parent facility providing support service are needed.

The costly overhead of acute hospital services, such as magnetic resonance imaging facilities, operating rooms, and emergency departments, is one reason that subacute care programs have been an attractive alternative for insurance company providers. Freestanding subacute care facilities that do not have convenient access to support services, however, should examine potential cost-escalating effects. For instance,

transporting patients to other sites for aggressive rehabilitation or diagnostic and treatment services can create liability problems and can cost time and money. More important, it can be a fearful and intimidating experience for the patient. Also, support services such as dietary, laundry, and housekeeping will need to be either absorbed into the facility's overhead or contracted with outside sources.[13]

CASE STUDY: FREESTANDING SUBACUTE CARE PROGRAM

St. Michael Rehabilitation Hospital, Texarkana, Texas

In the fall of 1993, St. Michael Hospital opened an 80-bed freestanding specialty hospital as part of their therapeutic model continuum of care. It is located on the same campus as their main 300-bed acute care hospital. Services include 30 general subacute beds (licensed as a skilled nursing facility) and 14 rehabilitation subacute beds. There are also 36 inpatient rehabilitation beds which are combined on the same floor with the 14 subacute rehabilitation beds. These nursing units are combined with the required therapeutic support areas of maintenance, engineering, food service, and administration. Other ancillary services are provided through satellite departments of the main hospital.

This freestanding facility totals 73,200 square feet at a construction cost of approximately $7.2 million excluding sitework and landscaping.[14]

Site Issues

The facility, nestled within a natural setting on the 62-acre St. Michael campus, is designed to promote healing of the body, mind, and spirit. Visual relief and interest are provided to the patients with views of landscaped courtyards and the natural beauty of the site. Courtyards and terraces are provided to patients with horticulture therapy programs implemented as well. The specialty hospital is positioned at the front door to the main hospital campus and provides discreet ambulance and service entrances.

Medical Planning Issues

The facility is designed around two types of care and three different patient types:

1. *Subacute care*: includes skilled nursing facility patients who are typically older and more confined and head injury patients who are of various ages and often have complicated neurologic damage.
2. *Rehabilitation care*: includes inpatient rehabilitation patients who are younger, more mobile, but are considered nonsick.

Because of the differences in care between these patients, the program required subacute beds to be physically separate from the rehabilitation beds. (Figures 5–2 and 5–3)

Patient Wing Design

Although the patient types are different (eg, general and rehabilitation subacute) their care requirements are similar. For this reason, the floor plans are almost identical, which improves the efficiency of the facility. The program also asked

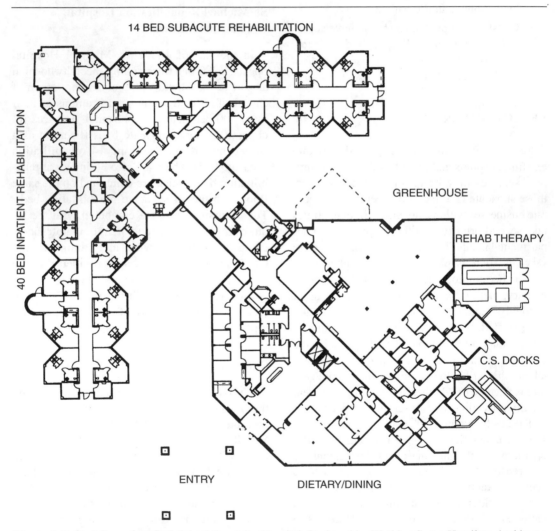

Figure 5–2 First floor plan: St. Michael Specialty Hospital. Designed by Watkins Carter Hamilton Architects. Courtesy of St. Michael Specialty Hospital, Texarkana, Texas.

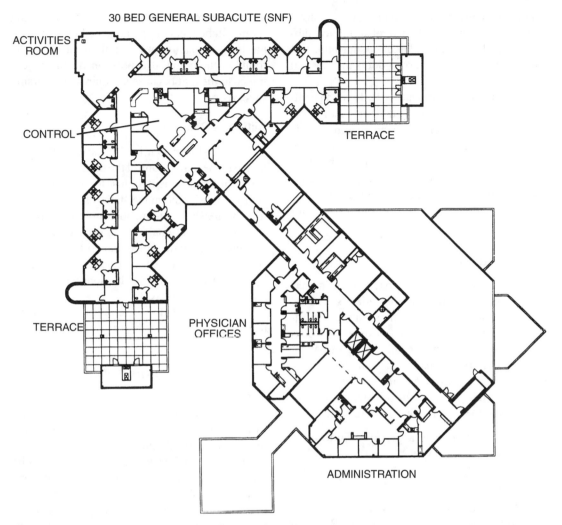

Figure 5–3 Second floor plan: St. Michael Specialty Hospital. Designed by Watkins Carter Hamilton Architects. Courtesy of St. Michael Specialty Hospital, Texarkana, Texas.

for the design to be easily converted to rehabilitation beds (ie, the design layout needed to be flexible). The rehabilitation unit is positioned on the first floor for easy accessibility to the outside. Although the rehabilitation program combines both subacute and inpatient rehabilitation beds on the same floor, the 14 rehab subacute beds act as their own nursing unit. They require their own nursing support, activity room, soil, clean, and other support facilities.

Both floor plans are designed around the triangle nursing unit which has been proven to re-

duce travel time for staff[14 (p. 338)]; it also helped facilitate the separation of the rehabilitation subacute unit and other rehabilitation beds. The nurse stations are positioned back-to-back so that at nonpeak hours (night), only one nurse station needs to function. Nursing support functions such as staff toilet, conference, lounge, and offices are also clustered between these two nurse stations for efficiency. The nurse support rooms, such as soiled and clean rooms, are also positioned centrally within the core of the triangle. A set of clean and soiled rooms are located at each side of the patient wing so that they are convenient to all rooms. The 14 bed rehabilitation subacute unit also shares the larger nursing units soil and clean rooms by the use of doors that open to both units.

The general subacute unit (skilled nursing facility) is located on the second floor because the patients are less mobile and do not require outside activities as much. Also, the unit is smaller with only 30 beds as opposed to the 50 beds below.

Because there are fewer general subacute beds on the second floor, terrace spaces were incorporated so that these patients could enjoy some outdoor activities.

Patient Bedrooms

The philosophy at St. Michael's Hospital has always been considerate of the patient's privacy, however, therapeutic reasoning led them to incorporate semi-private rooms. In order to be consistent with St. Michael's philosophy of patient privacy, each patient had to have amenities commonly found in a private room.

For this reason, the semi-private rooms were designed with the following (Figure 5–4):

- Each patient has a private window for views.
- Each patient has his or her own private cubicle curtain.
- Each patient has his own vanity for personal items and his own TV and VCR which eliminates the distraction from a neighbor's television.
- Each patient has equal access to the toilet room.
- The toilet room is large enough to accommodate a patient in a wheelchair and nursing staff at the same time.
- Optimum space is provided around each patient bed, allowing the opportunity for a family member to spend the night.

Transitional Apartment

In order to help the patient and caregiver prepare for the move back home, a transitional apartment was provided. It is designed with a living room, kitchen and dining area, bedroom and domestic style bathroom to mimic what is usually found in the home. It is positioned near the entrance to the unit because it requires less nursing supervision.

Activities Room

The activities room is also located at the entrance to the unit to control the number of visitors wandering past patient rooms (for more privacy). Being opposite the nurse station for visual control, the area can be more open and airy, allowing for a less institutional appearance as one enters the unit. It is multi-functional so that it can be sub-divided for more private activities or opened into one large room for celebrations with families (eg, holidays/birthdays).

Glass is provided at the ends of each corridor to give nurses' clear visibility to both patients and visitors.

Administrative/Support Building

The two-story administrative and support building is directly connected to the nursing units by a narrow circulation spine, allowing each unit to have its own entrance identity.

This structure houses the entrance lobby with a large barrel-vaulted skylight, admitting and counseling offices, a pantry style kitchen and dining facilities, rehabilitation gym and treatment facilities, speech pathology area, administration area, patient library, beauty shop, and a physician's office.

Also included in this structure are the hospital satellite support facilities including materials, management, housekeeping and pharmacy as well as the mechanical and electrical components necessary to operate the facility.

A separate discreet ambulance entrance is provided with close access to the elevators eliminating the need to transport stretcher-bound patients through the main lobby.

Rehabilitation Gym/Treatment Area

The rehabilitation gym area was treated as one large open area with views to the outdoors. Out-

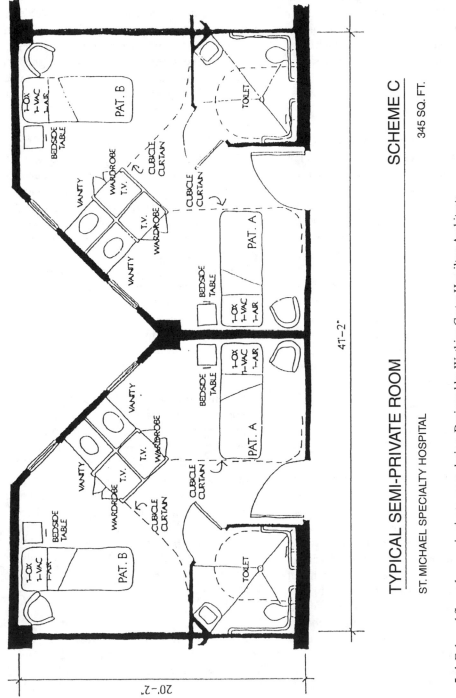

TYPICAL SEMI-PRIVATE ROOM

SCHEME C

ST. MICHAEL SPECIALTY HOSPITAL

345 SQ. FT.

Figure 5-4 Enlarged floor plan: semi-private room design. Designed by Watkins Carter Hamilton Architects. Courtesy of St Michael Specialty Hospital, Texarkana, Texas.

side of the gym is a greenhouse used for horticulture therapy (shown dashed on Figure 5–2). The speech-language pathology area is clustered together away from the gym for sound control. The therapist work room is positioned to control access to the unit as well as for visual supervision of the gym.

Exterior Design

Brick was used extensively throughout the campus on this facility not only because of its low cost, but also because of its high-touch, warm and friendly, thick appearance.

The specialty hospital was designed to compliment the architecture of the replacement facility being constructed at the north end of the campus. Being much smaller in scale than the main hospital, brick banding using different colored brick at various heights was incorporated for a more personal scale. Inlaid tiles offer a hint of color to the earth tones of the brick. Cast stone is used at the parapets to cap the brick facade. A green metal roof is also used at the canopy and at the central point of the nursing wing to add color and definition to the overall design.

CASE STUDY: HOSPITAL-BASED SUBACUTE CARE PROGRAM

The Pittsburgh Mercy Health System, which includes a 500-bed tertiary care hospital, wished to establish a subacute program within a hospital-based skilled nursing facility. The program was a component of an organizational vision to develop a more extensive continuum of care to serve its patients more effectively, many of whom are elderly. (Pittsburgh is reported to have the second highest per capita rate of elderly persons older than 85 years.) With a large Medicare population and longer lengths of stay related to the frailty and acuity of this age group, hospital administrators explored alternatives to the traditional acute care model. A decision was made to renovate designated space with a skilled nursing facility.

Environmental Design

It was determined early on that the elderly population requires special considerations. With age, visual and hearing acuity as well as dexterity diminish. The space needed to be designed to promote optimal functioning while at the same time abandoning an institutional environment (Figure 5–5).

Lounge Space

The lounge was designed with three types of lighting to create different atmospheres depending on activity or time of day. The combination of direct and indirect lighting reduced glare and created a warmer environment. Indirect lighting also provided an environment conducive to reflection and quiet time.

The furniture was selected to promote independence. For example, cushions provided firm support. The sofas and chairs were higher than residential furniture, allowing easier rising from a sitting position. Vinyl upholstery was selected to address infection control.

Dining Area

The dining area was designed to be bright and open. Windows and a cathedral type ceiling were selected to reduce an institutional atmosphere. The furniture was again selected to promote independence. The room was furnished with high-back chairs with arms to provide additional leverage for rising. The tables featured an adjustment mechanism to allow wheelchair-bound patients to enjoy group dining. Table tops were equipped with slightly raised ridges to prevent plates from sliding. Both round and square tables were selected to add variety to the environment.

Bedrooms

Bedrooms were designed to continue the homelike theme while promoting independence. The rooms were redecorated with wallpaper and borders to soften the surroundings. The cubicle curtains were softened in color, and quilted bedspreads coordinated to provide a cheery environ-

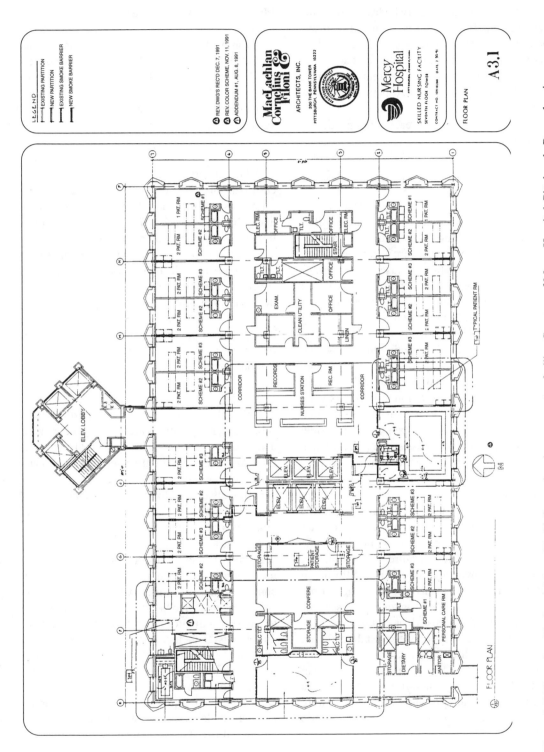

Figure 5–5 Floor plan: Pittsburgh Mercy Health System's subacute program facility. Courtesy of Mercy Hospital, Pittsburgh, Pennsylvania.

ment. An 18th century cherry bedroom grouping was selected. Beds could be adjusted to lower positions to make transfers easier. Each room was equipped with large touch-button telephones for easy dialing. Amplification sets were made available for hearing-impaired patients. Finally, high-back sitting chairs were added to provide support and to assist in decreasing fatigue during prolonged sitting.

Bathrooms and Grooming Facilities

When the existing space was constructed during the 1970s, the patient population in hospitals was younger. Bathtubs with high sides were installed at that time. This feature is not appropriate for the elderly population because it becomes difficult to negotiate the high step needed to get in or out of the tub. Commodes were not equipped to accommodate individuals who have difficulty with mobility. Sinks had cabinet fronts, which made them inaccessible for individuals in wheelchairs or those who need to sit when grooming. Modifications were made to remove these barriers to independence. Additional grab bars were installed to make movement in the toilet area easier. The grab bar on the open side of the toilet swivels to allow staff to assist the patient when necessary. Pull cords were placed in an easier to reach area. Additional night lighting was added to promote self-toileting.

A central shower was constructed to provide for wheelchair-accessible bathing. The modular bathing units have temperature controls outside the unit so that the temperature can be adjusted before the shower area is entered. Flip-down seating enables the patient to sit while showering. Hand-held or hands-free water sources allow individual bathing needs. Heat lamps in the ceiling outside the bathing unit were installed to keep patients warm while dressing. The sinks in each room were modified by removing the cabinet fronts. The height of the sink was lowered to accommodate chair grooming. Tilt mirrors were also installed to allow easy viewing while grooming.

Planning for Implementation

To prepare the unit for opening, a time line that included a process map (Figure 5–6) was developed. Work groups that focused on admissions, operations, human resources, medical practice, patient care policy, and management information systems were formed and met on a regular basis.

Admissions

Admission to the new unit was of central concern to the management team. It wanted the referral process to be smooth between the acute care and subacute care stay. The chair of rehabilitation medicine, the medical director of utilization review, a geriatrician, and a practicing physician were members of the management team. Admission criteria were developed by the team (Appendix 5A). A key to the success of opening was the inclusion of these team members, which ensured that areas of concern regarding patient referral patterns and patient care flow throughout the campus were addressed early in the process.

Operations

Unlike the situation for a freestanding facility, subacute care operations are interdependent with acute care services. Dietary, maintenance, housekeeping, rehabilitative services, and pharmacy services, to name a few, were important departments that had separate managers. Therefore, careful planning, communication, and coordination were essential.

A separate meeting with each department manager was held with members of the implementation team. Regulatory requirements were compared, and examples were given of differences that needed to be addressed to comply with the state's regulatory survey and licensure requirements. In dietary services, the current menu cycle was compared with the required one outlined in the long-term care regulations. Menu substitutions were considered to meet patient choice requirements. Pharmacy services worked to create the labeling necessary to meet the regulations. In the state of Pennsylvania, outpatient

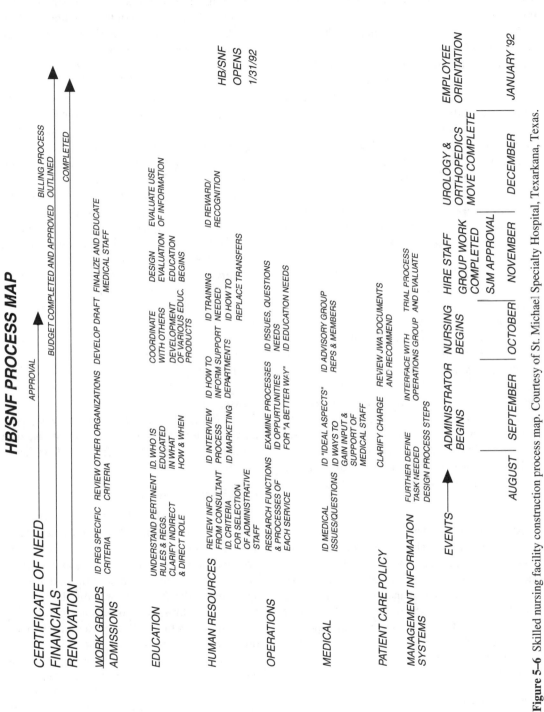

Figure 5–6 Skilled nursing facility construction process map. Courtesy of St. Michael Specialty Hospital, Texarkana, Texas.

labeling is required. The hospital pharmacy was accustomed to unit doses that did not require this type of labeling.

The chair of the rehabilitation medicine department, the manager of rehabilitation services, the unit's medical director, and other members of the implementation team met to discuss therapy requirements and how the unit would interact with the rehabilitation unit. A system of communication to identify and discuss eligible patients in the acute setting was established so that the patient was admitted to the appropriate unit. The elderly patient with lower endurance was determined to be a more appropriate match for the subacute unit because it is difficult for this patient to participate in 3 or more hours of therapy immediately after the acute care stay.

Human Resources

The human resources work group reviewed long-term care policies and compared them with the acute care campus practice. The same salary structure was maintained for all campus employees, which enhanced the job advertisements. Acute care employee salaries in the Allegheny County region tended to be higher for acute care than for long-term care. Nevertheless, a decision for an equal salary scale was made. This allowed experienced hospital staff to make a career change without losing vested benefits and salary. It also demonstrated a commitment to expanding the continuum of care within the system.

Medical Practice

An open admission policy to the subacute unit was set for all physicians on the hospital staff. Physicians not on staff were required to refer their patients to the hospital staff for admission. Prescreening for the unit and discharge planning collaboration were discussed by a work group of the medical staff. Thus a prescreening and discharge planning procedure was outlined. The role of the medical director of the unit was also defined.

Patient Care Policy

The patient care policy work group developed patient care standards, policies, and procedures to address regulations promulgated by the Omnibus Budget Reconciliation Act (OBRA) of 1987 as well as Medicare and state regulations. OBRA standards ensure that patient rights are preserved and independence is promoted.

Management Information Systems

The management information systems work group provided direction in statistical data collection and analysis and in interfacing with existing hospital programs. The inpatient pharmacy needed to adapt its labeling procedures for medication cassettes because of the regulation that there must be a prescription label for each patient. This differed from the hospital unit dose system. The outpatient pharmacy was already familiar with labeling requirements and was able to assist the work group in creating this system. The group also created a program that enabled the inpatient pharmacy computer profile to be transferred to a skilled unit profile upon patient discharge from the hospital. This enhanced continuity and prevented reentering of the same medication orders upon discharge.

The management information system work group determined which statistics and success measurements were needed for tracking over time. Census, pay mix, length of stay, and physician referral patterns were but a few of the data elements that were tracked from the first day of opening.

Unit Programming

Programming should include the discharge planning process and have community focus. The program addressed the need to include the primary care physician, families, and patients. On admission to the hospital, patients are screened by day 3 for possible eligibility by review of the admission and census records.

Close interaction with the exempt rehabilitation unit and social services helped identify potential candidates for the subacute unit. A registered nurse was hired as a care coordinator to oversee this process. This nurse coordinates the screening, admission, discharge, and chart review process by the fiscal intermediary. The interdisciplinary team provides a functional evaluation that assists the physician, family, and subacute care staff in planning for discharge to the community.

To prepare the family, the patient and family members are invited to participate in the interdisciplinary team meeting each week. This provides the opportunity to prepare for the future care needs of the patient. Evaluation of community needs is emphasized.

Continuity of care and case management were also emphasized to prepare the patient who leaves the acute care campus. A caregiver support group was organized to meet the needs of spouses or other family members in terms of information and emotional support. In addition, an educational health library was established for use by patients and families. Topics from how to renovate a house to adapt to the needs of an older adult to understanding long-term care insurance are available in publications and other consumer information materials.

To continue the philosophy of continued learning, faculty from a local university's school of nursing as well as staff from the hospital-based school of nursing were invited to participate in activities of the subacute unit by providing an educational experience for their students. Medical residents also participated on the unit during their rotation with the division of geriatrics.

CONCLUSION

Subacute health care programs are offered in many different facility types ranging in location from hospital-based facilities to freestanding skilled nursing facilities. The successful subacute care facility is designed to comply not only with the minimum licensure standards but also with the sensitivities of its patient population. The facility design should reflect amenities that enhance the overall health care experience for patients while also psychologically preparing them for transitions to other appropriate levels of care.

Careful consideration should be given to three design elements: the human touch, the natural environment, and the building environment. Patient amenities that reflect the human touch include family accommodations in the patient's room, patient/caregiver training spaces, patient/family access to medical information, and spaces that encourage patient socialization. Patient amenities designed to incorporate the natural environment include "positive distractions," outdoor views, greenhouses, flower gardens, and outdoor activity areas. Amenities within the building environment, which can provide therapeutic benefits for the patient, include site location, clear wayfinding, patient room privacy, medical space planning in relationship to staff ratios, and the interior design. Minimum licensure requirements such as disability accessibility, patient room sizes, corridor widths, entrances, number of isolation rooms, and support services must be followed closely, but in many situations these are exceeded to provide the patient with an ideal healing environment.

Because subacute care programs require designs that are patient oriented and often vary by facility type, it is beneficial to hire architects and other consultants with knowledge and experience in both acute and long-term care facilities. To expedite the approval process, the owner or administrator and consulting team should meet with local and state officials early on in the design process.

Subacute developers must consider the pros and cons of hospital-based versus freestanding facilities and new construction versus existing renovation before the program is finalized. This may be achieved by examining the intended subacute care goals, such as image, location, budget, and extent of patient amenities. Existing facility assessments can be evaluated quickly simply by looking for potential problems such as upgrades to comply with current building or health regulations, bed sizes and configurations, extent of renovation required, facility size, the condition of mechanical systems, disability accessibility, and support service availability.

If an existing facility has been selected to incorporate a subacute care program, consideration must be given to the construction of the facility if other parts of the facility remain in operation. These can include phasing and sequencing, dust and noise penetration, and construction personnel access to the operable parts of the facility.

Subacute care programs intended to share support services with other health care settings need to consider patient access and service availability. To avoid overrated expectations and/or inflated costs, support services should be evaluated for need, proximity to the facility, and patient transport convenience. Whether support services should be included or excluded in the subacute program varies depending on outside contract costs, facility overhead projections, and number of patient beds.

Successful subacute care facilities happen not by accident but with the combined teamwork of the owner or administrator and a qualified team of consultants, who work together to construct the facility on time and within the intended project budget. To accomplish this goal, the team must be familiar with facility licensure standards and certificate of need requirements, must be creative, and able to envision cost effective ways to introduce good design elements with patient therapeutic benefits, must work closely with local and state officials for timely project approval, and must involve construction contractors who have experience in health care projects and are interested in achieving the same goals of the project.

REFERENCES

1. Vaughan M. Transitional care environments. *Transitions.* 1994;1:8–11.

2. Tropp JE. The development of subacute services: Struggling to complete the continuum. *Strategic Health Care Market.* Jun 3, 1994:4.

3. Ulrich RS. How design impacts wellness. *Healthcare Forum J.* 1992;20–25.

4. Burnett J, Hamilton DK. *A Room in the Garden: Nature as a Stimulus to Recovery.* 1993 ASLA Merit Award for Research.

5. Tremain D. Planning a subacute care facility. *Transitions.* 1994;1:14.

6. Cope D, Sperling L. Fine tuning construction and design. *Provider.* 1990;17–21.

7. Vonderheide G. An architect's primer: Converting a unit to subacute. *Transitions.* 1994;1:16–18.

8. U.S. Architectural and Transportation Barriers Compliance Board. *Americans with Disabilities Act (ADA) Accessibility Guidelines for Buildings and Facilities.* Final Guidelines. Federal Register Vol. 56, No. 144; July 16, 1991: 35518.

9. Vaughan M. Transitional care: Definition and design. Presented at the symposium of the American Institute of Architects Academy of Architecture for Health; November 1993; San Diego, Calif.

10. Department of Health and Human Services, Centers for Disease Control. Guidelines for preventing the transmission of tuberculosis in health-care settings, with special focus on HIV-related issues. *MMWR.* 1990;39:1.

11. Shvetzoff S. No substitute for experience—Designing a hospital subacute unit can be full of pitfalls for the uninitiated. *Transitions.* 1994;1:12–13.

12. American Institute of Architects, Committee on Architecture for Health, with assistance from the US Department of Health and Human Services. *Guidelines for Construction and Equipment of Hospital and Medical Facilities.* Washington, DC: American Institute of Architects Press; 1992–1993.

13. Before you renovate, consider these points. *Subacute Care Newsl.* 1994;1:1–4.

14. Lockhart FP, Braud TL. Case study. In: Hamilton DK, ed., *Unit 2000 Patient Beds for the Future.* A Nursing Unit Design Symposium. Houston, Tex: Watkins Carter Hamilton Architects, March 7–9, 1990.

Patients will be considered for admission to the Mercy Hospital Skilled Nursing Facility from within the Pittsburgh Mercy Health System (eg, Mercy Hospital, St Joseph Nursing and Health Care Center), health care facilities external to the Pittsburgh Mercy Health System (eg, acute, skilled, or personal care facilities), or their own homes.

The facility follows an open admission policy for all residents regardless of race, color, nationality, handicap, religion, or age. Segregation of clients because of race, color, nationality, disability, religion, or age is not practiced. Patients with a primary diagnosis of known drug addiction, unstabilized mental disorders, alcoholism, or communicable diseases may not be admitted.

Inclusions

Patients considered for admission to the Mercy Hospital Skilled Nursing Facility will meet the following criteria:

- Patients must have had a prior hospital stay of 3 or more days within the last 30 days. This requirement can be waived if the patient's primary payer does not require it for reimbursement for hospital-based skilled care.
- Patients must have a Mercy physician who will be responsible for the primary medical care of the patient while in the facility.

- Patients must be medically stable and meet skilled care criteria as determined upon review by the skilled care coordinator.
- Patients must have a need for skilled care as defined by Medicare.
- If a patient's secondary diagnosis is a psychiatric disorder, mental retardation, or substance abuse, the patient must meet the exception criteria as defined in the Medicare skilled regulations for skilled care facilities.
- Patients must have a defined, realistic discharge plan for a posthospital-based skilled nursing facility stay that has been agreed upon by the patient and family. This plan must include the discharge location.
- If the planned discharge location is a nursing home or personal care home, eligibility for admission to that facility must be determined before admission to the unit. It is anticipated that the average length of stay in the hospital-based skilled nursing facility will be 20 days.
- Special considerations: Patients with the diagnosis of acquired immunodeficiency syndrome will be admitted only for care of a defined illness that requires a limited length of stay if other admission criteria are satisfied.

Courtesy of Mercy Hospital, Pittsburgh, Pennsylvania

81

Exclusions

Patients meeting at least one of the following criteria will not be considered eligible for admission to the Mercy Hospital Skilled Nursing Facility:

- Patients who require acute medical care
- Patients who require custodial care only
- Patients whose immediate prior hospital stay was in a psychiatric facility
- Patients with a primary diagnosis of a psychiatric disorder, mental retardation, or substance abuse unless they meet the exception criteria defined by Medicare regulations for skilled nursing facilities with a primary diagnosis of psychiatric disorder

- Patients who are ventilator dependent
- Special considerations:
  1. Patients may not be considered appropriate for admission if the unit does not have the capacity to provide services needed by the patient (eg, special physical therapy equipment not available, adequate personnel, etc).
  2. Patients awaiting placement at an intermediate care facility will not be considered for admission.

Patients with Medicaid as a primary insurer will not be admitted to this unit because it is not Medicaid certified.

6

Programs of Care

Phyllis A. Madigan

A programmatic approach employed in the subacute environment can be an invaluable tool to execute a consistent, cost-effective, quality product for large groups of patients. The challenge of providing subacute care to date is that it has no regulatory or reimbursement status. The subacute industry evolved as providers in the long-term care industry recognized that many of their referrals were patients who were stable enough to leave the acute care environment but too sick to go home. With no established delivery model or standards, many providers are left struggling to find the most efficient strategy to deliver this new category of care.

DEFINING THE SUBACUTE PRODUCT

The first step in establishing a programmatic approach in a subacute facility or unit is to define clearly what product is being delivered. A clear definition will save time and money in the development of the programs and will avoid operational confusion within the facility. Clear programmatic definition is also necessary for packaging the product for presentation to the health care market. Defining the type of subacute product begins with an evaluation of the services

presently offered to determine what must be modified. This can be clarified by reviewing the four types of subacute care that have evolved in the marketplace today: transitional, general, chronic, and long-term transitional. The principal feature of these four categories is licensure type. The first three are commonly delivered under a skilled nursing license, and the fourth is delivered under a chronic or acute rehabilitation hospital license.

The next step in defining the subacute product is to define the clinical components. One of the most common mistakes that subacute providers make in product definition is failing to recognize that this is a clinical product and must have a clinical definition. Some providers have attempted to define subacute patients financially or demographically. In these instances, the provider classifies subacute patients by the daily per diem, by payer classification, or by age. Examples of these classification systems define subacute patients as those with daily per diems over $400 per day, those with third party payment, or those younger than 65 years. This method of product definition not only can be perceived as a discriminatory practice but also will drastically limit the volume of patients available to the provider because younger individuals have fewer health problems. More important, however, there is no consistency in the services that the staff deliver. All clinical efficiencies are lost in the operational delivery by the fact that patients are not grouped together by their clinical needs.

When the category of subacute care that is best for a facility or unit is chosen, the focus should be the clinical resources that the patient will absorb. The first important element that must be defined is the number of nursing hours that the patient will need for care. An acceptable level of nursing for these types of patients can range from 3 to 8 hours of direct care per day (by a registered nurse, licensed practical nurse, or certified nursing assistant) depending on the delivery model chosen.

In selecting the level of direct care, there are two important points that must be kept in mind. The first is that subacute care is a cost-containment product, so as not to replicate the acute care setting. The second is that Medicare is a predominant payer initially in any subacute model chosen before a facility establishes a reputation in the market. In providing any level of subacute care, some negative impact on cash flow is expected. Consequently, there is a need for the facility to be well positioned financially to support the initial start-up phase.

A word of caution is offered to those providers that are designing a subacute program within the Medicare reimbursement system. Medicare is a cost-based system that provides little incentive for cost containment. Subacute care is designed to be a cost-containment product. This must be kept in the forefront of program design, or the distinction and cost savings between the acute and subacute settings will become blurred. A programmatic focus can help an organization develop the clinical criteria that will validate the medical necessity of care.

The second variable in defining a subacute product is the ancillary services necessary to treat program patients (eg, rehabilitation therapy, intravenous therapy, and wound care). These services must be delivered at a consistent level and executed at a volume that makes them clinically and economically feasible. Health care profes-

sionals must be able to keep their skills sharp, and to gain economies of scale in materials management, the facility must be caring for a sufficient volume of patients with the same diagnosis. Purchasing volume adds value to the cost-containment philosophy. Rehabilitation services will be one of the most vital ancillaries of this group and will need to be coordinated closely in an interdisciplinary fashion with nursing services. A consistent subacute product will be impossible to deliver if these two services are not functioning in concert.

The last and most important variable in defining a subacute product is the fact that the patient must be stable enough to leave the acute care environment. This is where a programmatic focus is advantageous. The provider can define what the patient's clinical status is on admission to the facility. The patient should not require physician intervention or diagnostic technology as frequently as in the acute care setting. Through a clear outline of what the clinical status of a patient will be at the time of discharge from the acute care environment, costly readmissions to the acute setting can be avoided.

THE RATIONALE FOR PROGRAM IMPLEMENTATION

The rationale for implementing a programmatic approach is to provide a consistent and standard approach to the delivery of subacute care. Standardization of care will allow the provider to predict outcomes both clinically and financially. By caring for groups of patients with similar problems, the provider can compare outcomes with established clinical variances. This will also allow the provider to predict the resources that the patient will absorb and thus to establish pricing strategies.

Implementing a plan of care for patients is not new to health care. Individual plans of care are established to outline for caregivers what services should be delivered to patients on a 24-hour basis. Individual plans, although effective for delivering services, can contain a number of shortfalls for the subacute patient. First, individual plans of care can be difficult to write. They are time consuming for the busy clinician on the floor, and the detail that is desirable in the document cannot be accomplished with the lean staffing patterns that are needed for today's service delivery. Second, patients with common problems will have common interventions, so that much of the care plan is a reiteration of the same information for several patients. Third, writing a plan of care has never been a priority for the health care professionals, so that plans lack detail and are not kept current.[1] Fourth, each clinician will interject his or her own personal experience and opinion into the plan for the patient, so that consistency in treatment of the same diagnoses can be lost. These four realities often render the individual plan of care an ineffective tool.

Standardized plans of care or a programmatic approach can circumvent many of the shortfalls in individual plans of care. As mentioned above, the first and most valuable asset of this tool is that the programmatic approach can standardize the product. A second advantage is that a programmatic approach can maximize the health care worker's productivity and will ultimately optimize proficiency and skill level.

IDENTIFYING A PROGRAM MODEL

The Operational Challenge of Delivering a Subacute Product

Subacute care can be a difficult product to deliver consistently. In fact, leading providers in the country cite that the biggest barrier to entering the subacute market is the execution of this product. As discussed above, subacute care has no designated licensure or reimbursement category. Thus providers are faced with trying to adapt other delivery systems in the health care system to this product. This poses a problem to providers because they must essentially merge two systems, one for the licensure category in which they choose to function, and one needed to deliver subacute care. These two systems will challenge operations and, if not effectively balanced, can defeat the provider both operationally

and financially by doubling the work for the clinician who is trying to deliver a subacute product.

In the long-term care setting, the focus has been restorative care. Delivery systems concentrate on maintaining an optimal functioning level for basic physical and social needs. Because the average length of stay in long-term facilities is up to 400 days, individuals entering this setting are essentially establishing residence. Consequently, there is ample time to establish long-term goals to meet their needs. Regulations and the required documentation are focused on 30- to 90-day cycles, thus allowing sufficient time for individual plans of care to be developed.

In the delivery of subacute care, the patients' needs are much different. For the most part, patients are admitted for short-term, specific medical problems and do not have the restorative needs of the traditional long-term resident. In many cases the length of stay is less than 30 days, so that patients are discharged before the paperwork required by long-term care regulators is due. A good example of this is illustrated in a recent long-term care survey of a subacute unit. The facility was given a deficiency for not complying with a regulation requiring the facility to give the patient a 30-day discharge notice. The patient was appropriate for subacute care, requiring a length of stay of only 8 days. This example, although extreme, is the tip of the iceberg when traditional systems are adapted to subacute care.

Under long-term hospital licensure the issues may differ, but the level of challenge remains the same. The acute environment, from a regulatory standpoint, is friendlier to subacute patients than the long-term care environment. However, difficulties can arise in competitive pricing, because of the high overhead associated with acute care delivery. The acute care systems tend to have more services available in the building, in contrast to the long-term environment, where services are brought in as they are needed. These services can be important cost centers to the system and, if not generating sufficient volume, can add significant overhead to the subacute product. The other challenge is the building itself. Because of the physical plant requirements in most acute settings for more complex mechanical supports, it is much more costly to operate these buildings. The reimbursement system takes this into account in that the acute long-term hospital is prospective payment system-exempt. Unless the patients require very complicated subacute care, however, it is difficult to be competitive in the managed care markets. Cost can exceed $1000 per day, which does not offer a reason to move the patient from the acute care setting. This is why a programmatic focus is so important. The programs selected have to be clinically and financially correct for the subacute environment.

Variables To Assess in Delivery Models

In identifying the programs that are suitable for an operation, it is first necessary to assess the present delivery model. As with any planning process, a clear picture of what services the present product delivers is needed. This analysis must consider both the strengths and the weaknesses of these products to determine what must be enhanced to reach the final delivery model. A programmatic approach provides advantages for planning the transition because the clinical needs of the patient are clearly outlined. The facility can guide its transition through careful planning of program implementation. In addition to identifying the subacute patients the facility can initially afford, the financial bottom line can be preserved. For those providing a traditional long-term product, this is a process of building up clinical delivery systems. For those in the acute long-term environment, the process will be realigning services already in place.

Long-term care providers must look at staffing patterns in all departments (nursing, medical, rehabilitation, dietary, housekeeping, laundry, and maintenance). These departments must be evaluated for the number of full-time equivalents but, more important, for how services are delivered. In a programmatic subacute delivery model, departments must understand that the patient is the central focus. The departments must structure their services around meeting the needs of the patient in a coordinated, interdisciplinary manner. They must also be focused on meeting the established patient goals in the most cost-efficient manner. Traditional delivery models tend to make the delivery of nursing care to specialized departments the central focus. A programmatic approach predetermines the tasks that each department must accomplish to predict a clinical outcome for the patient while securing a sound financial position.

The next step in the process is to decide which programs are to be delivered. This process is a two-step phase, analyzing both internal and external factors. As mentioned earlier, the first step is to conduct an internal analysis of the current resources within the facility clinically and financially and to establish what the facility can commit to. The second step is to assess what the local health care market will provide as referrals. One of the most common errors of providers is to assume that what they have to offer is needed by the community. The second most common mistake is that they may accept word-of-mouth information. In many instances, the needs outlined by one discharge planner are not the needs of the entire institution or community. Thus data analysis is the only valid method of assessing a market for subacute needs.

Data can be obtained in several ways. The first and most common method is to analyze the discharge patterns of the local hospitals. The quickest and easiest method to determine need is to utilize diagnosis-related groups (DRGs) for the analysis. This information can be obtained in a number of ways. The easiest method is by asking referral sources for DRG discharge data. If this is not possible, data can be purchased through a number of companies that compile data on hospital organizations, or reports compiled by the state hospital association can be obtained. Once these data are obtained, the analysis can be done by grouping the DRGs into categories that have common clinical needs. The provider can then establish patterns that will outline categories of patients with common needs and will produce sufficient patient referrals. Once these categories are established, each group must be analyzed for its clinical needs and the point at which the group can be transferred to the subacute environment. It is also helpful to look at the current lengths of stay in the acute environment to determine whether any of the groups show trends that exceed the targeted length of stay in the hospital. Another variable to assess is whether the acute length of stay targets can be shortened by early transfer to the subacute setting. In today's health care environment, it is imperative for the acute care hospital to justify the length of stay medically and economically.[2] Subacute care is a viable solution to this critical problem.

Once a community's baseline data have been established, specific goals to reduce the length of stay of particular patient groups can be developed. In these situations, there is an opportunity for the facility to work together with the hospital toward a common goal. Such a collaborative effort can help create the volume of patients necessary for the successful execution of a subacute program. Other data elements that can be helpful in the analysis include the demographic breakdown of the community and an examination of the health care pattern or trends of a community. A DRG analysis is the strongest predictor of success, however.

Once the external market is assessed and the provider feels confident as to what subacute programs are needed in the community, decisions must be made about how to support them financially. It must be remembered that subacute services under long-term care will significantly affect cash flow while sufficient data are gathered for presentation to the Medicare system. One strategy to avoid a cash shortfall while establishing a history with Medicare is to consider programs that are rehabilitation rather than nursing intensive. Rehabilitation is an ancillary service that is fully reimbursable through Medicare. Thus per diem rates can begin to rise while the facility is building a sufficient volume of Medicare utilization or census days that will allow it to apply for an atypical exemption for routine costs. The ability to apply for an atypical exemption usually arises when a facility is billing approximately $700,000 of rehabilitation annually. If

addressed aggressively, this can be accomplished within a 9-month period.

At this point, the facility can consider programs that will integrate patients with more complex nursing needs. Thus costs can be controlled by the identification of programs that may not dictate an immediate increase in routine costs. Programs that are rehabilitation intensive, such as those for orthopedic, stroke, and selected cardiac diagnoses, can necessitate fewer nursing hours. This will allow costs to be captured under ancillary services and paid by Medicare through an increase in interim per diem rates.

If a provider is functioning under an acute long-term care license, the financial profile of the patient programs offered is also important. As mentioned earlier, under this licensure category there is no payment from Medicare in the first 6 months. The key is to minimize the number of patient days and to accept more complicated patients during the start-up phase.

Regardless of the licensure category, there is one important principle in a long-term subacute strategy. The volume of referrals available in the community will dictate the success or failure of a program. The break-even point for the number of patients in a program is approximately five. As a result, once a subacute program is established each bed in a unit and program will turn over 16 to 18 times a year. This concept can be foreign to both the long-term care and the long-term acute care environments. This translates to a program where five beds will need approximately 70 to 90 admissions per year to keep a full census. Thus the basic market analysis will determine the size of the unit and programs. If programs are not selected on the basis of factual data, significant economies will be lost operationally, and the facility can become financially threatened.

One last consideration in assessing a delivery model is a cost-containment strategy. Although the Medicare system will be the largest payer source initially, it is important to develop a delivery model that provides the highest quality at the best price. Medicare is a cost-based system and as such does not promote a cost-containment philosophy. As a result, once a facility has established an atypical exemption, it is basically paid for what is spent on the patient. The market that is growing the fastest and is financially the most desirable, however, is the managed care payer. The managed care payer is a consumer, evaluating the patient's program on a concurrent basis. This evaluation scrutinizes the cost of services, the length of stay, and the outcome delivered to the patient. A programmatic approach will allow the provider to be competitive in this environment by predicting both clinical and financial outcomes of the patient groups that are treated. In the early evolution of subacute care, the ability to manage the care of patients was a desirable trait of providers. As the managed care penetration rate grows at astounding rates in this country, a cost-containment strategy is quickly becoming a baseline criterion for contracting with subacute providers.

Choosing Format Options

Once the number of beds has been determined, a delivery model chosen, and program types established, a format option for the subacute program must be selected. When a format option is chosen, the goal is to develop a model that will provide direction to the clinical staff, thereby producing a template for the delivery of services. There are three options currently used to accomplish this. A decision in this area once again is driven by the resources dedicated to program development and how well the format complements the clinical delivery model.

The most familiar format is the standardized nursing care plan (see Appendix 6A). The appealing feature of this format is that it is the accepted method for planning care taught in most settings. However effective the nursing care plan may be, historically it has not been utilized as a true interdisciplinary tool. Although it references other disciplines, it has been used almost exclusively by nursing departments. True exchange among the disciplines does not take place unless a nursing problem triggers interaction. If this for-

mat is to be successful in a subacute setting, it must be interdisciplinary.

A second disadvantage of this format of care is that it is not time sensitive and must be updated as the patient's condition changes. These plans usually identify the major nursing issues but do not benchmark goals for the patient or identify the date of discharge. Benchmarks have become an invaluable tool in health care when clinical patterns are standardized to ensure quality outcomes. They are interdisciplinary in that they identify the functional deficits that the patient must overcome before discharge. They are oriented toward the results for the patient and how the team can move toward the end result or outcome. A third disadvantage is that the nursing care plan format can be time consuming because frequent updates are necessary to solve problems as they arise. Most important, however, by not predetermining the resources that the patient should receive, it becomes impossible to predict what methods the clinician will opt to utilize while carrying out prescribed treatments. The length of stay variances combined with erratic use of resources pose difficulties in determining pricing strategies.

Standardization of nursing care plans occurred in the late 1970s, and they are now easily accessible and can be purchased at low cost. Because these plans were developed in acute and long-term care settings, they will need to be modified for the subacute setting. The development costs will be significantly lower than for other formats, however, because more material is available. The most significant advantage of this format is that it is still the most common method used in health care settings to outline the intended plan of care. Thus its level of acceptance among the staff will be high and the cost of training for the new system low. If a facility is providing a general or chronic subacute product, this format can be acceptable because the patient's length of stay is longer and Medicare is the primary payment source.

The critical path is a second format to support a programmatic approach (see Appendix 6B).

This critical path method did not originate in the health care setting. In fact, its beginnings are in the petroleum industry, and critical paths were used to coordinate the maintenance activity for equipment in the early 1950s[3] (see Chapter 10 for more information).

The definition of a critical path illustrates the advantages it can lend to the subacute setting. It is a time-sensitive, clearly outlined plan of care. More important, it is a multidisciplinary tool integrating all departments of the organization. The critical path provides caregivers the "big picture" of the overall goals for the patient and breaks this down into simple directives to be accomplished daily. This tool also allows the provider to quantify the input of resources in both materials and labor by segmenting each identified task. Outcomes are measurable, and data can be gathered easily to support or refute the feasibility of the plan. A critical path is designed and written for the majority of patients. Thus for some patients there will be a change in the sequence in which care is delivered. These changes are called variances. Variances can be positive or negative, depending on the sequence of events. The greatest use of variance data is that they can indicate to the clinician a weakness in the system or changes that need to be made in the path itself.[4] Variances are addressed in greater detail in the discussion of CareMaps™.

The critical path is a flowsheet that directs the clinical tasks to be followed daily in the normal course of a patient's recovery. An advantage of this format is that it is a progressive plan identifying what needs to be accomplished to move to the next day. It also is a tool that is used by all disciplines. Of the many formats available, the critical path is probably the most efficient in outlining the medical perspective. More important, however, it is simple. In most instances the entire plan for the patient's stay can be laid out on one page. It contains brief references as to what needs to be done for the patients, such as tests, procedures, and interventions.

The first step in the development of any of these tools is to identify the population for which

the facility is seeking to provide care. As mentioned earlier in the discussion of product development, resources must be directed to serve the highest volume of patients. All these formats must be developed for specific groups of patients. If the group is too broad, however, the tool's usefulness will decline. If too narrowly targeted, variances will increase. This will pose a significant problem in data collection. The two key elements in the development of any care path are to identify the patient population and to maintain a development team that is interdisciplinary.

The CareMap™ parallels the critical path in that it is time sensitive, with each day being outlined for each member of the team. The CareMap™ delves into a significant level of detail, however, providing specific directions to the multidisciplinary team. As Bower writes:

> Critical paths create a matrix that profiles interventions on one axis and time on another. Second-generation critical paths, which we call CareMaps™, incorporate usual patient problems, desired clinical outcomes, and intermediate goals into the matrix. In a CareMap™, the relationship between quality (as reflected in the clinical outcomes) and cost (as reflected in the length of stay and resource utilization) is clearly evident.[4(p61)]

The traditional CareMap™ (see Appendix 6C) is designed much like a critical path but with more of a focus on outcomes. In one modification of the traditional CareMap™ sections, seven sections have been used: admission criteria, evaluation tool, clinical benchmarks, actual day-to-day direction, discharge criteria, staff education, and patient education (see Appendix 6D).

The CareMap™ makes it clear to the health care professionals involved what needs to be done and how to accomplish it. With any CareMap™ format, it is the team that is being directed. Each patient with the same diagnosis will receive the same care and treatment. The CareMap™ can be individualized, but individualizations will be recorded as variances. As mentioned above, variances can be positive or negative and are classified in three ways: system, practitioner, and patient/family. Examples of negative system variances are equipment failure or lack of equipment, laboratory errors, and dietary errors. System variances can be positive when a new piece of therapy equipment or expedient service decreases the length of stay. Practitioner variances include short staffing or a clinician neglecting to do particular tasks indicated on the CareMap™. Positive variances could be ordering and administering the appropriate amount of medication, thus allowing the patient to participate appropriately in a therapy session. Patient/family variances could include a patient's diminished capacity to understand, a comorbid diagnosis that complicates the recovery process, or limited resources in the community that delay a discharge plan. Positive variances could be patient motivation or younger age, both of which may decrease the length of stay.

Tracking these variables can provide good information for improving quality and for indicating why patients are able to be discharged early or exceed the targeted length of stay for a particular diagnosis. This allows the facility to track variables that may affect outcomes. This information can also be used for reporting to managed care organizations on a timely basis whether the length of stay will be affected.

Choosing the right format options for a subacute program is an important step in securing reproducible clinical and financial outcomes. As in any system, however, the format is only one component in the overall implementation process.

The Importance of Case Management

Case management is a function that directs patient care across a continuum, allowing the patient to experience the integrated rather than fragmented care. This requires assembling an interdisciplinary team and maintaining a global perspective that is time sensitive. It is essentially a proactive function that ensures the patient is receiving the correct amount of resources at the correct time to achieve the clinical and financial outcomes predicted on admission.

The case manager should begin to assume responsibility for the patient before admission, identifying the clinical needs of the patient and choosing the correct plan of care. The case manager follows the plan of care, critical path, or CareMap™ on a daily basis, negotiating system changes as the variances are identified and involving applicable discipline. It is the case manager who should coordinate the team meetings, keeping the patient and/or family involved to ensure that the appropriate home services are available that will make possible a successful discharge.

Communication is critical for successful outcomes, and the case manager serves as the conduit for this communication. As Healey and colleagues write:

> A key problem is that staffing patterns have centered around the provider's needs rather than patient needs. Continuity of care is impeded by the use of temporary nursing staff, nurses displaced from one unit to another, alternative scheduling, and rotating shifts.[5(p68)]

As hard as any institution may strive to deliver patient-focused care, there will be instances when reality will make a situation less than perfect. It is in these instances that case management becomes invaluable.

Case management can also be utilized in assisting with the interpretation of outcome data. Once a product is developed, it will need ongoing evaluation that compares the clinical and financial outcomes of groups of patients. The delivery of subacute care, as for any other area of health care, can continually be improved. By measuring efficiency through length of stay, functional improvement, resource input, and patient satisfaction, data can be correlated to improve on the care path development. These outcomes can be communicated back to the staff, and change can be effected in practice patterns. This essentially will translate process into outcome.[6]

Education and Training: The Keys to Success

The biggest challenge that subacute care faces today is the education of the health care industry. Because this facet of health care is in its infancy, there is confusion about its definition and, more important, a scarcity of direct care workers who understand its basics. A provider cannot expect to hire a health care professional from another sector and expect him or her to understand immediately how to deliver the care necessary for the desired outcomes. Human nature dictates that, if an individual is hired into a new environment without proper education and understanding of its goals, he or she will begin to implement systems that resemble the environment from which he or she came. This can quickly derail the outcomes of a subacute program. Thus integral to a successful subacute program is the provider's strong commitment to education.

Staff education requires a financial commitment from the provider, but one that will be paid back many times. Education in health care has traditionally focused on delivering information that affects the functions of individual roles. In today's health care environment, education must be broadened to encompass the overall goals of the provider and must elucidate not just what has to be done but why. In the delivery of a subacute program, each task and function performed for the patient is critical. Operators are attempting to deliver a cost-effective product, and small deviations from the plan can quickly erode a marginal bottom line and the quality of the product delivered. Health care professionals have not historically been privy to this information. Their roles have been perceived as purely clinical. To deliver a successful subacute product, education must be broadened. Health care workers must be aware of outcomes and the critical importance of their roles in achieving these outcomes. Education programs must be structured and delivered in an organized fashion focusing on key roles and must

be extended to each employee in the facility. Once again, this will be a significant financial commitment for the provider, but it is essential to a successful programmatic approach.

CONCLUSION

A programmatic approach can put the subacute provider in control of the product that it delivers. It can implement intensive collaboration and coordination among disciplines and enhance the accountability of each health care worker. By establishing a range of diagnoses that the provider will care for and by instituting a targeted length of stay for each patient, the provider begins to collect the necessary data to identify where practice patterns need to be enhanced or changed. Through benchmarking, the expected functional independence to be achieved by the patient before discharge is established. All members of the interdisciplinary team have goals for which they are accountable. The case management function monitors patient improvement and gives feedback to the interdisciplinary team. The result is a focus on quality.

The collection of outcome data will provide management with the focus that is necessary for total quality management. Outcome data can begin with measures as simple as length of stay and grow to the analysis of common variances that will be the basis of future product development or indicators of programs that need to be discontinued. Outcome data will be the most valuable information to keep clinical delivery systems competitive.

A programmatic approach can be one of the most valuable marketing tools that a facility can utilize. The concept of subacute care can be confusing to many prospective referral sources. By utilizing a program-driven system, the facility groups the patients it is seeking into logical categories that are easily understood. The admissions criteria easily identify the patients the facility is able to accept, and benchmarks identify the progress that is expected. Clear patient identification allows for a strategic focus on what referral sources will support the volume of patients the facility will need for a program. More important, the facility is aware of the resources that patients will need to reach the desired goals. This will position the facility competitively for the managed care market. Pricing strategies have evolved quickly in the last few years. A variety of capitated arrangements will soon extend across the country. Quantifying clinical and financial outcomes through a programmatic approach will be necessary for providers to participate in the subacute industry of the future.

REFERENCES

1. Gish B, Campbell J. Introducing standardized care plans in an intermediate setting. *Focus Crit Care.* 1991;18:51–57.

2. Farren EA. Effects of early discharge planning on length of hospital stay. *Nurs Econ.* 1991;9:25–30.

3. Hoffman PA. Critical path method: An important tool for coordinating clinical care. *J Qual Improve.* 1993;19:235–246.

4. Bower KA. Developing and using critical paths. In: Lord J, ed. *The Physician Leader's Guide.* Rockville, Md: Bader; 1992:6.

5. Healey KM, Loukota SS, Sears TD, Miles RD. Innovations and dedication. *Hosp Health Networks.* 1994; 68–74.

6. Keatley MA. Managing patient care through outcomes analysis. *Inside Case Manage.* 1994;1:7–8.

Appendix 6A

Nursing Care Plan

CARE PLAN: *(Assumption: patient admitted postoperative day 3)*
CASE TYPE: **Total Knee Replacement**
LOS: Not determined

Nursing Diagnosis/ Clinical Problem	Expected Outcomes	Nursing Interventions	Date Intervention D/C'd	Date Problem Resolved	Initials
Potential for abnormal vascular instability	1. Patient will have the therapeutic efforts of prophylactic anticoagulant. PT will be 1 1/2 times normal or parameter as indicated by MD. 2. Patient will not develop a venous thrombus	1. Administer anticoagulant as ordered by MD. 2. Monitor lab values (daily PT) as indicated by MD. 3. Monitor for S&S of clot formulation—pain, swelling warmth in calf. 4. Apply antiembolism stockings per MD order, remove bid for 20 min or as ordered by MD. 5. Perform visual check for blood in stool, urine or excessive bruising.			
Impaired physical mobility/related to pain, stiffness, fatigue, restrictive equipment, and prescribed activity restrictions	1. Patient will have an increase in activity tolerance as indicated by ability to perform activity program. By discharge patient will be able to tolerate 30 min × 2/day of aerobic activity; will be able to ambulate w/assist device 150 ft × 3; and will climb 6–12 stairs w/assist device. 2. Patient will regain range of motion of affected extremity 90°. 3. Patient will have a decrease in pain and stiffness. 4. Patient will discharge with mild pain controlled by po medications.	1. Nursing collaborates with PT/OT to develop rehabilitation program and participates in weekly evaluations of treatment plan. 2. Nursing: —assists with transfers and reinforces proper transfer procedure. —encourages and ensures increasing ROM is performed until full ROM is achieved. —assists with gait training and wheelchair management. —assists patient to maintain proper positioning that maintains knee extension and ensures joint protection. 3. Nursing administers pain medication prn and documents effectiveness of pain medication.			

This is a partial example of the Total Knee Replacement Nursing Care Plan

Appendix 6B
Critical Path

CRITICAL PATH:
CASE TYPE: **Total Knee Replacement**
LOS: 8 days

(Assumption: patient admitted postoperative day 3)

Date of Stay	Admission/Day 1	Day 2	Day 3	Day 4
Category	Interventions/Outcomes	Interventions/Outcomes	Interventions/Outcomes	Interventions/Outcomes
1. Mobility	PT/OT eval begins. Out of bed to chair with assist × 1–2. Maintain proper alignment of affected extremity. Consult with PT/MD for specific knee precautions and orders for knee immobilizer. **Outcome:** Contact guard–supervised ambulation. Fall/risk assessment completed.	PT/OT eval completed. Out of bed to chair with assist × 1–2. Progressive gait and transfer training. Protective positioning. **Outcome:** Contact guard–supervised ambulation. Fall/risk assessment completed.	Out of bed to chair 30 min bid. Progressive gait and transfer training. Protective positioning. **Outcome:** Supervised ambulation with assistive device for 25 ft bid.	Out of bed to chair 45 min bid. Progressive gait and transfer training. Protective positioning. Begin prone lying if skin OK and staples intact. Add prone knee flex, bike without resistance, long- and closed-chain exercise. **Outcome:** Supervised ambulation with assistive device for 50 ft bid.
2. Flexion/ROM	Obtain MD orders for CPM machine and note degree of ROM.	CPM machine settings and prescribed times for usage documented. **Outcome:** Tolerates increased CPM flexion; target level = 5°	CPM machine settings and prescribed times for usage documented. **Outcome:** Tolerates increased CPM flexion; target level = 50°	CPM machine settings and prescribed times for usage documented. **Outcome:** Tolerates increased CPM flexion; target level = 60°
3. ADLs	Assessment of ADL abilities. Order equipment.	Instruction in the use of adaptive equipment. **Outcome:** Performs 50%–75% of ADL tasks with moderate assistance.	ADLs per OT plan of treatment. **Outcome:** Performs 75% or more of ADL tasks.	ADLs per OT plan of treatment. **Outcome:** Performs 75% or more of ADL tasks with minimal assistance.

This is a partial example of the Total Knee Replacement Critical Path

Appendix 6C
Traditional CareMap™

CareMap™: Congestive Heart Failure

Location	Day 1 ER 1–4 hours	Day 1 Floor Telemetry or CCU 6–24 hours	Day 2 Floor	Day 3 Floor	Day 4 Floor	Day 5 Floor	Day 6 Floor
			Benchmark Quality Criteria				
Problem							
Alteration in gas exchange/profusion and fluid balance due to decreased cardiac output, excess fluid volume	Reduced pain from admission or pain free; Uses pain scale; O₂ saturation improved over admission base line on O₂ therapy	Respirations equal to or less than on admission	O₂ saturation 90% Resp 20–22; Vital signs stable; Crackles at lung bases; Mild shortness of breath with activity	Does not require O₂; Vital signs stable; Crackles at base; Respiration 20–22; Mild shortness of breath with activity	Does not require O₂ (O₂ saturation on room air 90%); Vital signs stable; Crackles at base; Resp 20–22; Completes activities with no increase in respirations; No edema	Can lie in bed at base line position; Chest x-ray clear or at base line	No dyspnea
Potential for shock	No signs/symptoms of shock	No signs/symptoms of shock	No signs/symptoms of shock	No signs/symptoms of shock; Normal lab values	No signs/symptoms of shock	No signs/symptoms of shock	No signs/symptoms of shock
Potential for consequences of immobility and decreased activity: skin breakdown, DVT	No redness at pressure points; No falls	No redness at pressure points; No falls	Tolerates chair, washing, eating, and toileting	Has bowel movement; Up in room and bathroom with assist	Up ad lib for short periods	Activity increased to level used at home without shortness of breath	Activity increased to level used at home without shortness of breath
Alteration in nutritional intake due to nausea and vomiting, labored		No c/o nausea; No vomiting; Taking liquids as offered	Eating solids; Takes in 50% each meal	Taking 50% each meal	Taking 50% each meal; Weight 2 lbs from patient's normal base line	Taking 75% each meal	Taking 75% each meal
Potential for arrhythmias due to decreased cardiac output, increased irritable foci, valve problems, decreased gas exchange	No evidence of life-threatening dysrhythmias	Normal sinus rhythm with benign ectopy	K(WNL); Benign or no arrhythmias	Digoxin level WNL; Benign or no arrhythmias	Digoxin level WNL; Benign or no arrhythmias	Digoxin level WNL; Benign or no arrhythmias	Digoxin level WNL; Benign or no arrhythmias

continues

Appendix 6C continued

Location	Day 1 ER 1–4 hours	Day 1 Floor Telemetry or CCU 6–24 hours	Day 2 Floor	Day 3 Floor	Day 4 Floor	Day 5 Floor	Day 6 Floor
			Benchmark Quality Criteria				
Problem							
Patient/family response to future treatment and hospitalization	Patient/family expressing concern Following directions of staff	Patient/family expressing concerns Following directions of staff	Patient/family expressing concerns Following directions of staff	States reasons for and cooperates with rest periods Patient begins to assess own knowledge and ability to care for CHF at home	Patient decides whether he or she wants discussion with physician about advanced directives	States plan for 1–2 days postdischarge as to meds, diet, activity, follow-up appointments Expresses reaction to having CHF	Repeats plans States signs and symptoms to notify physician or ER Signs discharge consent
Individual problem: **Staff Tasks**							
Assessments/Consults	Vital signs q 15 min Nursing assessments focus on lung sounds, edema, color, skin integrity, jugular vein distention Cardiac monitor Arterial line if needed Swan-Ganz Intake and output	Vital signs q 15 min to 1 h Repeat nursing assessments Cardiac monitor Arterial line Swan-Ganz Daily weight Intake and output	Vital signs q 4 h Repeat nursing assessments D/C cardiac monitor every 24 h D/C arterial and Swan-Ganz Daily weight Intake and output	Vital signs q 6 h Repeat nursing assessments Daily weight Intake and output	Vital signs q 6 h Repeat nursing assessments Daily weight Intake and output Nutrition consult	Vital signs q 6 h Repeat nursing assessments Daily weight Intake and output	Vital signs q 6 h Repeat nursing assessments Daily weight Intake and output
Specimens/Tests	Consider TSH studies Chest x-ray EKG CPK q 8 hx 3 ABG if pulse Ox: (range) Electrolytes: Na, K, Cl, CO$_2$ Glucose, BUN, creatinine Digoxin: (range)	B/G	Evaluate for ECHO Electrolytes, BUN, creatinine			Chest x-ray Electrolytes, BUN, creatinine	

	Day 1	Day 1	Day 2	Day 3	Day 4	Day 5	Day 6
	ER	**Floor Telemetry or CCU**		**Benchmark Quality Criteria**			
	1–4 hours	**6–24 hours**					
Location	ER / 1–4 hours	Floor Telemetry or CCU / 6–24 hours	Floor	Floor	Floor	Floor	Floor
Staff Tasks							
Treatments	O₂ or intubate / IV or heparin lock	O₂ / IV or heparin lock	IV or heparin lock	DC pulse Ox if stable / D/C IV or heparin lock			
Medications	Evaluate for digoxin / Nitrodrip or paste / Diuretics IV / Evaluate for antiemetics / Evaluate for antiarrhythmics	Evaluate for digoxin / Nitrodrip or paste / Diuretics IV / Evaluate for pre-load/afterload reducers / K supplements / Stool softeners	D/C Nitrodrip or paste / Diuretics IV or PO / K supplements / Stool softeners / Evaluate for nicotine patch	Change to PO digoxin / PO diuretics / K supplements / Stool softeners / Nicotine patch if consent	PO diuretics / K supplement / Stool softeners / Nicotine patch if consent	PO diuretics / K supplement / Stool softeners / Nicotine patch if consent	PO diuretics / K supplement / Stool softeners / Nicotine patch if consent
Nutrition	None	Clear liquids	Cardiac, low-salt diet	Cardiac, low-salt diet	Cardiac, low-salt diet	Cardiac, low-salt diet	Cardiac, low-salt diet
Safety/Activity	Commode / Bed rest with head elevated / Reposition patient q 2 h / Bedrails up / Call light available	Commode / Bed rest with head elevated / Dangle / Reposition patient q 2 h / Enforce rest periods / Bedrails up / Call light available	Commode / Enforce rest periods / Chair with assist 1/2 h with feet elevated / Bedrails up / Call light available	Bathroom privileges / Chair × 3 / Bedrails up / Call light available	Ambulate in hall × 2 / Up ad lib between rest periods / Bedrails up / Call light available	Encourage ADLs that approximate activities at home / Bedrails up / Call light available	Encourage ADLs that approximate activities at home / Bedrails up / Call light available
Teaching	Explain procedures / Teach chest pain scale and importance of reporting	Explain course, need for energy conservation / Orient to unit and routine	Clarify CHF Dx and future teaching needs / Orient to unit and routine / Schedule rest periods / Begin medication teaching	Stress importance of weighing self every day / Provide smoking cessation information / Review energy conservation schedule	Cardiac rehab level as indicated by consult / Provide smoking cessation support / Dietary teaching	Review CHF education material with patient	Reinforce CHF teaching

continues

Appendix 6C continued

Location	Day 1 ER 1–4 hours	Day 1 Floor Telemetry or CCU 6–24 hours	Day 2 Floor	Day 3 Floor	Day 4 Floor	Day 5 Floor	Day 6 Floor
			Benchmark Quality Criteria				
Staff Tasks							
Transfer/Discharge Coordination	Assess home situation: notify significant other If no arrhythmias or chest pain, transfer to floor Otherwise transfer to ICU	Screen for discharge needs Transfer to floor	Consider home health care referral		Evaluate needs for diet and antismoking classes Physician offers discussion opportunities for advanced directives	Appointment and arrangement for follow-up care with home health care nurses Contact VNA	Reinforce follow-up appointment

Notes: ABG, arterial blood gas; B/G, blood gas; CPK, creatine phosphokinase; DVT, deep vein thrombosis; No c/o nausea, no complaints of nausea; OX, oximetry; TSH, thyroid stimulating hormone; WNL, within normal limits.

Source: The Center for Case Management, South Natick, Massachusetts. CareMap is a registered trademark of the Center for Case Management.

Appendix 6D

Modified CareMap™

Mariner Health Care	Patient Name:
Managed Care Protocol: Total Knee Replacement	(Last, First)
Fac. Admit Date:	Medical
Exp. LOS: 8 days	Record #:
Exp. Discharge Date:	Attending
Actual Discharge Date:	Physician:
Primary Nurse:	DOB:
	Facility:

NURSING (DAY 3)	Initials
1. Check VS, CSM, and incision q shift.	_____
2. CPM machine use as instructed by PT.	_____
3. Reinforce leg exercises taught by PT.	_____
4. Offer pain med 30–45 min before therapy time.	_____
5. Reinforce use of towel under ankle when out of CPM machine.	_____
6. Assist w/ transfers bed to chair. Use knee immobilizer if ordered by MD.	_____
7. OOB to chair 30 min bid.	_____
8. When sitting, encourage pt to alternate position of knee q30–60 min between full ext. & max flexion.	_____
9. Assist pt dress in street clothes w/ use of assistive device.	_____
10. Ambulate 25 f bid, PWB.	_____
11. Remove antiembolism stockings bid for 20 min.	_____
12. Give anticoagulant therapy as ordered.	_____
13. Assess bladder and bowel function; if no BM in 3 days, offer stool softener/laxative.	_____
14. Patient education; medication teaching.	_____

PHYSICAL THERAPY (DAY 3)	Initials
1. Continue active assisted to active exercises.	_____
2. Increase CPM flexion daily as tolerated.	_____
3. Instruct pt and nurses to alternate knee position between full ext. & max flexion q30–60 min. when pt sitting if quads strong enough.	_____
4. Gait training PWB w/ assistive device.	_____

Describe Variance: _____
_____
_____
_____

Probable Cause: _____
_____
_____
_____

Steps To Correct Variance: _____
_____
_____
_____

Signatures: Primary Nurse: _____
100/PD/01|KNEE3.wk1|REVISED: 4-15-93

Describe Variance: _____
_____
_____
_____

Probable Cause: _____
_____
_____
_____

Steps To Correct Variance: _____
_____
_____
_____

PT: _____
OT: _____

This is a partial example of the Total Knee Replacement CareMap™: Day 3 of 8
Courtesy of Mariner Health Care, Mystic, Connecticut.

7

Staffing Subacute Programs

Peg Pashkow

Some subacute programs may have a large interdisciplinary team that can share the responsibilities; others have only a small core team to cover the critical functions of the program. Critical qualities of the team members are those qualifications and competencies that allow the program to thrive and patients to reach optimal outcomes. To be cost effective, staff need to be flexible and open to fulfilling multifaceted roles by sharing responsibilities to meet program demands.

This chapter analyzes the critical functions, regulations, licensing, and certifications needed to staff each type of subacute program. It provides tools to assess staffing needs, set productivity standards for the team, and justify personnel costs.

THE SUBACUTE TEAM

The subacute team should be multidisciplinary to meet the demands of varied patient populations served in the subacute program. The pri-

The author wishes to thank Nancy Sementelli, RN, for her contributions to this chapter.

mary positions for the subacute team are listed in Exhibit 7–1. Additional medical and paramedical professionals may serve as consulting staff (Exhibit 7–2). The size and training of the subacute team will vary depending on program needs. This is discussed later in the chapter.

Program Director

At the helm, the subacute program needs a program director to provide leadership and direction. The program director is responsible for directing and maintaining clinical and operational systems of the program and therefore must understand factors affecting the quality and cost of care, especially resource appropriation and utilization. In facilities where the addition of subacute care has effected a change to decentralization of the management structure, the program director is responsible for budgeting, hiring, and managing the specialty unit. If management is centralized, the program director must determine the resources need and communicate this to the program's administrative staff.

Many states issue subacute beds under a long-term care (LTC) license and require that a nursing home administrator have responsibility for

Exhibit 7–1 Subacute Team Members

Program director
Medical director
Medical staff and consulting staff
    Physicians
    Physician assistants or nurse practitioners
Nursing staff
    Registered nurses
    Licensed practical nurses
    Nurse assistants
Registered dietitians
Physical therapy staff
    Physical therapists
    Licensed physical therapy assistants
    Therapy aides or rehabilitation technicians
Occupational therapy staff
    Occupational therapists
    Certified occupational therapy assistants
    Therapy aides or rehabilitation technicians
Speech-language pathologists
Respiratory therapists
Therapeutic recreation specialists
    Resident activity coordinators
Social workers
Case managers

the direction and management of the subacute program. This can be delegated to a program director. Because each state has different requirements, it is advisable to check the licensure regulations in the state.

Experience and training in health care and business management are important considerations when a program director is selected. Formal training may be in a variety of medical or allied medical professions, such as nursing, social work, case management, respiratory therapy, physical therapy, occupational therapy, speech-language pathology, nutrition, psychology, or nursing home administration. Because of the variety of internal and external contacts needed to build and maintain a strong program, excellent interpersonal skills and judgment are essential.

Some primary functions of the program director are to plan, organize, coordinate, and implement programs and services for patients; to develop a budget that ensures profit objectives; to provide high quality programs that meet market potential; to ensure quality care for patients; to develop a positive market position for the program; to establish and update policies and procedures in accordance with the Joint Commission on Accreditation of Healthcare Organizations, the Commission on Accreditation of Rehabilitation Facilities, Medicare, and other federal and state regulatory requirements; and to work with the internal case manager to identify and negotiate contracts with payers. Appendix 7A illustrates an example of a job description for this position.

To ensure the success of the subacute program, the program director must be afforded the staffing levels, supplies, and equipment necessary to provide the appropriate intensity of medical and rehabilitative interventions based on acuity to achieve desired patient outcomes. Only with this empowerment can the program director be held ultimately responsible for cost-effective service delivery, program evaluation, patient outcomes, and resource utilization in the subacute program.

Medical Director

The medical director of the facility or subacute program or a unit medical director with designated administrative responsibility is important in providing policy formulation, clinical oversight, and quality improvement and in ensuring regulatory compliance. Through consultation, approval, and guidance in the development and implementation of specific medical or rehabilita-

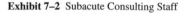

Exhibit 7–2 Subacute Consulting Staff

Physicians
Pharmacists
Radiologists
Laboratory technicians
Vocational specialists
Orthotists, prosthetists
Enterostomal therapists
Psychologists
Medical record experts
Chaplains

tive protocols, the medical director ensures the clinical integrity of the subacute program. The medical director should also be involved in quality improvement and utilization review.

The medical director may be the attending physician for some of the patients. A good option is to have a board-certified internist serve as the medical director, although a gerontologist may be equally appropriate for the patient population served. If the facility medical director or program medical director supervises patient care, patients are returned to the referring physician upon discharge with a detailed report and recommendations for follow-up care.

Medical directors whose personal and professional interests are aligned and congruent with those of the facility facilitate programmatic growth, marketing, and sound business decisions.

Medical Staff

Additional physician support may be full-time staff or consulting staff. An open staff policy permits private physicians to admit patients to the subacute program and to direct their care. Having 24-hour physician coverage is essential.

Board-certified physician specialists may serve as consultants. For example, in a ventilator weaning program a pulmonologist or internist is desirable. In a wound management program a plastic surgeon, vascular surgeon, or internist may give direction to the program. A physiatrist, neurologist, or orthopedic surgeon provides support for a rehabilitation program.

In addition, the use of physician assistants or nurse practitioners, as permitted by state licensure, can be a cost-effective, beneficial service that will assist the medical staff in daily operations, patient rounds, obtaining histories and physical examinations, emergencies, and discharge planning.

Director of Nursing

The director of nursing (DON) is responsible and accountable for the clinical care practices for every bed in the facility, whether acute, subacute, or LTC. Whether the new subacute program is to be established in an acute or LTC facility, the DON will be challenged with its addition. It is important that the DON support the subacute philosophy and direct the nursing staff in providing appropriate care in all programs offered within the organization. It is helpful if there can be uniform nursing policies throughout the facility.

The DON whose primary experience has been in LTC may need to become familiar with ventilator care, cardiac rehabilitation, postsurgical orthopedic rehabilitation, and other subacute patient needs. The DON with primarily acute care experience may need direction to train staff on issues such as patient assessment, care planning, and other documentation to meet state and federal regulations.

Nurses

Nursing staffing to ensure the appropriate level of care is one of the most important issues facing subacute providers. Services must be provided to patients whose conditions have stabilized but whose needs exceed what can be addressed in a traditional skilled nursing facility. Based on the needs of the patient population, it is important that the nursing staff have strong clinical backgrounds in the following areas: medical, surgical, intensive care, coronary care, and rehabilitation.

The nursing staff must be able to handle multisystem problems, recognize immediately any change in a patient's condition, and demonstrate competency in handling emergencies. Nurses whose experience has been in LTC may need a refresher in current assessment and technical skills. In addition, a subacute nurse needs to possess dynamic interpersonal skills to work successfully with families and members of the interdisciplinary team.

To ensure competency within the patient care team, the Rehabilitation Hospital at Heather Hill has developed nursing staff checklists. Exhibit

Exhibit 7–3 Competency checklist.

		Date Completed	Evaluator Signature
Employee Name _____	Date of Hire _____		
Department _____	License # _____		
	(professional)		
Unit/Program _____			

Competency	Date Completed	Evaluator Signature
Respiratory care (ventilator/tracheostomy care)	_____	_____
Wound Care/Enterostomal Therapy	_____	_____
Infusion Therapy (IVs, PICC lines, peripherals, catheters, pumps)	_____	_____
TPN, Tube Feeding	_____	_____
Blood Products, Peritoneal Dialysis	_____	_____
Orthopedic Program	_____	_____
Cardiac Program	_____	_____
Pulmonary Program	_____	_____
Emergency Protocols (Code Blue)	_____	_____
Dysphagia Program	_____	_____

Courtesy of the Rehabilitation Hospital at Heather Hill, Inc., Chardon, Ohio.

7–3 illustrates a general competency checklist and Exhibit 7–4, a specific competency checklist. When the nursing staff for a subacute program is being assembled, it is helpful to hire some staff with acute care experience and some with LTC experience. Acute care nurses have expertise in technical skills; LTC nurses have expertise in compliance issues surrounding patient assessment, care planning, and documentation that fulfills regulatory requirements. Both must be oriented toward working with the subacute patient in establishing goals with measurable outcomes, a common practice in rehabilitation nursing but an uncommon one for most acute and LTC nurses.

Levels of care must be identified in order to reflect the staffing patterns needed in the various categories of subacute care. At Heather Hill, an acuity-based assessment form is used to assist the medical director and the Admissions Department in placing the patient in either the general subacute or the long-term transitional subacute program.

Acuity-based staffing can be determined by using a system in which all patient-related tasks are weighted, thus ensuring that the number of hours needed on a particular unit are covered. The nurse-to-bed ratio is also used in many facilities to determine staffing. For example, a low ratio might be one nurse to 9 beds or fewer, and a high ratio might be one nurse to 14 beds. An illustration of staffing patterns in a 24-bed unit for the different categories of subacute care is presented in Table 7–1.

Exhibit 7–4 Competencies associated with ventilator care: Evaluation sheet.

Nurse _____   Date _____

Competency	Satisfactory/Comments	Unsatisfactory/Comments
Ventilator Alarm		
Alarm Activation		
Ventilator Adjustments		
Primary Controls		
Pressure Readings		
Humidification Device		
Adequacy of Ventilation		
Manual Resuscitator		
Oxygen Source		
Air Leak: Airway		
Suction with Ballard		
Blood Gas Analysis		
Pulse Oximeter		

Comments:

_____
Evaluator

Courtesy of the Rehabilitation Hospital at Heather Hill, Inc., Chardon, Ohio.

Registered Dietitians

The registered dietitian is a valuable member of the subacute team. He or she brings expertise in treating patients with diabetes, hypertension, hypercholesterolemia, pressure sores, non-healing wounds, enteral feedings, total parenteral nutrition, or poor dietary history or dietary habits.

Licensed Therapists

The number of licensed physical therapists, occupational therapists, and speech-language pathologists will be determined by the type and number of patients. Physical therapy is generally needed on every subacute unit. If the general subacute program primarily admits patients with a stroke and brain injury, speech-language pathologists will need to be among the primary members of the team. The speech-language pathologist is also an integral member of the team in a ventilator weaning program. In a general subacute program admitting mostly patients with orthopedic diagnoses for short-term rehabilitation, speech-language pathologists will only be needed occasionally and can be employed as needed or by contractual arrangement.

Table 7–1 Nursing Staff Ratios

| | | Percentage of Total Nursing Care Hours | | |
Program Type	Total Nursing Care Hours per Patient Day	Registered Nurse	Licensed Practical Nurse	Certified Nurse Assistant
Transitional subacute	5.5	30	30	40
General	4.5	30	20	50
Chronic subacute	3.5	25	15	60
Long-term transitional	7.0	60	20	20

Under the direct supervision of a licensed physical therapist, a licensed physical therapy assistant, a registered occupational therapist, or a certified occupational therapy assistant, trained rehabilitation aides can be utilized effectively to reinforce and supervise therapeutic treatment programs for gait, exercise, and activities of daily living. For example, a therapy aide can be assigned to reinforce adaptive techniques in patient dressing and bathing, to cue patients at risk for aspiration in feeding groups, or to assist and supervise patient ambulation.

Respiratory Therapists

If the subacute program supports a ventilator weaning program or if a large portion of the patient population has pulmonary diseases or chronic lung conditions, full-time, 24-hour respiratory therapy staff is advisable. Respiratory therapy patients who are alert and oriented can be seen during the first 24 hours, and then nursing can continue treatments throughout the patient stay to reduce costs and to make the respiratory therapists available for patients with a greater need for their expertise. Respiratory therapists can be cross-trained to take electrocardiograms, draw arterial blood gases, provide hyperbaric treatment, and otherwise supplement the nursing staff. If the program requires only occasional pulmonary services, such as aerosol treatments, tracheostomy care, or pulmonary rehabilitation, part-time respiratory therapy staff may suffice. In some facilities nursing supports the care for those

on mechanical ventilation, with respiratory therapists being shared with other parts of the hospital system or other nearby medical facilities.

Therapeutic Recreation Specialists and Activity Personnel

These important team members provide activities to meet patients' physical and psychosocial needs. Their focus is promoting community reentry, enhancing free time management planning, and teaching adaptive skills to provide continued enjoyment of past leisure pursuits.

Social Workers

Medical social workers are important in a subacute program to develop and provide patient and family counseling and support groups and to help prepare the family and patient for discharge to the community or to another level of care. In general subacute programs with many orthopedic rehabilitation patients with short stays, the social worker is primarily occupied with discharge planning, which includes arranging for coordinated services in the home and outpatient care in addition to preparing the family. In transitional and long-term transitional subacute programs with patients with more complex conditions, the social worker is more occupied with working with the patient and family on adjustment to illness, changes in life patterns, and possibly difficult placement issues. Because of their general role as patient advocates, they may be assigned the role of case manager.

Case Managers

Subacute case managers are patient care–focused, clinical practice–based, members of the interdisciplinary team. They are the liaison between the caregivers and the patient, the payer, and the external case manager; they are responsible for optimizing patient outcomes at the lowest cost to the payer. (The role of the case manager is described in Chapter 8.)

CONSULTING STAFF

Consulting Physicians

The medical specialists needed to serve on the consulting medical staff are determined by the diagnoses of the patients served. For example, subacute programs with a large number of patients with cardiac or pulmonary comorbidities will need a consulting cardiologist or pulmonologist. A specialist in infectious disease may be desirable for patients with iatrogenic infections, such as hospital-acquired pneumonia, complex wounds, or urinary tract infections, or those with infections and complex multisystem disease.

Consulting specialists may also assist in developing policies, serve on committees, market programs, or develop new programs. For example, the infectious disease specialist might help by serving on the infectious disease committee or by working with pharmacy for formulary development.

Some other medical specialists consulting in a subacute program might include orthopedists, neurologists, physiatrists, rheumatologists, hematologists, urologists, oncologists, endocrinologists, gerontologists, psychiatrists, radiologists, and dermatologists. Dentists, podiatrists, and optometrists are also desirable adjunct staff. Whether serving as attending physicians or as consultants, physicians will generally see the pa-

tients in subacute care three to seven times per week, depending on medical need and requirements for reimbursement.

Pharmacists

The pharmacist is important to subacute care. Twenty-four-hour access to a full pharmacy is essential, especially for transitional and long-term transitional subacute programs. These patients need 5 to 10 times more medications than the average LTC patient.

Enterostomal Therapists

Enterostomal therapists provide support for any wound issue. Some problems they address include decubitus ulcers and areas around stomas, feeding tubes, and tracheostomy tubes.

Psychologists

Some patients admitted to the subacute program will have emotional, mental, or psychiatric conditions. In addition to the psychiatric consultant, a licensed psychologist can provide psychometric testing, psychotherapy, or counseling. The psychologist can also work with the interdisciplinary team to suggest and monitor behavioral interventions. A master's prepared psychologist may be hired to work under the supervision and license of the psychologist, who will have a doctoral degree in clinical psychology.

Other Adjunct Staff

Orthotists and prosthetists are essential adjunct staff for programs with patients with amputations or neurologic or musculoskeletal deficits requiring bracing or splinting. Vocational specialists may be needed for programs serving patients desiring to return to work who will require adaptation or change.

Whether laboratory technicians are needed on site will depend on patient volume and whether the facility supports an on-site laboratory. Nursing or respiratory therapists may be cross-trained as phlebotomists to augment services, and an off-site laboratory can be contracted with to promote timely service.

Support Services

Many services can be shared with other components of the organization. These include laundry, housekeeping, maintenance, billing, payroll, human resources, reception, admissions, marketing, information systems, and medical records. Because of the complexity of documentation, a medical record specialist may prove to be invaluable to the subacute program.

CONTRACT AND EMPLOYED STAFF

If the census in the subacute program fluctuates greatly, or if the number of patients requiring specific services varies, contract staff will be the most cost-effective management decision. A high utilization of agency staff will raise the cost of care and can negatively affect the quality of care. Some facilities form an internal float pool for supplemental staffing to provide care at a lower cost.

Continuity of care is best achieved when there is consistency of staffing within the unit. This can be most cost efficient when patient care is provided by staff who are employed by the institution and involved with the coordination and delivery of care on a daily basis. The commitment, availability, knowledge of program goals and the education of employed staff are strong reasons to hire. Nevertheless, competencies for all staff must be checked and mentors provided to familiarize staff who are contracted or new to the subacute program.

EDUCATING STAFF ABOUT SUBACUTE CARE

The orientation and continuing education of all direct care staff should be carefully addressed to include the following:

- the organization's philosophy regarding subacute care
- a focus on rehabilitation to the patient's optimal ability
- care plans based on problems identified by the Minimum Data Set, the Health Care Financing Administration's mandated assessment tool for use in nursing facilities, and/or other comprehensive assessment tools
- interdisciplinary conferences including the patient and family
- multidisciplinary continuing education
- competency checks to ensure the established standard of care
- emergency response
- protocols, policies, and procedures
- information about new and existing programs within the organization

REPORTING STRUCTURE

Clear lines of authority must be defined for optimal operations. Under product line management, the program director is responsible for directing all staff on the subacute unit, eliminating layers of hierarchic management. Some organizations' program directors report to an administrative vice president; others report to the DON. Team members reporting to the subacute program director become collegially linked, communicating more openly with other disciplines to creatively resolve problems creatively and directly. Roles should be clear and congruent with both program and department needs and expectations.[1] The clinical nurse manager or head nurse who is accountable to the program director will generally still have a reporting relationship with the DON to ensure the DON's involvement in clinical operations. Some examples of matrix reporting structures for product line management are illustrated in Figures 7–1 and 7–2.

Figure 7-1 represents the current matrix model formerly used at the Rehabilitation Hospital at Heather Hill, with traditional department assignments and interdepartmental working relationships being developed along product lines.[2] The

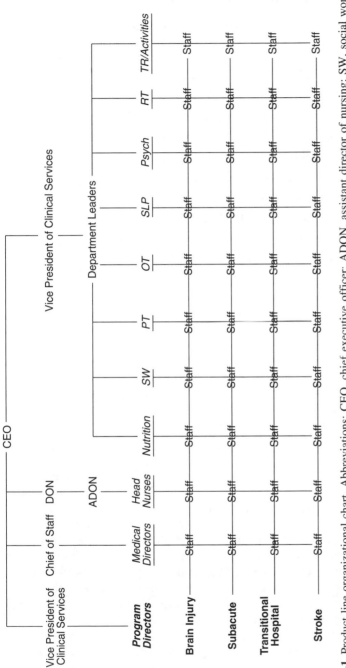

Figure 7–1 Product line organizational chart. Abbreviations: CEO, chief executive officer; ADON, assistant director of nursing; SW, social work; PT, physical therapy; OT, occupational therapy; Psych, psychology; RT, respiratory therapy; TR, therapeutic recreation; SLP, speech-language pathology.

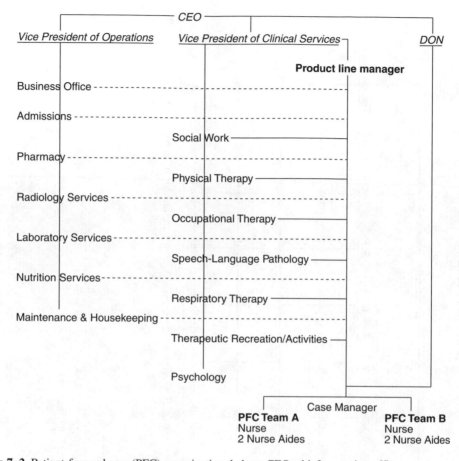

Figure 7–2 Patient-focused care (PFC) organizational chart. CEO, chief executive officer.

primary benefit of the matrix organization is that it offers administration the opportunity to focus its personnel resources on patient care and to decentralize decision making.[3] A drawback to this model is that the dual reporting relationship leaves staff accountable to both department directors and program directors, which may result in confusion and conflicts.

Figure 7-2 represents the current even more defined, decentralized product line structure utilizing the patient-focused care model of bedside care teams. This type of organization gives the team admission-to-discharge oversight of patient care, establishing greater accountability for patient outcomes.[4] The director of the product line, with support from functional departments

through a matrix relationship, is accountable for the cross-training of staff who provide most of the required care. Nursing aides, for example, may be cross-trained in basic nursing care, basic respiratory care, phlebotomy, electrocardiographic testing, patient transfers (to and from bed, wheelchair, and toilet), and supervision of ambulation. Some facilities have further cross-trained service associates to perform dietary duties, housekeeping, maintenance, and transport and administrative associates to cover admissions, financial counseling, medical record coding and abstracting, and unit secretary functions.[5] The risk in eliminating administrative positions at the departmental level is the loss of professional leaders to recruit and mentor new staff,

| | Transitional Subacute | | | General Subacute | | | Chronic Subacute | | | Long-Term Transitional Subacute | |
	Complex Medical	Extensive Wound Care	Chemo-therapy	Orthopedic Rehab	Intensive Rehab	Brain Injury Rehab	Post-surgery	AIDS Care	Hospice	Dialysis	Vent Weaning Pulmonary	Cardiac
Nursing Staff												
RNs	1:12	1:12	1:12	1:18	1:08	1:08	1:24	1:12	1:24	1:24	1:06	1:08
LPNs	1:08	1:06	1:12	1:12	1:12	1:12	1:12	1:12	1:12	1:08	1:12	1:08
CNAs	1:08	1:08	1:08	1:06	1:08	1:08	1:08	1:06	1:08	1:08	1:08	1:12
Respiratory Therapists	1:06	1:24**	prn	prn	prn	prn	prn	prn	prn	prn	1:03	1:06
Physical Therapy Staff												
PTs	1:24	1:24	1:24	1:48	1:08	1:12	1:24	1:24	1:24	1:24	1:10	1:10
PTAs	*	*	*	1:24	*	1:12	*	*	*	*	*	*
PT Aides	0	1:24	1:24	1:24	1:24	0	1:24	1:24	1:24	1:24	0	0
Occupational Therapy Staff												
OT or COTA	1:08	prn	prn	1:12	1:07	1:06	prn	prn	prn	prn	1:07	1:12
OT Aides	1:24	prn	prn	1:12	1:10	1:06	prn	prn	prn	prn	1:21	1:12
Speech-Language Pathologists	prn	prn	prn	NA	1:07	1:06	prn	prn	prn	prn	1:07	prn
Social Workers	1:15	1:15	1:15	1:15	1:10	1:10	1:15	1:15	1:15	1:15	1:10	1:15
Activities Personnel	1:24	1:24	1:24	1:24	1:24	1:24	1:24	1:24	1:24	1:24	1:24	1:24
Registered Dietitians	1:36	1:36	1:36	1:60	1:48	1:48	1:48	1:48	1:60	1:36	1:36	1:48

Figure 7–3 Sample ratios for staffing specific subacute programs. Abbreviations: RN, registered nurse; LPN, licensed practical nurse; CNA, certified nurse assistant; PT, licensed physical therapist; PTA, licensed physical therapy assistant; OT, registered occupational therapist; COTA, certified occupational therapy assistant; prn, as needed; AIDS, acquired immunodeficiency syndrome; NA, not applicable. *PT must evaluate and progress patient, but PTA could treat and document care. **If hyperbaric chamber available, respiratory therapist is part of treatment team.

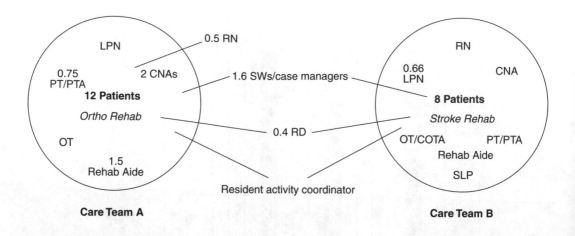

Figure 7–4 Patient-focused care team for 24-bed general subacute, 12 orthopedic rehabilitation patients, 8 stroke rehabilitation patients. Abbreviations: RN, registered nurse; LPN, licensed practical nurse; CNA, certified nurse assistant; PT, licensed physical therapist; PTA, licensed physical therapy assistant; OT, registered occupational therapist; COTA, certified occupational therapy assistant; SLP, speech–language pathologist; SW, social worker; RD, registered dietitian.

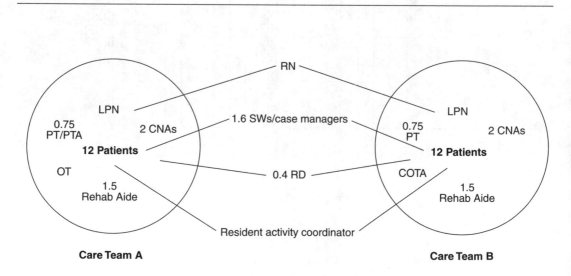

Figure 7–5 Patient-focused care team for 24-bed general subacute program, all orthopedic rehabilitation patients. Abbreviations: RN, registered nurse; LPN, licensed practical nurse; CNA, certified nurse assistant; PT, licensed physical therapist; PTA, licensed practical therapy assistant; OT, registered occupational therapist; COTA, certified occupational therapy assistant; SW, social worker; RD, registered dietitian.

perform evaluations, promote professional development, and evaluate quality service. The benefits are tighter control on costs and the assignment of direct responsibility and accountability.

Top level administrators facing the addition of subacute care to their organization have to be versatile in managing a more clinically and administratively complex facility. In cases where the management structure becomes decentralized, administrators are challenged with the responsibility to oversee and keep all self-directed units working together. No matter where the organizational authority lines are drawn, good communication is essential between and among the clinical and administrative staff.

STAFFING RATIOS FOR SPECIFIC SUBACUTE PROGRAMS

Depending on each program's needs, the number of members on the primary subacute team and the number of consulting staff will vary. Figure 7–3 illustrates the type and ratio of direct care staff needed to serve patients with various clinical needs based on the experience at the Rehabilitation Hospital at Heather Hill, which offers a continuum including each type of subacute care. Neither the program director nor the medical director is included in these numbers.

For example, a 24-bed general subacute program specializing in orthopedic rehabilitation, using the staffing ratio suggested in Figure 7–4,

would need 0.75 registered nurse, 2 licensed practical nurses, and 4 certified nurse assistants; 1 licensed physical therapist or licensed physical therapy assistant and 1 physical therapy aide; one registered occupational therapist or certified occupational therapy assistant and 1 occupational therapy aide; 1 resident activity coordinator; 0.4 full-time equivalent registered dietitian; and 1.6 social workers/case managers. The care team structure for this orthopedic rehabilitation program might be as illustrated in Figure 7–5.[4]

In a more complicated, but also more common, occurrence, the subacute program will have a mixed population. Should the program find itself with 12 patients needing orthopedic rehabilitation and 8 needing stroke rehabilitation, the care teams, using the patient-focused care team model, would be assigned as in Figure 7-4.

Ultimately, the program director has the authority and responsibility for hiring, contracting, and scheduling the staff to meet program needs in a cost-effective manner.

CONCLUSION

Subacute programs require qualified health personnel whose collective knowledge, skills, and clinical expertise reflect multidisciplinary competencies. Together, the team members must provide each patient with the services and education necessary for successful rehabilitation to effect the desired treatment outcome.

REFERENCES

1. Baptiste S. Clinical programme management: A model of promise? *Can J Occup Ther.* 1993;60:200–205.
2. Timm M, Wanetik M. Matrix organization: Design and development for a hospital organization. *Hosp Health Adm.* 1983;46–57.
3. Forer S. *Product Line Management in the Rehabilitation Industry.* Washington, DC: National Association of Rehabilitation Facilities; 1990.
4. Arthur P. Patient focused care: Acute orthopedic services. *PT Mag.* 1994;2(7)34–47.
5. Bullock K. Patient focused care. *PT Mag.* 1994;2(11):51–60.

Appendix 7A

Sample Job Description for Program Director

DIRECTOR OF SUBACUTE PROGRAMS

Purpose

The primary purpose of this position is to plan, organize, coordinate, implement, evaluate, and direct programs and services for patients with subacute needs for the Rehabilitation Hospital at Heather Hill.

General Information

The director of the subacute program is delegated the administrative authority, responsibility, and accountability necessary for carrying out the assigned duties.

Major Duties and Responsibilities

Administrative functions

- Manage the subacute programs.
- Ensure quality, quantity of, and effective goal-oriented programs that meet market potential.
- Prepare yearly program goals and objectives.
- Develop and implement strategies to provide relevant, cost-effective services.
- Develop, implement, and review annual budget to ensure profit objectives.
- Provide management reports that document effectiveness and efficiency of program operation, such as productivity and billing reports.
- Develop, implement, and review policies and procedures at least annually and participate in making recommended changes.
- Ensure compliance with accreditation certification and government standards relevant to subacute care, such as Joint Commission on Accreditation of Healthcare Organizations, Commission on Accreditation of Rehabilitation Facilities, Medicare, Medicaid, and other federal and state regulatory requirements.
- Ensure that staff, patients, residents, visitors, and others follow established policies and procedures at all times.
- Be responsible for quality patient treatment and patient, family, and community education.
- Optimally utilize personnel, space, and equipment.
- Work with internal case manager to identify and negotiate contracts with payers.

114

- Participate in interdepartmental development of systems, policies, and procedures. Identify dysfunctional systems or processes, and work with appropriate personnel to correct and improve them.
- Assess and respond to needs and trends through meeting with payers, case managers, physicians, and other customers.
- Develop a positive market position through marketing and public relations to improve referral base and case mix.
- Maintain an excellent working relationship with the medical profession and other health related personnel, facilities, and organizations.
- Meet with administration, medical, nursing, and therapy staff as well as staff from other related departments in planning subacute programs.
- Keep the president (chief executive officer), senior vice president (chief operating officer), chief financial officer, vice president of rehabilitation services, and DON informed about the status of subacute programs.

Staff development functions

- Work as a team builder and communicate with all levels of staff to plan and problem solve effectively.
- Hold regularly scheduled meetings for the subacute programs.
- Ensure that staff education programs are available to provide quality care and to meet the needs of the changing patient population.
- Create and maintain an atmosphere of warmth, personal interest, and positive emphasis as well as a calm environment throughout the facility.
- Participate with staff in implementing service programs.
- Facilitate continuing professional education and professional review for the team members from their various areas of specialization.

Committee functions

- Serve on selected committees of the facility as appointed or required.
- Evaluate recommendations from the facility's committees (eg, utilization review, infection control).
- Develop and implement quality improvement and program evaluation systems for the subacute programs.
- Recommend to a vice president the capital equipment needs for the programs.
- Provide for and document the maintenance and repair of all equipment.

Personnel functions

- Select, evaluate, and maintain competent staff. This includes interviewing, hiring, and orienting new staff, monitoring staff performance and attendance, and completing annual employee evaluations.
- Evaluate employee grievances, and institute disciplinary action as necessary.
- Monitor work distribution to ensure maximal productivity, including distribution and/or reassignment of work as necessary.
- Make arrangements for coverage when scheduled to be out of the facility.

Resident's rights functions

- Ensure that patients' rights to fair and equitable treatment, self-determination, individuality, privacy, property, and civil rights, including the right to make complaints, are well established and maintained at all times.
- Maintain confidentiality of all pertinent patient care information to ensure that resident rights are protected.

Experience

At least 2 years of management and 5 years in direct clinical experience or 5 years of hospital management. Strong managerial and communication skills. At least a BS in a health related field with an additional masters in business or management preferred.

8

Case Management for Subacute Programs

Peg Pashkow

The primary goal of case management is cost-effective care. Employed by private insurance companies, federal and state agencies that administer the Medicaid and Medicare programs, and managed care organizations, successful subacute care providers also are implementing case management strategies. This is accomplished by assessing the needs of the individual, estimating the cost of care and negotiating rates, and coordinating efficient care through treatment plans and alternatives. The focus must be the systematic achievement of outcomes within time and resource limitations. Manager of cost and quality, facilitator, liaison, gatekeeper, broker, educator, negotiator, and monitor are all roles for case managers.

Hospitals and long-term care facilities have little or no control over reimbursement, but they can control the use of resources. When a case is not managed, costs are uncontrolled. Case management has long been advocated in complex cases such as brain injury and spinal cord injury, but within today's cost-conscious environment it

can benefit even simple cases. This chapter addresses the justification for and return on investment of incorporating case management methods into routine operations in subacute health care facilities.

INTERNAL AND EXTERNAL CASE MANAGERS

Internal case managers are patient care–focused, clinical practice–based members of an interdisciplinary team. Based within facilities, they are the liaison between the caregivers and the patient, the payer, and/or the external case manager. Internal case managers are responsible for optimizing patient outcomes at the lowest cost to the payer. They provide a definitive representation of the services provided to the patient, which should translate into improved reimbursement levels and fewer denials for the provider.

External case managers are largely insurance company based and independent. If employed by an insurance company, they monitor quality of care and investigate any and all available cost-saving alternatives. They direct care to the contract provider, who may or may not be a part of a provider network. If there is no contracted pro-

The author wishes to thank Gail Anderson, Case Manager, for her assistance in providing the case studies for this chapter.

vider, they negotiate reasonable fees with the provider (also called a vendor) while ensuring quality care. External case managers assist the payer's provider relations personnel with credentialing to ensure that the provider has the appropriate and qualified staff, equipment, and outcome measures in place before a contract is made final. If there is no insurance benefit, but keeping patients in the acute facility rather than giving them a service outside their benefit package is more cost effective, external case managers are responsible for explaining this option to their company.

Independent case managers are often health care specialists with expertise in areas such as neonatology, obstetrics, or brain injury. They are employed by the stop-loss carriers for catastrophic events costing more than $100,000, for costs that are getting close to 50% of the life-time maximum, or if there is a probability of long-term costs.

In addition to working as a liaison with third party payers, internal case managers must work to control length of stay (LOS) for high-risk, high-cost Medicare patients. According to Sulden,[1] together with diagnosis-related group (DRG) reimbursement reductions, the additional reimbursement currently provided for patients with an abnormally long LOS will be phased out over 3 years beginning in fiscal year 1995. This will put additional pressure on subacute providers for early admission. Case managers in subacute units based in DRG-exempt hospitals will need to monitor the LOS closely to stay within target limitations set by the Tax Equity and Fiscal Responsibility Act. Case managers in subacute units utilizing skilled nursing facility beds need to monitor LOS closely for Medicare beneficiaries. Patients or their secondary insurance company, if they have one, will be required to make a copayment after day 20 of care and full payment when their skilled nursing benefit is exhausted after 100 days.

A flow diagram illustrating the integration and interaction of case management is shown in Figure 8–1. This chapter focuses on internal case managers in subacute settings.

THE CASE MANAGEMENT PROCESS

The National Association of Rehabilitation Professionals in the Private Sector (NARPPS) has defined successful case management as a process involving assessment, planning, negotiating, coordinating, monitoring, evaluating options and services, and reporting to meet the health needs of the individual. Thus case management promotes quality, cost-effective outcomes.[2]

Assessment

Before admission, case management involves a comprehensive assessment of each patient's individual needs. This includes assessing the referral for appropriateness, collecting data, verifying and precertifying insurance, screening the case, obtaining approval for contracts, interviewing individuals from the patient's support system, determining health needs, reviewing current status and the treatment plan, identifying barriers to wellness, reviewing history, and identifying resources such as insurance benefits and waiver programs.

Developing the Plan

Once the patient is admitted, an individualized treatment plan must be developed with the interdisciplinary team. NARPPS has published the *Professional Performance Criteria for Medical Case Management,*[2] which describes the following standards for plan development:

- The patient should be an active participant in the plan of care within his or her physical and/or psychosocial abilities.
- When the plan is written, all interested parties should agree before it is implemented.
- The plan should identify everyone's responsibilities, the action steps for which he or she is responsible, and the time frames for completion.
- A rationale for the plan integrating the elements of the evaluation as well as cost-benefit analyses should be included.

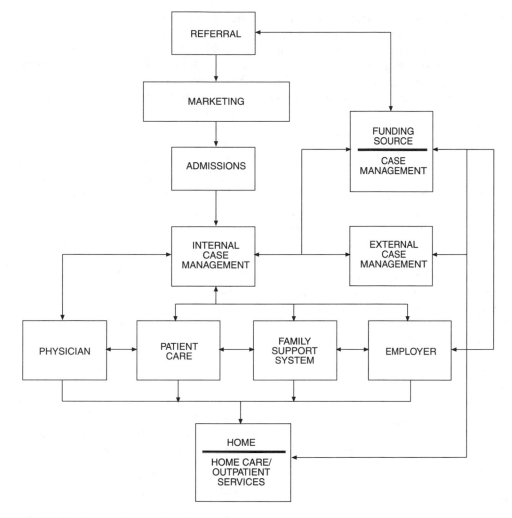

Figure 8–1 Integration and interaction of case management.

• Contingencies should be developed for likely problems and/or complications that may arise in any elements of the plan. This will allow utilization of new resources should the established processes not achieve the goals as stated.

The successful case manager must understand the clinical condition of the patient and the goals of the patient to work effectively with members of the treatment team. Services, treatments, and funding sources must be identified and prudently allocated to meet individual patient needs to move the patient expeditiously along the continuum of care to the least restrictive, most productive environment. The patient, family, physician, team, payer, and other interested parties must review the plan, and treatment gaps must be identified and corrected.

Negotiation

Although it is estimated that 25% of the payer mix in subacute care is commercial business, most subacute providers have a significantly higher goal of at least 50%. In many states, more than half of the commercial patients referred are insured with managed care contracts, which are expected to grow significantly over the next few years. Managed care reimbursement is responsible for the success of most organizations, and with the advent of health care reform it is expected to grow in importance and demand, especially through health maintenance organizations. This alone justifies the need for case management.

The case manager is responsible for maintaining good provider–payer relations. In contracting, it is essential that the negotiation format be prepared in a way that demonstrates the ability of the facility to meet the patient's requirements using provider-based managed care with comprehensive utilization management and performance criteria. Optimally, when the established performance accountability standards are followed carefully, additional external case managers, who are costly to the facility, can be eliminated.

The contract should be customized to the payer (see Chapter 19 for more information). The clarification of inclusions, exclusions, and criteria for precertification for ancillary services is a key consideration in the development of a contract. For a facility to receive reimbursement, a precertification must be done to determine the need for services as defined by medical necessity. A definition of what constitutes emergency services within the contract is essential.

It is important that the case manager understand different mechanisms of payment. These may include discounted fee for service, per diem charges based on acuity levels, a percentage of premiums, fixed rates versus a percentage of billable charges, or capitation. Capitation is a set fee by diagnosis for the entire care needed from surgery through rehabilitation. This may be individualized, for example, by age or medical history. It is only within the framework of individualization that the case manager has leverage to negotiate. The case manager has significant financial responsibility to negotiate the best possible rates for the subacute provider.

Implementation

The job of the case manager is then to coordinate the implementation of the treatment plan. The case manager communicates with the patient's caregivers and family members/significant others by functioning as a coordinator, facilitating communication among the care team members.

To ensure the cooperation of health professionals, case managers must show that, although they are financially driven, they are also clinically responsible. In team meetings, the case manager reviews progress, coordinates efforts, facilitates utilization of accelerated and/or alternative care options when appropriate, and revises treatment goals with the interdisciplinary team. Discharge planning is expedited because it begins early. At its best, case management fosters better collaboration among the staff involved in each patient's care. Using cost management strategies, the case manager promotes effective and coordinated care, determines resources, and identifies limitations of coverage and needs for added services and equipment. In this way, details are supervised to ensure that the patient's unique needs are met in the most appropriate, timely, cost-effective manner possible.

Monitoring

A good case manager is always monitoring for signs of potential problems and intervenes to prevent such problems from occurring. These problems may be found in the patient's chart or detected in interdisciplinary staff meetings. Once detected, indicators of potential problems must be acted upon immediately to avoid costly dilemmas. Some of these indicators include:

- inconsistent documentation and/or unquantifiable data regarding the patient's progress
- patient refusal to participate in therapies
- identical team reports week after week, signifying no change or progress
- a plateau in a patient's condition

- treatment for maintenance rather than improvement
- a patient awaiting placement
- a patient found on admission (during initial assessments) to have high functional capacity
- variations in team members' estimations of LOS
- therapeutic home visit several weeks before discharge rather than in preparation for discharge

Documentation

Effective case management documentation is designed to improve reimbursement and reduce costs. Acuity-based assessments (Exhibit 8–1) are valuable in estimating costs of care before admission. They provide the payer source with a justification for a rate other than the normal skilled nursing facility per diem rate, which does not account for the extra needs of the patient referred for subacute care. The acuity scale can also be used on an ongoing basis to document changing needs. It provides justification for adjusting charges based on reassessment of acuity, which is appreciated by the payer and health care administrator alike.

Case managers should be involved with the development and individualization of critical paths for patients (see Chapter 10 for a discussion of critical paths). Critical paths are important for continuity of care. They are effective in demonstrating the cost effectiveness of care plans to payers. They can also be used to motivate patients and keep staff directed toward treatment methods and goals. Computerized care plans that are easy to adapt to individual patients are especially effective.

Case managers must have a knowledge of reporting requirements for Medicare, Medicaid, and other insurers. Plans must be reported and reviewed often for continuity. The case manager facilitates plan modification between the team and the payer. Clear, concise, quantitative progress reports must be submitted as required to legally responsible payers, and guidelines of confidentiality must be followed.

Reports include:

- assessment of needs
- plan of care
- estimate of reasonable time frame for care
- estimated cost of care
- anticipated outcome of care
- suggestions and recommendations

Time frames for reports are when a significant change occurs, when an agreed-upon cost figure is reached, or no less than monthly without the payer's approval.

Outcome data should be recorded and used in negotiations with external case managers representing third party payers. This includes monitoring and evaluating the services and resources utilized in relation to the outcomes for assessing value. The case manager's goal is to demonstrate that value = cost/outcome.

For reporting purposes, it would be optimal to develop a method for illustrating cost analysis and cost savings. Documentation for utilization review management systems for LOS also provides valuable information. Other documentation that may be used for quality initiatives are patient surveys and provider feedback logs.

In 1987, the State University of New York at Buffalo developed the Functional Independence Measure (FIM) to measure the disability level of individuals. Cost and LOS are included among the data collected. Utilized widely in rehabilitation facilities and programs, the FIM is also being used in a number of subacute facilities as an outcome measurement tool. The State University of New York at Buffalo is currently developing an outcome measurement system specifically for subacute programs. (A detailed discussion of outcome measures can be found in Chapter 10.)

CASE STUDIES

The following case studies illustrate the multiple roles and responsibilities of internal case managers in subacute care facilities.

Exhibit 8–1 Heather Hill Acuity-Based Assessment Form

Services are required from nursing, respiratory therapy, rehabilitation, social services, dietitian services, and internal case management. The following includes the weighting scale for services only. Not included are supplies, medication, durable medical equipment, and physician services.

Nursing Assessment			Intermittent (Bolus)	05 ___	and/or Speech–		
Initial Assessment	15 ___		Bowel Training	11 ___	Language Pathology		
Update Care Plan and			Ostomy Care		Up to 1 hour qd	10 ___	
Documentation	05 ___		& Teaching	10 ___	1 to 2 hours qd	15 ___	
Cardiopulmonary			N/G Tube	04 ___	Dysphagia Mgt	15 ___	
Ventilator Monitoring			Peg Tube	04 ___	Integumentary		
Wean	15 ___	Genitourinary			Wound Management		
Stable	10 ___	Foley			Post Burn Mgt	20 ___	
Tracheotomy			Indwelling	05 ___	Simple	05 ___	
Wean	15 ___		External	03 ___	Moderate	10 ___	
Stable	10 ___	Intermittent			Complex	15 ___	
Suctioning			Catheterization	05 ___	Whirlpool (whole)	10 ___	
Infrequent	05 ___	Incontinent (Bladder)	10 ___		Whirlpool (part)	05 ___	
Moderate	10 ___	Bladder Training	10 ___		Medication Regimen		
Frequent	15 ___	Bladder Irrigation	05 ___		Intravenous Therapy		
Respiratory Therapy or		Dialysis			Continuous Infusion	06 ___	
Nursing Treatments			Peritoneal	15 ___	Continuous Med		
4 or more	10 ___		Hemo	10 ___	Infusion	07 ___	
2 or 3	07 ___	Musculoskeletal			Piggyback	04 ___	
Oxygen	07 ___	Traction			Intermittent Flush	03 ___	
Humidification for			Continuous	03 ___	CVP	10 ___	
Tracheotomy	05 ___		Intermittent	05 ___	Central/Line Care	03 ___	
Pulse Oximetry			Splints	05 ___	Blood Drawn	02 ___	
Infrequent	02 ___		Braces	05 ___	Oral/GT/Suppository		
Frequent	04 ___		Halo	10 ___	1–4 meds	02 ___	
Continuous	06 ___		Compress	05 ___	5–10 meds	04 ___	
Apnea Monitoring	05 ___		Heating Pad/Ice	05 ___	11+ meds	05 ___	
Cardiovascular			TENS Unit	05 ___	Intramuscular		
External BP Monitoring	05 ___		CPM Unit Setting	03 ___	Subcutaneous		
Telemetry	15 ___	Neurological			1–3 meds	03 ___	
ECG	03 ___		Neuro V/S	05 ___	4+ meds	05 ___	
Intermittent Telemetry			Dysreflexia Protocol	10 ___	PRN Medication		
Monitoring	10 ___		Dependent ADL		PO	02 ___	
Vital Signs			Partial	10 ___	IM/SC	03 ___	
Routine-qd-bid	03 ___		Total	15 ___	IV	05 ___	
Routine-4 hr	05 ___		Nonmobile, Markedly		Social Service		
Endocrine			Agitated/Disoriented	10 ___	Psychosocial		
Capillary Glucose			Mobile, Markedly		Basic	02 ___	
Monitoring	04 ___		Agitated/Disoriented	15 ___	Simple	05 ___	
Gastrointestinal		Patient/Family Education			Complex	09 ___	
Enteral Therapy			Complex	10 ___	Discharge Planning		
Weaning	03 ___		Simple	05 ___	Basic	03 ___	
Continuous (NG or		Rehabilitation			Simple	06 ___	
G Tube)	08 ___		Physical, Occupational,		Complex	09 ___	

Total Acuity Score   _____

Courtesy of the Rehabilitation Hospital at Heather Hill, Inc., Chardon, Ohio.

Mr C

Mr C was admitted to Heather Hill after hospitalization for the removal of an infected right knee and placement of antibiotic beads in the septic right knee joint. Benefits were verified with the self-insured employer, but precertification was completed by an agency providing medical review for the employer. An external case manager was assigned. Before admission, a per diem was established for placement of Mr C in Heather Hill's transitional hospital for care.

The case was reviewed on a weekly basis with the external case manager to assess continued need for inpatient services. When it was believed that the patient could be discharged, plans were finalized for the 300-mile trip home. Home health care visits were arranged. The patient was scheduled for surgery to replace the knee at a future date. Once home, the patient sought care from a local physician, whom he neglected to tell of his recent hospitalization. The physician lanced an antibiotic bead, thinking it was a boil. This resulted in Mr C's readmission to the acute care facility earlier than anticipated.

The physician at the acute care facility believed that Mr C was not safe at home with home care services to monitor the needed intravenous medication regimen. This resulted in a second admission to Heather Hill for general subacute care. When the antibiotic course of therapy was concluded, the physician, internal case manager, and external case manager believed that the patient was unsafe to return home again to await knee replacement surgery. The external case manager negotiated a respite per diem for the patient to remain at Heather Hill in chronic subacute care until his scheduled surgery.

After surgery, the surgeon recommended that Mr C stay in a subacute rehabilitation setting until he was safe to return home. The per diem was adjusted with the external case manager to accommodate the new plan of care.

Responsibilities of internal case management with this patient included the following:

- determine active insurance benefit, and verify coverage

- precertify the inpatient stay
- negotiate a per diem based on the plan of care, and adjust as indicated by the plan of care
- provide concurrent reviews
- assist in discharge planning, and verify benefits for services needed after discharge
- make the external case manager aware of other programs and provide information to generate future referrals

Table 8–1 illustrates the LOS and cost efficiency of using case management strategies with Mr C.

Mr S

Mr S was admitted to Heather Hill's Rehabilitation Hospital using his subacute benefit after a myocardial infarction. Benefits were verified with the insurance carrier, and concurrent reviews were provided to the review nurses at the insurance company.

Mr S remained in the facility for intensive rehabilitation until his return home with his wife a few weeks later. Because of the patient's interest in participating in an aggressive outpatient program to prepare him to return to work, funding for continued rehabilitation was pursued. He attended outpatient therapy from July until April of the following year. His employer remained instrumentally involved during the outpatient program and was supportive of a visit to the work site by the internal case manager and physiatrist. The patient maintained a strong desire to return to work, but as time went on and an evaluation of the job description was reviewed he decided to take early retirement. The new goal of the patient and his wife was to volunteer their time in a health care facility.

Responsibilities of case management with this patient included the following:

- verify status of insurance and verify benefits
- precertify admission
- provide concurrent reviews as requested

Table 8–1 Case Management of Mr C

Type of Care	Usual and Customary		Case Managed	
	LOS (days)	Charges ($)	LOS (days)	Charges ($)
Acute hospital	10	12,000	10	12,000
General subacute	46	20,700	36	16,200
Chronic subacute			10	2,950
Acute hospital	6	7,200	6	7,200
Subacute rehabilitation	14	6,300	10	3,950
Totals	76	46,200	72	42,300
Cost savings: $3,900 (9%)				

- assist in discharge planning
- maintain contact with employer as well as insurance company
- coordinate outpatient services out of the insurance contract with employer
- coordinate return to work program with appropriate staff and employer
- assist in referral process to appropriate community agencies (eg, find a place to take a driving test to ensure patient's safety on the road)
- increase employer awareness of programs offered at Heather Hill to encourage future referrals

Case management of Mr S allowed funds for inpatient care to be diverted to extend his outpatient coverage. Although the patient did not return to work, he and employer both believed that he was given every opportunity to achieve this.

QUALIFICATIONS OF A GOOD CASE MANAGER

The good case manager is trustworthy, mature, reliable, creative, flexible, and respected in the health care community and has a high degree of professionalism. He or she is a good communicator, understands quality improvement methodology, and is committed to the welfare of the patient and the organization. Knowledge of the reimbursement culture, including areas of eligibility, liability, plan design, and coverage, is essential. It is also important that the case manager

be aware of the types and availability of durable medical equipment; home health services; infusion therapy; psychology and psychiatry services; physical, occupational, speech-language, and recreation therapies; social work; and prescription drugs.

Case managers must conduct business, not just discuss clinical issues. They must be aggressive in cost cutting while being cognizant of quality care.

Who Qualifies As the Best Case Manager?

Some facilities do not have the financial resources to hire experienced case managers and must train existing staff to add this function to their present duties. The most difficult skill to learn is negotiation with the payer, although the role requires approximately 60% clinical skills and 40% financial skills. According to Kulik,[3] the best case manager is a clinical nurse specialist who has at least 1 year of experience in utilization review. Nevertheless, social workers, rehabilitation counselors, speech-language pathologists, and others have successfully served as case managers in subacute care facilities throughout the United States.

Credentials

The case manager's credentials may include the following:

- certified case manager, certified by the Certified Insurance Rehabilitation Specialist Commission

- certified registered rehabilitation nurse, sponsored by the Association of Rehabilitation Nurses
- certified rehabilitation counselor
- certified insurance rehabilitation specialist

Information about and sources of these certifications are given in Table 8–2.

Empowerment of case managers is essential to ensure their effectiveness. The organization that gives authority and flexibility to implement and follow through with these responsibilities will benefit from a case management program. A sample job description for an internal case manager is given in Appendix 8A.

CONCLUSION

The goal of case management is the same as the proposed goal of managed care: to achieve specific patient outcomes using a fiscally responsible time frame and appropriate resources for the specific case type and individual patient. In subacute programs, systems must be developed for managing and coordinating the care of patients in a cost-effective manner for discharge home or to a less expensive level of care, such as assisted living or long-term care. Facilities with case management will be best prepared for the future by utilizing cost containment strategies while providing effective, quality care.

Table 8–2 Certification Information for Case Managers

Credentials/Requirements	Credentialing Agency	Fees (as of November 1994)	
Certified case manager/Case management experience, licensure or certification in health/human services	Certified Insurance Rehabilitation Specialist Commission 1835 Rohlwing Road, Suite D Rolling Meadows, IL 60008 (708) 818-0292	Application: (nonrefundable) Examination:	$125 $150
Certified registered rehabilitation nurse	Rehabilitation Nursing Certification Board 5700 Old Orchard Road, First Floor Skokie, IL 60077-1057 (708) 966-3433 To obtain application for the examination, write: The Psychological Corporation, Project 651/CRRN 555 Academic Court San Antonio, TX 78204-2498 (800) 622-3231 or (210) 299-1061	Examination Association of Rehabilitation Nurses (ARN) ARN members: Nonmembers:	$185 $265
Certified rehabilitation counselor/Master's degree in rehabilitation counseling	Certified Insurance Rehabilitation Specialist Commission *(See address and phone number above.)*	Student application: (nonrefundable) All other applicants: (nonrefundable) Examination (all):	$85 $100 $125
Certified insurance rehabilitation specialist	Certified Insurance Rehabilitation Specialist Commission *(See address and phone number above.)*	Application: (nonrefundable) Examination:	$125 $150

REFERENCES

1. Suldan JI. Be aware of changes in Medicare. *Hosp Case Manage.* 1994;2:17.

2. National Association of Rehabilitation Professionals in the Private Sector. *Professional Performance Criteria for Medical Case Management.* Newton, Mass: National Directory of Rehabilitation Professionals; 1993.

3. Kulik T. The other CM customer—What does the payer expect? *Hosp Case Manage.* 1993;1:123–131.

Sample Job Description for Internal Case Manager

Position Description

The internal case manager is responsible for documenting the cost effectiveness of treatment provided, participating in utilization review, and preparing outcome reports. The person in this position communicates with the medical management team to coordinate the delivery of nursing and rehabilitative services to patients, to coordinate the discharge planning process, and generally to serve as the patient and family advocate. The case manager skillfully interacts with fiscal intermediaries and third party payers.

Qualifications

Education and experience

- College degree.
- Minimum of 2 years of clinical or health care experience.
- Experience in insurance, worker's compensation, medical management preferred.
- Knowledge of skilled care criteria for Medicare and other third party insurance plans.

Personal and physical expectations

- Ability to prioritize and work independently.
- Effective organization, coordination, and communication (written and verbal) skills.
- Ability to work as a team member in coordinating care within the interdisciplinary team.
- Professional and personal effectiveness in establishing relationships with referral sources and families.

Performance Responsibilities

Referrals and admissions

- Reviews inquiries for admission, and makes eligibility and coverage determinations.
- Verifies primary and secondary payer sources and eligibility for skilled care services under each benefit plan.
- Documents precertification authorization for private insurance plans and managed care contracts, including authorizing party and coverage limitations.

Coordination of cost-effective, quality care

- Collaborates with the attending physician to facilitate staffing conferences aimed at developing, monitoring, and refining the treatment plan to achieve identified patient outcomes.
- Schedules team conferences including all key team members.
- Maintains reports to update patients' progress.
- Ensures correct documentation on charts in coordination with policies and procedures, regulations, and utilization review, including, but not limited to, admission, transfer, and discharge data.
- Evaluates patient care plans and LOS for cost effectiveness and appropriateness.
- Participates in determining LOS and begins discharge planning process.

Payer liaison

- Negotiates case-by-case payment.
- Documents all payer interaction regarding precertification, expected outcomes and cost, and special instructions.
- Justifies the payment of skilled care by fiscal intermediaries and other third party payers.
- Communicates with insurance carrier for ongoing coverage, documenting all communication with insurance representatives.
- Invites representation at team conferences.

Monitoring and communication

- Ensures that the patient is oriented to the program, and conducts an orientation session with the family.
- Ensures that the patient participates, as feasible, in the development and implementation of his or her treatment plan.
- Ensures the quality and timeliness of medical record documentation in accordance with the hospital's defined policies and procedures.

- Within the program's philosophy, goals, and objectives, ensures that the patient is receiving individualized care to meet his or her needs.
- Maintains contact with the family, minimally weekly, to facilitate family involvement and to apprise the family of patient progress.

Discharge planning

- Ensures that discharge planning goals and objectives are developed and modified at each staffing conference.
- Ensures timely and appropriate discharge, coordinating placement issues.
- Maintains effective communication with the patient, family, and payer regarding the discharge plan and progress.
- Completes a program discharge summary and plan in collaboration with the attending physician. Submits this document to the payer and referral source.

Postdischarge planning

- Schedules patient's postdischarge appointment with the referring physician.
- Writes discharge and thank you letter with discharge summary.
- Contacts the insurance case manager by phone for follow-up of postdischarge status and care.
- Updates facility staff after postdischarge follow-up with patient, family, and physician.

Marketing

- Functions as contact person for all insurers, social workers, discharge planners, and outside case managers.
- Functions as in-house marketer, including maintaining relationships with referral sources, telemarketing, conducting tours, and seeing to guest relations.

9

Marketing and Admissions for Subacute Care

Kathleen M. Griffin

*If you build it, they will come. . . .*Unfortunately, that statement is not true for subacute care units and facilities. Referral sources must first know about the subacute unit or facility, and they must believe that the unit or facility truly solves their problems and meets their patients' needs. Marketing for subacute care or, more specifically, referral development is simply that: solving problems and meeting needs. People refer to people in whom they have trust.

Subacute care units or facilities that are integrated components of networks or health care systems must develop strategies to encourage referrals of patients from other provider entities within the system. Freestanding, nonaffiliated subacute units or facilities must be able to attract patient referrals from a wide variety of sources. As the health care system continues to change and become more payer driven, referral sources for subacute providers are expanding to include hospital discharge planners as well as insurance and managed care organizations' case managers, capitated physician groups, and utilization managers within hospitals.

This chapter focuses on marketing strategies that will result in the expected volume and types of referrals of patients to subacute providers and on admissions procedures that are user friendly to referral sources.

MARKETING AND REFERRAL DEVELOPMENT: DESCRIPTION

Although the term *marketing* encompasses all the activities that result in a mutually beneficial exchange of services for payment, referral development involves the long-term relationships that are essential to successful census development in subacute care units and facilities. A variety of factors influence census development, including the following:

- *The general reputation and knowledge of subacute care in the community and among referral sources.* This census development strategy usually involves an overall public relations and advertising program that is a component of the marketing plan for the subacute provider.
- *Patient/family satisfaction.* A dissatisfied patient or family can generate far-reaching negative publicity for the subacute provider. Such patients and families will convey their dissatisfaction not only to their

own physicians but also to other members of the public or the health care community. The physician who has received negative feedback from a patient or family will probably be reluctant to refer patients in the future and may even influence other physicians to discontinue referring patients to the subacute provider. On the other hand, satisfied patients and families will help educate others about subacute care.

- *Quality of care.* In addition to patient/family satisfaction, other components of quality of care are an optimal patient outcome, appropriate length of stay, competitive costs, and qualified and caring staff members.
- *Medical staff.* Because subacute care requires regular and relatively intensive physician management, the reputation of members of the medical staff in the community is an important factor influencing census development for the subacute provider.
- *Admissions system.* The manner in which inquiries and admissions are handled frequently is a key factor in the success of the marketing and referral development efforts.
- *Referral development and maintenance.* An active program of one-on-one relationship building, which includes providing regular feedback about patients admitted to the subacute programs, is required for successful census development for a subacute provider.

THE REFERRAL DEVELOPMENT PROCESS

The referral development process involves an integrated series of marketing activities that are focused on results. The results of the referral development process are measured by the volume and types of patients admitted to the subacute program in terms of the budgeted expectations for the subacute provider. Achieving the census expectations involves effective systems for referral development and maintenance as well as mar-

keting, encouraging inquiries, handling inquiries, development of an intake system, identifying prospects and qualifying leads, one-on-one referral development calls, and referral maintenance efforts. Figure 9–1 outlines the process for achieving census expectations.

THE REFERRAL DEVELOPMENT TEAM

The subacute referral development team involves the following individuals: a program director, a facility case manager, a nurse liaison, a medical director, a director of nursing, an admissions coordinator, an administrator, and others as needed. The program director, facility case manager, nurse liaison, and admissions coordinator are mandatory team members. Suggested roles for the program director and facility case manager are outlined in Exhibits 9–1 and 9–2. The nurse liaison usually focuses efforts on assessing patients before admission and referral development activities for hospitals. The admissions coordinator handles inquiries, maintains the referral source database, and manages the admissions process.

Other individuals may be involved in the referral development process, including social workers, nurses, physical therapists, occupational therapists, speech-language pathologists, and respiratory therapists. It may be appropriate for these individuals to target their peers and to conduct one-on-one meetings to discuss the subacute program. They may also give seminars and workshops. Their presence at the weekly referral development meeting allows them to become part of the overall referral development team.

REFERRAL DEVELOPMENT PLANNING

Annual and quarterly referral development plans are action-oriented, short documents developed to assist the referral development team in assessing current status, developing goals, and utilizing resources effectively. In other words, a referral development plan is a blueprint for all referral development efforts. The plan includes clear statements of goals, objectives, target audi-

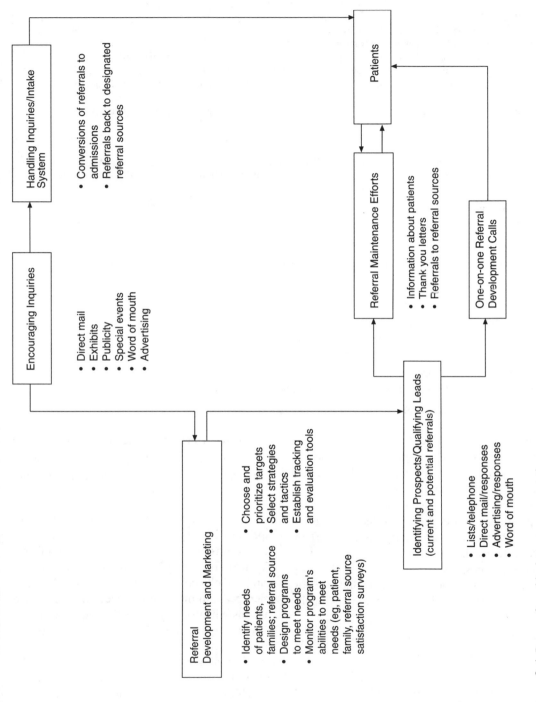

Figure 9–1 Process for achieving census expectations.

Exhibit 9–1 Program Director's Role(s) in Referral Development

Major Functions

One-on-one referral development and follow-up
- Cochairs referral development weekly meeting.
- Conducts an average of 20 one-on-one contacts per month that produce a significant number of admissions.
- Conducts an additional 4 to 6 one-on-one contacts per month jointly with a medical staff member.
- Sets referral development goals for staff. Reviews contact activities to ensure that there is a high conversion rate to admissions.
- Develops contracts with insurers, health maintenance organizations, and preferred provider organizations.

Management
- Supervises facility case manager.
- Ensures that marketing systems are implemented by setting an example and by reinforcing the importance of systems.
- Organizes and approves management staff vacations to avoid decline of program quality and referral activity.
- Motivates staff in referral development activities.

Recruitment
- Recruits medical staff.

Intake
- Monitors intake system daily for number/status of inquiries, evaluations, admissions, and problems.

Tracking
- Reviews tracking information weekly.

Advertising
- Reviews and approves quarterly media budgets for local area advertising.
- Reviews advertising effectiveness tracking.

Marketing Plan Development
- Reviews and approves quarterly and annual marketing plans.

ences, strategies, and tactics. It provides for specific ways to measure progress as well. The advantages to a referral development plan are that such a plan makes sure all staff know the answers to key questions about the subacute program, helps allocate scarce dollar and labor resources systematically and efficiently, assists staff in staying focused, and provides a systematic way to measure progress.

The referral development plan includes major goals to be achieved by year end. Goals might read as follows:

- Have the major market share of subacute patients in the catchment area.
- Be at breakeven financially by the _____ month of operations and be profitable by the _____ month.

- Have a managed care or insurance payer mix of _____ % by the end of the year.
- Have net revenues and a pretax profit at the end of the year of _____ and _____.

The referral development objectives are more specific. The objectives focus on the number of admissions on a monthly basis from various referral sources or types of referral sources. The monthly objectives allow the referral development team to measure its successes and to take actions when specific objectives are not met. A format for the sales objectives is suggested in Figure 9–2.

After the goals and objectives section of the referral development plan, the specific strategies to achieve those objectives are listed. The strategies involve primarily one-on-one, direct calls to

Exhibit 9–2 Facility Case Manager Role(s) in Referral Development

Job Summary

The facility case manager reports to the program director and is part of subacute unit management. The purpose of the position is to ensure that the facility achieves census objectives with the appropriate payer mix by setting up and coordinating the following census-producing systems:

- one-on-one referral development and maintenance
- intake
- tracking
- feedback to payers and referral sources
- annual and quarterly plans
- direct mail, exhibits, and local advertising

Major Functions

One-on-one referral development and follow-up
- Coordinates and participates in facility one-on-one referral development efforts.
- Cochairs referral development weekly meetings with program director.
- Organizes promotions such as inservices and direct mail activities for lead generation.
- Monitors referral source follow-up activities.
- Works with program director to develop contracts with insurers, health maintenance organizations, and preferred provider organizations.

Intake

- Sets up intake system with admissions coordinator and monitors via test calls and reviews of intake forms weekly.
- Provides intake training and refresher courses as needed (at least quarterly).

Tracking

- Completes monthly marketing report.
- Analyzes referral development trends.
- Maintains lists of weekly contacts made/planned and resultant admissions:
  1. Collects lists of contacts made the previous week and lists of contacts planned for next week from each member of the referral development team.
  2. Reviews lists for appropriateness/duplication/admission activity of each contact name and referral group. Redirects team activities as appropriate at meeting.
  3. Reviews referral source activity weekly and gives brief report at referral development weekly meetings.
  4. Reviews and analyzes weekly advertising tracking form.

Annual and Quarterly Marketing Plans

- Works with nurse liaison and program director to develop:
  1. annual facility referral development plan
  2. quarterly plans
- Monitors the implementation of plans and adjusts as necessary.
- Develops and monitors budget for department.

Advertising

- Develops local advertising budget based on approval from program director.
- Responds to media calls/questions.
- Positions subacute unit as a source of expert information about subacute care.

1) Achieve census and patient mix objectives as follows:

MONTH	INS/HMO/PPO (Incl. Worker's Comp)	MEDICARE	SELF-PAY	TOTAL
MONTH 1				
MONTH 2				
MONTH 3 (etc.)				

2) Achieve at least the following number of qualified referrals from these sources:

MONTH	INS/HMO/PPO CONTRACTS	INDEPENDENT INS/HMO/PPO CASE MANAGERS	DCPs OR NURSES ACUTE HOSPITALS	PHYSICIANS	OTHER	TOTAL
MONTH 1						
MONTH 2						
MONTH 3 (etc.)						

3) Complete contracts with insurers, PPOs, and HMOs as follows:

DATE	PAYER	CONTRACT START DATE	CONTRACT RENEWAL DATE	CONTRACT TERMS SUMMARY

4) Obtain at least _____ admissions from each completed contract within 6 months after contract is completed.

Figure 9–2 Format for referral development plan objectives.

---

referral sources. Direct referral development calls are supported by other marketing strategies, including direct mail, advertising, trade shows, presentations at medical staff meetings and seminars, and open houses. Figure 9–3 provides a sample format for the strategies section of the plan.

ORGANIZING AND MANAGING

The referral development team's energies must remain focused through a system that delegates specific tasks and provides for weekly reporting. The weekly subacute referral development team meeting is an appropriate mechanism for organizing and managing the referral devel-

opment efforts. The goals of the weekly referral development meeting are:

- to organize and direct the target staff's marketing efforts
- to establish expectations of each team member for referral development
- to provide follow-up and accountability for and to each team member
- to build and maintain enthusiasm at the staff level for referral development efforts

A sample agenda for the subacute referral development weekly team meeting is shown in Exhibit 9–3. During the subacute referral development

STRATEGIES	PERSON RESPONSIBLE	DIRECT COST	DATE TO BE COMPLETED

Figure 9–3 Format for strategies section of referral development plan.

team meeting, the following team members and their responsibilities during the meeting are as given in Table 9–1.

TRACKING AND EVALUATION

As the number of subacute providers continues to increase, automating the marketing and referral development functions is an increasingly important consideration for subacute providers. An automated sales management system, involvement of top level management in the referral development and marketing efforts, and effective accountability methods are essential components of the referral development program for the subacute provider.

The tracking and evaluation functions begin at the inquiry level with the maintenance of a daily referral log. Although the processes may be automated, as described in Chapter 12, there are certain data points that should be tracked by the admissions coordinator. Figure 9–4 provides an example of a tracking system for inquiries and referrals.

Another component of the tracking and evaluation system involves building the referral development database. Building a database is much more than collecting the names and addresses of current and potential referral sources for a mailing list. There are five basic steps in building a referral development database, whether or not the database is automated:

1. Compile a list of individual referral sources, including the information already in hand about each one of these referral sources. The information should include such items as the length of time the person has been a referral source, the volume of patients referred, the net revenues generated by those referrals, and the types of patients referred.

2. Review the data items to determine which ones can assist in improving the efficiency of the referral development efforts and which ones can be eliminated. The referral database needs to be as simple as possible so that it is useful.

3. Identify missing elements in the referral database. To find out more about the demographics, psychographics, and referral habits of referral sources, it may be necessary to conduct a survey.

4. Determine who the best referral sources are. Segment the database by the revenue value of the referral sources. By knowing the characteristics of the best referral sources, one can target potential referral sources who share those characteristics.

5. Keep the database up to date. A referral source database is a long-term relationship, not a one-night stand. Keeping it up to date will require money and constant maintenance, but the payoff should be greater profitability.

A third component of the tracking and evaluation system for referral development involves systematic contacts by telephone or in person.

Admission Coordinator _____   Date: _____   Total References: _____

Patient Name	Patient Location	Referral Source	Referral Source Phone #	Diagnosis	Patient Age	Payer	Preassessment Scheduled	Preassessment Completed	Financial Verification Completed	Next Steps

Figure 9–4 Daily referral log.

Table 9–1 Responsibilities of Team Members during Subacute Referral Development Team Meeting

Team Member	Responsibilities
Subacute program director	Cochairs meeting Reports on contacts Follows up on staff contacts Motivates and reinforces appropriate referral development activity Knows and monitors top referral sources Conducts and monitors top referral sources
Medical director	Reports on contacts Follows up with physician contacts
Facility case manager	Cochairs meeting Reports on contacts Coordinates the dissemination of new referral source names and maintains files on all contacts and resultant referral activity Maintains statistics on staff referral activity and results Conducts and participates in role playing/training in referral development Develops annual and quarterly plans Monitors referral/admission activity Follows up with all referral sources that have sent patients
Nurse liaison	Reports on contacts Follows up with referral sources
Business office manager or controller	Reports on contacts Prepares financial analyses for potential service contracts
Admissions coordinator	Reports on referral source feedback and activity Reports on admissions, including those pending

The contacts are made by a member of the referral development team. Individual team members may focus on selected targets. For example, the program director may contact provider relations persons from managed care organizations, and the facility case manager may target insurance case managers. The nurse liaison, who conducts the preadmissions assessments, may target hospital discharge planners. The subacute program medical director would probably target physicians. Tracking the contacts made by the members of the referral development team, ensuring the effectiveness of the call, and taking the next steps are essential to evaluate the efforts. Each time a contact is made, a call report should be completed by the contacting member of the referral development team. The results of the call report should be added to the database. Ideally, a tickler system, whether automated or manual, should be used to remind the referral team member that it is time to contact the targeted referral source again.

REFERRAL SOURCE MAINTENANCE PROGRAM

As a general rule, 80% of referrals come from 20% of the referral sources. It takes less time and energy per source to maintain a relationship than to establish a new one or to reestablish one. The current referral sources have already demonstrated trust and confidence in a subacute program and are excellent sources of positive public relations.

The referral source maintenance program includes two functions: feedback to referral sources, and user-friendly admissions procedures. One of the keys to success in maintaining referral relationships is to determine the types of information that referral sources desire from the

Exhibit 9–3 Subacute Referral Development Team Weekly Meeting: Sample Agenda for 1-Hour Meeting

Topics to be covered (20% of meeting time):	*Reported by:*
1. Review report of past week's statistics	Program director
• Admissions by payer type	
• Discharges by payer type	
• Census by payer type	
• Length of stay (LOS) by payer type	
2. Review of upcoming week	Facility case manager
• Potential admissions by payer	
• Potential discharges by payer	
3. Review of intake system	Admissions coordinator
• Any incomplete preassessments/conversions/glitches in system	
• Advertising currently running	
• Number of referrals to other providers	
• Inquiries/admissions—referral sources that need follow-up assigned to team members	
• New referral sources—assign to team members	
Topics to be covered (80% of meeting time):	*Reported by:*
4. Report on contacts	All team members
• Report of each member's past and planned week's contacts (not all contacts are reviewed, only ones with issues or follow-up needed from other team members); program director and facility case manager review all reports on contacts the day before the meeting and select ones to be discussed; additionally, each team member also prioritizes his or her contacts that require detailed review	
• Problem solving	
5. Priorities/summary	Program director
• Priorities for the week/month/quarter are covered (eg, quarterly planning, LOS, special concentrated efforts on target groups)	

subacute provider and to set up a system to ensure that the referral sources obtain that information. The information requested or required by referral sources may include:

- notification at the time of admission
- weekly progress reports
- participation in interdisciplinary team meetings
- involvement in discharge planning
- notification upon discharge of the patient
- discharge summary

Successful referral development also depends on having admissions procedures that are timely and responsive to referral sources. The admissions coordinator and the nurse liaison work together closely and with the other members of the referral development team to ensure that the admissions process is efficient and effective. The admissions coordinator is an inside person who handles the following functions:

- coordinates the efficient flow of information/activities beginning with a patient referral
- ensures that financial screening (including insurance verification and precertification) is properly completed in a timely manner and that the nurse liaison is notified for timely preassessment

- obtains signatures on admissions forms and notifies departments to facilitate information flow to department managers
- ensures that all information required to admit a patient properly is received by the business office before the patient's arrival
- ensures that financial responsibilities have been communicated to the family
- determines whether the number of days covered by insurance or third party payers is appropriate according to the diagnosis
- forwards information to the physician for admissions approval
- tracks demographic information (eg, location of referrals, referral source, age)
- provides tours for families and guests
- attends referral development meetings to discuss potential admissions and discharges
- follows up daily with potential referral sources for patients to be admitted and/or with a status check

The other key individual, the nurse liaison, has the following responsibilities:

- implements the referral development plan, which includes developing relationships with targeted referral sources (case managers, discharge planners, certain physician groups, etc) and obtaining qualified patient referrals to meet census and payer mix objectives of the region
- performs preassessments of referred patients to qualify for admission and ensures timely financial authorization and negotiation of favorable rates that meet the unit's profitability objectives; meets with family members and/or decision makers to effect the admission
- oversees the preadmissions process, including family tours, physician involvement, and financial authorization; works closely with the program director to ensure that the necessary equipment, supplies, and medications are available within the unit at the time of the patient's admission

- prepares reports demonstrating referral and admission trends and utilizes the data to refine sales targets; maintains current competitive analysis
- continually assesses market needs and recommends operational adjustments and additions in the unit to achieve and maintain the desired market share

The referral development process is graphically depicted in Figure 9–5 and includes the following procedures:

- *Intake:* Once a referral is received, the admissions coordinator formulates an intake record to determine diagnosis, medical stability, level of care, family involvement, reimbursement resources, and discharge options.
- *Patient preadmission assessment:* A preadmission assessment is scheduled with the referring party and the appropriate facility staff. It should be completed within 2 hours of referral. The nurse liaison then determines the appropriateness of clinical admission and either negotiates a daily rate with the payer or initiates financial verification procedures with the business office. The nurse liaison obtains physician's orders for admission and initial treatment orders. Appropriate medical records are obtained that include history/physical, discharge summary, current laboratory reports, current radiology reports, most recent 24-hour nursing assessment and notes, and therapy evaluations and progress notes. The subacute unit or facility may have criteria that trigger a review of potential admissions by the admissions committee. The criteria may relate to clinical or financial considerations. The admissions committee typically involves the medical director, the program director, and a business office representative. Unless there are complications related to an admission, however, the admissions decisions should be delegated to the nurse liaison, who utilizes approved criteria for admissions decisions.

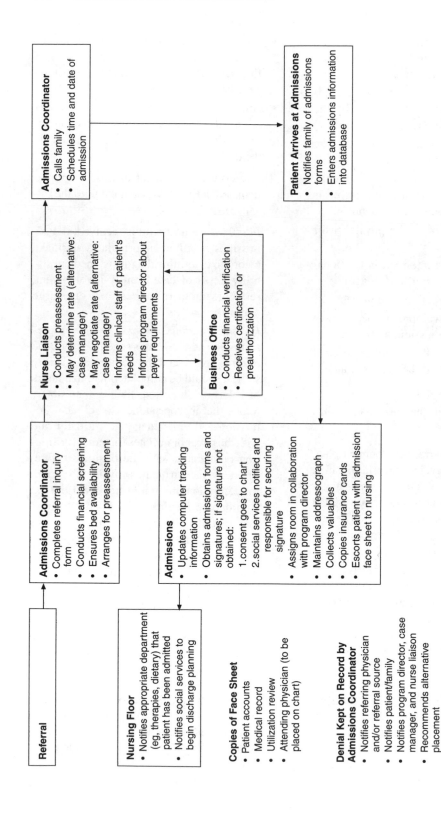

Referral

Admissions Coordinator
- Completes referral inquiry form
- Conducts financial screening
- Ensures bed availability
- Arranges for preassessment

Nurse Liaison
- Conducts preassessment
- May determine rate (alternative: case manager)
- May negotiate rate (alternative: case manager)
- Informs clinical staff of patient's needs
- Informs program director about payer requirements

Admissions Coordinator
- Calls family
- Schedules time and date of admission

Business Office
- Conducts financial verification
- Receives certification or preauthorization

Patient Arrives at Admissions
- Notifies family of admissions forms
- Enters admissions information into database

Nursing Floor
- Notifies appropriate department (eg, therapies, dietary) that patient has been admitted
- Notifies social services to begin discharge planning

Admissions
- Updates computer tracking information
- Obtains admissions forms and signatures; if signature not obtained:
  1. consent goes to chart
  2. social services notified and responsible for securing signature
- Assigns room in collaboration with program director
- Maintains addressograph
- Collects valuables
- Copies insurance cards
- Escorts patient with admission face sheet to nursing

Copies of Face Sheet
- Patient accounts
- Medical record
- Utilization review
- Attending physician (to be placed on chart)

Denial Kept on Record by Admissions Coordinator
- Notifies referring physician and/or referral source
- Notifies patient/family
- Notifies program director, case manager, and nurse liaison
- Recommends alternative placement

Figure 9–5 Subacute admissions process.

- *Initial treatment/care plan:* If the payer requires an initial care plan, the nurse liaison and/or program director develops an initial plan of care to reflect needed therapies, treatments, modalities, and medical supplies/equipment based upon the patient's current medical condition.
- *Benefits verification:* Primary and secondary coverage is verified by the business office concurrent with the development of the care plan. Eligibility and coverage are determined to include limitations, exclusions, deductibles, copays, reimbursement, billing preferences, and any external case management or utilization review needs. Medicare patient eligibility is determined by the admissions coordinator, who also verifies any secondary coverage. Billing requirements are communicated to the business office in writing.
- *Rate determination:* Daily per diems or per case rates may already by established by contract or provider agreements. If a per diem must be negotiated, the nurse liaison or case manager performs this task with the program director's approval. Per diem rates usually are tiered per patient acuity as determined by the preassessment (see Chapter 4).
- *Precertification/authorization:* A precertification number or a letter of agreement or understanding is obtained. A statement of medical necessity may be required from the referring physician or from the facility's medical director.
- *Site tours:* The admissions coordinator schedules facility/unit tours for the family, patient, or payer to facilitate the admission decision. Tour days and times must be available in the evenings and on weekends to accommodate all parties.

- *Admissions:* The actual admission is scheduled by the admissions coordinator, he or she handles all remaining tasks, such as obtaining copies of insurance cards, signing admissions agreements, ensuring the assignment of a physician (if necessary), and the like. Admission times must also be available 7 days a week.

If a patient is not accepted for admission, then it is the responsibility of the admissions coordinator to notify the referral source as to the reason(s) for denial of admission and to suggest alternative placements for the patient.

CONCLUSION

Marketing and, specifically, referral development are necessary to ensure that the census in the subacute unit or facility meets established financial objectives. The referral development process involves planning, organizing, tracking, and evaluating procedures in terms of their effectiveness. Referral development is not limited to a single individual. Rather, a team of individuals, including at least the facility case manager, the program director, the nurse liaison, the admissions coordinator, and the medical director should be involved in referral development efforts. Referral development in and of itself will not be successful without a timely and responsive admissions process. The admissions process typically is handled by an admissions coordinator, who serves as the internal person of the referral development team. Throughout the referral development and admissions process, there must be continual assessment and reassessment of referral source needs and interests as well as modifications of procedures to meet these needs and interests.

10

Subacute Outcome Measurement and Critical Paths Development and Use

Patricia Larkins Hicks and Carol Frattali

Escalating health care costs, pressures to contain them, and demands for accountability have placed the US health care system under a microscope. Every aspect of the system is being reexamined by one or more groups, including payers, regulators, legislators, employers, providers, and consumers. Each is seeking answers to a critical and multifaceted question: Who provides what service, to whom, in what setting, for how long, at what cost, and resulting in what benefit? The answers rely heavily on a need for collection and analysis of treatment outcome data and the development and use of critical paths.

As early as 1910, Ernest A. Codman, then a prominent surgeon at Massachusetts General Hospital, proposed a revolutionary idea that physicians should track the treatment outcomes of their patients and make this information public. Codman's outcome measurement concept was not popular with his colleagues, and subsequently he was forced out of the medical profession. Had his colleagues taken heed, adequate outcome data would perhaps be available today. Instead, these data are limited. It is essential that, in this emerging subacute environment, data are collected and analyzed that identify the professionals needed to provide specified services, the

types of patients who should be seen, the amount of time for which these patients should be required to be seen in the subacute environment, benefits to patients and caregivers, and the costs of services provided. This chapter defines the outcome data elements to be measured; identifies available outcome measures, projects, and systems; describes some ways in which outcome data can be used to effect change; provides tips to customize a system to meet specific needs; defines critical paths and a process for their development; and illustrates the use of critical paths as a case management tool in a subacute health care environment.

DEFINING OUTCOME MEASURES

To define appropriate outcome measures in the subacute environment, it is necessary to identify outcome parameters, what should be measured, and who conducts the measurement.

What Should Be Measured?

Since the early 1980s, the multidisciplinary field of medical rehabilitation has focused on measuring patient outcomes based on function.

Wilkerson et al[1] report that the World Health Organization (WHO) *International Classification of Impairments, Disabilities and Handicaps*[2] generally has been used as the framework for the development of outcome measures, including functional assessments. According to the WHO,[2-4] impairment is any loss or abnormality of psychologic, physiologic, or anatomic structure or function at the organ level. Examples include amputation, blindness, cognitive disorders, hearing loss, incontinence, paralysis, or speech or language disorders. Disability is any restriction or lack of ability to perform an activity in the manner or within the range considered normal for a human being. Hence a disability is the functional consequence of an impairment and as such reflects disturbances at the level of the person. Examples include difficulty in bathing, communicating, dressing, feeding, toileting, transferring, and walking. Handicap is a disadvantage for a given individual resulting from an impairment or a disability that limits or prevents the fulfillment of a role that is normal for that individual. Examples include dependency, joblessness, and social isolation.

On the basis of this framework, those areas of function typically assessed include activities of daily living (ADLs), cognition, communication, health maintenance, mobility, psychosocial well-being, self-care, and work. At issue is the level at which one measures function. Wilkerson et al[1] identify three levels of function. Microfunction focuses on increased skill (eg, range of motion, gait, or speech formation); measures used at this level are assessing impairment. Middle function focuses on increased functioning (eg, ADLs, walking, or communication needs); measures used at this level are assessing disability. Macrofunction focuses on increased return to chosen roles (eg, homemaking, recreation, or working); measures used at this level are assessing handicap. In the subacute setting, then, there is need to determine which level of function can be affected by services provided, with the recognition that if patients are coming from and being moved to other settings other levels of performance may be addressed more appropriately in those settings.

Also at issue is the definition of quality of life. Some researchers see it as synonymous with health status and functional status. Jette[5] suggests that the concept needs to be defined more narrowly as health-related quality of life. He cites an example that "persons in poor health may have a high quality of life and conversely persons in excellent health may not have a very good quality of life."[5(p530)] Measuring the effect of intervention on health-related quality of life addresses the consequences of disease, impairment, and/or disability as they affect the person. This broadens the assessment from what is typically measured when the effect on function alone is addressed.

Payers often are interested in paying only for those interventions that bring about meaningful change in the patient's behavior. Consumers also typically want professionals to intervene only if they can bring about a meaningful change in the patient's behavior. At issue here is the benefit of intervention when no meaningful change occurs. A lack of meaningful change, however, may result in prevention of further patient decline and thereby may decrease the burden of care on the part of the caregiver(s). In the subacute environment, it may be of equal importance to measure treatment effectiveness from two perspectives: improvement in status and prevention of further decline.

Measuring efficiency means determining the effectiveness of an intervention within a given time frame. No longer can the professional be concerned just with effectiveness; rather, he or she must look equally at what persons, procedures, techniques, materials, and equipment are being used in what time frame to be effective. The professional's goal needs to focus on achieving the best results in the shortest amount of time. At issue is how to facilitate the collection of these data by the professional intervening with the patient without creating an additional burden. Recently, single-subject experimental designs and case methods have proved to be useful methodologies in the clinical setting.[6-8]

One must be mindful that the time expended in caring for a patient is equated to the cost of the care. Hence as payers examine how costs can be contained, demands will increase for better time management in caring for patients. Measures of efficiency provide useful information in addressing these demands and provide direction regarding how costs can be contained without adversely affecting the patients.

Although there are many issues that make it difficult to define clearly what needs to be measured, it is certain that in the subacute setting outcome measures must assess both effectiveness and efficiency. Data from these assessments will facilitate decision making regarding personnel utilization, patient selection, frequency and type of intervention, length of stay, and discharge. For providers of services in the subacute setting, outcome data can guide in decision making regarding:

- appropriate use of skilled clinicians or technicians
- the case-mix that is appropriate for the facility
- the amount of time that must be scheduled for each patient
- best practices that can be employed at the lowest cost
- expected functional status of patients upon discharge

Who Conducts the Measurement?

In the subacute setting, there are a variety of individuals who can participate in outcome measurement. They may include, but are not restricted to, the case manager, the discharge planner, a family member/significant other, the nurse, the patient, the physician, the rehabilitation professional, and/or the social worker. What is measured will influence who participates in the measurement process. In this setting, however, the utilization of a team approach is an important consideration. If the goal is to optimize functioning as quickly as possible in a low-cost environment, then all key persons involved in the care process should be involved in determining what outcomes are measured, how outcomes will be measured, the frequency of measurement, and

their individual roles in the measurement process. If measurement is integrated into the care planning process, it will be easier to incorporate these key players because they meet regularly to plan for the patient's care. Involving all key players in outcome measurement at the point of service is critical because it defines the patient's status and facilitates appropriate and timely modifications in the care process to achieve outcomes at the lowest possible cost.

OUTCOME MEASURES, PROJECTS, AND SYSTEMS

The development of outcome measures, research projects, and data collection systems has increased over the past decade. The following discussion represents an overview of developments in outcome measurement and management.

Wilkerson et al[1] report that three functional status measures have emerged as the most frequently used outcome measures in medical rehabilitation. They are the Functional Independence Measure (FIM),[9] the Level of Rehabilitation Scale (LORS),[10–12] and the Patient Evaluation and Conference System.[13] Frattali[3] provides a description of selected functional status measures.[9–22] These are presented in Table 10–1.

There is much debate over the validity and reliability of these measures as well as the use of ordinal scales. Hence researchers question the usefulness of these measures in assessing functional status and the ability to utilize statistical analyses in interpreting the data collected.[3] Additionally, at issue is the applicability of these measures across health care settings. Data have been derived primarily from the inpatient acute care hospital setting. Given that different types of patients with different needs receive services in different settings, what needs to be measured and who measures it may also vary by setting. No one measure provides the data necessary to meet the diverse needs across work settings. One attempt to develop a measure for a different setting has been launched by the Focus on Therapeutic Outcomes corporation. This non-

Table 10–1 Characteristics of Selected Functional Status Measures

Instrument Name	Instrument Type	Areas Assessed	Scoring Method	Reliability/Validity
Katz Index of ADL[16]	ADL	Bathing, dressing, toileting, transfer, continence, feeding	Dichotomous scale of dependence/independence	High reliability based on unpublished data. Correlates with mobility and house confinement after discharge.
Barthel Index[17]	ADL	Feeding, grooming, moving to bed, bathing, toileting, walking, stair climbing, bowel and bladder control	Partial scores for performance with help, full scores for independent performance; items weighted	Information about reliability unavailable. Scores and changes in scores correlate with clinical judgment.
FIM version 3.0[9]	Rehabilitation oriented	Self-care sphincter control, mobility, locomotion, communication, social cognition	Seven-level ordinal scale from least independent to most independent	Interrater reliability ranges from 0.88 to 0.93 FIM domain scores and from 0.82 to 0.91 for item scores. For eligible subscribers who participate in the Uniform Data System, interrater reliability ranges from 0.96 to 0.98 for FIM domain scores and from 0.91 to 0.98 for FIM item scores. The FIM is reported to have face validity and predictive validity (for minutes of help per day).
Patient Evaluation and Conference System[13–15]	Rehabilitation oriented	Functions related to rehabilitation medicine, rehabilitation nursing, physical mobility, ADL, communication, medications, nutrition, assistive devices, psychology, neuropsychology, social issues, vocational/educational activity, therapeutic recreation, pain, pulmonary rehabilitation, pastoral care	Seven-level ordinal scale from dependent to independent function	Studies ongoing. Preliminary studies found wide range of interrater reliability from 0.68 to 0.80. Content and construct validity reported.
LORS-III[10–12]	Rehabilitation oriented	ADL, mobility, communication, cognitive ability	Five-level interval scale	Interrater reliability for LORS-IIB assessment domains ranges from 0.65 to 0.87. Interrater reliability for LORS-III is conducted on an ongoing basis. Face validity for LORS-III is reported.

Instrument	Type	Content	Scale	Reliability/Validity
Rehabilitation Institute of Chicago Functional Assessment Scale version II[18]	Rehabilitation oriented	Functions related to the following services: nursing, physical therapy, occupational therapy, communicative disorders, psychology, social work, vocational rehabilitation, therapeutic, recreational	Seven-level ordinal scale ranging from normal ability to severe disability	Interrater reliability ranges from 0.66 to 1.00 across items scores, with better than 75% to 100% agreement on most items. Studies on validity underway.
Functional Assessment Measure, revised[19]	Rehabilitation oriented	Self-care, sphincter control, mobility, communication, psychosocial adjustment, cognitive function	Seven-level ordinal scale ranging from least independent to most independent	Studies ongoing. Based on unpublished data. Interrater reliability ranges from 0.89 to 0.95. Preliminary studies found face validity and concurrent validity with clinical observations, Disability Rating Scale,[23] Barthel Index, and FIM.
Assessment of Needs for Continuing Care[20]	Global	Health status, functional status (ADL, independent ADL, communication, assistive devices used), environmental factors in postdischarge care, nursing and other care requirements, family and community support, patient/family goals and preferences, options for continuing care	Functional status section: four-level ordinal scale (for ADL and communication), three-level scale (for independent ADL) from independent to dependent function	Ongoing studies. Information currently unavailable.
Minimal Data Set	Global	Cognitive patterns, communication/hearing patterns, vision patterns, physical functioning and structural problems (include ADL), continence, psychosocial well-being, mood and behavioral patterns, activity pursuit patterns, disease diagnoses, health conditions, oral/dental status, skin condition, medication use, special treatment and procedures.	Four-level ordinal scale for physical functioning, cognitive patterns, communication/hearing patterns	Based on published field test results, interrater reliability for key functional indicators in each assessment domain ranges from 0.47 to 0.91. Studies on validity underway.

Source: Reprinted from C. Frattali, "Perspectives on Functional Assessment: Its Use for Policymaking," *Disability and Rehabilitation*, Vol. 15, pp. 1–9, with permission of Taylor and Francis, © 1993.

profit corporation, comprising six founding members (Caremark, Healthfocus, HealthSouth, MedRehab, Rehab Clinics, and RehabWorks), was founded for the purpose of developing a standard process to measure functional outcomes in outpatient physical and occupational therapy. Additionally, in the long-term care setting, some investigators are utilizing the Resident Assessment Instrument and its Minimum Data Set (MDS) to determine residents' functional status.[23] These measures were developed by a research team under contract with the Health Care Financing Administration (HCFA). Their initial purpose was for use in the development of resident care plans, not for outcome monitoring. At issue, then, is their validity and reliability as outcome measures. Jette[5] suggests that health-related quality of life instruments[24–31] should be utilized when effects on quality of life are being measured and has reviewed a selected group of these measures. Table 10–2 provides a description of these measures.

At issue with these measures is their sensitivity to disease-specific, clinically important changes as well as their validity and reliability. Also of concern is their practicability, that is to say the time it takes to complete administration of the tool, training requirements, burden on the respondent, and scoring complexity. In many situations, the patient is unable to be respondent (eg, because of his or her medical condition, cognitive status, or cultural differences); hence the appropriate person to represent the patient is an issue that needs to be considered for accurate assessment.[5]

Given differing service delivery settings, geographic locations, patient conditions, and sources of data requirements, there is no one outcome measure that adequately provides all necessary data. When one selects an outcome measure, it is important to determine the domain it assesses; its reliability and validity, whether the scoring method allows for statistical analysis, the measure's practicality, training requirements, scoring complexity, the burden on the respondent and/or the person(s) administering the measure, and resources needed.

Several professional associations have launched outcome measurement projects that are discipline specific. For example, in 1991 the American Occupational Therapy Association (AOTA) partnered with the American Occupational Therapy Foundation (AOTF) to convene a panel of experts for the purpose of proposing short- and long-term strategies for obtaining outcome data that would demonstrate the effectiveness of occupational therapy intervention. As a result of the recommendations made, AOTA/AOTF prioritized its actions toward examining existing databases that might yield information concerning the effectiveness of occupational therapy and toward considering clinical intervention studies that would specifically examine occupational therapy strategies for care.

With respect to existing databases, initial data from a study comparing the FIM and the LORS[32] showed great similarity and indicated that function, at the time of admission, may be the best prediction of length of stay now available for long-term care and rehabilitation patients. In addition, a study to explore FIM data implications for occupational therapy is under review. Since 1988, outcome studies by occupational therapists have been funded by AOTA and AOTF. These studies focused on preschoolers, children, and adults. Another major focus of these studies has been the fields of mental health, stroke rehabilitation, head injury, and assistive technology. Additionally, AOTF has supported the development of the Assessment of Motor and Process Skills, an occupational therapy assessment instrument. Given occupational therapists' lack of training in data collection, the AOTF has provided a training resource and sponsored workshops to encourage the development of clinical studies.[32]

The American Speech-Language-Hearing Association (ASHA) launched its outcome measurement project in 1986 with the development of an automated program evaluation system.[33] This system contains an eight-level scale that addresses 13 different areas related to communication referred to as the Functional Communication Measures. An expert panel was convened in 1992 to refine these scales. The ASHA Functional

Table 10–2 Characteristics of Health-Related Quality of Life Measures

Measure	Content	Length	Mode	Time (minutes)
Medical Outcomes Study Health Status Questionnaire[24]	Physical, role limitations due to physical and emotional problems, social functioning, general mental health, pain, energy/fatigue, general health perceptions	36 items	Self-report	10
COOP Charts[25]	Physical, mental, role, social, pain, overall health change, social resources, life quality	9 items	Self-report or clinical rating	8–10
Duke–University of North Carolina Health Profile[26]	Symptom status, physical function, emotional function, social function	64 items	Self-report	15–20
Sickness Impact Profile[27]	Physical ambulation, mobility, body care Psychosocial: social interaction, communication, alertness, emotional behavioral Other: sleep/rest, eating, work, home management, recreational pastimes	136 items	Self-report	30
McMaster Health Index Questionnaire[28]	Physical: mobility, self-care, communication, global physical function Social: general well-being work/social role, performance, social support and participation, global self-function Emotional: self-esteem, personal relationships, critical life events, global life events, global emotional function	59 items	Self-report	20
Nottingham Health Profile[29]	Six domains of experience: pain, physical mobility, sleep, emotional reactions, energy, social isolation Seven domains of daily life: employment, household work, relationships, personal life, sex, hobbies, vacations	45 items	Self-report	10
Quality of Well-Being Scale[30]	Functional performance: self-care, mobility, institutionalization, social activities Symptoms and problems	50 items	Self-report	12
Functional Status Questionnaire[31]	Physical: basic and intermediate ADLs Emotional function: anxiety and depression, quality of social interaction Social performance: Occupational function, social activities Others: sexual global disability, global health satisfaction, social contacts	34 items	Self-report	10

Assessment of Communication Skills for Adults is a more comprehensive measure and therefore is anticipated to be more sensitive to overall changes in functional communication. In 1993, ASHA developed a project to document the efficacy of treatment in 10 areas: hearing loss in children, communication disorders resulting from traumatic brain injury, fluency, phonologic dis-

orders in children, child language disorders, aphasia, dysphagia, voice disorders, hearing aid use in adults, and motor speech disorders. The technical reports are currently in development. Additionally, in 1993 a task force on treatment outcome and cost effectiveness in speech-language pathology and audiology was established to work with a consulting firm to be hired by

ASHA to generate an outcome database for the professions.[34]

Another critical decision confronting practitioners in the subacute setting is whether to base their outcome data on a provider–centered or consumer–centered approach. Lansky et al[35] suggest that good data originate with the patient and the provider, so that the two must collaborate. They identify three data collection methods that can be employed to accomplish their objective: consumer satisfaction measures, provider activity records, and clinical databases. In a managed care environment, the consumer selects a health plan based upon both cost and demonstrated quality. Providers in a subacute setting therefore need to give consideration to measuring both functional status and consumer satisfaction with services provided.

It is important to collect and analyze outcome data in the subacute environment, but it is equally important to be capable of making comparisons of data from other providers. There are two organizations that maintain large national databanks of outcome information: the Center for Functional Assessment Research, Department of Rehabilitation Medicine, State University of New York at Buffalo, and Formations in Health Care, Inc., Chicago, Illinois. The Center for Functional Assessment Research manages the Uniform Data System (UDS) for Medical Rehabilitation. The UDS consists of the Uniform Data Set, which contains the FIM and demographic, functional, financial, and diagnostic data, and the Data Management Service, which analyzes and reports data. The database comprises primarily data submitted from rehabilitation hospitals. Formations in Health Care is a national company with experience in managing and developing outcome measurement systems in inpatient, outpatient, subacute, and industrial rehabilitation. In 1993, Formations was contracted by nine subacute care and rehabilitation providers to develop a national outcome measurement system for medical subacute care. A program evaluation model served as the framework for the Medical Outcomes System. It consists primarily of outcome measures that reflect the collective effort of the patient care

team. The system includes two types of outcome measures: efficiency, or resource utilization, and effectiveness, or health status change. Areas of health status change include wounds, respiratory, infection, nutrition, and pain.[36]

The Medical Outcomes System is expected to be available to other subacute care providers in the spring of 1995, with comparative reports becoming available in the summer. Formations' goal is that the database will be accepted as the national benchmark for subacute outcomes.[36] Both the Center for Functional Assessment Research and Formations hold and maintain national databanks of outcome information that are used to compare the cost effectiveness of rehabilitation programs.

DATA USES

Providers in the subacute environment are challenged to maintain quality and at the same time contain costs. Perhaps the single most important use of outcome data needs to be directed toward addressing this issue. Wilkerson et al[1] identify several critical questions that, if answered on an ongoing basis, will equip the provider with information that permits more appropriate decision making and will ensure that quality of care is not diminished while costs are lowered:

- To what extent does admission status predict resource utilization and costs of care?
- How much of the variance in resource utilization can be explained by a specific functional status measure relative to other variables, such as impairment or diagnosis?
- What is the relationship between functional outcome (in rehabilitation) and the resources needed to produce such outcomes?
- What are the effects of the environment and support network on length of stay, cost of care, and discharge planning?
- What are the rates and patterns of functional gains typical for various impairment groups?

- What are indicators that patients have achieved their optimal level of function and need to be discharged?
- What is the optimum service mix and length of time needed to produce maximum gains for any given patient considering functional status, impairment group, social and environmental circumstances after being discharged, personal skills, capacity to learn, and motivation?
- Which of the following best predicts resource utilization and costs of care: admission, discharge, admission/discharge, or admission/follow-up?

Based upon the answers to these questions, providers can reexamine staffing patterns, techniques, and equipment used and the frequency, intensity, and duration of interventions and modify their practice models and programs accordingly. It is essential that providers continually improve their practice models and programs and communicate their findings to case managers, consumers, employers, payers, referral sources, and other professionals, thereby demonstrating value and subsequently using their data to influence decisions regarding reimbursement utilization and access. It will become increasingly important for providers in the subacute setting to create a collaborative partnership with case managers. Case managers are responsible for ensuring that patients are receiving the right services by the right professional in the right setting at the right time. Outcome data are necessary if case managers are to be convinced that the subacute environment is the right setting for specific patients who are in need of particular professionals to provide certain services for a given period of time that will facilitate achieving their optimal level of functioning.

In a managed competition environment, utilization of services will more than likely be determined by someone other than the provider. The need to create interdependent partnerships with referral sources cannot be overemphasized.[37] Using outcome data to market to these potential partners is critical to ensuring that patients have access to services in the subacute environment. Additionally, these data are being demanded by accrediting agencies such as the Commission on Accreditation of Rehabilitation Facilities (CARF) and the Joint Commission on Accreditation of Healthcare Organizations. Accreditation from these agencies distinguishes the provider as meeting industry standards and, in some cases, ensures reimbursement (see Chapter 13).

Although there has been intense interest in and focus on selecting the appropriate outcome measures, collecting and analyzing data, and using a system that will allow comparisons, it is equally important that providers focus on how to use these data to effect change. There is inconsistency in measurement, resulting in a lack of a national frame of reference for using outcome data. It is important to realize, however, that at a local level these data can be used by the provider to contain costs, ensure quality, maintain appropriate utilization and access to services, and meet accreditation standards. Furthermore, providers can differentiate themselves from their competitors.

DESIGNING AN OUTCOME MEASUREMENT SYSTEM

There are five steps involved in designing an outcome measurement system: defining objectives, selecting an outcome measure(s), determining systems specifications, defining training needs, and determining funding requirements. A description of each of these steps follows.

Step 1: Defining Objectives

Determining what data need to be collected is the first task in defining the objectives for an outcome measurement system. Data needs should be defined primarily by customer expectations. Identify both internal and external customers, and then determine their data needs. For example, internal customers may include nursing staff, the program administrator, and/or patients/residents. External customers may include case managers, payers, family members, and/or significant others. Customer needs vary. Thus the nursing staff may want more time to provide patient care duties, and the case manager may want to know how many therapy visits it will take for the patient to improve function.

- *Tip:* Do not anticipate customer needs. Ask the customers. Use either informal (eg, telephone call) or formal (eg, customer survey) means to determine customer needs.

Decide who will be involved in the data collection process. Identify the key players involved in providing patient care, and have them play an active role in carrying out their responsibilities. For example, the admissions coordinator may have certain data collection responsibilities when the patient is admitted, and the nurse or social worker may collect additional data on an ongoing basis.

- *Tip:* Utilizing a team approach will facilitate a multidimensional measurement perspective. The collection of data needs to be at the point of service so that collection is not viewed by the provider as a burden or an additional responsibility. As staff are providing services, all necessary data elements should be identified so that the information is collected only once. This reduces the likelihood of errors. As much as possible, the information should be collected in a closed field format. For example, rather than writing the gender of the patient, the staff person selects either male or female. Closed fields facilitate a consistent assessment of the patient and allow for data to be aggregated.
- *Tip:* Make data collection a one-step process with closed fields.

Decide what information to provide to customers based upon the data collection. Customers are more responsive to graphic reports than tabular reports.

- *Tip:* Provide user-friendly reports for all customers when they need them.

Being clear about objectives up front will lay the foundation for designing a system that will ultimately meet the organization's needs and provide benefit to both the organization and its customers.

Step 2: Selecting an Outcome Measure(s)

Identify all tools currently available that will assist in meeting objectives. Compare them across these parameters. Do not forget to identify pros and cons of each measure from other users. Table 10–3 provides an example of a comparison of widely used functional outcome measures. Rank the measures, and then reach consensus on what measure will best meet data needs.

- *Tip:* Identify an expert team to select an outcome measure(s). Preferably, use individuals within the work environment. Utilize outside expertise if it does not exist within.

Step 3: Determining Systems Specifications

Given the rapid changes in technology, a variety of systems are available. These systems may include utilization of an optical scanning form, laptop computers, a personal computer–based system, or pen computers. Regardless of the choice of system, there are common data elements that need to be collected. Exhibit 10–1 provides a list of elements that are typically included in an outcome system.

- *Tip:* Select a system that will be compatible with the customer's system. That is, make sure the customer's data can be integrated with data collected by the facility. This is critical so that data can be prepared. Utilize an information systems expert.

Step 4: Defining Training Needs

Identify who needs to be trained, what needs to be trained, how best to train, who trains, when training will need to occur, how long training will take, and expectations of trained participants

Table 10–3 Analysis of Four Outcome Measures

Outcome Measurement

	FIM	MDS	LORS	Patient Evaluation and Conferences System
Environment	Acute	Skilled nursing facility	Acute	Acute
Function Area	6	15	7	16
Number of Items	18	71	18	115
Scale Level	Seven ordinal	Two to four ordinal	Five interval	Seven ordinal
Validity	Face validity	Construct validity	Face validity	Face validity
Reliability	0.88 to 0.98	0.47 to 0.91	0.65 to 0.87	0.68 to 0.80
Frequency of Assessment	Admission, discharge, follow-up	Quarterly	Admission, discharge, follow-up	Admission, team meetings, discharge
Time To Administer (minutes)	30	30	30	90
Training Time (hours)	6	4	6	8
Personnel*	RN/other	RN/other	OT, PT, SP, RN	Entire team
Report Format	Data graphics	Graphic	Data graphics	Data graphics
Measures	Central tendency	Raw scores	Regression analysis	Central tendency
External Database	200,000	None	14,000	35,000
Current Use	+150 acute care facilities	All skilled nursing facilities	58 facilities	12 facilities

Courtesy of Reg Warren, NovaCare Contract Services Division, King of Prussia, Pennsylvania.

*RN, registered nurse; OT, occupational therapist; PT, physical therapist; SP, speech-language pathologist.

Exhibit 10–1 Examples of Outcome System Data Elements

Facility	Payer source
Name	Admission date
Location (ZIP code)	Start of care date
Number of beds	Onset
Census	Frequency of treatment
Payer mix	Intensity of treatment
Accreditation status (eg, Joint Commission, CARF, state)	Length of stay
	Projected discharge
Referral sources and ZIP code	Actual discharge
Admission hours	Discharge location
Nurse:patient ratio	Admission functional status
Resident/Patient	Discharge functional status
Name	Follow-up functional status
Social Security number	Charges
Gender	Plan of Care
Birth date	Short- and long-term goals
Address (ZIP code)	Expected outcome
Race/ethnicity	Service providers (type, credentials)
Marital status	Interventions (frequency, intensity, duration)
Education	Equipment/materials used
Vocational status	Progress
Primary language	Follow-Up
Living situation	Date
Medical diagnosis	Informer
Rehabilitation diagnosis	Method
Impairment group	Maintenance
Major surgical procedures	

when training is completed. Initially, staff need to understand the clinical value of the data collection process. Why the data are important and how they can be used to improve patient care are important considerations for the service provider. Understanding the rationale will facilitate the staff's willingness to participate. Next, it is critical that staff are trained to administer the outcome measure(s) reliably. Customers want data that are accurate, reliable, and complete and that have integrity. Equally important in the training process is ensuring that staff not only have technical skills but also learn how to use the data to effect meaningful change in the services they provide. This means improving their patients' functional status as well as improving their service to their patients. Ultimately, staff need to know how to use their data to ensure that all customers are satisfied.

- *Tip:* To ensure that the desired results are obtained, remember that training is a process, not an event.

Step 5: Determining Funding Requirements

Now that needs have been identified, all costs associated with developing and implementing the system must be determined. The benefits associated with these costs are then quantified. Think in terms of both tangible (eg, improved retention of employees) and intangible benefits (eg, increased volume of patients, satisfied staff).

- *Tip:* Develop a budget to ensure that all costs associated with the outcome measurement system have been taken into account.

Developing a system that will meet particular needs is not easy. It takes considerable time, commitment, and resources.

CRITICAL PATHS

Definition of Critical Path

Today, most health systems and networks view critical paths in a context of continuous quality improvement and systemwide clinical integration.[38] The process involves analysis of variances and outcomes, patient satisfaction, and the experience of a team of health professionals. In essence, the knowledge gained from the process is used to change the course of care through revision of paths as necessary.

Critical paths are treatment regimes, based on a consensus of clinicians and supported ideally by patient outcomes research, that include only those vital elements that have been proved to affect patient outcomes.[39] They are clinical management tools that organize, sequence, and time the major interventions of nursing staff, physicians, and other health professionals for a particular case type or condition.[40] According to Zander,[40] when length of stay is graphed on an axis against an intervention axis, a basic critical path is born.

Although the terms are sometimes used interchangeably, critical paths are differentiated from clinical paths and CareMaps™. According to Kaine,[39] clinical paths (or pathways or path methods) are treatment regimes, agreed upon by consensus, that include all the elements of care regardless of the effect on patient outcomes. It is a broader look at care and may, for example, include tests and radiographic studies that do not affect patient recovery. CareMaps™ are more elaborate critical paths that reflect the patient's and/or family's baseline responses expected by the staff as a result of their interventions along the same time line as those interventions. Thus they show the relationship of sets of interventions to sets of intermediate outcomes along a time line and are considered superior to critical paths. As a matter of simplicity, the term *critical paths* is used throughout the remainder of this chapter.

Origins and Purposes of Critical Paths

The concept of critical paths originated in the mid-1950s.[41] The approach "uses a specialized form to delineate the various activities involved in a specific project from start to finish and the time anticipated to complete each of these activities."[41(p235)] Critical paths were first used to manage the annual maintenance work in an oil and chemical refinery. They were proved to be valuable for charting projects requiring the coordination of hundreds of separate contractors and were commonly used in engineering, construction, and computer work.

The earliest use of critical paths reported in the health care literature was in the mid-1980s. Zander[40] adapted the concept to review the delivery of patient care at the New England Medical Center. Grudich[42] later reported a major improvement in operating room efficiency by the application of critical paths at St Cloud Hospital in Minnesota. Similarly, Hofmann[41] reported, after a 6-month pilot project at Mount Clemens General Hospital in Detroit, that use of a critical path for coronary artery bypass graft resulted in a reduction in complication rates from 16.6% to 5.0%. In addition, patients whose care was in compliance with the critical path had an overall shorter length of stay.

Several deficiencies in health care management converged to spur the development of critical paths. Zander[40] identified three:

1. the inability of existing documentation systems to assist clinicians in integrating the work of each clinical discipline

2. limitations of the diagnosis-related group system in potentially setting limits on total work load

3. limitations of current care management tools and professional roles that do not recognize advances in knowledge

These deficiencies promoted alternative case management methods designed to integrate services while tracking patient outcomes. Thus the goals of critical paths, as detailed by Kimball[43] are to:

- strengthen the collaborative nature of patient care through mutually agreed upon outcomes, time lines, and processes

- direct the contributions of all care providers toward the achievement of positive patient outcomes
- provide outcome-oriented patient care within a fiscally responsible time frame
- use the resources that are appropriate, in amount and sequence, to the specific case type
- ensure that critical areas of patient care are carried out

Thus quality improvement is built into the system, and variances in patient care or outcome are identified and acted upon as soon as they occur.

Developing a Critical Path

Hofmann[41] sequenced the critical path developmental process, which she believes comprises activities in nine primary categories (Table 10–4):

1. literature search (review treatment efficacy and outcome studies)
2. steering committee (convene a committee to oversee project implementation)
3. targeting strategy (select a target diagnosis or clinical condition)
4. model design (create a form and procedure for use of the critical path)
5. organizational support (enlist support of key people)
6. pilot test (test the critical path on a trial basis)
7. preliminary findings (gather and review pilot data)
8. refinements (measure, adjust, and refine the critical path)
9. full-scale implementation (standardize the procedure)

Overall, an average of 4 months was spent in research, 6 months were devoted to planning and preparation, and 6 months were devoted to piloting. Another 6 months were targeted for critical path refinement and standardization on a full scale.

Procedures for Critical Path Development

An account of time-tested and research-based procedures to facilitate the development and use of critical paths for subacute care is offered by McDermott and Toerge.[44] The following procedures, ordered sequentially, are recommended:

1. Create organizational structures to support the programmatic focus of critical paths. For subacute care, programs can include, for example, stroke, orthopedic, spinal cord injury, respiratory, and wound management.

Table 10–4 Critical Path Task Force Activities and Time Frame

Steps	Months 1	2	3	4	5	6	7	8	9	10	11	12	13	14	15	16	17	18	19	20	21	22
Literature search	•	•	•	•	•	•	•	•	•	•	•	•	•	•	•	•	•	•	•	•	•	•
Steering committee						•	•	•	•	•	•	•	•	•		•	•	•	•	•	•	•
Targeting strategy						•		•	•					•	•	•	•	•	•	•	•	•
Model design						•	•	•	•	•	•	•										
Organizational support						•	•		•	•	•	•	•						•	•		•
Pilot test										•	•	•	•	•	•	•						
Preliminary findings														•	•	•	•	•	•	•	•	•
Refinements														•	•	•	•	•	•	•	•	•
Full-scale implementation																•	•	•	•	•	•	•

Source: Adapted from P.A. Hofmann, Critical Path Method: An Important Tool for Coordinating Clinical Care. *Journal on Quality Improvement,* Vol. 19, pp. 235–246, with permission of Mosby-Year Book, © 1993.

2. Each program develops explicit criteria for admission, continued stay, and discharge. For example, admission criteria can address appropriate diagnoses, age ranges, comorbidities, respiratory status, infectious processes, and skin integrity. Wherever possible, criteria should be data based. For example, the mean length of stay could be determined by program evaluation data collected over a period of years to determine a norm.

3. Create functional categories that parallel the types of interventions. These categories make up the *y* axis on the critical path. Functional categories, for example, can include mobility, self-care, medical homeostasis, communication, nutrition, cognition, education, community reintegration, and continued care and discharge planning.

4. Next, determine the time intervals for initiation/completion of interventions, which make up the *x* axis. Time intervals can, for example, be set at day 1, day 2, week 1, week 2, and week 3. Time on the critical path can be extended for day treatment, outpatient care, and follow-up care.

5. Weekly team conferences are built into the critical path to document the most recent treatment process and outcomes. During these conferences, each patient is rated along functional categories (using outcome measures identified and agreed to by team members), and intervention goals are stated/restated. Thus change is measured and documented at regular time intervals for each functional category.

6. Variances from the critical path are documented on a regular basis by a coordinator in the appropriate section on the critical path. These variances can result, for example, from patient or family elements (eg, preferences, individual needs), clinical providers (eg, modification of a treatment procedure), system elements (eg, availability of resources, management

variances, or staffing patterns), or community/external elements (eg, lack of community placement).

7. A surveillance and monitoring system is put in place to collect and analyze data from the critical path to determine its utility and the need for modifications.

Rao reports that his facility pilots a new critical path for a 6-month period (Rao P, 1994. Personal communication). During this time the critical path is not changed, but data are collected continuously and analyzed only after a sufficient period of time is allowed to test the critical path. Subsequent data analysis dictates refinements to the critical path. Overall, the critical path development time ranges from 1 to 2 years. McDermott and Toerge[44] identify the advantages and disadvantages to critical path development and use and offer a set of recommendations that support the developmental process and minimize problems (Exhibits 10–2 and 10–3).

Consistent with Rao's assertion that, wherever possible, patient management criteria should be data based, Metzler[45] believes that a wealth of information to develop critical paths is found in billing files. Metzler states, "The financial databases that generate patient bills are vast repositories of usable and easily retrievable patient facts that are often overlooked as data sources for critical path development."[45(p4)] For example, information about duration of treatment, use of anticoagulation therapy, and laboratory work ordered for total hip replacement can be gleaned easily to identify similarities and differences in clinical practice. These data can then be grouped to establish an average case on which to structure practice patterns. Metzler believes that use of billing data can accelerate the path development and increase the relevance of path because of the direct correlation to cost.

Design Parameters

Critical paths typically follow the same basic format (Figure 10–1). The time frame for the path forms the top of each column. It usually is ex-

Exhibit 10–2 Advantages and Disadvantages of Critical
Paths

Advantages
- Approach is uniform across all services and programs
- A map of care for patients, payers, and providers is provided
- Case managers have an effective tool to deal with external relations and internal quality issues
- Comprehensive information and data on the treatment process are provided
- Program evaluation is enhanced
- Critical paths are a management tool to examine utilization and resource allocation
- Critical paths are an excellent marketing tool for managed care and to improve payer mix
- Care delivery and quality improvement efforts are improved

Disadvantages
- Critical paths suggest a "cookbook" approach to care
- Critical paths threaten functioning and existing roles of staff
- Explicit delineation of process may lead to punitive actions
- There is increased pressure to perform and document
- Resistance to change may be encountered
- There is a risk of being used primarily to decrease lengths of stay
- Large investment in time and energy is required to develop and implement

Source: Reprinted from *Developing Critical Paths of Rehabilitation Care* by J McDermott and J Toerge with permission of National Rehabilitation Hospital, Washington, DC, © 1994.

---

pressed in patient days, although the time frame can also be expressed as hours, geographic locations, or phases of care along the continuum from acute to outpatient care or home care.[41] The functional categories of care are listed in the left margin and can include, for example, assessments or evaluations, consultations, treatments, medications, activity, diet, patient/family education, and discharge planning. The main body of the grid contains specific actions, tests, assessments, and so forth that are expected to be completed within a specified time period. An area for initials and check marks to show any variations also is included (see Appendix 10A for design format).

Documentation of Variance

Hofmann[41] has used the opposite side of the critical path form to record variances from expected actions. Other forms incorporate tracking of variances directly on the critical path grid (see Appendix 10A). Variances are differences between what is projected and what occurs and allow the health care team to take immediate actions. According to Kimball,[43] there are three major types of variances: system variance, in which the institution cannot provide care (usually in the form of tests, medications, or procedures) in a timely manner; patient variance, in which the patient does not respond to uniform treatment, requiring modification of the plan to meet the need; and practitioner variance, in which the practitioner prefers a pattern of treatment other than that outlined on the critical path.

Typically, the critical path form is placed on

Exhibit 10–3 Recommendations To Facilitate Critical
Path Development and Use

---

1. Build secure top management buy-in.
2. Establish clear goals and objectives for critical path development.
3. Select three to four outcomes that need to be achieved by the facility/program.
4. Establish an oversight committee (eg, comprising program directors and medical director).
5. Identify and support a project manager for the development of each critical path.
6. Select a critical path design team for each homogeneous population.
7. Select an appropriate number or size of populations to be covered by the critical path.
8. Use time as an organizing principle, not as a deadline.
9. Identify variances from the critical path.
10. Organize team conferences around critical paths. Require team communication to mirror the critical path.
11. Institute an aggressive training protocol for critical path development and use.
12. Establish cost analysis procedures.

Source: Reprinted from *Developing Critical Paths of Rehabilitation Care* by J McDermott and J Toerge with permission of National Rehabilitation Hospital, Washington, DC, © 1994.

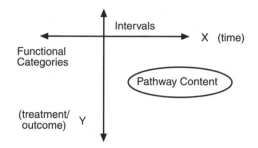

Figure 10–1 Critical path of care.

Source: Adapted with permission from National Rehabilitation Hospital, Washington, DC.

---

the patient's clipboard and is reviewed daily by the patient's staff nurse, utilization review nurse, or other case coordinator/manager. Any variance from the outlined path is noted and appropriate action is taken. The form is sent to the medical record department with the patient's chart after discharge. It is then removed and sent to the quality improvement coordinator for monitoring. Appropriate data are extracted from each form and entered into a computer system. Findings are then reported to the interdisciplinary team as well as to external sources, such as payers.

Applications to Subacute Health Care: An Example

One of the primary uses of critical paths in subacute care is utilization management. It therefore becomes important to link the critical path at the subacute level of care to acute, home health, and outpatient care. Otherwise, there cannot be effective utilization management using the critical path. In health care, critical paths emerged at the acute level of care. What is needed is better overall organization and communication across settings and thus facilitation of integrated delivery networks. The critical path process therefore needs to be defined and designed along the continuum of care, beginning with the patient's entry into the health care system and ending with the patient's exit from the system. Furthermore, the ultimate outcome

in critical path development and use will be the addition of financial information. Thus resource utilization can be anticipated, and the overall design of clinical process management can be integrated.[38]

A critical path for total hip arthroplasty, developed by SubAcute Care of America,[46] offers a good example of a path that links acute care to subacute care (Appendix 10A). The critical path begins with the preoperative day and proceeds to the day of surgery, postoperative days 1 through 3, and subacute care from postoperative day 4 to postoperative days 12 and 13. For both acute and subacute care, the path is organized by the following activities: diagnostics, activity/safety, nutrition, procedures/treatment, medications, therapy, discharge planning, education, and nursing assessment.

The critical path reflects the interdisciplinary nature of patient care, involving the orthopedic surgeon, nurse, dietitian, social worker, physical therapist, occupational therapist, laboratory technician, and case manager. Variations in patient care are documented on the critical path in the "U" column for unmet goals with reasons documented in the progress notes section of the medical record.

Special Considerations

Two special considerations must be noted when one is developing or using critical paths: clinical practice variation and difficult diagnoses. Both embody some of the nuances of critical path development and deserve some elaboration.[39] Relative to practice variation, the reader should be advised that critical paths are not intended to standardize care among all health practitioners or to police practitioners in any way. If acceptable practice patterns vary, these can be reflected in separate critical paths as necessary. Alternatively, the differences can be noted on a generic critical path by asterisks or other symbols. Practitioners, however, should remain cognizant of how these variations affect cost and patient outcomes to justify their means. It is important to understand that the use of critical paths is a continual process; the information gleaned, with variations noted, can be used to refine clinical paths as more becomes known about the clinical care process and outcomes (including resource use).

Difficult diagnoses present problems for mapping care because so many exceptions to the rule may exist compared with "clean" diagnoses. Zander[40] believes that the best way to handle difficult diagnoses is to ask the main question "What is the purpose of admission?" and to develop critical paths that are organized by treatment stage, central theme, or problem. This strategy allows more flexibility. Examples of such case types, which are common to subacute health care, include terminal care, burn treatment, bowel/bladder training, and ventilator weaning.

If a critical path seems unworkable, it probably has been conceptualized too narrowly or too broadly. For example, stroke is too broad and should be identified as left hemisphere or right hemisphere, or even as mild, moderate, or severe. Conversely, trying to describe postdiagnostic treatment and outcomes for Guillain-Barré syndrome day by day may be too narrow.

A fine degree of flexibility must be found in developing critical paths. Zander states:

> Keeping a [critical path] rigid enough to reveal variances but dynamic enough to be usable in the real clinical world is the challenge. As patients move from one treatment stage to the next, there should be a new [critical path]. When there are no standard [critical paths] available that describe the new purpose for staying in the institution, blank forms can be used anecdotally. There will, of course, be no variances, but these anecdotal records will eventually become a data

base for new [critical path] development."[40(p309)]

CONCLUSION

Subacute outcome measurement and critical paths provide a patient-centered system that is currently being used to define, structure, and manage clinical interventions so that desired outcomes can be attained within an average time frame for most patients. In short, outcome measurement and critical path development and use constitute a form of managed care. This approach requires an intellectual level of curiosity about patient responses to care in the presence of diverse staffing arrangements in subacute health care settings. The process generates a set of questions that require answers on a continual basis:

- What interventions and outcomes should be occurring?
- What is actually occurring?
- What did not happen and why?
- What should be done about it?
- Who will do it and when?

Thus the critical path and outcome measurement approach structures and integrates care into a continual cycle of planning, action, and evaluation. Zander aptly concludes, "Quality improvement actually begins with the first component [critical paths] and proceeds like detective work through the other components of the system [to optimize patient outcomes]"[40(p310)] During a time when the growth of managed care organizations is unprecedented, the critical paths/outcome measurement approach carries considerable weight in demonstrating the quality and cost effectiveness of subacute care.

REFERENCES

1. Wilkerson DL, Batavia AI, DeJong G. The use of functional status measures for payment of medical rehabilitation services. *Arch Phys Med Rehabil.* 1992;73:111–120.

2. World Health Organization. *International Classification of Impairments, Disabilities and Handicaps.* Geneva, Switzerland: World Health Organization; 1980.

3. Frattali CM. Perspectives on functional assessment: Its use for policymaking. *Disabil Rehabil.* 1993;15:1–9.

4. Fuhrer M. Overview of outcome analysis in rehabilitation. In: Fuhrer M, ed. *Rehabilitation Outcomes.* Baltimore, Md: Brookes; 1987:1–15.

5. Jette AM. Using health-related quality of life measures in physical therapy outcomes research. *Phys Ther.* 1993;73:528–537.

6. Olswang LB. *Treatment Efficacy Research: A Path to Quality Assurance.* Rockville, Md: American Speech-Language-Hearing Association; 1990.

7. McReynolds L, Kearns K. *Single-Subject Experimental Designs in Communicative Disorders.* Baltimore, Md: University Park Press; 1983.

8. Kazdin A. Drawing valid inferences from case studies. *J Consult Clin Psychol.* 1981;49:183–192.

9. State University of New York at Buffalo, Research Foundation. *Guide for Use of the Uniform Data Set for Medical Rehabilitation: Functional Independence Measure.* Buffalo, NY: Research Foundation; 1994.

10. Carey RG, Posavac EJ. Rehabilitation program evaluation using a revised level rehabilitation scale (LORS-II). *Arch Phys Med Rehabil.* 1982;63:367–376.

11. Parkside Associates, Inc. *Level of Rehabilitation Scale–II.* Park Ridge, Ill: Parkside Associates; 1986.

12. Formations in Health Care, Inc. *Level of Rehabilitation Scale–III.* Chicago, Ill: Formation in Health Care; 1991.

13. Harvey RF, Jellinek HM. *PECS: Patient Evaluation and Conference System.* Wheaton, Ill: Marianjoy Rehabilitation Center; 1979.

14. Harvey RF, Jellinek HM. Functional performance assessment: A program approach. *Arch Phys Med Rehabil.* 1981;63:43–52.

15. Harvey RF, Jellinek HM. Patient profiles: Utilization in functional performance assessment. *Arch Phys Med Rehabil.* 1983;64:268–271.

16. Katz S, Ford AB, Moskowitz RW, Jackson BA, Jaffee MW. Studies of illness in the aged. The index of ADL: A standardized measure of biological and psychological function. *JAMA.* 1963:185:94–101.

17. Mahoney FI, Barthel DW. Functional evaluation: The Barthel Index. *MD State Med J.* 1965;14:61–68.

18. Heinemann AW. *Rehabilitation Institute of Chicago Functional Assessment Scale–Revised.* Chicago, Ill: Rehabilitation Institute of Chicago; 1989.

19. Forer S. *Functional Assessment Measures–Revised.* Santa Clara, Calif: Santa Clara Valley Medical Center; 1990.

20. Health Care Financing Administration. *Assessments of Needs for Continuing Care.* Baltimore, Md: Health Care Financing Administration; 1989. Form HCFA 32 (10-89).

21. Morris JN, Hawes C, Murphy K, Nonemaker S, et al. *Minimum Data Set for Nursing Home Resident Assessment and Care Screening (MDS): Training Manual and Resource Guide.* Natick, Mass: Eliot; 1991.

22. Hawes C, Morris JN, Phillips C, Pries B, Mor V. *Development of Resident Assessment System and Data Base for Nursing Home Residents: Report on the Field Test of the Resident Assessment Instrument (FAI).* Research Triangle Park, NC: Research Triangle Institute; 1991.

23. Mor V. Long-term care outcomes research-in-progress. In: *Data Needs for Outcomes Research in Long-Term Care.* American Society of Consultant Pharmacists Research and Education Foundation; 1993:51–62.

24. Ware J, Sherbourne C. The MOS 36-item Short Form Health Survey (SF-36). *Med Care.* 1992;30:473–483.

25. Nelson E, Wasson J, Kirk J, et al. Assessment of function in routine clinical practice description of the COOP Chart method and preliminary findings. *J Chronic Disabil.* 1987;40(suppl 1):55S–69S.

26. Parkerson GR, Gehlbach SH, Wagner EH, et al. The Duke–UNC Health Profile: An adult health status instrument for primary care. *Med Care.* 1981;19:806–828.

27. Bergner MB, Bobbitt RA, Carter WB, Gilson BS. The SIP: Development and final revision of a health status measure. *Med Care.* 1981;19:787–805.

28. Chambers LW, MacDonald LA, Tugwell P, et al. The McMaster Health Index Questionnaire as a measure of quality of life for patients with rheumatoid disease. *J Rheumatol.* 1982;9:780–784.

29. McEwen J. The Nottingham Health Profile. In: Walker S, Rosser R, eds. *Quality of Life Assessment and Application.* Lancaster, England: MTP Press; 1988:95.

30. Fanshel S, Bush JW. A health-status index and its application to health-services outcomes. *Oper Res.* 1970;18:1021–1066.

31. Jette AM, Davies AR, Cleary PD, et al. The Functional Status Questionnaire: Reliability and validity when used in primary care. *J Gen Intern Med.* 1986;1:143–149.

32. American Occupational Therapy Foundation. *Progress with Outcomes: Research Strategies for the American Occupational Therapy Association and the American Occupational Therapy Foundation.* Gaithersburg, Md: American Occupational Therapy Foundation; 1993.

33. Larkins P. *Determining Quality of Speech-Language-Hearing Services.* Rockville, Md: American Speech-Language-Hearing Association; 1987.

34. Logemann J. *Treatment Efficacy and Outcome: Everybody's Job.* Rockville, Md: American Speech-Language-Hearing Association; 1994.

35. Lansky D, Knudsen K, Wetzler H. *Health Outcomes Accountability: Methods for Demonstrating and Improving Healthcare.* (unpublished manuscript, 1993).

36. Santopoalo R. New measurement tool will enhance subacute competitiveness. In: Larkin H, ed. *Physical Rehabilitation Update.* Chicago, Ill: Formations in Health Care, 1994.

37. Larkins P. Playing hardball in a managed competition environment. *Adv Dir Rehabil.* 1994;3:17–19.

38. Lumsdon K, Hagland M. Mapping care. *Hosp Health Networks.* 1993;34–40.

39. Kaine R. Practice protocols by a different name are not quite the same. *Hosp Rehabil.* 1993;2:124.

40. Zander K. Critical pathways. In: Melum MM and Finioris MK, eds. *Total Quality Management: The Health Care Pioneers.* Chicago, Ill: American Hospital Association, 1994; 305–314.

41. Hofmann PA. Critical path method: An important tool for coordinating clinical care. *J Qual Improve.* 1993;19:235–246.

42. Grudich G. The critical path system: The road toward an efficient OR. *AORN J.* 1991;53:705–714.

43. Kimball L. Collaborative care: A quality improvement and cost reduction tool. *J Health Care.* 1993;15:6–9.

44. McDermott M, Toerge J. *Developing Critical Paths for Rehabilitation Care: An Instruction Manual.* Washington, DC: National Rehabilitation Hospital; 1994.

45. Metzler S. Using detailed billing data to develop critical paths. *QRC Advis.* 1994;10:4–6.

46. SubAcute Care of America. *Total Hip Arthroplasty Critical Path.* El Cajon, Calif: SubAcute Care of America; 1994.

Appendix 10A

Total Hip Arthroplasty Critical Path

Date: Day: Activities	PreAdm	U*	Day 1/OR	U*	Day 2/POD 1	U*	Day 3/POD 2	U*	Day 4/POD 3	U*
Diagnostics	Hemogram; PTT; TCM; chest X-ray; EKG/UA; chem panel 7		PO hip X-ray		Hemogram					
Activity/Safety	Ambulatory		Bed rest; hip precautions		WC bid; bedside commode; no bedpans; prog amb 75 ft		BRP toilet extender; ambulate 75 ft; begin stairs		Ambulate BR; climb stairs; amb 75–100 ft; Functional Independence Measure (FIM): modified independence	
Nutrition	Regular		NPO/ice chips, clear liquids		Push fluids; ^ fluids		Regular		Eating 75% diet; FIM: comp indep	
Procedures/Treatment			Adm wt; I&O periph pulses; VS q4 hr & neuro; Hemovac; CPM if ordered		I&O VS q4hrs periph pulses; DC Foley; CPM adj per order		I&O; VS qid; dressing change daily; DC hemovac; CPM adj per order		I&O; dressing change; afebrile; VS stable; CPM adj per order	
Medications			IV; Ancef; anticoag; PCA/IM pain, antiemetics		Blood transfusion; DC IV; PO pain med		Pain meds; anticoag		Pain med PRN	
Therapy	Physical therapy (PT) eval; incentive spiro		TED hose, incent spiro q1hr; refer to protocols		PT bid; amb w/ walker; bed mobility; transfers		PT bid; Amb w/ walker; transfers		PT bid; curb & stairs; amb, car transfer; therapeutic exercise; FIM: mod indep	
Discharge Plan	Case manager assessment; begin discharge planning; home assessment				Social work assessment		Finalize plan; order equipment; toilet extender		Discharge home or to subacute care unit; equipment delivered	

continues

Appendix 10A continued

Date: Day:	PreAdm	U*	Day 1/OR	U*	Day 2/POD 1	U*	Day 3/POD 2	U*	Day 4/POD 3	U*
Activities										
Education	Preop teaching		PCA; incentive spiro; ankle pump		Walker; TED; diet; elimination; hip precautions		s/s infection; incision care; dressing stick		v/u hip precautions; infection; elimination; PT program	
Nursing Assessment			Comfort; tissue perfusion; fluids; infection; neuromuscular; elimination; skin integrity; dislocation; refer to practice guidelines		PO tol meds; continue to assess from previous list		Continue to assess from previous list		Normal elimination; minimal pain; amb to BR; lab work normal; no extremity edema; no infection; neuromuscular intact; no skin breakdown; VS stable; no fluid imbalance; no phlebitis/emboli; minimal assistance w/ drug; FIM: complete/modified independence	

Date: / Day:	Day 1/POD 4	U*	Day 2/POD 5	U*	Days 3–4/POD 6–7	U*	Days 5–6/POD 8–9	U*	Days 7–8/POD 10–11	U*	Days 9–10/ POD 12–13	U*
Activities												
Consults							Rehab team review					
Diagnostics	PT & PTT as ordered											
Activity/Safety	Ambulate w/ walker; BRP or bedside commode		Transfer; gait training; activities of daily living (ADLs); dress/groom		Prog ambulate 75 ft (ADLs)		Amb 100 ft; begin stairs/curb; (ADLs)		Climb stairs; uneven surf; ambulate 150 ft		Gait 200–300 ft; car transfer; climb stairs; ADL; FIM: comp mod ind	
Nutrition	Nutritional assess		Diet as planned; adequate fluids		Diet as planned		Diet as planned		Diet as planned		Eating/ tolerating diet; FIM: comp ind	
Procedures/ Treatment	VS q shift; wt; I&O; TED; incision care; Assess bowel & bladder; CPM if ord		Incision care; I&O: VS & neuro q shift; CPM adj per order		I&O; incision; VS q shift; elim; CPM adj order		I&O; VS bid; incision; elim; check neuromusc status; CPM/order		I&O; VS bid; incision; CPM/ order		VS norm; incision clean; norm elim; CPM adj/order	
Medications	Antibiotics; anticoags; antiemetics PRN; pain meds PRN; laxative/softener		Pain meds PRN; meds as ordered		Pain meds PRN; meds as ordered		Pain meds PRN; meds as ordered		Pain meds PRN; meds as ordered		PRNs; meds as ordered	

continues

Appendix 10A continued

Date: Day:	Day 1/POD 4	U*	Day 2/POD 5	U*	Days 3–4/POD 6–7	U*	Days 5–6/POD 8–9	U*	Days 7–8/POD 10–11	U*	Days 9–10/POD 12–13	U*
Activities												
Therapy	PT eval; occupational therapy assess; refer to protocols		PT bid; ambulate; therapeut exercise; bed mob/transf; OT as needed		PT bid; Transf; gait training; therapeut exercise		PT bid; ambulate w/walker; therapeut exercise		PT bid; curb & stairs; ambulate w/walker		Ready for discharge; home exercise prog; FIM: comp mod ind	
Discharge Plan	Begin discharge plan		Interview family				Finalize plan; home assess; order equip		Order home health as needed		Equipment delivered; discharge home	
Education	Assess knowledge		Hip precaut ADLs		Walker; safety; diet; elim; hip precaut		s/s infection; incision care; elim		v/u hip precaut; infection; elim; PT program		Understands and demonstrates knowledge	
Nursing Assessment	Skin integ; periph pulses; color; sensation; movement of extrem; hip precaut; elim; incision; infection; nutrition; lung sounds; refer to practice guidelines		Continue to assess from previous list		Continue to assess from previous list		Continue to assess from previous list		Continue to assess from previous list		Minimal pain; no skin breakdown; no infect; normal elim; I&O normal; neuromusc intact; no phlebitis; VS stable; min assist ADLs; FIM: comp mod ind	

*With any variation, check and initial in column U. Document any unmet (U) activities in progress notes on back of critical path form.

Source: Adapted with permission from **SubAcute Care of America, El Cajon, California.**

11

Business Office Operations for Subacute Providers

Mary M. Marshall

Business office functions are critical to the successful operation of the subacute unit. It will be necessary to make changes and additions to the current business office functions of the hospital or nursing facility to handle the increased payer sources and number of admissions and discharges. These changes will necessitate an increase in staffing as well as intensive staff training.

Because the subacute unit will function separately, there should be specific staff dedicated to this unit for verifying insurance; preparing billing; following up with problem claims; managing accounts receivable (A/R) and collections, accounts payable, and statistical tracking; and addressing other aspects of daily operations. As the unit grows in patients and payer sources, it may be necessary to separate completely the subacute unit business office functions from those of the nursing facility or hospital. In the hospital, it

is more likely that the billing and collection procedures will be integrated into the established systems. However, all areas discussed in this chapter should be addressed in planning for the subacute unit, regardless of setting.

STAFFING AND TRAINING

Basic staffing should include the business office manager, bookkeeper, and billing specialist. These staff are dedicated to the subacute unit and should be trained in Medicare, Medicaid, managed care, private insurance, and per diem billing. As contracts are negotiated, these staff will implement billing and collection procedures. The business office staffing will be limited when the unit opens but may increase depending on changes in payer mix and census. This section describes the basic requirements for the staff.

Business Office Manager

Requirements

- Bachelor's degree
- Thorough understanding of Medicare, Medicaid, and insurance/managed care payment systems

Appreciation is expressed to the following people for their contribution of information: Roxanne Urfer, Assistant Administrator/Controller, Specialty Hospital, Jacksonville, Florida; Marilyn Martz, Business Office Manager, Specialty Hospital, Jacksonville, Florida; and Diana Cooke, Senior Manager, Central Business Office, Transitional Hospital, Atlanta, Georgia.

- Experience in managing a business office in a hospital or nursing facility, including hiring and training of staff
- Experience with computer management of business office procedures, including word processing
- Excellent organizational skills, ability to motivate staff, self-starter

Responsible to: Administrator

Job Summary

- Hire and train staff
- Coordinate office functions
- Negotiate and manage vendors
- Manage third party payers
- Coordinate establishment of costs for categories of patients as well as for individual patients
- Coordinate with case manager and nurse liaison in negotiating per diem rates, if not covered through contracts or provider agreements with Medicare or Medicaid
- Manage and monitor contracts
- Manage payroll (payroll may be handled through the general office service for the entire facility)
- Coordinate coding with the medical records department
- Establish financial logs and other statistical tracking systems
- Facilitate monthly flow of financial information to accountant/controller for preparation of financial statements
- Establish written procedures for billing and collections
- Ensure that collection procedures are up to date and fully implemented
- Request and receive certifications and preauthorizations for treatment
- Establish, with accountant, ways to track cost-to-charges ratios
- Train other hospital/facility personnel regarding what is needed by the business office

- Perform other tasks as assigned by the administrator and agreed to by each party

Bookkeeper

Requirements

- High school diploma
- Knowledge of basic accounting procedures, including chart of accounts, general ledger, and financial statements
- Experience with collections and A/R management
- Basic computer knowledge and experience
- Ability to interact with people
- Willingness to learn new skills and procedures

Responsible to: Business Office Manager

Job Summary

- Manage accounts payable
- Input payables to accounting system
- Code checks to the chart of accounts
- Manage accounts receivable (A/R)
- Monitor collections and follow up as needed (A/R management includes follow-up on problem claims with the billing specialist)
- Maintain statistical logs and tracking systems, including financial logs for Medicare Parts A and B, bad debt logs, therapy service logs, and therapy labor logs
- Perform other responsibilities as assigned by the business office manager and agreed to by each party

Billing Specialist/Patient Account Representative

Requirements

- High school diploma
- Experience with billing, using the Health Care Financing Administration (HCFA)

forms 1450 and 1500, to intermediaries and carriers; preferable experience in a skilled nursing facility or hospital (HCFA forms 1450 (UB-92) and 1500 are found in Appendix 11A).

- Experience with verification of insurance
- Basic computer knowledge and experience
- Willingness to learn

Responsible to: Business Office Manager

Job Summary

- Manage billing pending and payment pending files
- Verify detailed primary and secondary insurance requirements, including deductibles, coinsurance, billing forms, documentation, and payment schedules
- Process claims
- Follow up on problem claims (eg, claims paid incorrectly or not at all)
- Input charges to accounting system
- Perform other responsibilities as assigned by the business office manager and agreed to by each party

Because of the complexity of billing several payment sources for one patient (eg, Medicare Parts A and B and supplemental insurance), the billing specialist may be involved in both billing and collections. This provides continuity with the accounts because one person is responsible for verification, billing, and collections. The title *patient account representative* could describe this combined position.

Additional Facility Staff Who Will Be Involved in Business Office Functions

Other hospital/facility staff, such as an admissions coordinator, medical records coordinator, and central supply clerk, will handle functions that will support and be necessary for the operations of the business office. The activities of each of these positions that affect the business office function are described below.

Admissions Coordinator

The following functions are usually handled by the admissions office as part of the general admissions process. The business office manager must coordinate with admissions personnel to ensure that procedures are in place to transfer the required information to billing. During preadmission and admission interviews, when financial responsibilities are explained to the beneficiary and/or responsible party, any data not collected through the admissions process will be requested by the business office person conducting the interview.

The tasks for the admissions coordinator that pertain particularly to billing are as follows:

- Identify the person legally responsible for the account
- Explain charges
- Copy insurance cards
- Copy Medicare and Medicaid cards
- Complete Medicare secondary payer forms
- Complete face sheets for the clinical record and submit copies to the bookkeeper
- Coordinate with medical records staff for codes needed for billing (eg, ICD-9 codes and CPT codes)
- Obtain signed insurance forms and authorizations to bill
- Obtain written authorization when the Medicare life reserve days will not be used (long-term care hospital)

The interaction between the admissions office and the business office is ongoing and active to ensure timely billing and collections.

Medical Records Coordinator

The medical records coordinator will provide information about the coding required for billing, including ICD-9 and CPT codes. When the payer requests documentation to support the claim, the medical records personnel will assist the billing specialist in determining what should be sent and will copy the information.

Central Supply Coordinator

The central supply coordinator will track the usage of supplies and provide this information to the billing specialist.

EXPERIENCE

Billing and Collections

Because of the variety of payer sources and the complexity of the patients in a subacute unit, it is necessary that the key staff have experience in billing and collections with Medicare, Medicaid, private insurance, and managed care organizations.

Costs and Charges

Business office personnel, particularly the office manager, must understand costs and establishing charges because the cost of services must be assessed for reimbursement and for negotiating managed care contracts. Costs include both the direct and the indirect costs of providing services and supplies. The charges are based on direct and indirect costs plus a margin of profit (or an add-on for nonprofit companies) to ensure that charges are more than costs.

Direct costs are the out-of-pocket costs of providing the services. For example, for physical therapy the direct costs include the therapist's fee or salary/benefits and supplies used in the therapy department. Hospital/facility staff, such as the physical therapy aide, may also be included in the direct costs.

Indirect costs are those costs associated with providing the services and supplies. For physical therapy, indirect costs include the costs associated with the physical therapy room, such as a portion of the building depreciation, mortgage interest, property insurance, property taxes, maintenance, utility and housekeeping expenses, and an allocation of administrative and general costs. All these costs contribute to the hospital/facility's ability to provide physical therapy services.

When negotiating contracts with managed care organizations and other payer sources (eg, Medicaid), it is critical that the facility be able to identify the basic costs and set a charge depending on the level of care. There may also be charges for ancillary add-ons (eg, therapy, pharmacy, and medical supplies). It is critical to be aware of the special needs of the subacute patient in determining the charges and negotiating the rates. The business office manager will be involved in, and possibly responsible for, establishing these charges.

PAYERS

The payer sources available for the subacute unit will vary according to the geographic area, the type of patient mix, and the referral sources. The following payers are available for subacute patients. Issues related to billing and payment are discussed.

Medicaid

Because of the higher acuity of the subacute patient, special rates may be negotiated with the Medicaid program where the state plan has provisions for this. It is important to determine whether there are special billing procedures required for the negotiated rates. Often, the state Medicaid program will have forms and procedures that are different from the standard requirements. It is necessary to research carefully the state regulations related to negotiated rates and related circumstances if the unit is certified for participation in the Medicaid program.

Medicare

Medicare will be the payer covering the majority of patients in the long-term care hospital and the subacute unit at start up. The proportion of Medicare may become more equal with that of managed care as the unit grows and the referral base is diversified. Many units, particularly those based in an acute hospital, may remain primarily Medicare.

Medicare is a cost-based system with specific criteria for eligibility and coverage. In a short-term, transitional skilled nursing facility subacute unit, whether freestanding or hospital-based, patients will usually be discharged before using the full 100-day benefit period and will usually be discharged in fewer than 20 days. In the long-term care hospital, the length of stay will often be longer as a result of regulatory requirements for a 25-day average length of stay. The long-term care hospital benefit period is 150 days with 60 full covered days, 30 coinsurance days, and 60 life time reserve days. The number of days available to the beneficiary at the time of admission must be determined. For the long-term care hospital, if the beneficiary does not want to use the life reserve days, written authorization must be obtained.

The business office personnel must be knowledgeable in the requirements of Medicare for the skilled nursing facility or long-term care hospital because, when a claim is sent to Medicare, the facility is verifying that all Medicare regulations are being met. This requires communication with nursing and all appropriate departments.

Commercial Insurance

There is currently limited commercial insurance available for patients in a skilled nursing facility. When a subacute unit is initiated, insurance as a payer source will increase and will require training of personnel and additions to procedures. Most hospitals are experienced in insurance billing.

Managed Care Organizations

The biggest challenge for subacute care business operations will be understanding and managing the contracts and agreements with managed care organizations. The arrangements for payment can be in many forms, including an individual rate for a specific patient, capitated rates and negotiated rates for an individual or a group of patients. The organizations with which such arrangements are made include health mainte-nance organizations (HMOs) and preferred provider organizations (PPOs). It is important that the business office manager understand the types of agreements that have been negotiated because each can dictate specific billing requirements and accounting considerations.

Tracking Payers

It is recommended that a database be established to track information needed about each payer source, including names, address, contact person, billing forms, documentation requirements, and the like. The payer sources will be listed alphabetically and will include Medicare and Medicaid as well as all insurance companies. Hard copies of the information can be maintained in a notebook, if this facilitates accessibility. The database and notebook must be kept current. The bookkeeper will monitor this information. A sample payer information sheet is found in Appendix 11A.

INQUIRY/ADMISSIONS PROCEDURES

Part of the establishment of the subacute unit is evaluating and planning admission procedures. The requirements of each payer source will affect what is done during the inquiry/admission process to facilitate optimum business office functions. The key areas that overlap among the departments are described in this section.

Responsibilities

Depending on the size of the subacute unit and the philosophy of its management, the admissions process may be the responsibility of the general admissions staff for the hospital/facility or there could be dedicated separate admissions staff for the unit. The admissions office of the hospital/facility is usually separate from the business office. Regardless of the arrangements, active communication between admissions and billing is critical, particularly because the admissions office personnel are obtaining data needed for billing.

The business office manager should be involved in the inquiry and preadmission interviews and decisions regarding admitting the potential patient, particularly as these relate to payment verification, certifications, and preauthorizations. Once the decision to admit is made, the business office manager or representative will be involved in the preadmission and admission processes so that the family and patient understand the financial responsibilities associated with placement for subacute care.

Documents obtained through the admissions process that relate to financial management and billing should be transferred to the business office as they are received and upon completion of the admission. The material needed by the business office will be obtained during the preadmission and admission interviews by the admissions office personnel and the business office personnel. It is important to make a decision as to who will obtain the billing and financial information needed.

A checklist of financial-related items to be included in the admission process and sent to billing is given in Appendix 11A. This list will be modified with additions and deletions to fit the exact nature of a specific program. For example, there may be a contract with a managed care organization that requires a particular form to be signed by the beneficiary/member. This form would be added to the admission checklist.

Payer/Payment Verification

When an inquiry is received by the hospital/facility, payer/payment verification is begun immediately and conducted concurrently with the assessment of medical needs so that a decision regarding admission can be completed as quickly as possible. Primary and secondary coverage should be verified. The verification continues throughout the billing process. For example, if Medicare benefits are exhausted and a secondary payer is to be billed, the insurance is verified again. It is not uncommon for insurance to pay differently from what was verified on admission. A written agreement is helpful to support the payment that is verified by telephone. The payer (eg,

Medicare, insurance, HMO, or PPO) is identified at the time of the inquiry regarding admission.

Insurance

The verification procedure for insurance coverage will minimally include obtaining information regarding a contact at the insurance company, deductibles that have been met, coverage requirements, certifications, and preauthorization from the beneficiary or the responsible party. If the payer is an HMO or other entity with which the nursing facility or hospital has a contract, appropriate information will be requested as dictated by the agreement. Specifically, the following steps will be included in the insurance verification procedure:

1. The billing specialist (or other business office personnel identified by the business office manager) will call the insurance company to verify benefits and the current status of premium payments. All information obtained about the primary insurance must also be requested for secondary payers.

2. Once coverage is confirmed through the initial telephone contact, all additional information on the verification form is requested or determined to be not applicable. A separate verification form is completed for each payer. A sample insurance verification form is found in Appendix 11A.

   Information to be requested includes coinsurance, deductibles, billing forms required, documentation required with claim, special billing instructions, certification or preauthorization requirements, payment schedules, electronic billing available, utilization review requirements, and any other information pertinent to making an admission decision and billing efficiently.

   Once the patient is admitted, more detail regarding billing and collections will be researched and secured.

3. Decisions regarding payment arrangements made with the family, case managers, and insurers, including negotiated rates and discounts, are recorded in writing.

4. A precertification or preauthorization is requested from the insurance company. If this cannot be provided, approval of data received by phone is requested in writing.

5. Any pertinent information needed to make the admission decision is communicated to the admissions office and the case manager. This information may include the need for preauthorization, physician certification, prepayment by the patient, initial plan of care for the payer, or the like.

6. With this information, data from the nurse liaison, and other details gathered by the admission staff, a decision is made regarding admission of the patient to the subacute unit or hospital. The business office manager is party to these decisions.

7. With the admission decision made, the process immediately proceeds to obtaining other information to set up billing and collections. Any missing material for the verification form is researched and obtained. Additional detail about billing requirements is secured.

Medicare

Skilled Nursing Facility

For the patient to be covered by Medicare Part A in the freestanding and hospital-based skilled nursing facility, the following criteria must be met:

- The beneficiary must be eligible for Medicare Part A as determined by review of the Medicare card. The Medicare card will indicate whether the patient has Part A (inpatient) and/or Part B (outpatient) benefits. A copy of the Medicare card will be made on admission.
- The beneficiary requires skilled nursing or rehabilitation services on a daily basis.

Coverage requirements are determined by the nursing staff with the nurse liaison and the rehabilitation program manager. Daily requirements mean 7 days per week for nursing and 5 days per week for rehabilitation.

- The beneficiary requires, as a practical matter, placement in a skilled nursing facility.
- There has been a 3-day hospital stay in an acute hospital with the day of discharge not included.
- Admission to the skilled nursing facility is within 30 days of discharge from the acute hospital.
- Certification for nursing facility placement from the hospital's discharging physician or the admitting skilled nursing facility physician is obtained.
- A physician order for placement in a skilled nursing facility is written on the admitting order sheet.
- The coverage in the skilled nursing facility is for the same or a related condition as the condition for which the patient was covered in the acute hospital.
- Services are reasonable and necessary for the condition for which the patient is to be admitted.
- There are available days in the benefit period. If the beneficiary has been out of a hospital or nursing facility or has been below a Medicare-covered level of care in a nursing facility for 60 consecutive days, there are 100 days available in the benefit period. Otherwise, available days must be determined.

Long-Term Care Hospital

There are no specific admission criteria in the regulations for the patient to be covered in a long-term care hospital for Medicare Part A. However, the certification status of the hospital dictates review criteria for the state peer review organization (PRO). During the preliminary precertification period while a hospital attempts to establish its long-term care status, all facilities are reviewed by the PRO under the acute care criteria which is the 1993 InterQual crtieria. Once a facility has achieved certification as a long-term care diagnostic-related group (DRG) exempt provider, it is reviewed under the group long-term care criteria. Therefore, the guiding factor in appropriate criteria application is dictated by the provider's status.

Once the provider has met the long-term care criteria, specific coverage expectations will be applied. An example of this criterion is based on the PRO in Florida. The long-term care hospital is required to have an average length of stay of 25 days. Twenty meet the long-term care criteria in Florida. According to the PRO in Florida, the patient must meet *at least one* of the following five conditions:

1. The patient has a chronic illness that requires long-term medical care that cannot be reasonably provided in a less acute setting.
2. The patient has multisystem disease requiring careful and frequent monitoring of laboratory and physical parameters.
3. The patient is of extreme age and/or condition and subsequently lacks the capability of normal response to infection.
4. The patient requires long-term regulation of medications, requiring close observation and adjustment, that is not possible at a lower level of care.
5. The patient requires long-term isolation from the general public in cases of infectious disease or the like.

Through the admissions process, it is verified that all conditions have been met. This information is communicated to the business office.

If all criteria are met, a preadmission meeting with the beneficiary and/or the beneficiary's responsible party will be scheduled to explain Medicare-related issues as well as other admission requirements. The Medicare issues include:

- Coinsurance requirements
- Covered and noncovered services
- Payment schedules

At this preadmission meeting with the beneficiary and/or the beneficiary's responsible party or at the time of admission, the following documents, in addition to any other required admission documents, will be explained and signed:

- the Medicare secondary payer form
- the authorization to bill the Medicare program form

BOOKKEEPING/BILLING

Once the admission is completed, information is sent to the business office to set up the financial file and start the billing process. The components of this process, including financial data, billing, collections, and overall A/R management, are addressed in this section.

Financial File

The initial set-up of the financial file will include minimally the following items:

- the face sheet with ICD-9 codes
- a copy of the Medicare card
- a copy of insurance cards
- a signed explanation of financial responsibilities (facility's procedures)
- the completed financial questionnaire
- the denial letter (notice of noncoverage) if the patient is not being covered by Medicare (skilled nursing facility)
- the authorization to bill the insurance company and/or Medicare
- the authorization to release the medical records and other information that may be requested by an insurance company or government agency
- the certification and/or preauthorization for treatment

For patients admitted under Medicare Part A, the following will also be needed:

- the Medicare secondary payer questionnaire

- a physician's certification
- a physician's order for Medicare-certified bed placement (skilled nursing facility)

All information regarding the account will be maintained in the patient's financial file, including claims submitted, records of collection efforts, and correspondence.

Billing

Billing will be prepared by the billing department according to the procedures for each payer source. Billing should be submitted as frequently as possible to facilitate cash flow.

All private accounts will be billed within the first week of each month for services provided during the previous month. Insurance will be billed weekly or according to the insurance company's procedure or negotiated contract.

Medicare patients will be billed at least monthly and more often if accepted by the fiscal intermediary.

Procedures

1. Services are billed on HCFA form 1450 (UB-92) or 1500. Samples of these forms are found in Appendix 11A.
2. Basic patient information is entered into the computerized billing/accounting system at the time of admission.
3. At the end of the billing period, the submitted claim will include all routine and ancillary charges incurred during the service period. Only charges for the service period stated should be included on the claim. Appropriate revenue and diagnosis codes, and the unit's uniform charges, are used.
4. Charges received after the bill has been submitted should be handled according to the correction and/or adjustment policies of the payer. This can involve submitting an adjusted claim or adding items to the next bill (insurance).
5. The completed claim is submitted to the insurance company or Medicare interme-

diary. A copy of the primary payer remittance advise is included when secondary payers are billed, if required. A copy of the claim is maintained in the patient's payment pending file until all payment has been received.

6. All documentation required by the payer should be in the clinical record. If documentation is required with the claim, these data should be requested by billing following a specific schedule. There is specific documentation that is required by Medicare and should be on file (eg, therapy plan of treatment). Other payer sources often have documentation requirements that should be in place before billing.

7. For Medicare patients, the information on HCFA form 1450 (UB-92) is entered on the Medicare Part A and/or Part B financial log and into the facility's A/R system. Financial logs needed by skilled nursing facilities are not always maintained by the billing/accounting system and can be set up in a database with the capacity to produce a spreadsheet.

8. When payment is received:
   - Deposit the check.
   - Mark the claim with:
     — the date of payment
     — the rate paid times the number of days, if paid on a per diem base
     — any coinsurance deducted, if applicable
     — adjustments made, if any
     — interest paid, if any, for Medicare patients
   - Reconcile the remittance advise with the claim.
   - Post the payment to A/R.

9. If payment is not received within 30 days of billing:
   - Follow the insurance company's or intermediary's procedure for tracing the claim.

- Review the claim status report from the insurance company or intermediary regularly, if available. The claim may have been dropped from the system because the hospital or facility did not send required information.

Request for Additional Medical Information

When a determination of coverage cannot be made based upon the information on the claim and any attachments submitted with it, the insurance company or the intermediary may request additional documentation. This information will be sent immediately.

Failure To Submit Documentation

The insurance company or intermediary may reject or deny the claim for lack of medical necessity if requested information is not received. In the case of Medicare, the hospital/facility can be held liable for the denied services. If a claim is rejected, the hospital/facility must start the billing process over (ie, resubmit the claim). If the claim cannot be resubmitted, it will be necessary to begin the appropriate appeal process.

HCFA Forms 1450 (UB-92) and 1500

Most billing is done on HCFA claim forms 1450 (UB-92) and 1500. It is critical for the bookkeeper and the billing specialist to understand completion of both these forms. Coordination with the medical records department will be important to ensure that appropriate coding is done on the billing form.

Electronic Transmittals

Claim forms should be submitted electronically to expedite the payment of claims. Electronic transfer can be made directly or through a clearinghouse. When multiple insurance companies will be billed, a clearinghouse should be investigated.

Coinsurance and Deductibles

Medicare and most insurance plans will have coinsurance and deductible requirements that must be met by the beneficiary. At the time of verification of payment, these qualifications will be identified. It is critical that the coinsurance and deductibles be billed in a timely fashion. The same collection procedures that apply to primary billing will apply to the coinsurance and deductibles. Coinsurance and deductibles are paid by the beneficiary, a supplemental insurance plan, or the state Medicaid program.

For Medicare in the skilled nursing facility, there is a coinsurance amount due for days 21 through 100 that the patient is covered under Part A and a coinsurance of 20% and a deductible of $100 per year for Part B. These amounts must be billed. If the coinsurance and deductible are not collected and the facility follows the regulations related to Medicare bad debt, the Medicare program will reimburse the amounts not collected as a part of the cost report settlement. Some intermediaries will make interim settlements on Medicare bad debt or allow for Medicare bad debt in the interim rate.

For the long-term care hospital, there is a coinsurance payment for the 30 coinsurance days that follow the 60 full covered days. This amount is set at the beginning of each year. Deductible and coinsurance requirements for Part B are the same as for the skilled nursing facility.

A/R Management

Payment pending files will be set up by the billing specialist. For A/R to be managed on a timely basis, these files will be reviewed and appropriate follow-up done at least monthly, with weekly review preferred.

There are times when the insurance company or intermediary does not pay the claim properly or does not pay the claim at all. To monitor what is being done to resolve the problem, a problem claim log is used (see Appendix 11A). A separate problem claim log is used for each claim. The information can be maintained in a database or on a hard copy in the payment pending file with the unsettled claim until the problem is resolved. After the claim is settled, hard copies of all the records are filed in the patient's financial file. (A sample form showing the necessary information to track and monitor these "problem claims" is in Appendix 11A.)

Every transaction involved in correcting errors in payment or in collection is entered on the log, including phone calls, letters, exchanges of documentation, and so forth. The full name and phone number of the person contacted at the insurance company or intermediary should always be recorded. At the time of review of problem claims, the problem claim logs as well as the outstanding claims will be analyzed to determine whether the claim should be pursued further and to determine an appropriate plan of action.

The A/R report will be examined at least monthly, and written collection procedures will be implemented on a timely and consistent basis. With Medicare, any coinsurance or deductibles that have not been paid after specified Medicare requirements have been met will be entered on the Medicare bad debt log and deleted from A/R.

Sample Collection Procedures

To expedite the resolution of problem claims and to ensure that collections are timely, each hospital/facility must develop written collection procedures. The following collection guidelines are samples and should be modified to fit the systems in place at the hospital or nursing facility. The time frames may be modified to conform to appropriate strategies for each unit.

General procedures can be as follows:

1. All balances due from the patient (eg, deductibles, coinsurance, and services not covered by insurance or Medicare) will be billed to the patient or the patient's representative as soon as the patient's liability can be determined.
2. Statements are sent on the second day of the month after the month of service and every 30 days thereafter.
3. The patient or the patient's representative will be contacted by telephone 7 days after the second billing.
4. A letter will follow the phone call, with a second letter to be sent when the account is 60 days outstanding. These letters will inform the patient that the account will be

sent to a collection agency if payment is not received within 7 days.

It is important to determine whether the company will use a collection agency and what the procedures for submitting to the collection agency will be. It may be more acceptable for accounts to go to an outside collection agency after 90 days.

5. Documentation of the collection efforts expended will be maintained in the patient's file with dates of billings, copies of any correspondence, and reports of telephone contact or personal contact.
6. All accounts with a balance of less than $5 after insurance or other payment will be written off because the cost of collection will exceed the potential amount of collection.
7. For accounts where the patient is deceased, the guarantor is pursued in an attempt to bring about satisfactory settlement.
8. For accounts of deceased patients without a guarantor and in cases of extreme hardship, normal collection efforts are carried out and documented with an explanation of action taken and disposition.
9. Collection efforts are to be documented in the patient's financial file with copies of follow-up letters, telephone reports, and the like.

Copayment/Deductibles

Coinsurance and deductible collection procedures will be the same as those given above.

Collection procedures for insurance billing may be as follows:

1. Billing to insurance companies will be done at a minimum of every 2 weeks.
2. Fifteen days after the first claim is submitted, a follow-up phone call will be made to the insurance company for a claim status.
3. If payment is not received within 30 days of billing, another phone call should be made.

4. If after 45 days a payment is not received, the patient is contacted, and a payment plan is set up.

5. The patient will be billed until the insurance company responds with payment.

6. If a patient's coverage consists of two or more insurance companies, only the primary company will be billed, and the patient will be responsible for billing the secondary insurance. Documentation will be provided to the patient to expedite secondary insurance billing, if requested.

Managed Care Organizations

When there is a negotiated contract, billing will be according to the terms of the contract. For example, an HMO may require weekly billing or billing at the time of discharge. Many organizations have specific times to issue payment checks. Billing at these times will expedite payment if claims are received within a predetermined period. It is important for the business office to determine at the time of admission whether there are special billing requirements and procedures set up by the payer or the contract with the payer.

Payment Plans

Accounts should be collected in a timely manner. If an account is overdue and a payment plan is necessary, the patient will be responsible to pay a minimum of 15% of the balance each month.

Approval for Write-Off of Accounts

All accounts deemed uncollectible will be reviewed and approved for write-off by the business manager. The bookkeeper will notify the business manager in writing of the status of the account and will provide a summary of all efforts to collect the account and the date of proposed write-off. Written approval for write-off will be signed by the business manager. In some systems, the administrator or other staff will be designated to approve write-offs of outstanding accounts. Accounts are considered current if

arrangements have been made to pay and payment is being received according to plan.

CONTRACT MANAGEMENT

Systems for contract management and monitoring should be established to include therapy contracts, supply vendor contracts, and managed care contracts. Because contracts are directly related to expenses and revenues, the business office manager is responsible for setting up contract management procedures and for assigning a person to be responsible. Minimally, the following contract parameters should be monitored carefully:

• Dates of renewal
• Changes in fees/prices
• Termination stipulations
• Negotiable provisions

HARDWARE AND SOFTWARE NEEDS

It is not within the scope of this chapter to review all the hardware and software that is available on the market. The important consideration is that, with the implementation of a subacute unit, upgrading of the business software and possibly the hardware available to the hospital/facility will be necessary. For the hospital-based unit, changes will involve meeting regulations for the skilled nursing facility. As a part of the planning process, planners should evaluate the present system, analyze the projected needs for the subacute unit, and make appropriate decisions regarding needs and costs.

CONCLUSION

This chapter has presented basic considerations for the subacute unit business office relative to staffing and procedures. It is important to have adequate staff for the subacute unit, even if this requires adding dedicated staff for the unit. The hospital or nursing facility must evaluate the capabilities of current staff and systems to ensure that the added demands of the subacute unit can be met. These additional needs will be related to increased admissions, a different patient mix, added payer sources, increased claims, and accounts receivable. Further, plans must be in place to handle possible growth.

Each subacute unit will have unique needs depending on the setting and system structures. The need for carefully made projections cannot be overstated. Although the daily operations of the business office are the responsibility of the business office manager, the administrator or executive director will be ultimately accountable for the success of the business office and its integration into the total functioning of the subacute unit. A cooperative team must be in place.

Appendix 11A
HCFA Form 1450 (UB-92)

UB-92 HCFA-1450   OCR/ORIGINAL   790-0201   I CERTIFY THE CERTIFICATION ON THE REVERSE APPLY TO THIS BILL AND ARE MADE A PART HEREOF.

HCFA Form 1500

PLEASE
DO NOT
STAPLE
IN THIS
AREA

APPROVED OMB-0938-0008

CARRIER

| | PICA | | | | | | | HEALTH INSURANCE CLAIM FORM | | | PICA | |

| 1. MEDICARE | MEDICAID | CHAMPUS | CHAMPVA | GROUP HEALTH PLAN | FECA BLK LUNG | OTHER | 1a. INSURED'S I.D. NUMBER | (FOR PROGRAM IN ITEM 1) |
| *(Medicare #)* | *(Medicaid #)* | *(Sponser's SSN)* | *(VA file #)* | *(SSN or ID)* | *(SSN)* | *(ID)* | | |

2. PATIENTS Name (Last Name, First Name, Middle Initial)

3. PATIENTS BIRTH DATE   MM DD YY   SEX   M   F

4. INSURED'S NAME (Last Name, First Name, Middle Initial)

5. PATIENT'S ADDRESS (No., Street)

6. PATIENT RELATIONSHIP TO INSURED   Self   Spouse   Child   Other

7. INSURED'S ADDRESS (No., Street)

CITY   STATE

8. PATIENT STATUS   Spouse   Married   Other

CITY   STATE

ZIP CODE   TELEPHONE (Include Area Code) ( )

Employed   Full-Time Student   Part-Time Student

ZIP CODE   TELEPHONE (Include Area Code) ( )

9. OTHER INSURED'S NAME (Last Name, First Name, Middle Initial)

10. IS PATIENT'S CONDITION RELATED TO:

11. INSURED'S POLICY GROUP OR FECA NUMBER

a. OTHER INSURED'S POLICY OR GROUP NUMBER

a. EMPLOYMENT (CURRENT OR PREVIOUS)   YES   NO

a. INSURED'S DATE OF BIRTH   MM DD YY   SEX   M   F

b. OTHER INSURED'S DATE OF BIRTH   MM DD YY   SEX   M   F

b. AUTO ACCIDENT?   YES   NO   Place (State)

b. EMPLOYER'S NAME OR SCHOOL NAME

c. EMPLOYER'S NAME OR SCHOOL NAME

c. OTHER ACCIDENT?   YES   NO

c. INSURANCE PLAN OR PROGRAM NAME

d. INSURANCE PLAN NAME OR PROGRAM

10d. RESERVED FOR LOCAL USE

d. IS THERE ANOTHER HEALTH BENEFIT PLAN?   YES   NO   *If yes, return to and complete item 9 a–d*

READ BACK OF FORM BEFORE COMPLETING & SIGNING

12. PATIENTS OR AUTHORIZED PERSON'S SIGNATURE I authorize the release of any medical or other information necessary to process this claim. I also request payment of government benefits either to myself or to the party who accepts assignment below.

SIGNED _____   DATE _____

13. INSURED OR AUTHORIZED PERSONS SIGNATURE I authorize payment of medical benefits to the undersigned physician or supplier for services described below.

SIGNED _____

14. DATE OF CURRENT: MM DD YY   ILLNESS (First symptom) OR INJURY (Accident) OR PREGNANCY (LMP)

15. IF PATIENT HAS HAD SAME OR SIMILAR ILLNESS, GIVE FIRST DATE MM DD YY

16. DATES PATIENT UNABLE TO WORK IN CURRENT OCCUPATION   FROM MM DD YY   TO MM DD YY

17. NAME OF REFERRING PHYSICIAN OR OTHER SOURCE

17a. I.D. NUMBER OF REFERRING PHYSICIAN

18. HOSPITALIZATION DATES RELATED TO CURRENT SERVICES   FROM MM DD YY   TO MM DD YY

19. RESERVED FOR LOCAL USE

20. OUTSIDE LAB/ $ CHARGES   YES   NO

21. DIAGNOSIS OR NATURE OF ILLNESS OR INJURY (RELATE ITEMS 1, 2, 3, OR 4 TO ITEM 24E BY LINE
1. |___.__   3. |___.__
2. |___.__   4. |___.__

22. MEDICAID RESUBMISSION CODE   ORIGINAL REF. NO.

23. PRIOR AUTHORIZATION NUMBER

PATIENT AND INSURED INFORMATION

24.	A			B	C	D			E	F	G	H	I	J	K
	DATE(S) OF SERVICE			PLACE OF SERVICE	TYPE OF SERVICE	PROCEDURES, SERVICES, OR SUPPLIES (Explain unusual circumstances)			DIAGNOSIS CODE	$ CHARGES	DAYS OR UNITS	EPSDT Family Plan	EMG	COB	RESERVED FOR LOCAL USE
	FROM		TO			CPT/HCPCS	MODIFIER								
	MM	DD	YY	MM	DD	YY													
1																
2																
3																
4																
5																
6																

| 25. FEDERAL TAX I.D. NUMBER   SSN   EIN | 26. PATIENT'S ACCOUNT NO. | 27. ACCEPT ASSIGNMENT? *(For gov't claims, see back)*   YES   NO | 28. TOTAL CHARGE $ | 29. AMOUNT PAID $ | 30. BALANCE DUE $ |

31. SIGNATURE OF PHYSICIAN OR SUPPLIER INCLUDING DEGREES OR CREDENTIALS (I certify that the statements on the reverse side apply to this bill and are made a part hereof.)

32. NAME AND ADDRESS OF FACILITY WHERE SERVICES WERE RENDERED (If other than home or office)

33. PHYSICIAN'S, SUPPLIER'S BILLING NAME, ADDRESS, ZIP CODE, & PHONE #

SIGNED _____   DATE _____

PIN # _____   GRP # _____

PHYSICIAN OR SUPPLIER INFORMATION

(APPROVED BY AMA COUNCIL ON MEDICAL SERVICES 8/88)   **PLEASE PRINT OR TYPE**   FORM HCFA-1500 (12-90)   FORM OWCP-1500   FORM RRB-1500

continues

Appendix 11A continued

Payer Information Sheet

Updated _____

(use pencil)

Name of Company _____

Address _____

City _____ State _____ Zip _____

Phone # (____) _____ Fax # (____) _____

Contact Person _____

Title _____ Phone # (____) _____

Contact Person _____

Title _____ Phone # (____) _____

Billing Form ☐ UB-92   ☐ 1500   ☐ Other _____

☐   Accept Electronic Claims Submission

Documentation Required with Claim _____

_____

_____

Appeals Process _____

_____

_____

Comments _____

_____

_____

Note: This information can be maintained in a database.

Courtesy of MAPS, Management and Planning Services, Atlanta, Georgia.

Information from Admissions to Billing

Patient's name _____ Admission date _____

Medical record # _____ Accounting # _____

_____ 1. Primary payment source _____

_____ 2. Secondary payment source _____

_____ 3. Copy of the Medicare card, if applicable

_____ 4. Beneficiary's signed authorization to bill

_____ 5. Medicare secondary payer form completed, if applicable

_____ 6. Insurance information (e.g. copy of insurance cards, name
            of contact at insurance company)

_____ 7. Copy of face sheet with ICD-9 and other appropriate codes

_____ 8. Number of Medicare days available: _____

_____ 9. Has the patient been in a hospital or skilled nursing
            facility in the last 60 days? yes _____   no _____

            If yes, give name of hospital or skilled nursing facility
            and number of Medicare days used:

            _____

_____ 10. Hospital stay dates _____

_____ 11. Was insurance coverage verified? yes _____ no _____

Comments/explanation: _____

_____

_____

Person Completing Admission: _____

Date form completed _____

**THIS INFORMATION SHOULD BE SENT TO THE BUSINESS OFFICE AS QUICKLY
AS IT IS AVAILABLE AND NO LATER THAN THE DATE OF ADMISSION.**

Courtesy of MAPS, Management and Planning Services, Atlanta, Georgia.

continues

Appendix 11A continued

Insurance Verification

☐ Primary Payer
☐ Secondary Payer

Patient name_____ Admission date_____

Social Security #_____ Medical record #_____

Insured's name_____ Relation to patient____

Name of Insurance Company_____

Policy Number_____ Group number _____

Effective Date of Policy_____

Are premiums current? yes ☐   no☐   Paid through_____ (date)

Coinsurance required? yes ☐   no☐   Amount _____

Deductible required? yes ☐   no☐   Has it been met? yes ☐   no☐

Comments_____

_____

Mailing address for claims

Company _____

Address _____

Telephone #_____ Fax #_____

Contact Person(s)
(1)_____   Phone_____

(2)_____   Phone_____

(3)_____   Phone_____

Is hospitalization required for payment? yes ☐   no ☐
If yes, how long?_____

Courtesy of MAPS, Management and Planning Services, Atlanta, Georgia.

INSURANCE VERIFICATION   **PAGE 2 OF 3**

Method of payment:

☐ Per diem   ☐ Per unit   ☐ All-inclusive   ☐ Add-ons

Describe Add-ons —————————————————————————

Billing forms accepted? —————————————————————

☐ UB-92   ☐ 1500   Other ——————————————

Documentation required with claim ————————————————

————————————————————————————————————

————————————————————————————————————

Electronic transmission accepted?   yes ☐   no ☐

Contact person to set up electronic billing

Name ——————————————— Phone —————————————

Payment schedule ——————————————————————————

————————————————————————————————————

Covered services ———————————————————————————

————————————————————————————————————

————————————————————————————————————

Is prior authorization required?   yes ☐   no ☐

Explain how precertification or preauthorization is obtained

————————————————————————————————————

————————————————————————————————————

————————————————————————————————————

Appeals procedures ——————————————————————————

————————————————————————————————————

————————————————————————————————————

continues

Appendix 11A continued

INSURANCE VERIFICATION   **PAGE 3 OF 3**

Other information/special instructions _____

_____

_____

_____

Recommendations for admission personnel _____

_____

_____

_____

Person completing form _____ Date _____

Problem Claim Log

**FOLLOW-UP LOG FOR
PAST DUE/PROBLEM CLAIMS**

KEEP THIS LOG WITH THE FINANCIAL LOG FOR MEDICARE CLAIMS

FACILITY/AGENCY _____ PROVIDER NO. _____

PATIENT/RESIDENT _____ HIC INS NO. _____

SERVICE DATES _____ DATE CLAIM SENT _____

INTERMEDIARY/INSURANCE COMP _____

CONTACT _____ PHONE _____

PROBLEM _____

_____

_____

FOLLOW-UP INQUIRY/RESPONSE

DATE	

DATE RESOLVED _____

SOLUTION _____

_____

_____

_____

FACILITY/AGENCY REPRESENTATIVE _____

Courtesy of MAPS, Management and Planning Services, Atlanta, Georgia.

12

Management Information Systems for Subacute Care

John F. Heller and Murry Mercier

Demands placed on information management systems by subacute care delivery strategies reflect overall changes in the delivery of health care services today. Constituent groups that include payers, employers, patients, physicians, and regulatory agents are demanding that health care providers assume financial risks through payment capitation and demonstrate the clinical and financial value of their services. In an industry that has traditionally underinvested in technology and has implemented stand-alone systems for each area of the institution, the need for integration between clinical and financial data will challenge even the most sophisticated health care provider.

The impact of providing subacute care services in a hospital environment should be considerably less than that experienced by long-term care providers. In general, hospital information systems are more capable than those in long-term care environments of dealing with large-volume business transactions and accommodating sophisticated insurance and managed care contract administration and billing. In addition, long-term care providers that decide to focus on subacute services will do so in smaller, geographically dispersed units.

Long-term care providers will face several major changes in business pressures. For one, the addition of a subacute unit will significantly increase the volume of admissions and will decrease the average length of stay. In addition, higher-acuity patients will require much more intense ancillary services than general long-term care patients. Business processes and the information systems that support them need to change to accommodate these factors. Also, payer sources will expand from traditional Medicare, Medicaid, and private pay to include insurance and managed care entities. Systems need to address complex contractual calculations and billing processes. Finally, as with all areas of health care reimbursement, payers are requiring higher levels of risk sharing, including all-inclusive per diems, case rates, and full population capitation. Systems need to support preadmission pricing, timely and concurrent review of clinical and financial data, and product line cost analysis.

The impact on hospitals providing subacute services will vary depending on licensure. If a hospital chooses to provide such services as a distinct skilled nursing unit, it will be faced with complying with the many regulatory issues associated with long-term care, including:

- accurate collection of costs associated with the distinct unit to facilitate the completion of cost reports
- compliance with Minimum Data Set (MDS) data collection requirements as defined by the Omnibus Budget Reconciliation Act (OBRA) of 1987 as well as the documentation of care planning
- integration of systems supporting the above processes with existing admission/discharge/transfer, patient accounting, nursing, and medical records applications

Hospitals and long-term care facilities face distinctly different pressures related to the decision to provide subacute care services. Hospitals will need to implement systems to support new regulatory and cost collection requirements and to integrate those with existing systems. In contrast, long-term care providers will need to replace all systems to support redefined business processes. In addition, the typical long-term care facility has fewer, less experienced business office and management staff and scarce financial resources to upgrade these positions. Implementation is also complicated because systems typically must be implemented in multiple facilities (if a chain), whereas a hospital generally involves a single location.

As discussed above, providing subacute services from a hospital platform will have a much smaller effect on existing information systems. Issues associated with managed care and outcome data management are the same as with all other hospital product lines. In contrast, long-term care providers and their system vendors are generally unprepared to cope with all the factors related to providing subacute care services in a managed care environment. These providers are faced with the difficulty of implementing systems in smaller facilities that historically have invested less in information systems than the health care industry overall. Because of this low level investment, packaged systems are less sophisticated and not designed to support the requirements of the subacute care business model.

Although this chapter focuses primarily on system requirements related to subacute care

provided from a long-term care platform, the principles discussed apply to all subacute providers regardless of licensure.

OVERVIEW OF INFORMATION SYSTEMS FOR SUBACUTE CARE

The delivery of subacute services from a long-term care platform requires significant changes to both clinical and financial delivery models. These changes drive the need to implement and utilize information systems that fully integrate patient demographic, clinical, and financial information. These systems must provide the sophistication and flexibility to adapt to ever-changing subacute clinical product offerings and reimbursement conditions. Subacute providers must focus on implementation of systems that enhance the ability to predict, measure, and manage the cost and quality of care.

Figure 12–1 provides an overview of the fundamental components of the patient and subacute business management systems. This overview mirrors traditional hospital and long-term care patient management system models, with the distinct difference of providing a single, integrated patient database as well as the ability to manage clinical and financial data appropriately for individual patient cases. Additionally, to respond to increasing demands from regional and national health care buying groups, it is necessary to support companywide patient, product line, and payer data management for both clinical and financial outcomes.

Major requirements of subacute management information systems include the support of the following system modules:

- Census management
  1. Streamlined admission processing, including production of internal face sheets and payer-mandated admission forms
  2. Modeling of individual proposed contracts and negotiated per diems to determine whether it is in the provider's best interests to agree to them

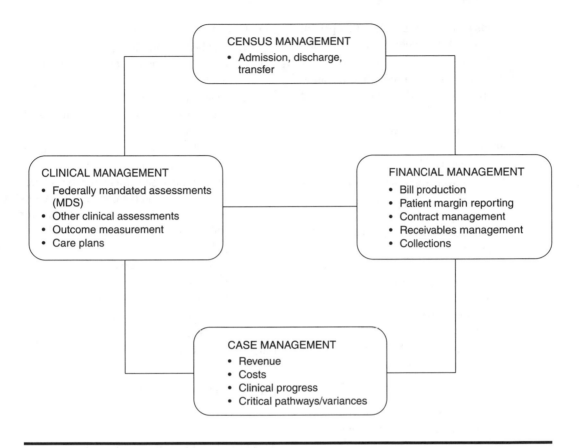

Figure 12–1   Subacute care system components.

3. Certification of benefits at time of admission

4. Accurate census reporting for Medicare distinct unit, including available Medicare days, Medicare patient census, and non-Medicare patients in certified beds

• Clinical management
    1. Preadmission clinical evaluation required to determine appropriateness of patient and pricing
    2. Collection and management of clinical data including comprehensive assess-

ments using the MDS and other patient assessment instruments, care plans, and outcomes

3. Production of required documentation for regulatory bodies and the internal medical record

4. Support of acuity-based staffing measures

- Financial management

1. Acuity-based reimbursement and per diem, case-rate, and capitated pricing and billing

2. Data collection, billing, and receivables management

3. Concurrent review of costs versus anticipated reimbursement for contract-covered patients to ensure that resource utilization is consistent with contract requirements

4. Audit of billings to health maintenance organizations (HMOs), preferred provider organizations, and other contract payers

5. Follow-up of bills to contract payers and auditing of payments to ensure full reimbursement

- Case management

1. Measurement of patient outcomes and linking of clinical goals achieved with the cost of providing the care

2. Support of critical pathway methodology for managing product lines

3. Monitoring of patient care against standard care plans and standard critical pathways

- Business management

1. Census and labor data reporting across all entries on a daily basis

2. Measurement of payer-specific issues, including Medicare unit percentage of occupancy and disparity

3. Marketing contact and referral management and reporting

4. Cash and accounts receivable management and reporting

- Outcomes management

1. Analysis of provider performance relative to each contract and to each negotiated case

2. Identification of utilization patterns for services most intensely used in providing covered services

3. Modeling of the effects of changes in variables such as case mix, patient demographics, physician behavior, services, costs, and contract arrangements to guide the provider in planning for future managed care contracts and negotiations

4. Incorporation of quality improvement methodologies into the delivery of patient care as well as evaluation of the care delivered

The remainder of this chapter expands on these functional requirements as they relate to these six system modules.

CENSUS MANAGEMENT

Referral and admission systems in the traditional nursing facility are designed to accommodate a low volume of private pay, Medicaid, and Medicare admissions. The typical nursing facility may process 10 to 20 admissions per month. In contrast, a subacute facility with an average length of stay of 15 to 20 days may process 200 to 300 admissions per month. This increased volume requires a more sophisticated and streamlined admission and census management system. Payers for patient care in a subacute unit may include a significant number of insurers and managed care organizations. The billing and documentation requirements for these payers necessitate capabilities not available in most existing long-term care systems.

Unlike fee arrangements in traditional nursing facilities, subacute providers are required to negotiate patient-specific pricing, often with limited turnaround time. Pricing may take the form of discounts from charges, all-inclusive per diems, per diems with caps and exclusions, case rates, and capitated pricing. Providers must develop pricing systems that facilitate estimation of patient resource needs, charges, and associated costs. Figure 12–2 illustrates the major functional components of census management necessary to support the subacute unit's business management environment.

Referral Tracking System

Contact with the subacute patient is initiated through daily prospecting with referral sources. These include insurance company case managers, independent case management firms, HMOs and other managed care entities, hospital discharge planners, physicians, Medicaid case managers, and family members. A referral system should support and monitor marketing program activities performed in the subacute care facility. In addition, for multifacility companies the system should allow for extraction of referral data for corporate reporting and national contract management purposes.

To facilitate cost-benefit analysis of marketing efforts, referral system capabilities should include cost factors for determining cost per project and cost per marketing program. These cost factors are linked to the contract management system to determine a return on investment for each marketing program. At the time of initial contact, it is important to support the collection of information detailed in Exhibit 12–1.

When the referral results in evaluation or immediate admission to the subacute care center, the referral status is monitored. Evaluations, family tours, and admissions are logged and scheduled, and all related correspondence is generated through the referral system. Reasons for nonadmission should be categorized and tracked to revise the marketing strategies as needed. Categories to include are listed in Exhibit 12–2.

An important component of the referral tracking system involves screening for appropriate funding. The system must facilitate verification of insurance coverage, Medicare eligibility, Medicaid eligibility, and personal asset analysis. Funding verification is maintained by financial class, payer, and plan category.

Exhibit 12–1 Data Requirements for Initial Referral Contact

Type of contact (phone, letter)
Source of referral (HMO, insurance company, hospital, etc)
Referral contact name
Date of referral
Type of request (general information, referral information)
Patient demographics
Mailing address for literature
Way in which contact was referred to subacute center
Primary and secondary diagnoses
Contributing factors

Preadmission Pricing

In many cases, the referral source may request the subacute care center to quote a per diem or case rate for a patient. To ensure desired financial margins, the provider must have a pricing system to facilitate estimations of the cost, both direct and fully allocated, for the duration of the patient's stay. This is achieved by linking a clinical resource assessment with a cost accounting and pricing system.

Typically, a clinical evaluation is conducted, either verbally or at the referral site, to assess the patient's acuity, appropriate program placement, and resource profile. Nursing intensity and ancillary resource needs are matched to the provider's charge matrix to estimate standard charges for room and board and ancillary services. Cost-to-

Exhibit 12–2 Nonadmission Tracking

No funding available
Alternative center selected
    Price
    Family decision
    Lack of amenities
    Location
Needed services not available at center
Does not meet subacute criteria
Other

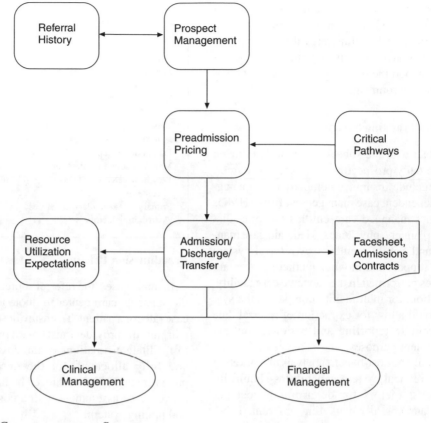

Figure 12–2 Census management flow.

charge ratios are then used to calculate the cost of providing the care. Application of Medicare cost methodologies and cost-to-charge ratios results in a reasonable estimation of costs and may be used until the provider has implemented a fully integrated cost accounting system. Once such a system is implemented, cost data should be used along with critical pathways to support patient-specific pricing.

A simplified per diem pricing worksheet is presented in Table 12–1. In this example, the estimated gross charges for the patient are $530 per patient day. Using cost-to-charge ratios from a current Medicare cost report, the estimated cost for the patient is $374 per patient day. With these estimates, a pricing matrix similar to that presented in Table 12–2 may be used to calculate profit margins at various per diem price quotes.

This allows the provider to determine a pricing range for negotiation with the managed care entity. This pricing system minimizes the risk associated with per diem and case rate payment methodologies.

Once a per diem is successfully negotiated, the contract terms must be documented and entered into the registration and patient accounting systems. It is particularly important to document all exceptions to the per diem rate, such as excluded or capped services.

Admission/Discharge/Transfer

Once the referral has been accepted for admission, the patient is processed through the registration system. During the registration process, financial information is collected, and admission

Table 12–1 Per Diem Cost Estimate

Service Provided	Estimated Charge ($)	Cost Factor	Estimated Cost ($)
Room and board	200	0.68	136
Therapies (6 days per week)			
Physical therapy, 4 units @ $20 per unit	34	0.75	26
Occupational therapy, 2 units @ $25 per unit	43	0.65	28
Speech-language pathology, 2 units @ $25 per unit	43	0.70	30
Respiratory therapy	0	0.00	0
Medications			
Oral	30	0.80	24
Intravenous	130	0.80	104
Nutrition	20	0.60	12
Supplies	30	0.45	14
Total	530		374

documents and notices are produced and sent to the appropriate departments. The registration system accesses the referral system to pull historical data into a new preadmission or admission file. Certain demographic and funding data are integrated with the patient accounting system. Data elements captured during the admissions process are listed in Exhibit 12–3.

In addition to the standard admission, discharge, and transfer functions, subacute care systems should facilitate reporting of Medicare remaining days, insurance coverage thresholds, and census reporting by product line, by payer, and by plan.

CLINICAL MANAGEMENT

The definition of clinical management in long-term care has traditionally been driven by federal and state regulations stemming from OBRA 1987. These regulations provide for minimum standards for patient assessment, problem identification, and development of care plans. As a result, both long-term care providers and information system vendors have focused development and implementation efforts on systems that primarily support these government requirements. This contrasts with the hospital environment, where systems have been developed to support clinical processes meeting the functional requirements of providing care to higher-acuity patients.

Figure 12–3 provides an overview of key information flows required to support the delivery of services to subacute patients. The objectives of the clinical information systems are to:

- accumulate clinical data necessary to predict patient resource requirements and clinical outcomes
- compile service and outcome data to support concurrent case management
- collect service and patient assessment data to feed financial systems

Table 12–2 Per Diem Pricing Matrix*

Negotiated Rate ($)	Percentage Discount	Profit Margin (%)
530	0	29
515	3	27
500	**6**	**25**
485	**8**	**23**
470	**11**	**20**
455	**14**	**18**
440	**17**	**15**
425	20	12
410	23	9
395	25	5
380	28	2

*Estimated gross charges, $530; estimated cost, $374. Values in boldface are in the targeted negotiation range.

Exhibit 12–3 Registration Data Elements

Patient demographics
Business unit (if multifacility company)
Product line (eg, ventilator, cardiac, oncology, renal)
Payer data
Plan and contract data
Diagnoses (ICD-9 codes, discharge diagnosis-related
    group)
Billing account number
Guarantor data (eg, name, address)
Physician data
Billing-related data (eg, address, billing cycle, docu-
    mentation requirements)

- support consistency and quality of clinical systems

Starting with the preadmission patient screening, the provider must be able to predict the resources required by the patient and the expected clinical outcomes. It is critical for the subacute provider to confirm its ability to care adequately for the patient as well as to predict associated costs and the expected length of stay before admission. Application of standardized critical pathways for specific product lines and/or diagnoses provides a basis for accurately forecasting patient service requirements and associated costs. Critical pathways also provide a basis for measuring compliance with organization, state, and federal quality of care standards.

After admission, the clinical management system must support the completion of the required MDS as defined by federal OBRA regulations and various state-specific variations as well as diagnosis-specific patient assessments. The assessment process must support changing clinical product offerings as well as different assessments for each product line. For example, a patient classified as a weanable ventilator patient may undergo a complete respiratory assessment but only receive a shortened orthopedic assessment. Conversely, a patient admitted for orthopedic rehabilitative services may not require the full respiratory assessment. Systems built with traditional hard coded assessment process flows

will require greater time and expense to implement and support.

Closely associated with the patient assessment process is the process of collecting clinical outcome indicators. This process is normally completed at admission and is updated at discharge. Additionally, concurrent as well as postdischarge follow-up may be desired.

As with all systems, it is desirable to implement a business and system model that integrates patient assessments into the fewest number of process flows. Because of the rigid structure of regulatory requirements and the difficulty associated with merging comprehensive and other outcome assessments, however, it may be necessary to implement multiple, stand-alone assessment processes. Depending on the subacute provider's licensure and accreditation, patient assessment systems may be required to support the automation of one or more of the data sets specified in Exhibit 12–4.

Based on completion of the MDS, there are regulated formulas for the generation of triggered resident assessment protocols (RAPs). RAPs indicate potential patient problems that should be considered during the development of the patient care plan. As with the MDS itself, these triggers are required but inadequate for higher-acuity patients. It is necessary for systems to support easy implementation of additional formulas based on the answers provided in organization-specific comprehensive assessment tools. Once again, these capabilities will support enforcement of clinical standards. In addition, if the organization chooses to complete interdisciplinary assessments and care plans, the ability easily to compare assessment data across disciplines will improve clinical outcomes by suggesting potential patient problems based on such analysis.

Care planning requirements for subacute providers are similar to those of long-term care providers, with the added dimension of a standardized critical pathway. In a fully developed subacute environment, care plans are developed with the following inputs:

- standardized critical pathway (product line/ specific diagnosis, including standard treat-

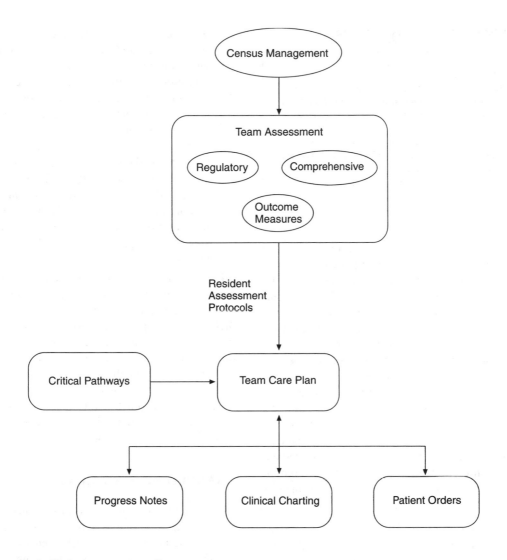

Figure 12–3 Clinical management flow.

ment interventions, goals, and potential order sets)

- suggested treatment goals and interventions
  based on regulated RAPs
- suggested treatment goals and interventions
  based on organization assessment formulas

Systems supporting the care plan development
process must be carefully designed to support
clinical standards and efficient care plan cre-
ation/maintenance and, most important, to en-

sure that plans appropriately address each
patient's unique clinical requirements.

Perhaps the weakest portion of all health care
information systems, but particularly those of
long-term care systems, are modules supporting
the delivery and documentation of patient care.
Long-term care systems have traditionally been
implemented to support minimal clinical documentation in response to government-regulated
reporting and survey requirements. These systems do not improve the delivery of patient care.

Exhibit 12–4 Patient Assessment Data Sets

MDS criteria
Resource utilization group criteria
Subacute accreditation standards of the Joint Commission on Accreditation of Healthcare Organizations
Joint Commission hospital accreditation standards
Standards of the Commission on Accreditation of Rehabilitation Facilities
Comprehensive assessment criteria
Outcome data

In a facility providing subacute services to higher-acuity and less stable patients, it is imperative to integrate automated systems into the clinical decision-making process. This will result in improved consistency and quality of those decisions and will reduce the time and effort required to deliver and account for services.

Federal guidelines and systems developed for monitoring and documenting changes in patient conditions are manageable for stable patients with lengths of stay averaging more than 150 days. These guidelines, however, are overly cumbersome when applied to subacute patients who are more acute and less stable and have a much shorter length of stay. Key system components for supporting the delivery of subacute services include the following:

- *progress notes:* This entails charting associated with delivery of key medical, nursing, and rehabilitative services relating to patient progress. These notes are differentiated from daily, minute-by-minute patient care charting. Progress notes are generally completed with the delivery of major services and should be directly tied to care plan updates (goal date updates and changes in interventions).

- *clinical charting:* This is charting supporting minute-by-minute documentation of primary nursing services supplied. Automation of clinical charting will probably require access to system resources in the patient's room.

- *orders management:* In long-term care, this function has traditionally been limited to physician orders documented by medication administration records. Unlike acute care providers, long-term care providers typically use contract services for rehabilitation, laboratory, pharmacy, and other ancillary services. As a result, no support systems are available to feed a long-term care orders management system. Expansion of functionality to include orders from all disciplines and development of a direct interface to billing and receivable systems should be a high priority for subacute providers.

In summary, clinical management systems supporting subacute services in an acute hospital setting will need to be expanded to support OBRA regulations if delivered from a Medicare distinct skilled nursing unit. Long-term care providers will require a complete overhaul of both the clinical service delivery model and the systems supporting that model. Providers need to focus on system functionality that supports the collection of clinical service and outcome data, which feed case management systems.

FINANCIAL MANAGEMENT

The complexity and high risk associated with managed care contracting require that subacute care providers develop sophisticated financial management systems. These systems must link with clinical and outcome data to facilitate more complex billing arrangements, estimates of the profitability of case managed per diem contracts, and evaluations of the profitability of managed care provider agreements. This section defines the system functionality needed by subacute providers (Figure 12–4) to support this complex financial environment.

Bill Production

Adapting general long-term care systems to bill for the more complex contract arrangements

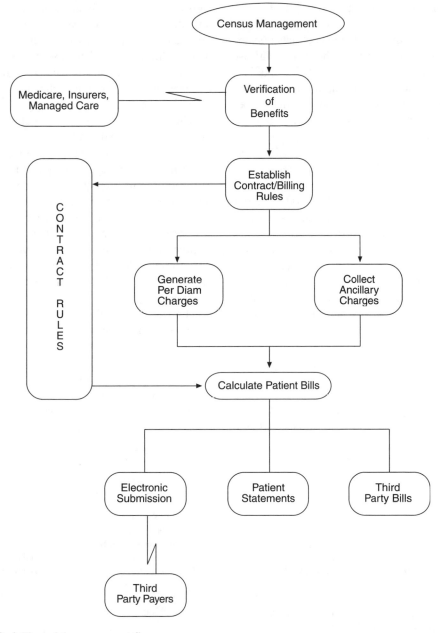

Figure 12–4 Financial management flow.

negotiated with payers is a critical but often problematic issue for subacute care providers. There
is no standard contract between subacute providers and managed care organizations. Reimbursement may be based on percentage discounts from
standard charges, per diem rates for defined levels of care with certain ancillary services capped
or excluded, case rates, or capitated arrangements. Billing systems must be adapted to accommodate the increased complexity and high

transaction volume unique to the subacute environment.

The terms of the negotiated contracts must be clearly communicated from the marketing/case management personnel to the business office. Ancillary services that are capped at a specified dollar amount per day, exclusions from base per diem rates, and per diem rates that fluctuate within the billing cycle are examples of such contract arrangements that challenge the facility billing office. In addition, although typical long-term care systems are designed to bill on a monthly cycle, with lengths of stay often shorter than 10 days subacute billing systems must be prepared to generate bills on demand.

Although Medicare and some charge-based insurance patients will be billed by means of the UB-92 format, patients billed on a per diem, case rate, or capitated basis may require alternative formats. A sample per diem billing summary is presented in Exhibit 12–5.

Patient Margin and Accounts Receivable Reporting

Because most payer arrangements shift some or all of the financial risk of providing care to the subacute provider, financial systems must facilitate financial performance reporting at the individual patient level. Contribution and profit margins may be calculated by applying the same cost-finding principles discussed in the census management section of this chapter to actual incurred charges.

The financial system *must* calculate gross room and board and ancillary charges, marginal costs, full costs, contribution margin, and profit margin for all managed care patients. Although most long-term care systems are designed for a monthly charge collection and billing cycle, providers should strive toward daily charge capture and profit margin analysis. Daily collection of charges supports both discharge (versus monthly) billing cycles and concurrent financial management of patients reimbursed through capitated payment contracts. The complex contract arrangements also require a more sophisticated accounts receivable management system. Policy and prior authorization numbers must be documented, and policy limitations and caps *must* be monitored to ensure appropriate financial results and timely payment. A sample patient profit margin and accounts receivable report is presented in Exhibit 12–6.

Exhibit 12–5 Per Diem Billing Summary

Bill Date	mo/day/yr	Patient Number	xxxx
Patient Name	John Smith	Policy Number	xxx-xx
Payer	Central Health Plan	Authorization Number	xxxx
Address	Main Street	Admission Date	mo/day/yr
City, State, ZIP	Hometown, USA 11111	Discharge Date	mo/day/yr

Per Diem Charge		
Respiratory Therapy—Level I	13 days @ $750.00	$9,750.00
Exclusions from Per Diem		
Total Parenteral Nutrition		$2,178.37
Air-Fluidized Therapy		$1,500.00
		$3,678.37
Less: 10% Discount on Exclusions		($367.84)
Net Excluded Items		$3,310.53
Total Contract Charges		**$13,060.53**

Exhibit 12–6 Patient Profit Margin and Accounts Receivable Report

Patient Data			Payer Data	
Admit Date	mo/day/yr		**Name**	HMO #10
Discharge Date	mo/day/yr		**Contact #**	xxxx
Est/Actual LOS	50/59		**Insured's Name**	Last, First
Referral Source	Hospital #10		**Insured's Relation**	Mother
Referring Physician	Physician #20		**Policy #**	xxxx
Hospital DRG	090 Simple Pneumonia		**Policy Dollar Limit**	$1,500,000
Prognosis	Fair		**Policy Dollars Used**	$500,000
ICD-9 Codes			**Policy Day Limit**	150 days
V46.1	Vent Dependent		**Policy Days Used**	60 days
V55.0	Atten to Tracheostomy		**Exclusions**	IVs, High-Cost DME
93.99	Other Resp Procedures		**A/R Balance**	$10,500
V57.1	Physical Therapy Nec		**A/R Age**	75 days

Financial Data	Current Period	Stay to Date
Total		
Gross Charges	$16,098	$32,508
Deductions	($3,498)	($5,958)
Net Revenue	$12,600	$26,550
Full Cost	$9,700	$20,822
Margin	$2,900	$5,728
Days	28	59
Per Patient Day		
Gross Charges	$575	$551
Deductions	($125)	($101)
Net Revenue	$450	$450
Full Cost	$346	$353
Margin	$104	$97
Margin Percentage	23%	22%

Product Line and Contract Management

Individual subacute care centers may contract with as many as 30 different managed care and insurance companies, and corporate offices may administer hundreds of contracts. Because there is no standard for how subacute care providers classify and contract for services, each contract is likely to have unique pricing structures, exclusions, caps, and payment terms. Therefore, it is imperative that providers develop sophisticated contract management capabilities. The system should allow for the evaluation of contract utilization, profitability, and accounts receivable. The system should also link with clinical data to

allow profitability evaluation of different products or service lines. A sample product line profitable report is presented in Exhibit 12–7.

CASE MANAGEMENT

Case management functions use input from the other three subsystems to support concurrent clinical and financial review for each patient. Three components combine as primary input: admission expectations and reimbursement rules, a patient-specific care plan, and actual services delivered and outcomes achieved.

The key to these systems is supporting the prediction of patient outcomes and the services re-

Exhibit 12–7 Product Line Profitability Report

6 Months Ending June 10, 19xx	Respiratory	Oncology	Wound Management
Number of Cases	161	261	230
Average Length of Stay	53.10	31.90	27.23
Patient Days	8,549	8,326	6,263
Total			
Gross Charges	$4,958,478	$3,829,960	$3,288,023
Deductions	($897,656)	($541,190)	($551,135)
Net Revenue	$4,060,822	$3,288,770	$2,736,887
Full Cost	$2,957,989	$2,556,082	$2,054,231
Margin	$1,102,833	$732,688	$682,657
Per Patient Day			
Gross Charges	$580	460	525
Deductions	($105)	($65)	($88)
Net Revenue	$475	395	437
Full Cost	$346	307	328
Margin	$129	$88	$109
Margin Percentage	27%	22%	25%

quired to achieve those outcomes and then providing the earliest warning when actual experience does not match expectations. Figure 12–5 provides a breakdown of key variances that should be addressed. These variances should be available to case managers for each patient at any point during the stay. The following variances correspond to Figure 12–5 and describe the content and purpose for each:

A. Patients are admitted with expectations related to acuity, standard and patient-specific outcome-oriented goals, and service levels to achieve outcomes. These expectations can be compared with the resulting plan of care to identify discrepancies.

B. After a care plan is determined, deviations from that plan should be monitored carefully. Missed or excessive treatments and/or lack of progress toward discharge goals should be monitored closely as well.

C. Ultimately, what determines the profitability of the patient case is the relationship among admission expectations, actual treatment delivered, and outcomes achieved.

BUSINESS MANAGEMENT

Multifacility subacute care organizations face the additional task of consolidating facility data into consolidated corporate level business management systems. Data extracts of interfaces to the corporate databases facilitate corporate-based monitoring and management of key operational issues, including marketing, census, labor, and accounts receivable. For example, multifacility chains may extract data from the facility referral tracking system to evaluate the cost effectiveness of various marketing programs. The data may include leads and referrals by representative, lost referrals, cost per marketing program, and referrals by product line.

Acuity-based staffing systems allow corporate office personnel to implement and monitor facility staffing standards. Interfaces with facility time and attendance systems facilitate daily monitoring of nursing hours per patient day.

OUTCOMES MANAGEMENT

As subacute care continues to play an increasing role in the health care reform process, provid-

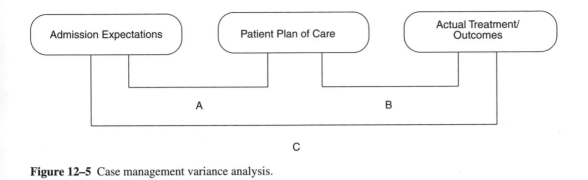

Figure 12–5 Case management variance analysis.

ers are being required to demonstrate the value and cost effectiveness of their services. Constituents are demanding proof of clinical quality tied to financial results. Complicating the delivery of this information is the need to collect and consolidate data from multiple locations.

In traditional acute care settings, outcome data have been managed by a combination of decision support and medical record abstracting systems. These systems are typically not integrated and are managed by separate departments. Therefore, for most health care providers outcome data repositories and the links to financial and clinical feeder systems will need to be developed and implemented from the ground up. This repository will need to support analysis of patient level data for external constituents and internal quality improvement programs. Data included should allow organizations to measure clinical and financial outcomes as well as provide the basis for comparing the organizational experience against market and/or national experience. Analysis will include the following breakdowns:

- product line management
- diagnoses and diagnostic groupings
- third party contracting
- facility/operating unit
- patient characteristics

Data elements collected for each of the above should support the identification of the clinical outcomes achieved, the services provided to achieve those outcomes and the related costs to provide the services. Key uses of the data repository will include support for continuous quality improvement programs, marketing to payer and patient groups, and internal product line and contract management. (See Chapter 10.)

CONCLUSION

Subacute care's impact on management information systems reflects the pressures that health care providers face from the industry as a whole. Continued development of alternative delivery mechanisms that emphasize distributed locations, along with the impact of managed care and capitated payment schemes, will overrun health care information systems that are, in general, currently underfunded and fragmented.

Systems developed to support the subacute environment must emphasize integration of financial and clinical information. In addition, these systems must support timely concurrent review at a level of detail that ensures that clinical goals are met with an appropriate use of human and financial resources. Overall, the development and implementation of a comprehensive information system will be the keys to securing a place in the subacute environment.

13

Joint Commission and CARF Accreditation for Subacute Care

Mary Tellis-Nayak and Christine M. MacDonell

The emergence of subacute care as a defined entity along the continuum of care has spurred the need for an agreed upon set of national standards against which to judge performance, monitor service delivery, and determine the outcomes of care. Subacute care is currently being delivered in nursing facilities, freestanding subacute centers (typically licensed as nursing facilities), and acute as well as long-term care hospitals. It was estimated to be a $1 billion industry in 1993 and is projected to grow to a more than $10 billion industry before the end of the decade. In the current health care climate aimed at containing costs, subacute care is seen as a viable alternative to more costly acute care services for many types of cases, including orthopedic rehabilitation (eg, total hip or knee replacement), neuro-rehab, cardiac rehabilitation, respiratory complications, cancer pain management, and infectious diseases such as tuberculosis and acquired immunodeficiency syndrome.[1]

To date, subacute care largely has been unmonitored. Although some states are exploring special licensing categories for subacute

units, the Health Care Financing Administration (HCFA) has not established any specific regulations for subacute care. Currently, subacute care programs that are housed in nursing facilities are surveyed using the same regulations. In addition, although providers may negotiate rates with Medicare or Medicaid for patients receiving subacute care, it is not a reimbursement category recognized by the HCFA.

Until January 1995, the Joint Commission on Accreditation of Healthcare Organizations surveyors had been applying standards from the *Accreditation Manual for Long-Term Care*[2] to subacute patients. The Commission on Accreditation of Rehabilitation Facilities (CARF) also has been applying its standards for comprehensive inpatient rehabilitation programs.[3] Many of the organizations applying for these accreditations, however, are delivering subacute services.

Service delivery trends in and growth predictions about the subacute industry have led both the Joint Commission and CARF to pursue the development of subacute standards. This chapter provides an overview of the new standards for subacute care from both the Joint Commission and CARF.

JOINT COMMISSION STANDARDS: AN OVERVIEW

In May 1993, an expert panel on subacute care was convened to determine the feasibility of developing a new set of standards for subacute care. The panel determined that, with revisions to some intent statements, the Joint Commission standards for long-term care could be applied, and the addition of certain standards from the *Accreditation Manual for Hospitals* (rehabilitation, physician credentialing and privileging, and respiratory services), to subacute care. Optional surveys of subacute programs began in January, 1995. Organizations currently accredited may apply for a special extension survey for their subacute program in 1995 and 1996. An overview of the protocol, which underwent field review and incorporates suggested changes, follows.

The protocol reflects agreement that the subacute patient no longer requires inpatient acute care services yet needs a higher level of care than is available in traditional skilled nursing facilities or at home. The protocol also is based on these recommendations of the panel:

- Subacute programs are currently required to comply with the federal regulations emanating from the Omnibus Budget Reconciliation Act of 1987; therefore, the *Accreditation Manual for Long-Term Care* must form the foundation for a subacute protocol.
- The intent of some of the standards are tailored to the needs of the subacute patient specifically in the areas of time frames, staff qualifications, organizational structure, leadership, and safety and equipment management.
- Standards for comprehensive rehabilitation, medical credentialing and privileging, and respiratory care need to be added.

These standards exist in the *Accreditation Manual for Hospitals* and were added, as appropriate, to the subacute protocol.

Thus new subacute care standards per se have not been developed. Rather, the protocol uses existing standards tailored by new interpretations and the survey process to emphasize the needs of subacute patients. According to the protocol, subacute care is defined as:

> [c]omprehensive inpatient care designed for someone who has had an acute illness, injury, or exacerbation of a disease process. It is goal-oriented treatment rendered immediately after, or instead of, acute hospitalization to treat one or more specific active complex medical conditions or to administer one or more technically complex treatments, in the context of a person's underlying long-term conditions and overall situation. Generally, the individual's condition is such that the care does not depend heavily on high-technology monitoring or complex diagnostic procedures. It requires the coordinated services of an interdisciplinary team including physicians, nurses, and other relevant professional disciplines, who are trained and knowledgeable to assess and manage these specific conditions and perform the necessary procedures. It is given as part of a specifically defined program, regardless of the site.

> Subacute care is generally more intensive than traditional nursing facility care and less intensive than acute care. It requires frequent (daily or weekly) recurrent patient assessment and review of the clinical course and treatment plan for a limited (several days to several months) time period, until a condition is stabilized or a predetermined treatment course is completed.[4]

The protocol recognizes that not every sub-acute facility has the same capabilities or services the same types of patients. Thus the protocol is designed to encourage facilities to be creative in developing approaches to patient care that fit their case mix and capabilities.

The Joint Commission's subacute protocol, consistent with its long-term care standards, incorporates the following major sections:

- patient rights and responsibilities
- admission
- patient assessment and evaluation
- patient care
- continuity of care
- leadership
- human resources management
- information management
- quality assessment and improvement
- plant, technology, and safety management
- infection control

A summary of the standards for each section follows.

Patient/Resident Rights and Responsibilities

Consistent with federal regulations for Medicare- and Medicaid-certified nursing facilities, these standards and corresponding intent statements convey that patients have the right to be supported to reach their highest practicable level of function. Thus these standards support heavily the notion of quality of life and support services aimed at improvement as well as maintenance of function.

Standard PR.1.1.2 states that the patient has the right to an environment that contributes to a positive self-image and preserves dignity. An intent statement to the effect that facilities will "create a home-like environment for those patients who are preparing to transition to their homes with a full resumption of life in familiar and personal surroundings" was added (PR2). Another statement (PR.1.1.4) relates to impartial access to treatment or accommodations with the intent that patients are not designated or restricted to certain areas based on payer mix.

According to the standards, the patient has the right to inspect and obtain copies of all records pertaining to his or her care. According to the new intent statement, a licensed professional should be available for interpretive purposes. Consistent with the Americans with Disabilities Act, the standards state that patients have the right to free and private communication with persons of their choice (PR.1.1.7). A corresponding intent statement was added to make provisions for the hearing impaired and those with disabilities.

The standards specify that the patient has the right to refuse treatment to the extent permitted by law. According to the intent statement, however, refusal of treatment should be based on informed consent of the possible consequences and alternative treatments currently available.

PR.1.2.20 requires freedom from chemical and physical restraints except as authorized in writing by a physician. The intent statement, however, explains that, when patients are restrained, there is evidence that all less restrictive means have been evaluated, the decision has been approved by the team, and the patient and/or family has been informed. When restraints are used, the process must be consistent with guidelines as stated in the *Accreditation Manual for Long-Term Care*.[2]

Regarding standards for transfer or discharge (ie, PR.1.1.22), the new intent statement states that the subacute program should be an environment with an emphasis on the healing process. When treatment is completed, the patient will be discharged. Other reasons for discharge could include the need for only one-to-one care, repeated injury to other residents or staff, inability to obtain qualified licensed or unlicensed staff trained in necessary therapies, lack of a therapy program tailored to the patient's needs, refusal of the patient to participate in the recommended plan for which the admission was designed, participation in activities that are contrary to medical recommendations, or exceeding physiologic parameters and/or criteria of the program.

The establishment of a patient council to assist patients in voicing and resolving complaints and participating in decision making, although a requirement in nursing facilities, may not be the best mechanism for resolving complaints of subacute patients. Therefore, if the subacute program is not within a nursing facility, other alternatives may be established (eg, establishment of a grievance protocol or voicing of complaints through a case manager, program director, or social worker).

Admission

The organization must develop a statement that clearly states the philosophy and scope of services on the subacute unit. The statement must clearly delineate the type of patients who can be admitted to the unit. Peer reviewers of the section proposed added language that the philosophy and scope must address the expected rate of progress and the final functional outcome. This statement must include criteria not only for admission but also for continued stay and discharge. Finally, the statement must distinguish the subacute patient from the traditional skilled nursing patient based on services being delivered.

The subacute program must ensure that it can meet the patient's needs. Thus, consideration must be given to qualified staff, appropriate therapy programs, physical plant and equipment, policies and procedures supporting the patient's needs, appropriate therapeutic and diagnostic support (including pharmacy, respiratory, laboratory, and radiology), appropriate support for care management, family support and discharge planning, and nutritional care.

The admission process must be defined in writing and include:

- definitions of the categories of patients accepted and not accepted by the organization
- criteria for determining admission eligibility
- information to be obtained before admission
- the procedure for conducting an assessment, before the patient's admission, of the scope of services he or she requires

- the procedure for accepting referrals
- the procedure for conducting an initial assessment on admission and for developing an interim plan of care based on that assessment
- delegation of responsibility for the initial assessment and interim plan of care to a designated member of the interdisciplinary team

The admission standards require that patients be admitted only on the recommendation of a qualified physician currently licensed by the state to practice medicine. The attending physician must prescribe the medical regimen of care for the patients he or she admits and must submit (before or on admission) information pertaining to the admitting diagnosis or diagnoses, current medical findings, the diet prescribed, medication and treatment orders, and the patient's functional status.

Patient Assessment and Evaluation

An assessment process must be defined and designed to ensure comprehensive assessment of each patient's needs. The assessment must describe the patient's capacity to perform daily life functions and any significant impairments. The assessment must involve the patient and, when available, his or her family.

The standards emphasize that assessments must be performed by appropriately qualified persons. For example, the appropriate rehabilitation professional should be involved in the assessment when functional deficits are noted. At a minimum, the subacute program's policy should require initiation of assessments within 24 hours and completion within 48 hours. Also at a minimum, assessments are reviewed within 30 days or in response to changes in the patient's condition.

The assessment includes both physical and psychiatric status and needs. In addition, the initial medical assessment includes at least the following:

- medical history
- physical examination

- mental status
- diagnosis or diagnoses
- prognosis and estimation of rehabilitation potential
- attending or referring physician's plan of medical care
- overall treatment plan

The assessment process for each patient also includes assessment of nursing status and needs, nutritional status and needs, oral health status and needs, rehabilitation status and needs, and activities status and needs. The intent statement regarding therapeutic recreation states that each subacute patient who has or anticipates a length of stay exceeding 14 days will receive an activity/recreation therapy assessment. Finally, the assessment of each patient is coordinated by a registered nurse.

Patient Care

The patient care standards contain sections pertaining to care management, care planning, care of dying patients, patient/family education, medical care, nursing care, oral health, nutritional care, therapeutic activities, rehabilitation, and other standards.

Care Management

Because of the short length of stay for subacute patients, it is essential that the care management system be organized in such a way that patient care needs are met from the time of admission. Thus care management must be an integral part of the organization's patient care program. According to the standards, the care management system is directed toward achieving and maintaining the patient's optimal status. For most subacute patients, optimal status pertains to progressing the patient to a lesser level of care.

The care management system is implemented by members of an interdisciplinary team and is designed to ensure coordinated participation of all appropriate health care professionals. One of the distinguishing features of the nursing facility subacute program is the interdisciplinary nature of the care management system. In addition, the patient and/or family should be an integral member of the team. Either or both should be actively involved in the care management process and have a role in determining the direction of the care plan. Achieving optimal function and quality of life for patients is the primary goal of a subacute program.

The standards specify that the medical director or a registered nurse is designated, in writing, to be responsible for implementing patient care policies. This can be interpreted to mean that the physician, nurse, or other appropriate professional is in charge of the subacute program. However, this person must be qualified by experience or education in the subacute program areas (such as ventilator, traumatic brain injury, rehabilitation, or medical).

Patient care policies must be reviewed at least annually and revised as necessary. When the subacute program is a distinct part of the organization and offers services different from those of other parts of the organization, policies and procedures should address the unique requirements for the care of subacute patients as outlined in these standards.

Care Planning

Based on information obtained during the admission process, an interim plan of care is developed as soon as possible after admission. Development of an interim plan of care should not exceed 24 hours. The interdisciplinary plan of care is developed as soon as possible after admission but not later than 72 hours after completion of the comprehensive assessments. The interdisciplinary plan of care includes at least the following:

- identified patient needs
- identified goals that are realistic and measurable
- approach to meeting identified goals
- specification of interdisciplinary team members
- frequency with which services are to be provided

- expected date(s) for achievement of goals
- plan for discharge

The plan of care should be reviewed every 2 weeks for the first quarter, every month for the second quarter, and quarterly thereafter or more frequently as indicated by the patient's condition.

Care of Dying Patients

The care of dying patients is designed to optimize patient comfort and dignity. The patient is cared for in a supportive, homelike environment that supports the patient's decision-making ability.

Patient/Family Education

Patients are trained in self-care as appropriate for their status. Self-care as part of the recovery process is emphasized. In addition, the patient's family is involved in the training for patient self-care. This training should start early in the subacute stay.

Medical Care

The standards specify that a qualified physician supervises the health care of every patient. The attending physician establishes an appropriate visiting schedule that complies with applicable law and regulation. By definition, the subacute patient requires closer monitoring and more frequent medical intervention than a traditional skilled nursing patient. Therefore, medical monitoring and intervention are needed to achieve optimal patient outcomes.

Nursing Care

Assisting with the management of complex medical conditions is a critical role of the nurse on the subacute unit. Nursing care requires sufficient levels of appropriately trained and qualified staff so that each patient's nursing and medical treatments are evaluated for their effectiveness. Nursing care standards are designed to meet certain conditions, including rendering of all prescribed treatments and medications, appropriate nursing interventions, rehabilitative/restorative nursing care, care designed to prevent complications of immobility, and assistance in self-care.

Oral Health

These standards are designed to meet oral health needs and require an initial assessment by a qualified individual.

Nutritional Care

The subacute patient has special dietary needs due to his or her medical complexity that require the registered dietitian to have primary responsibility for responding to the patient's nutritional needs. Nutrition and hydration status is monitored on an ongoing basis and documented in each patient's medical record. Patients who require help with eating should be evaluated by occupational therapy, and patients exhibiting swallowing difficulty are referred to the speech-language pathologist. Patients are assisted to sit in a regular dining chair when possible.

Therapeutic Activities

The standards require an activities program suited to patient needs, abilities, and interests. These services are designed to enhance functional life activities and add to quality of life. Activities are provided in individual and group settings. Patients are encouraged but not obliged to participate in planned activities.

Rehabilitation

Rehabilitation services must be available at least 5 days per week with 6- or 7-day coverage available as dictated by patient need. Rehabilitative care includes physical therapy, speech-language pathology, occupational therapy, and other specialized services to meet patients' rehabilitation needs. Other specialized services include psychology, therapeutic recreation, vocational rehabilitation, orthotics, prosthetics, rehabilitation nursing, respiratory therapy, and neuropsychology. Therapy is provided only on the attending physician's written order. Rehabilitation services are provided as part of interdisciplinary team activities by qualified professionals, consistent with applicable professional licensure laws, regulations, registration, and/or certification.

Other Standards

In addition to the above, specific standards outlining the provision of respiratory services, pharmaceutical activities, social services, spiritual services, and diagnostic services are detailed.

Continuity of Care

These standards ensure that procedures are in place for discharge planning and transfer of information as part of the care management system. The transitional nature of subacute care makes it necessary for programs to establish a system to address the continuity of care needs of subacute patients in a timely and effective manner. Thus organizations are encouraged to determine discharge criteria and to collect data pertaining to their outcomes. The organization must also define an individual responsible for financial resource monitoring, which is done in collaboration with the patient, family, and interdisciplinary team. Finally, communication protocols as defined by the organization should be established with area hospitals to coordinate outpatient services.

Leadership

These standards require licensure and certification by appropriate agencies when applicable. Administrative policies and procedures relate at least to admissions; charges, payments, and refunds; transfers; and discharges. Criteria for admission, continued stay, and discharge from the subacute program are clearly written to delineate the subacute patient from the traditional skilled nursing patient. These standards do not prescribe organizational structure (ie, the standards do not require that the subacute program be a geographically distinct part of the facility), but a description of the organizational structure and how the subacute program interfaces with the organization is required.

A governing body is appointed and is responsible for approving the appointment of a medical director who has the education, training, and/or experience appropriate to the scope of the subacute program. The physical plant, equipment, and staff must be appropriate to the needs of patients and the community served. Standards are written to prevent any health care worker from practicing outside the scope of his or her license or certification.

The leadership standards provide sufficient detail for the activities of medical staff, nursing personnel as well as other subacute care specialists. Specific standards relate to credentialing and privileging of medical staff. Among the credentialing and privileging principles established by the Joint Commission for subacute care are the following:

- Privileges may be delineated by category and should address cognitive as well as technical skills.
- Each facility must define the scope of its care and define it so that a practitioner can request privileges consistent with the scope of care.
- A facility that has a general credentialing process can apply it in determining subacute care credentials, but the privileges granted must be program- and category-specific.
- The transfer of credentials information is permissible when obtained from another accredited organization. The assessment of that information, however, and recommendations for privileges must be undertaken by the organization that is providing subacute care services.
- When the subacute program is part of a facility that does not currently have a credentialing process, the program or facility must develop one.

The standards for credentialing and privileging specify that: Medical staff membership and delineated clinical privileges are granted by the governing body, based on medical staff recommendations in accordance with applicable bylaws, rules and regulations, and policies (MS.2.1); all individuals who provide patient care services independently must have delineated clinical privileges, whether or not they are members of the medical staff (MS.2.2); there is a mechanism designed to assure that all individuals with clinical privileges provide services within the scope of privileges granted (MS 2.2.1); there are mechanisms for appointment/ reappointment and initial granting or renewal/revision of clinical privileges (MS.2.3).

Clinical privileges may be defined in several ways, including by patient category (eg, ventilator patients, ortho rehabilitation patients) or practitioner specialty (eg, physiatry, pulmonology). Finally, appointment or reappointment to the medical staff and the granting or renewal/revision of clinical privileges are made for a period of not more than 2 years.

Human Resources Management

These standards ensure that care is organized and staffed to meet the needs of all patients. For example, nursing care is provided 24 hours a day, 7 days a week. There must be a registered nurse available 24 hours a day, 7 days a week to provide care if needed. In addition, a sufficient number of qualified rehabilitation professionals is available to meet the rehabilitation needs of all patients. These individuals have been determined to be competent to provide rehabilitation services by reason of education, training, experience, and demonstrated adherence to current standards of care. Furthermore, there is evidence that each individual who provides rehabilitation services meets all applicable licensure, certification, or registration requirements. Staff are required to receive in-service programs and to attend educational programs to ensure that they have current clinical information regarding the care of patients in the subacute program.

The governing body endeavors to ensure that all professional personnel who provide patient care in the subacute program are currently licensed or otherwise authorized by the state to practice, have a defined scope of practice, and are competent to provide the services that the organization allows them to provide. Thus all organization personnel meet the legal requirements of licensure, certification, and/or registration for their occupations in accordance with applicable law and regulation. Performance evaluations need to evaluate technical skills, interpersonal skills, and behaviors that support patient rights.

Information Management

These standards were taken, with few changes, from the information management chapter of the *Accreditation Manual for Long-Term Care*.[2] Medical records must be complete, readily accessible, and systematically organized to facilitate the retrieval and compilation of information. Furthermore, a complete medical record is maintained for each patient in accordance with accepted professional standards and applicable law. Initial assessments must be completed within 48 hours of admission.

The changes specify the requirement of policies related to documentation of care. At a minimum, documentation should be every 30 days and/or in response to a change in the patient's condition. Physician's written orders must be recorded and signed. All verbal and telephone orders must be reviewed and signed by the attending physician. At the time of discharge, the transfer form and discharge summary must be completed, and the patient's medical record must be signed as soon as practicable by the attending physician. Finally, a report of progress is documented in the medical record within 10 days after rehabilitation services are initiated. In addition, the patient's progress is reported and reevaluated by the physician and the appropriate rehabilitation professional every 2 weeks for the first quarter, every month for the second quarter, and quarterly thereafter, or more frequently when indicated by a change in the patient's condition.

Quality Assessment and Improvement

These standards were also taken, with one intent statement added, from the *Accreditation Manual for Long-Term Care*.[2] The intent statement specifies that the scope of care of the subacute program is specifically reflected in monitoring and evaluation activities. That is, all patient care activities provided by the subacute program are monitored and evaluated as an integral part of the quality assessment and improvement function.

Plant, Technology, and Safety Management

These standards ensure that a safety management program is designed to provide a physical environment free of hazards. The standards for the *Accreditation Manual for Long-Term Care* [2] are combined with standards for food preparation and dining areas.

Infection Control

An effective, facility-wide program for the surveillance, prevention, and control of infection is required. Furthermore, there must be written policies and procedures for infection surveillance, prevention, and control for all patient care departments/services.

CARF STANDARDS: AN OVERVIEW

CARF is the national accrediting agency that establishes standards for organizations serving people with disabilities. CARF officially began in 1966 as a nonprofit standard-setting and accreditation system for the rehabilitation industry. Its programs are representative of five broad categories in rehabilitation: medical rehabilitation, vocational/employment, developmental disabilities, alcohol and other drugs, and mental health programs. The arena of subacute rehabilitation falls in the medical rehabilitation category and is the latest addition to standards for CARF.

Development of CARF Subacute Standards

CARF approached its board of trustees in August, 1992 with a request to convene a national advisory committee in 1993 to develop standards for subacute rehabilitation. A national advisory committee, which is the first step in the development of standards, was formed. The first meeting of the National Advisory Committee for Subacute Rehabilitation was held in 1993. The following questions were addressed: Who can provide subacute rehabilitation? How does subacute rehabilitation differ from acute rehabilitation? What are the primary concerns of consumers and funders with this new arena?

The committee prepared a set of standards that attempted to answer these questions, and the first draft was distributed for peer review. After this review, it became apparent that the field had serious concerns about the delineation between what was being proposed for subacute standards and what currently existed as standards for comprehensive inpatient rehabilitation programs. Several organized rehabilitation groups urged CARF not to go forward with the standards but to study the issue further. The board of trustees then convened another national advisory committee. The second committee met in the fall of 1993 for the development of subacute standards.

The second advisory committee identified key issues that crossed the entire continuum of rehabilitation. In doing so, it developed a new approach for CARF. That is, it developed standards that eventually could be applied to all medical rehabilitation programs. After these more global standards were developed, a distinction between comprehensive inpatient rehabilitation and subacute rehabilitation was made in terms of intensity of physician contacts, nursing hours, and mix of professional and nonprofessional staff and therapy hours.

After a second field review, the prescriptive nature of the proposed standards (ie, daily physician visits and a defined number of nursing hours per person served) was removed. Subsequently, the CARF board of trustees passed unanimously a set of comprehensive inpatient medical rehabilitation standards in three categories. These standards were published in July 1994 and were used in surveys beginning January 1, 1995.

Accreditation Conditions, Principles, and Criteria

All subacute programs that apply for CARF accreditation must comply with its accreditation conditions, principles, and criteria.[3] These focus on the person served as a major decision maker in all aspects of the program. They also focus on receiving input from the person served, ensuring total accessibility (including architectural, employment, and attitudinal accessibility), establishing an outcome measurement and management system, and complying with safety and legal requirements.

Organizational Standards

Subacute programs must also meet organizational standards, which are detailed in Section 1 of the accreditation manual,[3] that address the mission, governance, management, planning, safety, accessibility, information management system, fiscal, personnel, and personnel development issues of the organization.

The next set of standards applied is the Section 2 standards. These address the system that a subacute program has to have so that an individual can enter its system; become oriented to the system; be assessed; have an individual plan developed, reviewed, and managed; be referred for additional services as needed; and be discharged and followed after discharge.

The Section 3 standards, on promoting outcome measurement and management, focus on the systems that are necessary to develop outcome measurement systems and how to analyze and use the information throughout the organization. The medical rehabilitation program standards (discussed below) are found in Section 4.

A subacute program would then choose from Section 5 which standards would apply for accreditation. This section contains the new standards for comprehensive inpatient categories 1 through 3.[5]

Medical Rehabilitation Programs

Medical rehabilitation programs are defined by the coordinated, interdisciplinary, and integrated nature of services that include the following activities: evaluation, treatment, education, and training of persons served and their families. They are designed to promote outcomes that will minimize and/or prevent impairment, reduce disability, and lessen handicap. Subacute programs

seeking accreditation need to measure themselves against this definition to ensure a match with the standards. Medical rehabilitation programs need to state clearly their mission and purpose and must be able to identify who has responsibility and authority to maintain the operation of the program.

The CARF standards also require programs to be responsible for developing outcome systems. This has been a focus of CARF for the last 20 years. These standards address specific outcomes that should be included in the program evaluation system, including program efficiency, effectiveness, and consumer satisfaction. Also included are standards that address admission procedures and initial evaluation areas that must be covered. Another standard addresses the patient's opportunity to visit a program before admission, when feasible.

The medical rehabilitation program standards apply to the medical and rehabilitation components of the program. That is, there must be appropriate medical services to meet the pathophysiologic needs of persons served. The program must also have procedures to obtain emergency medical procedures.

The standards also call for measurable criteria for initiating and terminating specific rehabilitative services. The survey team will review these criteria and ascertain conformance with the standard.

These standards emphasize issues related to the environment: where services are offered and what staff are needed to deliver rehabilitative services effectively. For the first time, CARF standards also require that medical rehabilitation programs establish and document a system for determining the types and number of staff members needed by each discipline. The standards also specify the need for orientation and ongoing training and development of staff to enhance their interpersonal interactions with persons served.

Families are also emphasized in the standards. Programs must have in place organized educational programs for families and must have information available about advocacy, support groups, and assistance in accommodations if necessary. Protocols must also be in place to ensure the safety of persons served. These protocols need to reflect the behavioral and cognitive needs of patients.

Follow-up after discharge is a key component of the program evaluation system. The follow-up plan must be written and sent to a designated physician and/or service program. Appropriate recommendations specific to the needs of the persons served must be stated in the report.

All medical rehabilitation program standards must be met, regardless of the level of rehabilitation represented by the specific program and which category of accreditation is chosen. The following standards were written for both acute and subacute comprehensive inpatient programs.

Comprehensive inpatient programs are 24-hour programs that coordinate medical and rehabilitation services. Programs may seek accreditation in a category dependent on the licenses they hold. Programs can be accredited in more than one category. Category 1 is reserved for acute rehabilitation programs within facilities licensed as hospitals. Categories 2 and 3 are reserved for subacute rehabilitation (see Appendix 13A for an outline of the necessary components for each category).

Category 2 accreditation is available for subacute rehabilitation programs located in facilities that are licensed as hospitals, hospital-based skilled nursing facilities, or freestanding skilled nursing facilities. Persons served in these programs have outcomes that focus on returning home or advancing to another level of rehabilitative care (eg, home health; comprehensive inpatient Category 1). These individuals typically have diagnoses including, but not limited to, stroke, neuromuscular diseases, brain injury, orthopedic conditions, and multiple trauma.

The Category 3 designation is for subacute rehabilitation programs located in facilities licensed as hospital-based skilled nursing facilities or freestanding skilled nursing facilities. Persons served in this category have expected outcomes of returning to the community with or without support (eg, board and care, home). Examples of diagnoses are

orthopedic conditions, amputations, and multiple trauma without complications.

The differences in these standards involve intensity issues only. The only prescriptive standards that remain detail the minimum of therapy hours required from the core team. For Category 1, therapy must be provided for a minimum of 5 days per week for a minimum of 3 hours per day. This is in addition to the education component of an individual's program. For Categories 2 and 3, therapy from the core team for a minimum of 5 days per week for a minimum of 1 to 3 hours is required. Standards that cross all categories identify specific program evaluation measures, including percentage of unplanned transfers to acute medical facilities and percentage of patients discharged to long-term care.

The core team must be identified. The standards clearly state that the list should not be limited to those identified in the standards. Rather (and as is the case with all CARF standards), the core team is defined by the needs of the persons served. CARF standards do not state that core team members need to be full or part time; they can be either as well as on contract. The survey team will look for the involvement of the core team in all areas of decision making as well as the core team's commitment to the program. The standards do state clearly that these core team members are the primary providers of therapy services. They also state that state practice acts for the therapies should be in force. Finally, the team must meet in weekly conferences unless it is documented that the needs of persons served will be met if the conference is every other week.

Many standards address physician issues. For the first time, CARF standards now require that comprehensive inpatient programs have a medical director. The standards clearly outline the requirements to be met for this position. Organizations must have a formal credentialing process to determine physician privileges. The standards also outline the rehabilitation physician's role on the team. Physician contact with patients is also addressed. The standard across all categories is that the physician will decide the medical and rehabilitation needs of the person served and the number of direct, individual contacts the physician will have with the person served. These contacts should be appropriate to justify the need for continued comprehensive rehabilitation within the category for accreditation. Physician standards also address concurrent care, such as the need for physician medical management 7 days per week, 24 hours per day and the consultative medical services that need to be available (eg, cardiology, family practice, neurology, and rheumatology).

The standards for all three accreditation categories also, and for the first time, address the need for a director of nursing services. This individual should not be confused with an organization's director of nursing, who has overall responsibility for all nursing within the organization. The individual referred to by this standard could be the overall director of nursing but most likely will be the individual(s) responsible for the nursing services in the comprehensive inpatient program, Categories 1 through 3. This person is responsible for ensuring staff competency, adequate number of staff, and adequate staff levels to meet the rehabilitation and complex needs of the person served; developing and implementing the nursing care plan; ensuring that services are coordinated; and providing orientation and ongoing training for rehabilitation nursing. Rehabilitation nursing should be available 24 hours per day. The nursing service in each accreditation category must develop an acuity system that will translate into hours of care per person served. The survey team will assess whether the appropriate intensity of services has been delivered within 10% of the assessed need that has been established. The standards emphasize the need for nursing policies and procedures that demonstrate coordination with other services.

Because subacute programs may not be based in hospitals, policies and procedures must be written to address access to both emergency medical services and ancillary services to meet the needs of the populations served. The beds of subacute programs also need to be in designated areas, and the program should be occurring in an environment that supports a rehabilitative approach to care. The rehabilitation portion of the subacute program must be structured and scheduled to achieve maximum interaction with persons served.

CONCLUSION

Both the Joint Commission and the CARF standards for subacute care emphasize coordinated and integrated services using an interdisciplinary approach to subacute care, specify roles and responsibilities at the level of the medical director and director of nursing, promote an outcome-oriented approach to care designed to reduce the level of disability and enhance quality of life, focus on the patient and family as active participants in that care, and detail differentiation in terms of intensity of care compared with acute and long-term care. Both sets of standards were designed to benefit providers, consumers, and funders alike in the following ways:

- to provide assurance that a monitoring and evaluation system is in place and focused on the best interests of consumers
- to provide assurance that the programs and services offered have met consumer-focused, national state-of-the-art standards of performance
- to provide assurance that the accredited organization is focused on optimal outcomes for each person served
- to provide assurance that the accredited program actively involves persons served and significant others, as appropriate, in the decision-making processes that affect the planning and implementation of services

Neither set of standards is overly prescriptive. Rather, each allows sufficient latitude to tailor a subacute program to best fit the needs of the populations served. (Appendix 13B provides presurvey subacute care database forms for facilities interested in Joint Commission Accreditation.)

Because standards can change, the reader is well advised to consult the Joint Commission or CARF or to refer to the most current accreditation manuals in print to determine the standards with which to comply.

REFERENCES

1. Joint Commission on Accreditation of Healthcare Organizations. *Standards for Surveying Subacute Health Programs.* Oakbrook Terrace, Ill: Joint Commission; 1994.

2. Joint Commission on Accreditation of Healthcare Organizations. *Accreditation Manual for Long-Term Care.* Oakbrook Terrace, Ill: Joint Commission; 1994.

3. Commission on Accreditation of Rehabilitation Facilities (CARF). Standards for comprehensive inpatient rehabilitation programs. In: *1995 Standards Manual and Interpretive Guidelines for Medical Rehabilitation.* Tucson, Ariz: CARF; 1995.

4. Joint Commission on Accreditation of Healthcare Organizations. *Subacute Care Protocol.* Oakbrook Terrace, Ill: Joint Commission; 1994.

5. Commission on Accreditation of Rehabilitation Facilities (CARF). *Supplement to the 1994 Standards Manual and Interpretive Guidelines for Organizations Serving People with Disabilities.* Tucson, Ariz: CARF; 1994.

Appendix 13A

CARF Comprehensive Inpatient Categories 1 through 3

CATEGORY	CATEGORY ONE ACUTE	CATEGORY TWO SUBACUTE	CATEGORY THREE SUBACUTE
LOCATION	Hospital	Hospital* Hospital-based SNF* SNF	Hospital-based SNF* SNF
MEDICAL NEEDS	Risk for medical instability is high	Risk for medical instability is variable	Risk for medical instability is low
REHAB PHYSICIAN NEEDS	Across all categories regular, direct, individual contact determined by medical & rehabilitation needs		
REHAB NURSING NEEDS	Multiple and/or complex rehab nursing needs, potential for high medical acuity skilled nursing	Multiple and/or complex rehab nursing needs, potential for high medical acuity skilled nursing	Routine rehab nursing needs, low potential for high medical acuity skilled nursing
PT, OT, SPEECH, SS, PSYCH, TR	Should receive, determined by need, minimum 3 hours	Should receive, determined by need, minimum 1 to 3 hours	Should receive, determined by need, minimum 1 to 3 hours
AVAILABILITY OF CORE TEAM	5 days a week minimum	5 days a week minimum	5 days a week minimum
OUTCOMES EXPECTED	Progress to another level or community with support as needed	Progress to another level or community with support as needed	Community with support as needed
ED/TRNG OF PT/FAMILY	Ongoing	Ongoing	Ongoing
EXAMPLES OF PATIENTS (BUT NOT LIMITED TO THOSE LISTED)	CVA, SCI, TBI, neurologic dxs, multiple trauma, etc	CVA, multiple trauma, TBI, neuromuscular diseases, etc	Uncomplicated total hip replacements, amputations, uncomplicated multiple trauma, etc.

*A hospital is defined as a unit of a larger entity and/or a freestanding hospital.
Courtesy of the Commission on Accreditation of Rehabilitation Facilities, Tucson, Arizona.

Appendix 13B

Presurvey Subacute Care Database

Facility Name _____

Address _____

City _____ State _____ ZIP _____

JCAHO Identification Number _____

1. Ownership:

Corporate Name _____

Corporate Address (if different from above)_____

_____

_____

_____

2. Facility type (please check one):	**3. Our subacute program is operated (please check):**
For Profit _____	Within a nursing home _____
Non-Profit _____	Within an acute care hospital _____
Government _____	As freestanding _____
Other (please specify) _____	Within a rehab. hospital _____
_____	Other (please (specify) _____
	_____

4ai. Our subacute program operates in a designated unit which has _____ beds.

aii. Our subacute program does not operate using a designated unit but has the capacity for _____ patients.

b. The information on the matrix covers _____ year(s) or _____ months.

Please complete the attached matrix and return it within three weeks to:

Joint Commission on Accreditation of Healthcare Organizations
Attn: LTCAS
One Renaissance Blvd.
Oakbrook Terrace, IL 60181

The survey of subacute programs will be guided by the information contained on this database and matrix. Please be as complete as possible in completing the matrix, using patient information from the last year or for as long as the program has been in operation, if less than one year. We hope, through your participation, to collect valid data on subacute care. Instructions for completing the matrix are attached. If you have any questions, please call 708-916-5723.

continues

Appendix 13B continued

	Patient Categories	Cardiac	Post Surg.	Pulmonary	Renal	Infect. Disease	TBI	Complex Med.	Ortho Rehab.	Neuro	Other
AT	Total Number of Admits										
AP	Admissions (Total %)										
A1	From Hospital										
A2	From Lower Level Care										
A3	From Emergency Room										
A4	From Rehabilitation										
A5	From Home										
A6	Other										
B1	Length of Stay (Avg.)										
B2	Min/Max										
C	Interruption in Tx Plan										
C1	Develop Infection										
C2	Sent to Emergency Room										
C3	Expired while in Program										
C4	Other Interruptions										
D1	D/C Hospital										
D2	D/C Home										
D3	D/C Lower Level Care										
D4	D/C Rehab and LTC Service										
D5	D/C Other										
E	Payer Source										
E1	Medicare										
E2	Medicaid										
E3	Managed Care (HMO, PPO)										
E4	Self										
E5	Insurance										
E6	Workmen's Compensation										
E7	Other										
F1	Gender Male										
F2	Female										
G1	Age <12										
G2	13–21										
G3	22–64										
G4	65–84										
G5	85+										

Source: *1995 Survey Protocol for Subacute Programs.* Oakbrook Terrace, Ill: Joint Commission on Accreditation of Healthcare Organizations, 1995, pp. 16–17. Reprinted with permission.

Part III

Development

Development

14

Market Assessment for Subacute Care

Kathleen M. Griffin

The basic purposes of the market assessment for subacute care are to reduce risk and to enhance profitability. Before assessing the financial feasibility of subacute care, a provider requires answers to the following five questions:

1. Does a set of purchaser "wants" for subacute care exist in the community?
2. On what scale does the "want" exist?
3. What economic value (price) will purchasers attach to the satisfaction of these wants?
4. What costs are involved in providing satisfaction of these wants?
5. To what degree are these wants unsatisfied?

The market assessment provides information that allows the provider to determine the following: the existence and size of the market potential, a demand function (ie, a range of reasonable prices at different levels of demand), a cost function (ie, the cost of different levels of services), profitability, and a description of the competitive marketplace.

This chapter provides guidelines for conducting both internal and external market assessments. An internal market assessment is conducted whenever the subacute provider expects that all admissions will be transfers from an acute hospital and physicians within the institution or the health care system. An external market assessment is required whenever the subacute provider expects to attract referrals and admissions from unrelated providers.

INTERNAL MARKET ASSESSMENT

The internal market assessment is performed when the subacute provider expects that all, or nearly all, admissions to the subacute care setting will come directly from related institutions. The focus of the internal market assessment is threefold:

1. Assess the volume, types, and expected lengths of stay of patients who would be candidates for transfer to the subacute care setting.
2. Identify the physicians who would be attending the highest volumes of potential subacute patients.
3. Assess the forces within the hospital or within the system that are favorable and

223

the forces that would be unfavorable to the development of a subacute care level within the institution or within the system.

By determining the potential subacute patient volume, patient types, and length of stay, the subacute provider derives an estimate of the number of beds required to meet the internal need. This is a five step process.

Identify the Relevant Diagnosis-Related Groups

The vast majority of admissions to subacute settings are from hospitals. Therefore, the diagnosis-related groups (DRGs) are utilized in estimating bed need. The specific DRGs utilized in the bed need analysis depend on the subacute provider's mission and capabilities. Hospital-based subacute skilled nursing units, which typically focus initially on Medicare patients, involve a review of between 50 and 75 DRGs. The DRGs may be clustered by program as shown in Table 14–1.

Subacute providers that plan to specialize only in rehabilitation, for example, may focus only on the DRGs that reflect orthopedic or neurologic rehabilitation needs. Freestanding nursing facility–based subacute providers within an integrated delivery system may desire to eliminate the DRGs expected to require highly skilled nursing or daily medical interventions. Finally, long-term care DRG-exempt hospitals may focus only on the DRGs that tend to have significant volumes of patients who require more than 25 days of hospital care.

Define Potential Subacute Candidates

The next step in the bed need analysis is to define the parameters of patients who would be candidates for transfer to the subacute setting. In an assessment of the bed need for a hospital-based subacute skilled nursing unit, which will be eligible for an exemption from the Medicare routine cost limits as a new provider, the analysis may include only Medicare patients who exceeded a 3-day overall length of stay in the acute

hospital and exceeded the mean DRG length of stay for that geographic region.

Long-term care DRG-exempt hospitals that expect to be subacute providers within an integrated system may define candidates for admission differently. For example, patients may be counted for admission to the long-term care DRG-exempt hospital only if they exceeded a 30-day length of stay. The assumption is that these patients would have been transferred to the long-term care DRG-exempt hospital subacute provider after 3 to 5 days of acute hospitalization, thus meeting the 25-day average length of stay requirement for the long-term care hospital to obtain or continue its exemption from the prospective payment system.

Typically, after identification of the DRGs and definition of characteristics and subacute patient candidates, discharges from the referring hospital(s) for a specified time period (usually the previous 6 months or the previous year) are reviewed.

Determine the Number of Subacute Days

Two types of subacute days should be identified: the number of days that patients remained in the acute hospital when they could have received care in a subacute setting, and the number of days patients would be expected to spend in the subacute setting. The days that the subacute patient spent in the acute hospital that could have been spent in a subacute setting may be estimated from the number of days that the patient exceeded the geometric mean length of stay in the acute hospital.

To determine the number of days that the subacute patient would be expected to remain in the subacute setting, an estimated length of stay by diagnosis must be determined. The estimated length of stay will be influenced by a number of factors, including patient diagnosis, patient acuity, availability of postacute discharge options, and reimbursement issues. Typically, the estimated length of stay in a hospital-based subacute unit will not exceed 20 days. Free-standing nursing facilities and long-term care hospitals should estimate the length of stay on the basis of typical stays in subacute settings in the area.

Estimate the Market Share of Potential Admissions

By their very nature, market assessments tend to be estimates rather than guarantees. Good market assessors, however, combine objective data with their intuitive judgment and experience to develop the best possible estimate of subacute bed need. Certain factors will promote, and other factors will hinder, achieving a significant share of the potential subacute patient admissions. For example, if the subacute setting is on an attractive floor within the acute hospital and the medical staff favor the development of the subacute unit, a significant portion of the market share would be expected. On the other hand, if the subacute setting is expected to be in a nursing facility that is not convenient to the acute hospital and the facility is not particularly attractive, then the potential share of the subacute patient volume that would be expected to convert to admissions to that subacute setting would be far less.

After the identification of potential subacute days with an adjustment for the estimated market share, the bed need is determined simply by dividing the total days by the number of days in the time period during which patient discharges were reviewed. Subacute care settings, whether they are units or facilities, do not run at 100% occupancy. Therefore, to obtain a real bed need, the number of beds derived from the above process should be divided by the expected occupancy. For example, if the bed need was assessed to be 19 and the subacute provider expects to run at a 95% occupancy, the real bed need would be 20 (19 divided by 95%).

Assess Contributing and Barrier Forces

An internal market assessment involves an evaluation of forces that would be expected to promote, and forces that may serve as barriers to, the development, operations, and utilization of the subacute setting. A force that might serve to promote utilization of the subacute setting would be a well-coordinated utilization management system within the hospital. A force that may serve as a barrier to utilization of a new subacute setting might be the fact that a large number of physicians have a financial interest in a community-based subacute provider. Once these forces are determined, planning for the subacute unit can include steps to overcome the barriers and to build on the forces that promote development and utilization of the subacute setting.

EXTERNAL ASSESSMENT

The subacute provider that expects to attract referrals from a variety of acute hospitals, rehabilitation hospitals, and physicians in the community must conduct an external market assessment. The subacute provider utilizes the external market assessment to estimate bed need, patient volume, patient type, and operations that must be in place to attract the referrals from the external referral sources.

The external market assessment involves interviews with potential referral sources (eg, insurance case managers, hospital discharge planners, and physicians) and an analysis of competitors. Referrals to subacute care providers may come from a number of sources. Increasingly, however, referrals of managed care patients are made by the case managers employed by or working under contractual arrangements with the managed care organization.

Referrals from Managed Care Organizations

Surveying the market for managed care patients involves finding the answers to nine questions:

1. Who has the patients?
2. How are patient placement decisions made?
3. Who controls or influences patient placement decisions?
4. What diagnoses or problems constitute the largest volume of patients with long hospital stays?

Table 14–1 DRGs by Program Groupings for Subacute Bed Need Analysis

Pulmonary Rehabilitation	Medically Complex/ Postoperative	Rehabilitation	Cardiac Recovery	Oncology	Wound Management
75 Major Chest Procedure	130 Peripheral Vascular Disorders w/cc	14 Specific Cerebrovas Dis Ex Tia	104 Cardiac Valve Proc w/Pump & Cardiac Cath	10 Nervous System Neoplasms w/cc	217 WND Debrid & Skin Grft Exc Hand Musc & Co
76 Other Resp System or Procedures w/cc	141 Syncope & Collapse	113 Amputate Circ Disorder Exc Upper Limb/Toe	105 Cardiac Valve Proc w/Pump & w/o Cardiac Cath	82 Respiratory Neoplasm	238 Osteomyelitis
79 Resp Infections & Inflammations	148 Major SM & LG Bowel Proc w/cc	209 Major Joint & Limb Reattachment Proc	106 Coronary Bypass w/CA	172 Digestive Malignancy w/cc	263 Skin Grafts &/or Debrid for Skin Ulcer w/cc
85 Pleural Effusion	149 Major Small & Large	210 Hip & Femur Proc Except Major Joint AG	107 Coronary Bypass w/o Cardiac Cath	199 Hepatobiliary DX Proc for Malig	264 Skin Grafts &/or Debrid for Skin Ulcer w/o cc
87 Pulmonary Edema & Resp Failure	154 Stomach Esophageal & Duodenal Procedures	211 Hip & Femur Proc w/o cc	121 Circ Disorder w/ Acute MI & CV Comp D/C Alive	203 Malignancy of Hepatobiliary System	271 Skin Ulcers
88 Chronic Obstructive Pulmonary Disease	160 Hernia Proc Exc Inguinal & Femoral	213 Amputation for Musculoskeletal System	122 Circulatory Disorders w/AMI	257 Total Mastectomy for Malignancy w/cc	277 Cellulitis Age > 17 w/cc
89 Simple Pneumonia & Pleurisy AG	170 Other Digestive OR Proc w/cc	223 Upper Extremity Proc	126 Acute & Subacute Endocarditis	346 Malignancy of Male Reproductive System	287 Skin Grafts & Wound Debrid for Endoc, Nutr
96 Bronchitis & Asthma Age > 17 w/cc	174 GI Hemorrhage Age >69	235 Fractures of Femur	127 Heart Failure & Shock	366 Malignancy, Female Reprod	439 Skin Grafts for Injuries
475 Resp System Diagnosis w/ Ventilator	179 Inflammatory Bowel Disease	236 Fractures of Hip & Pelvis	144 Other Circulatory Diagnosis w/cc	400 Lymphoma or Leuk w/Major OR Proc	440 Wound Debrid for Injuries
482 Tracheostomy w/ mouth, Larynx, or Pharynx	180 GI Obstruction	239 Pathologic Fractures & Musculoskeletal		401 Lymphoma or Leuk w/Other OR Proc & cc	

continues

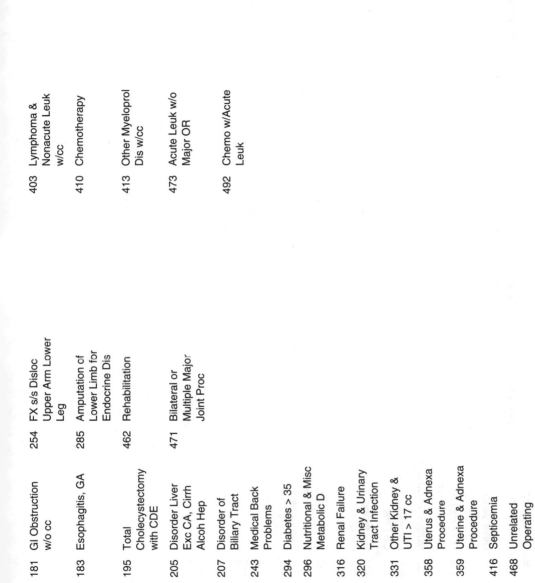

181 GI Obstruction w/o cc

183 Esophagitis, GA

195 Total Cholecystectomy with CDE

205 Disorder Liver Exc CA, Cirrh Alcoh Hep

207 Disorder of Biliary Tract

243 Medical Back Problems

294 Diabetes > 35

296 Nutritional & Misc Metabolic D

316 Renal Failure

320 Kidney & Urinary Tract Infection

331 Other Kidney & UTI > 17 cc

358 Uterus & Adnexa Procedure

359 Uterine & Adnexa Procedure

416 Septicemia

468 Unrelated Operating

254 FX s/s Disloc Upper Arm Lower Leg

285 Amputation of Lower Limb for Endocrine Dis

462 Rehabilitation

471 Bilateral or Multiple Major Joint Proc

403 Lymphoma & Nonacute Leuk w/cc

410 Chemotherapy

413 Other Myeloprol Dis w/cc

473 Acute Leuk w/o Major OR

492 Chemo w/Acute Leuk

Table 14–1 continued

Pulmonary Rehabilitation	Medically Complex/ Postoperative	Rehabilitation	Cardiac Recovery	Oncology	Wound Management
	478 Other Vascular Proc w/cc				
	486 OR Proc for Multiple Trauma				
	487 Multiple Trauma				
	488 HIV w/Extensive OR Proc				
	489 HIV w/Major Related Condition				
	490 HIV w/or w/o Other Related Conditions				

5. How are hospitals paid, and what is the average hospital payment for these types of patients?

6. What happens to these patients now relative to placement?

7. Which of these (or other) patients would the managed care organization send, and how many per month?

8. What does the managed care organization consider a fair per diem price for the care of these patients, and/or what is it paying other providers now?

9. What would it take to realize those potential referrals to the subacute unit?

Who Has the Patients?

This question is answered by first identifying the health maintenance organizations (HMOs), preferred provider organizations (PPOs), and managed indemnity plans that have the most lives in the area. Typically, the HMOs will have employed case managers and will have more aggressive utilization management procedures than PPOs and managed indemnity insurers. It is also important to determine which hospitals and physician groups are providers for the managed care organizations with the most lives and the location of these providers relative to the proposed subacute care facility. The geographic area of the managed care organizations with the most lives should be determined, as should the location of the administrative offices that serve the covered lives in that area.

How Are Patient Placement Decisions Made? Who Controls or Influences Patient Placement Decisions?

Patient placement decision making and decision makers vary among managed care organizations. Although primary care physicians are identified as the gatekeepers for HMOs, in reality case managers or utilization managers may have a strong influence on when patients are discharged from hospitals and where they are placed. Case managers or utilization managers may be employed by the HMO and operate on the premises of major provider hospitals. Alternatively, these managers may operate out of a local, regional, or national office of the HMO; may operate on the premises of a capitated physician group provider; or may be directly employed by a physician group. Utilization management focusing on minimizing hospital days and case management focusing on placement of patients at the time of discharge may be grouped together as job responsibilities for the same individual, or there may be separate positions dedicated specifically to utilization management and other positions dedicated to case management. Although utilization management and case management usually are performed by nurses, HMO medical directors also may become involved in the utilization management process.

The timing and extent of case management are even more highly variable among PPOs, managed indemnity plans, and self-insured plans. Utilization management and case management may be performed by employees of the plan or may be contracted to a case management firm or to independent case managers. Typically, the physician and family influence the discharge decisions in terms of time and placement to a significant extent in PPOs, managed indemnity plans, and self-insured plans. Triple-option payers (HMO, PPO, and managed indemnity options) may utilize the same individuals and systems for utilization management and case management, or there may be one group performing those responsibilities for the HMO option and another group performing the tasks for the PPO and managed indemnity option. Learning the systems and potential purchasers as well as purchase influencers is essential for the subacute provider, so that the operations can be market driven and the educational sales effort can be appropriately targeted.

What Diagnoses or Problems Constitute the Largest Volume of Patients with Long Hospital Stays?

As managed care organizations continue to increase their utilization of transitional subacute units as alternatives to hospital days, providers will want to focus on solving the problem for the managed care organization that yields the most savings to the organization. Most HMOs and many other managed care organizations have sophisticated tracking systems to identify long–hospital stay "problems." Providers may desire to assist managed care organizations in clinically reviewing records of long-stay hospital patients to determine the point in the hospital stay at which many of these problem cases could be safely transferred to a transitional subacute unit. This review can occur concurrently on present long-stay hospital patients and can be performed retrospectively to determine the volume of patients and patient days over the period of a year.

How Are Hospitals Paid, and What Is the Average Hospital Payment for These Types of Patients?

Payments by managed care organizations to acute hospitals take a variety of forms, including discounts from charges, per diems with or without stay limits, per case (similar to DRGs), per diagnosis with or without outlier payments, and capitated payments. Hospitals that are paid on a per case, per diagnosis, or capitated basis have a strong incentive to utilize their own transitional subacute units as a step-down placement, particularly if they have negotiated with the managed care organization to do their own internal utilization management.

Hospitals that are reimbursed by managed care organizations through discounted charges or per diems without stay limits will view the subacute unit in the community nursing facility as a competitor; but the managed care organization's costs for hospital stays are probably relatively high under these payment systems. Therefore, the managed care organizations will be motivated to work with the subacute provider for early transfer of hospital patients, so long as the per diem cost of the subacute care is significantly lower than that for continued hospital stays. When hospital per diem costs are in the $1000 per day range, even a 30% to 40% savings is significant. In areas in which hospital reimbursement

rates have been reduced through aggressive negotiations by HMOs, however, the competing subacute provider probably will have to offer savings of at least 50% or more over the cost of continued hospital stays.

When managed care organizations have negotiated per case or per diagnosis payments with caps on outlier payments with hospitals, then there is little incentive for the managed care organizations to transfer patients to another setting that requires additional payments beyond the fixed payment already made to the acute hospital. On the other hand, hospitals that are reimbursed at a fixed rate and do not have their own transitional subacute units are highly motivated to transfer long-stay patients to another setting as soon as the transfer can safely occur. The partnership in this event would be between the subacute provider and the hospital. Hospitals that are reimbursed on a capitated basis have no incentive to transfer patients to subacute providers that are outside the capitated network. In these situations, the subacute provider must become a member of that capitated network.

What Happens to These Patients Now Relative to Placement?

Providers that are assessing the managed care marketplace must ascertain practice patterns as well as potential or actual competitors. Practice patterns regarding the placement of subacute patients vary considerably throughout the country. Discharge to home with home health services is increasing as hospitals create or purchase home health agencies, but frequently patients will remain in the acute hospital for additional days to be transferred home safely. In this scenario, the subacute provider may create programs for transitional patients with short stays as a 1- or 2-week step-down before transfer to home, or the subacute provider may work with a major hospital under a management agreement to develop and manage a hospital-based subacute unit by converting empty hospital beds to skilled nursing beds. The subacute provider also may develop a relationship with the key home health agencies in the area so that patients whose health deteriorates at home can be admitted directly to the subacute unit rather than readmitted to the acute hospital.

The market feasibility study must also assess real and potential competitors by discovering where managed care organizations now place patients for subacute care. The competitors are not necessarily limited to transitional hospitals and subacute units in nursing facilities. In some areas of the country where traditional health care practice patterns prevail, managed care organizations may be transferring subacute patients to rehabilitation hospitals that have geared up to care for ventilator-dependent and medically complex patients. To position a new subacute unit effectively, providers must determine what will persuade case managers and utilization managers from managed care organizations to transfer patients to the new subacute provider instead of to the current competitor.

Which of These (or Other) Patients Would the Managed Care Organization Refer, and How Many per Month?

Case managers and utilization managers for managed care organizations handle monthly caseloads that vary in number as well as in patient types. Some managed care organizations use case managers only for patients who are difficult to place. In other managed care organizations, case managers may specialize in patient types (eg, pediatric, orthopedic, or rehabilitation patients). The market assessment must provide accurate information about potential patient volumes and types for the subacute provider to determine the financial feasibility of creating a subacute unit or facility. If the marketplace has more than one established subacute provider, some managed care organizations may decline to contract with new providers or may be willing to contract only for certain types of patients.

Individual interviews with provider relations and contract personnel as well as with case managers and utilization managers for managed care organizations are essential in the market assessment. Specific data from the records of case managers about numbers and types of patients placed

during a prior period can assist the case manager and the potential subacute provider in targeting the patient types that constitute the largest volume of potential subacute patients for each of the major managed care organizations in the area.

What Does the Managed Care Organization Consider a Fair per Diem Price for the Care of These Patients, and/or What Is It Paying Other Providers Now?

Not all managed care organizations are willing to share information about the prices that they have negotiated with acute hospitals or with potential subacute provider competitors; typically, however, they will provide information about the price range that they consider fair and equitable for subacute care and would serve as an incentive for them to transfer patients to the new subacute care provider.

What Would It Take To Realize Those Potential Referrals to the Subacute Unit?

Case managers throughout the country have become sophisticated during the past several years in managing the cost of care for patients in subacute care settings. These case managers realize that there is little savings to be had in transferring a patient from the higher-cost acute hospital to the lower-cost subacute unit in a nursing facility if the length of stay of the patient is not managed by the subacute provider. Determining case managers' expectations about length of stay, frequency of therapies, nursing staffing, physician management, clinical protocols, and frequency and types of reports will furnish the potential subacute provider with valuable information about program operations that will attract patients from managed care payers.

Referrals from Hospitals

The potential number of referrals from hospitals may be determined in two ways. First, the subacute provider may obtain from surrounding hospitals the same kinds of discharge data described in the internal assessment section of this chapter. These data may be obtained directly from the hospitals or by reviewing the information that is on the Medicare database at the Health Care Financing Administration. Second, subacute providers will want to interview discharge planners, utilization managers, or case managers employed by area hospitals to determine the potential referral volume and patient types. Exhibit 14–1 lists questions to be investigated with hospital discharge planners, utilization mangers, or case managers.

Referrals from Other Sources

Physicians, employee benefit managers, rehabilitation providers, and others may be potential referral sources for subacute providers. The ex-

ternal market assessment includes interviews with all key potential referral sources. The interviews, when completed, are analyzed, and the potential volume and types of referrals from each referral source are totaled. The total constitutes the potential market share, a number that may be adjusted downward on the basis of perceived barriers to admissions to the subacute unit. Experience shows that interviewers tend to overestimate referral volumes. Therefore, rarely is the total estimated volume adjusted upward.

Competitive Analysis

The subacute provider must assess the strengths and weaknesses of potential competitors as part of the external assessment. Information about competitors can be obtained through a

---

Exhibit 14–1 Sample Interview Questions for Hospital Discharge Planners and Hospital Case Managers

1. What types of subacute services are you familiar with?
2. Which patient diagnoses are associated with the longest stays in your hospital?
   Which are the most difficult to place?
   What happens to these patients now?
3. Does your hospital have a large number of geriatric/Medicare patients? What percentage of your patients are:
   • Medicare?
   • commercial insurance?
   • managed care?
   • Medicaid?
   • indigent?
4. Which managed care plans have a lot of patients in your hospital?
5. Does your hospital have a physician–hospital organization?
   Does it own any physician practices or clinics?
6. If there were a subacute unit developed to meet your needs, what would you want to see as far as:
   • nursing?
   • staff qualifications?
   • admission hours?
   • response time?
   • therapy staff?
   • respiratory therapy?
   • location (relative to hospital and family)?
   • physician coverage?
7. What need do you see for a new subacute provider in your area?
8. You mentioned _____ patients as having long stays in your hospital. How many of these patients would you refer to this subacute provider per month (by diagnosis or problem)?
9. Who is involved in making the discharge placement decision?
   How involved are physicians, and will they consider placement in a subacute unit that is adjacent to a nursing facility?
   Do families and geographic preference come into the decision?
   How involved are case managers (do HMOs direct discharge placements)?
   Who actually makes the final discharge decision?
10. How is utilization review (management) conducted in your hospital?
11. Can you recommend anyone else in your hospital or in the community that I should talk with, such as:
    • physicians?
    • physician clinics?
    • case managers?
    • HMOs or PPOs?
    • hospital staff?

"mystery shopping call" or by scheduling an appointment and requesting a tour. The purpose of either the "mystery shopping call" or the tour is to obtain as much information as possible. Competitive facilities rarely divulge information about their census, rates, and referral sources to a potential competitor. Therefore, the subacute provider must use judgment in determining the best way to obtain information.

Before a tour or "mystery shopping call," the subacute provider should drive by the potential competitor to assess the relationship to medical-surgical hospitals and medical office buildings, the condition of the physical plant, the surrounding neighborhood, parking availability, and access to major thoroughfares. During the "mystery shopping call" or tour, the objective is to obtain as much of the following information as possible:

- Is there a separate subacute care unit?
- If so, how many beds does it have? What is the average census? If not, how many patients typically receive subacute services? How long has the facility offered subacute care?
- What types of patients does the facility treat (by diagnosis, by acuity level, or in special programs)?
- What is the average length of stay of these patients? Where are the most common patient dispositions at discharge (eg, nursing home, home, rehabilitation, hospital, death)?
- What services/programs does the provider offer in the subacute unit or as subacute services?
- What is the ratio of licensed nurses to patients? What is the ratio of licensed nurses plus certified nurse assistants to patients?
- What is the rehabilitation staffing (eg, contract or employee, number of staff, special skills)?
- Is there a respiratory therapist? What is the coverage (eg, 8 hours with evening and night back-up, 24 hours a day)? Is the therapist under arrangements with a hospital? Which one?

- Who are the medical staff? Is there a medical director for the subacute care unit? Are there medical program directors for the specific programs?
- What are the daily rates for subacute care?
- What is the payer mix for subacute care (eg, how many Medicare, commercial insurance, and managed care patients does the facility treat; which commercial insurers and managed care organizations contract with the facility; does the facility take Medicaid patients in the subacute unit; if so, what percentage)?
- Who are the referral sources for the subacute unit (eg, which case managers, which hospitals and discharge planners, which physicians, which HMOs)?
- What marketing and sales strategies does the facility use to obtain subacute care patients? Does it have one or more nurse liaison marketers and/or assessor/marketers? Whom does the facility target market (discharge planners, case managers, physicians, others)? How does the facility position itself in its literature?

CONCLUSION

A comprehensive market assessment before a subacute care unit or facility is opened helps reduce financial risk and enhance profitability. The subacute provider that expects to receive referrals only from within a system should focus on the current discharges from the related acute hospitals to estimate subacute patient volume and bed need. The subacute provider that is not affiliated with one or more acute hospitals and expects to attract referrals from a wide variety of hospitals in the area must conduct an external market assessment. Referral potential from managed care organizations, hospitals, physicians, and employers that contract directly with subacute providers must be estimated by means of an extensive interview process. In addition, the strengths, weaknesses, and positioning strategies of potential competitors should be determined.

15

Legal and Regulatory Analysis for Subacute Units and Facilities

Theodore N. McDowell, Jr.

Traditionally, the legal and regulatory analysis for the development of a subacute unit or facility has focused on four core areas: certificate of need (CON) requirements, Medicare certification, Medicaid certification and admission restrictions, and state licensure requirements. As part of the development process, providers must examine the interaction of these core issues to develop an appropriate legal structure for the subacute facility.

With the growth of the subacute industry and the increasing integration of acute care services and long-term care (LTC) services, however, the legal and regulatory analysis is expanding to include examination of joint venture arrangements and strategies to affiliate with integrated delivery systems (IDSs). The implementation of a joint venture between a hospital and an LTC provider to develop subacute programs requires a complex analysis. Similarly, participation in an IDS expands the legal analysis to include a number of developing and unresolved issues facing these new networks, such as antitrust and insurance requirements.

This chapter discusses the core legal issues that apply to the development of any subacute facility. The chapter also examines six common joint venture models. The analysis involves a dis-

cussion of the structure of each joint venture model as well as the key legal issues affecting such models. Finally, the chapter provides a conceptual framework for understanding IDSs and the role of subacute providers in such systems.

THE LEGAL AND REGULATORY BASICS

The development of any subacute facility requires an analysis of the following four key legal issues: CON requirements, Medicare certification, Medicaid certification and admission restrictions, and state licensure requirements.

In addition to the four core areas stated above, accreditation guidelines may become a key component of the analysis as national organizations such as the Joint Commission on Accreditation of Healthcare Organizations and the Commission on Accreditation of Rehabilitation Facilities (CARF) develop specific accreditation criteria for subacute providers (see Chapter 13 for additional information).

CON Requirements

CON laws regulate the development of new health care services and capital expenditures over cost thresholds based upon various standards, such as medical need for the service in the area and cost effectiveness. Although CON regulation has been eliminated in some states and may become obsolete under a managed competition reform model, a CON will be required in many states before the construction and development of a new subacute facility or the implementation of a new subacute program. During the application and review process, documentation that a provider plans to offer specialized subacute programs often can be used as a feature to distinguish the provider's application from competing applications. The CON process can become costly and time consuming, especially if a CON application is contested by other providers.

The CON review process often serves as a barrier to entry for subacute providers attempting to develop new facilities or programs. Restrictive CON regulations have been criticized as being based on a state's need to control its Medicaid budget rather than on medical care considerations.[1] This criticism often is aimed at CON regulations that inhibit the development of new nursing facility beds or place a moratorium on new beds. For instance, research studies during the late 1980s found that states with restrictive CON policies tend to experience an undersupply of nursing facility beds and a correspondingly high nursing facility occupancy rate.[2] As a result, demand for nursing facility care in those states exceeds the supply of available beds. The studies found that, when such a situation occurs, nursing facilities have an increased incentive and ability to select those applicants who are most profitable, such as higher-paying private payers or applicants who need relatively limited care. Applicants with greater care needs, such as subacute patients, may have trouble gaining access to a nursing facility. The research concluded that restrictive CON requirements for nursing facility beds are an underlying causative factor for many of the placement delays and access problems experienced by hospitals as they try to discharge subacute and heavy care patients into postacute settings.

In states with restrictive CON regulations, many providers attempt to structure the develop-

ment of a subacute facility to avoid CON review or to fall within an applicable exemption to the review process. For instance, a provider may choose to acquire an existing facility to avoid CON review rather than construct a new facility, which in most cases will be subject to CON regulations. Other strategies that may avoid CON review include management or leasing of an existing facility by a subacute provider. Typically, the contractual management arrangement or leasing arrangement allows the subacute provider to gain operational and management control over subacute programs and to generate revenues without having to go through the CON process.

Subacute providers entering a new market also should review the state's CON statute and regulations for any applicable exemptions. Many states have exemptions for the following procedures or arrangements: the development of skilled nursing facility (SNF) beds or swing beds in a rural area, the conversion of a hospital's acute care beds to SNF beds, the conversion of acute care hospital beds to long-term care hospital (LTH) beds, the addition of a limited number of new beds to an existing facility, and the conversion of an entire facility from a hospital to a SNF.

The exemptions to CON review often become the focus of conflict between competing segments of the health care industry. For instance, until 1994 acute care hospitals in Florida were authorized to convert beds to LTH beds without CON review. Such conversions were criticized as loopholes, and consequently the Florida CON regulations were modified to require a CON for the conversion of a general acute care hospital to an LTH.[3]

An exemption for hospitals converting acute care beds to SNF beds was the source of conflict during the late 1980s in both North Carolina and Louisiana.[3] In Louisiana, a controversial interpretation of the state's CON regulations allowed hospitals to bypass review of bed conversions if Medicaid certification was not sought. A controversy between hospitals and nursing facilities over such conversions surfaced in the 1987 legislative session. The nursing home association introduced a bill that would have blocked such conversions, but the bill did not pass. As a result of the lack of review for conversions, 24% of Louisiana hospitals had developed hospital-based SNFs as of 1988.

In North Carolina, hospitals and nursing facilities attempted a compromise that would have resulted in a situation similar to that in Louisiana. In early 1987, North Carolina amended its state medical facilities plan to allow hospitals to convert acute beds to skilled beds exclusively for Medicare patients for a stay of 60 days or less. This amendment was adopted in an attempt to be responsive to hospitals' concerns about their inability to discharge patients to a Medicare skilled level of care. The original amendment, however, was rejected by the US Office of Civil Rights because it was discriminatory against non-Medicare patients. North Carolina subsequently broadened the provision in the 1988 medical facilities plan to allow hospitals to accept patients of all payer classes for 30 days or less.

As the hospital industry, the rehabilitation industry, and the nursing facility industry compete for subacute business, CON review and criteria are likely to continue to be points of controversy. Each segment of the health care industry will attempt to ensure a level playing field with respect to CON criteria.

Medicare Certification

Because Medicare does not have a certification category for subacute providers, a subacute facility must comply with a preexisting Medicare certification category. As shown in Table 15–1, subacute providers usually comply with Medicare certification criteria relating to prospective payment system (PPS)–exempt specialty hospitals, freestanding SNFs, hospital-based SNFs, or swing bed programs. The certification requirements differ for each type of provider, and the different standards will have a significant impact on the business and operational aspects of the provider. Furthermore, the lack of criteria tailored to subacute facilities requires subacute providers to comply with many inapplicable or inappropriate standards.

Table 15–1 Subacute Providers

Hospital	SNF
Swing beds	Freestanding SNF
LTH	Hospital-based SNF
• Hospital-within-a-hospital	
• Freestanding LTH	
Rehabilitation hospital	
Rehabilitation unit	

Specialty Hospitals

The Medicare regulations currently exclude the following five types of hospitals from Medicare PPS for hospitals: psychiatric hospitals, rehabilitation hospitals, children's hospitals, LTHs, and cancer hospitals.[4] In addition, rehabilitation distinct part units within a hospital also are exempt from PPS reimbursement.[5] Although LTHs and rehabilitation hospitals/units presently are the most active specialty hospitals in the subacute industry, children's hospitals and cancer hospitals also may be vehicles for specialized subacute programs related to oncology and pediatric patients.

LTHs. To be excluded from PPS as an LTH, the facility must have a provider agreement with Medicare to participate as a hospital and have an average length of inpatient stay greater than 25 days. The average length of inpatient stay is determined by dividing the number of total inpatient days (less leave or pass days) by the number of total discharges for the hospital's most recent complete cost reporting period.[6] If, however, a hospital has experienced changes in its average length of stay, the same computation can be made for the immediately proceeding 6-month period.[7]

The 25-day length of stay requirement and the 6-month qualification period raise operational and financial issues for LTHs. The average length of stay requirement forces these hospitals to develop programs targeting long-term transitional subacute patients or chronic subacute patients rather than short-stay transitional subacute patients or general subacute patients. Furthermore, compliance with the requirement may become more difficult as managed care utilization review and Medicare peer review procedures continue to reduce inpatient lengths of stay.

The 6-month qualification period has been criticized by hospitals as producing cash flow difficulties. During the 6-month period, the provider will be reimbursed under PPS. Consequently, hospitals attempting to qualify often reduce losses on Medicare cases during the 6-month period by operating the facility at a reduced Medicare census for the first 6 months.

On September 1, 1994, the Health Care Financing Administration (HCFA) issued a final rule modifying the conditions of participation for LTHs.[8] The preamble to the rule indicates that the HCFA intends to restrict the hospital-within-a-hospital model under which an LTH operates on the campus of a PPS hospital or in space leased from a PPS hospital and arranges for the host hospital to furnish most of the employees and services. The rule contains organizational and functional separateness criteria designed to ensure that the LTH is functioning as a separate entity from the host acute care hospital. The organizational standards require the LTH to have a separate governing body, chief medical officer, medical staff, and chief executive officer. The functional separateness standard contains two alternative tests. First, the LTH can meet a core services test by separately performing specified hospital services. As an alternative, the LTH can share services and employees with the host hospital and still obtain an exclusion by showing that at least 75% of the LTH's inpatient population is referred to it from sources other than the host hospital.

Although these requirements will not affect freestanding LTHs, the requirements will affect LTHs that are operating as part of a hospital system. The rule applies to entities seeking exclusion as an LTH for cost reporting periods beginning on or after October 1, 1994. Hospitals seeking reapprovals of LTH exclusions that were approved before October 1, 1994 must comply with the new conditions as of October 1, 1995. This extension is meant to provide existing hospital-within-a-hospital arrangements sufficient time to restructure or unwind the arrangement.

Rehabilitation hospitals and units. A PPS-exempt rehabilitation hospital must have a provider agreement with Medicare to participate as a hospital, must meet various treatment requirements, and must serve an inpatient population at least 75% of which requires intensive rehabilitation services and meets 10 specified medical conditions (the 75% rule).[9] The treatment requirements and the 75% rule will shape and restrict the subacute programs developed by rehabilitation hospitals.

Subacute programs within rehabilitation hospitals obviously will be oriented toward rehabilitation services rather than medical or nursing services. The programs also will emphasize the following 10 medical conditions, which are included as part of the 75% rule: strokes, spinal cord injuries, congenital deformities, amputations, major multiple traumas, fractures of the femur (hip fractures), brain injuries, polyarthritis, neurologic disorders, and burns.[10] To increase the ability of rehabilitation facilities to develop subacute and other programs, the American Rehabilitation Association has recommended expanding the 75% rule to include additional conditions, such as oncology cases, pulmonary disorders, cardiac disorders, and chronic pain.

In addition to the 75% rule, the Medicare guideline requiring rehabilitation inpatients to receive a minimum of 3 hours of therapy services per day (the 3-hour rule) significantly affects subacute programs.[11] The required intensity of rehabilitation therapy often forces patients initially to receive services at another facility to build up enough stamina for the therapy levels provided in the hospital. Disabled patients may receive services in an SNF during a period in which they do not have the stamina to tolerate 3 hours of therapy services per day. After stabilizing, the patient may be moved to a rehabilitation hospital. Such a treatment path seems to contradict the concepts of intensity and mix of services relating to SNFs and rehabilitation hospitals. From a business perspective, this treatment path often results in joint venture or affiliation arrangements between rehabilitation hospitals and SNFs.

Subacute programs must be developed to comply with the treatment procedures and requirements relating to preadmission screening procedures; close medical supervision for patients; the furnishing of rehabilitation nursing, physical therapy, and occupational therapy; and the provision of speech-language pathology services, social or psychologic services, and orthotic and prosthetic services on an as-needed basis.[12] The Medicare regulations also require qualified personnel, set forth requirements concerning the plan of treatment for each inpatient and the use of coordinated multidisciplinary teams, and establish four qualification standards for a director.[13]

Distinct part rehabilitation units within a hospital are required to meet the 75% rule and treatment standards similar to those applicable to rehabilitation hospitals to be exempt from PPS.[14] In addition, the rehabilitation unit must meet distinct part requirements intended to ensure that the unit is effectively operated as a distinct and separate part of the larger hospital.[15]

Medicare regulations implemented in 1992 modify the rules concerning new rehabilitation hospitals and hospitals attempting to exclude new distinct part rehabilitation units or seeking to expand the bed capacity of alrcady excluded units. To obtain PPS exemption for the initial 12-month cost reporting period, the hospital may certify that the new hospital, the new unit, or the new beds in an already excluded unit, as the case may be, will meet the 75% rule for the initial cost reporting period.[16] The hospital or unit will retain the payments to it under the exclusion for its first year as long as the hospital or unit actually meets the 75% rule during its first year. If a hospital or unit fails to meet the 75% rule, the HCFA will determine the amount of actual payment under the exclusion, compute the payment that would have been made under PPS, and recover any difference in accordance with the rules of recoupment of Medicare overpayments.[17]

The concepts of a new rehabilitation hospital and a new unit have created problems for hospitals and units attempting to obtain an initial exclusion. Many recent reimbursement cases have denied new provider status in various situations, such as the shifting of a hospital's Medicare status from LTH status to rehabilitation hospital status.[18]

Children's hospitals. Children's hospitals are excluded from PPS if they predominantly serve patients younger than age 19.[19] The term *predominantly* is usually interpreted to mean more than 50%. Given the patient population, children's hospitals are not Medicare oriented. A Prospective Payment Assessment Commission (ProPAC) report found that children's hospitals treat about 12% of all pediatric patients but that Medicare discharges represent only 1% of total discharges from these hospitals.[20]

The ProPAC report also identified key characteristics of children's hospitals. The three most common diagnoses of Medicare patients in children's hospitals are complications of an organ transplant, chronic renal failure, and asthma. These three diagnoses account for one quarter of Medicare cases. The medium age of Medicare patients in children's hospitals is 18 years, and this finding suggests that some children's hospitals also treat substantial numbers of adults. In recent years these hospitals appear to be experiencing increases in case complexity. In contrast to LTHs, children's hospitals serve a shorter-stay Medicare patient. The children's hospitals' average length of stay for Medicare beneficiaries is approximately 9 days.

Industry experts suggest that pediatric subacute programs should be developed to meet the unique needs of children, and children's hospitals may become the focus of efforts to develop such programs.[21] A potentially effective strategy involves a children's hospital creating a continuum of care by developing an SNF designed to treat subacute pediatric patients. As an example, in 1994 California issued regulations and reimbursement roles for pediatric subacute care provided to technology-dependent Medi-Cal patients younger than 21 years of age. The California program estimated that treating pediatric subacute patients in an SNF rather than in an acute care hospital would save the state and federal governments more than $11 million annually.[21]

Cancer hospitals. A cancer hospital is excluded from PPS if it meets the following criteria: it was recognized as a comprehensive cancer center or clinical cancer research center by the National Cancer Institute of the National Institutes of Health as of April 20, 1983; the entire facility is organized primarily for treatment of and research on cancer; at least 50% of the facility's total discharges reflect a principal diagnosis of neoplastic disease; and the facility was classified as a PPS-excluded cancer hospital on or before December 31, 1990 (or December 31, 1991 for hospitals in states operating demonstration projects).[22] These conditions of participation are extremely restrictive and essentially foreclose the cancer hospital classification as an option for new hospitals. Furthermore, as of 1989 there were only nine cancer hospitals across the nation, and these hospitals were extremely specialized in nature. Consequently, it is likely that the growing need for subacute oncology programs will be filled to a large extent by alternative providers, such as other specialty hospitals, hospital-based SNFs, or freestanding subacute SNFs.

Freestanding SNFs

Freestanding subacute SNFs are subject to the same Medicare regulations and requirements of participation as all other SNFs under Medicare (as well as nursing facilities under Medicaid). The subacute SNF is subject to the survey, certification, and enforcement procedures and the requirements of participation developed under the Omnibus Budget Reconciliation Act (OBRA) of 1987.[23] The OBRA 1987 requirements of participation represent dramatic changes to the previous conditions of participation for SNFs and nursing facilities. The new requirements of participation emphasize treatment outcomes rather than treatment process, as was the case under the previous conditions of participation. The requirements of participation are extensive and impose standards covering virtually every aspect of a nursing facility's operations.

In addition to facing the problems experienced by all providers with respect to the requirements of participation, subacute facilities must comply with requirements that often are inapplicable or inappropriate to short-stay subacute programs.

For instance, the present time period (14 days) for completing a minimum data set is inappropriate for short-stay subacute patients. There is a growing consensus that requirements of participation and other regulatory schemes designed for traditional SNFs should be modified and tailored to the different services and programs delivered in a subacute SNF.

Hospital-Based SNFs

The development of a hospital-based SNF requires compliance with three Medicare regulatory areas: the hospital-based status criterion, Medicare requirements of participation and other OBRA 1987 requirements, and Medicare distinct part requirements.

The term *hospital based* refers to a reimbursement category established by the HCFA, and the category does not depend on geographic location. The *Federal Register* defines a "hospital-based SNF" as follows: "A SNF is determined to be hospital-based when it is an integral and subordinate part of a hospital and is operated with the other departments of the hospital under common licensure, governance and professional supervision. (All services of both the hospital and the SNF are fully integrated.)"[24(p292)] The *Federal Register* also requires the hospital and the SNF to submit a combined Medicare cost report. As a practical matter, a hospital attempting to obtain hospital-based status from the HCFA for a nursing facility must show that there will be common governance between the hospital and the SNF, integrated services between the SNF and the hospital, and a common cost report filed each year by the hospital and the SNF.

In terms of the Medicare requirements of participation and the other OBRA 1987 requirements, the preamble discussion to the OBRA 1987 requirements in the *Federal Register* specifically rejects industry comments that hospital-based SNFs should have separate requirements because of differences in case mix and other factors.[25] Consequently, the hospital-based facility must comply with all the OBRA 1987 requirements that are applicable to freestanding SNFs. As a practical matter, hospitals often find it difficult to function within the highly regulated nursing facility industry.

Finally, hospital-based SNFs may be subject to Medicare distinct part requirements if the SNF is developed as part of the hospital facility. Many hospital-based facilities are developed by hospitals converting acute care hospital beds and space to SNF beds and space, and these units must satisfy distinct part guidelines. The unit must be physically separate from the rest of the institution and be an entire, physically identified unit consisting of all beds within the unit. Examples include a separate building, floor, wing, or ward.[26] The unit, however, does not necessarily need to be confined to a single location within the hospital's physical plant.

Swing Bed Hospitals

The Medicare eligibility provisions for the swing bed program recognize two categories of swing bed hospitals.[27] The first category covers rural hospitals with fewer than 50 beds. The second category includes rural hospitals with a 50- to 99-bed capacity. The calculation of bed capacity excludes newborn, intensive care unit, coronary care unit, and distinct part psychiatric or rehabilitation unit beds because the special nature of such beds makes them unavailable for swing bed use.

To participate in the swing bed program, both the 1- to 49-bed hospital and the 50- to 99-bed hospitals must meet the following requirements: the hospital must have a Medicare provider number and a Medicaid provider number (if the applicable state plan authorizes the swing bed concept); the hospital must be located in a rural, nonurbanized region based on the most recent census; the hospital must have obtained a CON, if necessary under applicable state law; the hospital must not have in effect a 24-hour nursing waiver under 42 CFR §405.1910(c); the hospital must not have had swing bed approval terminated within the previous 2 years; and the hospital must meet selected requirements of participation for SNFs under the Medicare program.[28] The applicable Medicare requirements of participation include resident rights; admission, transfer,

and discharge rights; resident behavior and facility practices; specialized rehabilitation services; dental services; social services; and patient activities. The applicable SNF requirements of participation were selected by the HCFA with the goal of ensuring quality extended care services while excluding conditions that duplicate existing hospital requirements, which require extensive structural modifications or are unnecessary in an inpatient hospital setting.[29]

OBRA 1987 expanded the swing bed program to include the 50- to 99-bed category hospitals and established additional eligibility requirements for the larger rural hospitals.[30] For instance, 50- to 99-bed hospitals must enter into availability or transfer agreements with all SNFs in the geographic region unless the SNF is unwilling to enter into an agreement. Pursuant to the transfer agreement, the swing bed patient must be transferred in 5 week days to an SNF in the hospital's geographic area if there is an available SNF bed unless the patient's physician certifies that such a transfer is medically inappropriate.

Medicaid Requirements

Any provider considering the development of a subacute facility must review and comply with applicable Medicaid regulations to participate in the Medicaid program. Medicaid requirements will vary considerably from state to state. Providers should pay particular attention to Medicaid regulatory requirements that go beyond existing certification and admission standards implemented by federal Medicaid regulations as well as by Medicare regulations. Given the scope of this issue, this section does not attempt to provide a comprehensive survey of Medicaid regulatory issues; rather, it provides some relevant examples to familiarize providers with some of the possible issues.

In the nursing facility industry, two important issues involve Medicaid certification and admission policies. Federal statutory and regulatory provisions under Medicaid prohibit certain admission practices with respect to Medicaid nursing facility residents. For instance, the provisions prohibit nursing facilities from requiring a resident to waive Medicaid benefits and prohibit a nursing facility from requiring a Medicaid resident to pay a fee as a precondition of admission or as a requirement for continued stay in the facility.[31] Many states have supplemented the federal provisions through first-come, first-served statutes that prohibit discrimination in admission policies based on payment source and prescribe the priority of admissions based on an individual's chronological position on a waiting list.[1,32] Such restrictions may hinder the ability of a subacute SNF to modify its payer mix toward Medicare and managed care patients and away from Medicaid patients. Although these first-come, first-served statutes attempt to address serious access problems for Medicaid patients to SNFs, the end result may be the refusal of many specialty oriented facilities to participate in a state's Medicaid program.

A second restrictive Medicaid certification requirement found in some states requires SNFs with certified Medicaid beds to certify all its beds for participation in the Medicaid program. Subacute SNFs in such states will not be able to distinguish between Medicaid units and other units. Perhaps the best example of this policy is seen in Tennessee. In *Linton v Tennessee Commissioner of Health and Environment*,[33] the court examined Tennessee's policy of allowing Medicaid participating nursing facilities to certify fewer than all available beds for Medicaid participation. The court found that the policy was contrary to federal law, created a disparate impact on minority Medicaid patients, and violated the federal statutory Medicaid requirements. The court approved a remedial plan that requires a Medicaid participating nursing facility to certify all available licensed beds as Medicaid beds; prohibits involuntary transfer or discharge based on payment source; imposes admission practices to regulate and enforce full certification and first-come, first-served admission requirements; establishes procedures for orderly provider withdrawal from the Medicaid program; and includes policies and procedures implementing the *Linton* standards.

An example of a Medicaid certification issue outside the nursing facility industry is seen in Alabama's Medicaid requirements for LTHs. The Medicaid requirements increase the Medicare standard average length of stay of 25 days to 30 days. The 5-day increase may be significant as LTHs face pressures from managed care utilization review and peer review procedures to reduce inpatient lengths of stay. The increased average length of stay also may force Alabama LTHs to reject some shorter-stay patients who would be admitted to an LTH in other states.

State Licensure Standards

State licensure statutes and regulations will impose standards on health care providers. Although the standards will vary depending upon the type of provider, licensure standards generally cover areas such as governing body; administration; nursing services; professional services; dietary services; social services; pharmacy services; rehabilitation services; medical, dental, and nursing care; medical records; equipment; safety; environmental sanitation and housekeeping; recreation; patient capacity; and physical plant standards. The regulations also will set forth procedures for a provider to obtain and maintain a permit to operate the facility.

Accreditation Standards

As subacute facilities strive to achieve recognition as a legitimate, distinct level of care, compliance with applicable accreditation standards being developed by national organizations is likely to become a priority. The reader should refer to Chapter 13 for a full discussion of the accreditation standards being developed by the Joint Commission and CARF.

Interrelationship of the Legal and Regulatory Issues

The legal and regulatory issues discussed in this section are interrelated, and the final subacute strategy developed by a provider will depend, to a large extent, on the coordination of these legal and regulatory areas. A good example of this principle is the hospital-within-a-hospital strategy, which evolved during the late 1980s and early 1990s in response to many of the restrictions and limitations contained in the various legal and regulatory areas.

The hospital-within-a-hospital strategy involves the development by an acute care hospital of a separate LTH within the acute hospital's physical plant or on the same campus as the acute hospital. The LTH may occupy a floor or separate portion of the acute hospital. As part of the hospital system, the LTH serves as a transitional facility treating long-stay transitional subacute patients and chronic subacute patients.

The LTH will be certified as a separate LTH under Medicare regulations because Medicare does not allow an LTH unit within a PPS hospital. The Medicare regulations only authorize rehabilitation and psychiatric units. Medicare certification of the LTH as a separate hospital, however, depends upon the state licensure department's willingness to license a portion of the acute care hospital as a separate hospital. Consequently, the hospital-within-a-hospital strategy involves the coordination of Medicare certification requirements and state licensure requirements. In addition, in many states CON review may be an issue. In some cases, the hospital-within-a-hospital strategy has avoided CON review because the conversion of beds from acute care beds to LTH beds may not trigger CON review. On the other hand, some states specifically require CON review for the conversion of general acute care beds to LTH beds.

The popularity of the strategy has led to increased scrutiny by the HCFA. On October 13, 1993, the HCFA issued a bulletin calling on all HCFA regional offices to scrutinize closely any provider attempting to establish a hospital-within-a-hospital.[34] The bulletin described three hospitals that had created a new entity designated as an LTH. The new LTH did not have a separate facility. Rather, the LTH leased a floor in each of the acute care hospitals and contracted for services with the host hospital. The bulletin suggested that such arrangements may be an attempt to circumvent the Medicare regulations concerning LTHs and the prohibition on LTH units.

The concerns expressed in the bulletin were reinforced in a final rule issued in the *Federal Register* on September 1, 1994 that restricts the use of the hospital-within-a-hospital strategy.[8] The preamble discussion criticizes the strategy as inappropriately allowing PPS hospitals to establish an LTH unit and to abuse and circumvent PPS by diverting long-stay cases to the LTH unit, leaving only the shorter, less costly cases to be paid under PPS. To ensure that LTHs are legitimate, independent entities, the rule requires an LTH located in an acute hospital or on the same campus as an acute hospital to adhere to organizational and functional separateness criteria.[8] These criteria were discussed earlier in this chapter; they essentially prohibit the strategy.

JOINT VENTURE ARRANGEMENTS

In many ways, subacute care represents a bridge between the acute care industry and the nursing facility industry. This integration creates opportunities for innovative joint venture arrangements between hospitals and SNFs or freestanding subacute providers. This section highlights some of the joint venture models presently being utilized to provide subacute services. There are no "cookie cutter" models for joint ventures, and there are unlimited ways to structure such arrangements.

From a legal and regulatory perspective, joint ventures increase the complexity and sophistication of the analysis. A checklist of legal issues relating to joint ventures is included in Appendix 15A. Although every joint venture should be analyzed based upon the entire checklist, different models will raise different concerns. Furthermore, the checklist contained in Appendix 15A is by no means comprehensive, and additional issues may be raised depending on the actual structure or implementation of a joint venture. The legal and regulatory issues that become prominent in any joint venture will vary depending upon factors such as the state in which the venture is being developed, the identity of the joint venturers, the actual structure of the joint venture arrangement, and the classification of the new subacute facility. Finally, given the complexity of the analysis, the checklist has not been applied to each model discussed in this section.

Joint Ownership Model

Under a joint ownership model (Figure 15–1), the hospital and the LTC provider create a new legal entity jointly owned by the hospital and the LTC provider. The new, jointly owned entity will be the subacute provider and could be classified for Medicare/Medicaid purposes as an LTH, a rehabilitation hospital, or a SNF. The subacute entity will be separately licensed and considered a separate provider under Medicare and Medicaid.

Both the hospital and LTC provider will contribute capital to the new subacute provider to be used for the construction, development, and operation of the subacute facility. The hospital and LTC provider also will share governance. As a practical matter, allocating control between the joint venture participants will be a significant business issue. Finally, both the hospital and the LTC provider will share in the profits, revenues, and losses of the subacute facility.

Leasing Model

Under the leasing model (Figure 15–2), a subacute provider will lease space in a hospital (or a SNF) and develop a subacute program. The subacute provider may lease a floor of the hospital or

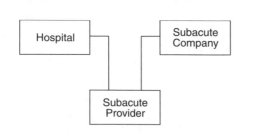

Figure 15–1 Joint ownership model.

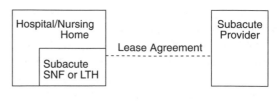

Figure 15–2 Leasing model.

a distinct portion of the hospital. Some subacute providers actually lease the entire facility, in which case the joint venture is transformed into a pure lessor–lessee relationship.

In most leasing arrangements involving a portion of the hospital facility, the subacute provider will be licensed separately under state law and will be considered a separate provider for Medicare and Medicaid purposes. The subacute provider will have complete control over the governance of its programs and operations. For Medicare purposes, the subacute program may be classified as an LTH or a SNF. Although the subacute provider will have a separate governance structure from the hospital, in most cases the subacute provider will share management and administrative services, personnel, and medical equipment with the hospital. The shared services arrangement is implemented under a shared services contract. The contract will set forth the services, personnel, and equipment to be provided by the hospital to the subacute provider and the fees charged by the hospital for such services, personnel, and equipment.

From the hospital's perspective, the leasing arrangement improves access to a continuum of care and transitional programs for its hospital inpatients. This arrangement may allow the hospital to reduce its Medicare inpatient lengths of stay and thus improve its performance under PPS. The hospital may be able to oversee, at least partially, the quality of care in the subacute facility based upon the shared services arrangement. The shared services arrangement also may produce a limited source of revenues for the hospital. A disadvantage of the leasing arrangement from the hospital's perspective involves the hospital's reduced control over the subacute services compared with a joint ownership model. Also, the hospital will not share in the revenues generated by the subacute provider, and the hospital's revenues will be restricted to the lease payments and the shared services contracts.

From the subacute provider's perspective, the benefits of a leasing arrangement include the development of a subacute program without significant capital costs related to construction and start-up development; reliance on the hospital as a predictable source of appropriate patients; access to hospital expertise, personnel, and resources; and separate control over the governance structure of the subacute facility as well as the revenue from the subacute programs. The subacute provider, however, also must recognize certain disadvantages associated with the leasing model. For instance, the provider's close association with the lessor hospital may hinder the provider's ability to develop working relationships with other referral sources in the community, especially any facilities that compete with the lessor hospital. It may be difficult for the provider to establish a separate identity in the community for marketing and recognition purposes.

Management Model

At the present time, perhaps the most common joint venture arrangement between hospitals and LTC providers is the management model (Figure 15–3). Under this model, the hospital develops a hospital-based SNF and engages the LTC provider or subacute provider to manage the SNF. The management contract usually involves turnkey management services. The LTC provider will be responsible for providing management and administrative services, billing and collecting for SNF services, developing the subacute programs, marketing the programs, negotiating managed care contracts, staffing and operating the facility, and ensuring compliance with legal and regulatory guidelines. In exchange for the management services, the LTC provider receives a management fee from the hospital. The management fee usually

represents a percentage of the revenues generated from the SNF's operation.

In most cases, the management arrangement can be structured to retain hospital-based status for the SNF. Consequently, the hospital enjoys the benefits associated with a hospital-based SNF and also benefits from the expertise of the LTC provider. Although the arrangement may dilute the hospital's control over the SNF, the management agreement can be structured to require hospital consent for certain key business and operational decisions and expenditures.

LTC providers find the management model attractive as a low-cost strategy. The LTC provider avoids extensive capital costs. As is the case with the leasing model, the provider retains control over its own operations and can rely on a predictable source of appropriate patient referrals. Some disadvantages include possible limitations on marketing the subacute programs to sources outside the hospital system and the necessity of working closely with hospital administration to ensure that the hospital-based SNF is achieving overall hospital benefits. The management arrangement also may be subject to closer scrutiny by the hospital compared with the leasing model in terms of the financial and operational performance of the SNF. Consequently, the management arrangement may be less stable than other models because continued management of the SNF may be dependent upon the achievement of certain performance criteria.

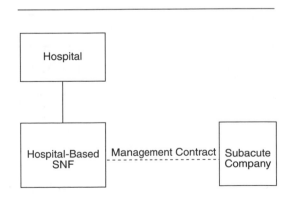

Figure 15–3 Management model.

Shared Services Model

The shared services model (Figure 15–4) emphasizes the contractual sharing of services between a hospital and an LTC provider in an effort to develop subacute programs that will benefit both entities. Under this model, a new legal entity is not created, and typically a new facility is not constructed. Rather, a subacute program will be developed in one of the facilities. For instance, a unit within an SNF could be designated as a subacute unit, and the subacute programs in the unit would be developed under the shared services contract. Consequently, one of the entities will be designated as the provider for Medicare, Medicaid, and other reimbursement purposes and will be the primary beneficiary of revenues.

Under a shared services agreement, the hospital and the LTC provider provide designated services, equipment, and personnel for the subacute program. The agreements allow flexibility for the parties to maximize the expertise and resources of each party. Although the financial arrangements under any shared services agreement will vary considerably, each party will receive some fee for its services. The parties generally confine the shared services arrangement to a specified unit and agreed upon programs. For instance, the parties may decide to dedicate 10 beds in the SNF to a wound management program. Given the need to limit the scope of the shared programs, admission criteria and procedures should be carefully set forth in the agreement.

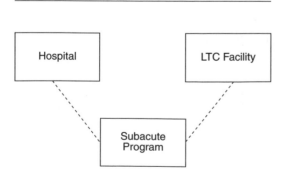

Figure 15–4 Shared services model.

Bed Reserve and Priority Agreements

A bed reserve agreement (Figure 15–5) is a contractual arrangement under which a hospital or other provider pays a nursing facility to reserve a fixed number of beds for patients being discharged from that hospital or provider. The hospital's reservation fee can be a cash payment, in kind services, or discounts on services. A priority agreement varies slightly from a bed reserve agreement by requiring that the hospital pay a nursing facility to guarantee priority placement of patients discharged from the hospital. Under the priority agreement, no beds are reserved. Rather, the hospital is given priority over other potential admissions for the next available nursing facility bed.

Bed reserve and priority agreements represent a low-cost, low-risk option for hospitals to gain access to LTC beds for their difficult-to-place subacute patients. From the nursing facility's perspective, these agreements may increase revenue, upgrade service capabilities, and avoid more intrusive and competitive threats from the hospital industry. The agreements, however, are usually restricted to situations where the hospital is experiencing extreme access issues and does not have the capabilities to develop subacute and LTC services within its own system. The agreements often will be used as a transitional strategy while the hospital is developing its own subacute or LTC facilities. As health care reform encourages hospitals to develop an entire continuum of care within an IDS, these bed reserve and priority agreements are likely to become less common or useful.

The bed reserve or priority agreement must be carefully structured within legal guidelines developed from the following legal areas: Medicare provider agreement restrictions, Medicaid antisupplementation provisions, OBRA 1987 admission requirements, and state and Medicaid antidiscrimination statutes.[35] Recently, the HCFA issued a bulletin questioning the validity of bed reserve agreements because such agreements restrict access to LTC services for Medicaid recipients. The bulletin, however, was with-

Figure 15–5 Bed reserve agreements.

drawn by the central HCFA office. Thus, carefully structured bed reserve and priority agreements continue to be a viable option within the industry.

The negotiation of a bed reserve or priority agreement typically will focus on three issues: the number of beds reserved, the reservation fee, and admission criteria. In terms of subacute services, admission criteria often become a focal point of negotiation. The hospital has an incentive to ensure that its difficult to place subacute patients will not be excluded from reserved beds. The hospital's incentives may conflict with the nursing facility's concern that the hospital will dump inappropriate extensive care patients on the facility. Consequently, the agreement should contain admission criteria specifying and defining the type of subacute patients the nursing facility has the capability to treat. The admission criteria also should limit the medical conditions of hospital patients being admitted to reserved beds. The specification of medical conditions will allow the nursing facility to develop subacute programs designed for the identified medical conditions and will avoid any problems associated with expectations that the nursing facility will provide a full continuum of subacute programs.

Managed Care Organization Model

An increasingly common arrangement among providers involves the development of a managed care organization (MCO) formed to negotiate managed care contracts with health maintenance organizations (HMOs), insurers, employers, and other MCOs (Figure 15–6). This model is unique in that the MCO is not the direct provider of subacute services or other health care services. Rather, the MCO functions as a managed care contracting entity for the various providers associated with the MCO. Providers can affiliate with the MCO by becoming a shareholder in a for-profit MCO or a member in a nonprofit MCO. As an alternative, some providers may affiliate with the MCO on a contractual basis pursuant to a provider agreement. Under the provider agreement, the provider agrees to provide specified services to managed care enrollees referred in accordance with the managed care contract between the MCO and the HMO/insurer/employer.

A threshold issue is whether the MCO should be organized as a for-profit or a nonprofit organization. For-profit organizations are often chosen if the providers contemplate generating revenue and accumulating assets in the organization by expanding the purposes of the MCO beyond its original contracting purpose. For instance, the MCO may begin to purchase physician practices, provide ancillary services, and manage providers. On the other hand, if the MCO is expected to remain confined to its managed care contracting function, then nonprofit status is often chosen because most of the revenues generated under the negotiated contracts will flow directly through to the affiliated providers. In addition, nonprofit status often avoids securities law issues associated with a for-profit venture.

To attract HMOs and other managed care organizations, the MCO usually attempts to develop a full continuum of care through the affiliated providers. This allows the HMO to provide a full package of benefits to its enrollees through a single arrangement with the MCO. Consequently, the MCO may affiliate with a wide range of providers, including hospitals, rehabilitation units, subacute providers, SNFs, home health agencies, ancillary providers, and physicians.

This model is particularly effective in situations where providers desire to maintain autonomy with respect to operations and services. Each provider will be responsible for providing its particular set of services to patients funneled to the provider under the managed care arrangements negotiated between the HMO/insurer/employee and the MCO. A disadvantage often experienced by an MCO relates to difficulties in coordinating services among the loosely affiliated providers. It may be difficult to integrate protocols, referrals, and services effectively among the participating providers. In some cases, the providers may continue to compete with each other for referrals until the MCO begins to negotiate capitation arrangements. Another potential disadvantage involves the inability of the providers to share revenues for services, as is the case under many of the joint venture arrangements.

Integrated Delivery Systems

Many of the joint venture models discussed in this chapter can be viewed as transitional steps toward an IDS. Managed care and health care reform incentives are encouraging providers to become part of an IDS. Consequently, it is important for subacute providers to recognize the structural components of an IDS and the legal/regulatory issues associated with an IDS.

The purpose of an IDS is to bring the entire continuum of health care services into one system. An IDS essentially is a managed care strategy that allows the IDS to approach managed care payers with a comprehensive range of health care services. The MCO can engage in "one-stop shopping." The IDS also represents a positioning strategy for health care reform and managed competition. Under a managed competition

model, the IDS could become a health plan or a component of a larger health plan.

An IDS involves the integration of four components of the health care system (Figure 15–7). The first component involves hospital services. Hospitals affiliate to develop a network of hospitals covering a wide geographic area. The integration process occurs through acquisitions, mergers, or affiliation agreements. This integration step is evidenced by the explosion of hospital mergers and acquisitions during the early 1990s.

The second component involves hospital–physician integration. Much of the integration activity during the early 1990s focused on this area. Integration strategies include the development of physician–hospital organizations, management services organizations, medical foundations, and direct employment of physicians by hospitals. A continuum of hospital–physician integration strategies is developing as shown in Figure 15–8.

The third component of the health care industry involved in an IDS is the financial/insurance component. Increasingly, integrated systems are developing insurance capabilities to take on capitation and financing risk. The integration of insurance capabilities can be achieved through a joint venture between a provider and an HMO/insurer or by the provider network itself obtaining an HMO or insurance license. Many IDSs in Florida are obtaining an HMO license to become health plans within Florida's managed competi-

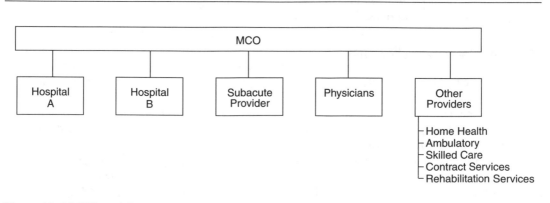

Figure 15–6 MCO model.

Figure 15–7 IDS.

tion reform model. The integration of insurance capabilities into an IDS overcomes the conflicting financial incentives in the present system between payers and providers. As the IDS moves toward capitation, all the participants have the common incentive of controlling costs and providing quality care in the appropriate setting. The development of insurance expertise allows the IDS to share the expertise of the insurer, including financing risk analysis, information management, quality assurance, and utilization review functions (Exhibit 15–1).

The final component of an IDS involves the development of a continuum of care from acute care, to subacute care, to skilled nursing care, to home health services. The IDS must affiliate with providers along this continuum (Exhibit 15–2). Many subacute providers are developing strategies to fit within this component of the IDS. In terms of the role of subacute providers in an IDS, the following points should be kept in mind.

Uncertainty

Presently, the final role of subacute providers in an IDS remains uncertain because of the lack of definitive health care reform. For instance, it is uncertain whether subacute care will be recognized as part of a health benefit package. Uncertainty also is created by the present transitional nature of the health care industry. Although the industry is moving toward capitation, providers

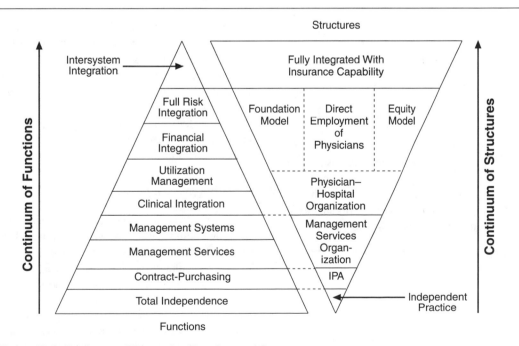

Figure 15–8 Continuum of Integration Functions and Structures.
Source: Arthur Anderson, Fall 1994.

Exhibit 15–1 Benefits of Developing Insurance
             Capabilities

Create common incentives
Capitation risk
Sharing of expertise
Utilization review
Information management

and networks must simultaneously deal with Medicare reimbursement incentives, Medicaid reimbursement systems, and fee-for-service arrangements. Finally, uncertainty will continue as long as the government struggles with how it should respond to subacute care.

Managed Care

It seems probable that subacute care will play an important role in many IDSs given the importance of managed care as the driving force behind both integration and subacute care. Consequently, if managed care incentives control the new system, present experience suggests that subacute providers will continue to be viewed as attractive, low-cost, quality alternatives to the acute care setting.

Coordinator of the System

The role of subacute care in an IDS may vary depending on the identity of the coordinator of the IDS. Although all parties participating in an IDS must relinquish some control and share control, in most cases one party will be the coordinator of the IDS. The most common coordinators include hospitals, managed care organizations, and physicians. Systems with a hospital as coor-

Exhibit 15–2 The Vertical Continuum of Care

Acute care
Subacute care
Skilled care
Outpatient care
Home care

dinator may develop subacute providers as a discharge option. For instance, the IDS could develop a hospital-based SNF as a transitional facility. In contrast, an IDS controlled by an HMO may view subacute facilities as an alternative to the hospital setting.

Specialty Niche and System Integration

Many freestanding subacute providers are struggling with a choice between remaining outside any particular IDS and becoming part of a designated IDS. If the provider remains outside an IDS, it can position itself as a specialty facility and market itself to a number of systems. The risk with such a strategy involves the possibility that the IDS will develop its own subacute capabilities, leaving the specialty provider without any strong affiliations. The trend toward full service capabilities within a capitated system seems to favor the inclusion of a subacute provider in one designated IDS.

Capitation

The development of IDSs operating within true capitated systems will be the ultimate test of the legitimacy of subacute providers. A capitation-driven system will move patients to the low-cost, appropriate setting. If the subacute industry's claim that it provides low-cost, quality care is legitimate, then a capitated system should establish a subacute level of care as one of its components.

Legal/Regulatory Issues

As IDSs proliferate, new legal and regulatory issues are being raised that will affect the future structure of such systems. In some cases, existing legal and regulatory schemes must be applied to the new arrangements generated by an IDS, and often regulators and the industry are unsure as to how such schemes should be appropriately applied to the new environment. In other cases, unique legal and regulatory issues are raised by an IDS. For instance, many providers are struggling with the issue of whether an IDS should be regulated as an insurer or an HMO under various state laws. This issue remains unresolved in many states.

CONCLUSION

The legal and regulatory analysis for subacute facilities reflects the dynamic nature of the industry. As subacute providers participate in joint venture arrangements and IDSs, the legal/regulatory analysis expands beyond the core issues (CON requirements, Medicare certification, Medicaid certification and admission restrictions, and state licensure requirements) to include complex and often unresolved issues. As part of the strategic planning process, providers must monitor changes in applicable laws and regulations. Any changes could establish new barriers for a particular strategy (as evidenced by the regulatory response to the hospital-within-a-hospital strategy) or create new opportunities. To survive the current restructuring of the health care industry, providers must be prepared to respond to the rapidly changing legal and regulatory guidelines for subacute care.

REFERENCES

1. US General Accounting Office. *Nursing Homes: Admission Problems for Medicaid Recipients and Attempts To Solve Them* (report to HM Metzenbaum, US Senate). Washington, DC: Government Printing Office; 1990. General Accounting Office Rep HRD-90-135.

2. Lewin-ICF. *Subacute Care in Hospitals, Synthesis of Findings* (report prepared for the Prospective Payment Assessment Commission). Washington, DC: Lewin-ICF; 1988.

3. Fla Stat Ann §408.036(1)(h); Fla Agency for Health Care Administration Reg §59C-1.002(63).

4. 42 CFR §412.23.

5. 42 CFR §412.25 and §412.29.

6. 42 CFR §412.23(e)(i).

7. 42 CFR §412.23(e)(ii).

8. 59 *Federal Register* 45330–01.

9. 42 CFR §412.23(b).

10. 42 CFR §412.23(b)(2).

11. Gill H. Strategies for Providing Subacute Care. Presented at the American Association of Homes for the Aging 22nd Spring Legislative/Management Conference; March 15, 1994; Washington, DC.

12. 42 CFR §412.23(b)(3), (4).

13. 42 CFR §412.23(b)(5), (6), (7).

14. 42 CFR §412.29.

15. 42 CFR §412.25.

16. 42 CFR §412.23(b)(8); 42 CFR §412.30.

17. 42 CFR §412.130.

18. Wynn B, Zollar C. PPS Excluded Hospitals—Current Payment Issues. Presented at the 15th Annual Institute on Medicare and Medicaid Payment Issues; March 16–18, 1994; Baltimore, Md.

19. 42 CFR §412.25(d).

20. Prospective Payment Assessment Commission. *Interim Report on Payment Reform for PPS-Excluded Facilities.* Washington, DC: Prospective Payment Assessment Commission; 1992. Cong Rep C-92-05.

21. Lellis M. Tapping into the undeveloped market niche of pediatric subacute care. *Natl Rep Subacute Care.* 1994;2:2–3.

22. 42 CFR §412.23(f).

23. Omnibus Budget Reconciliation Act of 1987. PL 100-203.

24. McDowell TN. The subacute patient: Hospital responses to the challenge. *J Health Hosp Law.* 1990;23:289–294.

25. 54 *Federal Register* 5316 at 5318.

26. Health Care Financing Administration. *Skilled Nursing Facility Manual* (section 201.1), Washington, DC: Health Care Financing Administration, 1989.

27. 42 CFR §482.66.

28. 42 CFR §482.66(a)(1–5), (b).

29. 47 *Federal Register* 31518 at 31520.

30. 42 CFR §482.66(a)(6), (7).

31. 42 USC §1320a–7b(d); 42 CFR §483.12(d).

32. Connecticut Gen Stat Ann §19A-533; Ohio Rev Code Ann §74.42.055.

33. *Linton v Tennessee Commissioner of Health and Environment*, US District Court, MD of Tenn No 3-87-0941, July 5, 1990.

34. Department of Health and Human Services, Deputy Director, Bureau of Policy Development. *Circumvention of PPS-Exclusion Criteria.* Washington, DC: Department of Health and Human Services; 1993. Ref No FQA-812.

35. McDowell TN. Subacute care providers: Filling a treatment gap. In: Gosfield A, ed. *1992 Health Law Handbook.* New York, NY: Clark Boardman Callaghan; 1992:173–204.

Appendix 15A

Checklist of Legal Issues Concerning Joint Ventures

Federal Tax Exemption Issues

- *Applicability:* Applies if one of the joint venture participants is a 501(c)(3) tax exempt organization
- *Private inurement:*
  1. 501(c)(3) qualification that no part of the net earnings of the organization inures to the benefit of any private shareholder or individual.
  2. Restricts inurement of an organization's assets to an insider.
  3. In essence, the prohibition means that an insider cannot pocket the organization's funds except as reasonable payment for goods or services.
  4. The existence of any private inurement may jeopardize tax exempt status.
- *Private benefit:*
  1. The organization must be organized and operated to serve a public rather than a private interest.
  2. Broader in scope than private inurement prohibition, but not as strict as private inurement prohibition.

  3. Private benefit of an arrangement must be incidental to the accomplishment of the organization's larger exempt purposes.
  4. Private benefit requires a balancing of the public and the private interests served by a given activity.
- *Unrelated business income (UBI) tax:*
  1. The Internal Revenue Service (IRS) recognizes that exempt organizations may engage in business activities that are unrelated to their exempt functions; generally, the income from such activities is taxed.
  2. IRC §512 establishes three conditions that must be satisfied for such income to be subject to the UBI tax:
     —The income is from a trade or business.
     —The trade or business is regularly carried on by the organization.
     —The trade or business is not substantially related to the organization's performance of its exempt function.

252

- *Use of taxable subsidiaries (attribution):*
  1. The issue is whether activities of the taxable subsidiary will be attributed to the parent, thereby jeopardizing the parent's exempt status.
  2. Hands-off approach: The parent and subsidiary must be seen as separate entities from an organizational and operational standpoint.
- *Key sources for a joint venture analysis:*
  1. General Counsel Memorandum (GCM) 39005 (June 28, 1983; joint venture arrangement)
  2. GCM 39732 (November 4, 1987; joint ownership arrangement)
  3. GCM 39862 (December 2, 1991; hospital–physician revenue stream joint ventures)
  4. GCM 39598 (December 8, 1986; lease arrangement and use of subsidiary issue)
  5. GCM 37789 (December 18, 1978; lease arrangement)
  6. Rev Rule 73-313 (lease arrangement)
  7. Private Letter Ruling 8629045 (loan arrangement)
  8. Private Letter Ruling 9204033 (January 24, 1992; management contract)
  9. GCM 39646 (July 13, 1987; use of subsidiary issue)
  10. IDS rulings:
      —Friendly Hills
      —Facey Foundation
      —Billings Clinic
      —Harriman Jones
      —Rockford

Tax Exempt Financing

- *Applicability:*
  1. Applies if one of the joint venture participants is a 501(c)(3) tax exempt organization and the joint venture partici-

pants want to use tax exempt bonds to finance the joint venture.
  2. Nonprofit organizations generally are able to utilize the proceeds from tax exempt bonds, which substantially reduces borrowing costs. The lower rates on borrowing lower the cost of capital and increase the investment in plant and equipment by nonprofit organizations.
  3. Joint venture arrangements with a for-profit entity often will restrict the tax exempt organization's ability to utilize tax exempt bond financing.
- *Use of proceeds restriction:*
  1. The Tax Reform Act of 1986 imposed new restrictions on the issuance of bonds to finance 501(c)(3) facilities.
  2. Bonds issued for an exempt organization must be qualified 501(c)(3) bonds.
  3. Ninety-five percent of the proceeds must be used to provide the facility, and the other 5% will be available to pay other nonqualifying costs.
  4. This restriction often restricts availability of bond financing for joint ventures with a for-profit entity.
- *Rev Proc 90-13:*
  1. If tax exempt bonds are available and utilized for a joint venture that involves a management contract, Rev Proc 90-13 contains restrictions on the terms of the management contract and the governance of the joint venture entity.
  2. If tax exempt bonds are available and used for a transaction and the new organization has contracts with independent contractor physicians, then the Rev Proc 90-13 contains certain restrictions on the contracts and on the governance of the joint venture entity.
- *IR-90-60 (April 3, 1990):* IRS publication warning as to three potentially abusive acquisition transactions relating to health care

facilities financed with tax exempt bonds:

1. One transaction involved a charitable organization acquiring a nursing facility or a hospital with the proceeds of tax exempt bonds.
2. A second scenario involved a charitable organization leasing or selling a facility that was financed with the proceeds of tax exempt bonds.
3. A third scenario involved a private entity selling an unprofitable facility to a charitable organization.

Medicare/Medicaid Antifraud and Abuse Statutes

- *Applicability:* Applies if there are referrals among the participants or from the participants to the joint venture entity.
- *Prohibition (42 USC §1320a-7b):*
  1. Prohibits the offering or paying of any remuneration (eg, any benefit) intended to induce the referral of Medicare or Medicaid business.
  2. Prohibits the solicitation or receipt of any remuneration that is in return for the referral of Medicare or Medicaid business.
- *Case law interpreting the statute:*
  1. *United States v Perlstein*, 632 F2d 661 (6th Cir 1980)
  2. *United States v Ruttenberg*, 625 F2d 173 (7th Cir 1980)
  3. *United States v Greber*, 760 F2d 68 (3d Cir 1985), *cert denied*, 474 US 988 (1985)
  4. *United States v Lipkis*, 770 F2d 1447 (9th Cir 1985)
  5. *United States v Bay State Ambulance and Hospital Rental Service, Inc*, 874 F2d 20 (1st Cir 1989)
  6. *United States v Kats*, 871 F2d 105 (9th Cir 1989)
  7. *Polk County, Texas v Peters*, DC E Texas, 9:92CV45 (August 28, 1992)

8. *Inspector General v Hanlester Network* (Initial Decision, Case No C-186 through C-192, C-208, C-213, March 1, 1991); (Department Appeals Board, Dec No 1275, September 18, 1991); (Administrative Law Judge [ALJ] Decision on Remand No CR181, March 10, 1992); (Departmental Appeals Board, Dec 1347, July 24, 1992); (Summary Judgment in favor of Department of Health and Human Services by Federal District Court, DC C Calif, No CV-92-4552 WGR, February 10, 1993)

- *Safe harbor regulations:*
  1. Final regulations published in the *Federal Register* on July 29, 1991 (56 *Federal Register* 35952).
  2. Interim final rule for managed care plans published in the *Federal Register* on November 5, 1992 (57 *Federal Register* 52723).
  3. Proposed regulations published in the *Federal Register* on September 21, 1993 (58 *Federal Register* 49008–01).
  4. Final safe harbors address investment interests (eg, joint ventures), space rentals, equipment rentals, personal services and management contracts, sale of physician practices, referral services, warranties, discounts, employment arrangements, group purchasing organizations, waiver of beneficiary coinsurance and deductibles, and managed care plans.
  5. Proposed safe harbors would add provisions covering additional investment interests, practitioner recruitment, obstetric malpractice insurance subsidies, referral agreements for specialty services, and cooperative hospital service organizations.

- *Fraud alerts, reports, and informal guidance:*
  1. Office of Inspector General (OIG) fraud alert: Joint venture arrangements
  2. OIG, Department of Health and Human Services report on financial arrange-

ment between physicians and health care businesses (OAI-12-88-01410; May 1, 1989)

3. Florida Health Care Cost Containment Board joint venture study report (1991)
4. OIG fraud alert: Hospital incentives to physicians (May 1992)
5. Settlement agreement between OIG and Semi-Valley Hospital and Healthcare Services (joint venture settlement)
6. OIG fraud alert: Routine waiver of copayments or deductibles under Medicare Part B
7. OIG management advisory report to the HCFA on financial arrangements between hospitals and hospital-based physicians
8. OIG fraud alert: Prescription drug marketing

Ethics in Patient Referrals Act (the "Stark Prohibition"; 42 USC §1395nn)

- *Applicability:*
  1. Applies if joint venture entity provides designated health services.
  2. Applies if the referral-source physician has a financial relationship with the entity.
     —Financial relationship includes an ownership or investment interest.
     —Financial relationship includes a compensation arrangement.
- *Prohibition:* Prohibits physicians having a financial relationship with an entity providing designated health services from making Medicare/Medicaid referrals to the entity.
- *Designated health services:*
  1. Clinical laboratory services
  2. Physical therapy services
  3. Occupational therapy services
  4. Radiology or other diagnostic services
  5. Radiation therapy services
  6. Durable medical equipment

7. Parenteral and enteral nutrients, equipment, and supplies
8. Prosthetics, orthotics, and prosthetic devices
9. Home health services
10. Outpatient prescription drugs
11. Inpatient and outpatient hospital services

- *Exceptions:* The statute contains various exceptions to the prohibition.

State Self-Referral Restrictions

- *Applicability:* Many states have prohibitions similar to the Stark Prohibition.
- *Examples:* Georgia Patient Self-Referral Act of 1993; Florida Patient Self-Referral Act of 1992.

Antitrust

- *Applicability:* Antitrust restrictions probably apply to joint activities that capture a large percentage of the market share and to negotiation activity relating to managed care contracts.
  1. Price fixing
  2. Group boycotts
  3. Joint ventures
  4. Monopolization
- *Resources:* Given the extensive nature of an antitrust analysis, the reader should refer to resources such as:
  1. Mots W, Leibenluft R. Antitrust applications of managed care contracting. In: American Association of Homes and Services for the Aging, Ernst & Young, eds. *Dare To Discover Managed Care.* Washington, DC: American Association of Homes and Services for the Aging and Ernst & Young LLP; 1994.
  2. Miles J. Healthcare antitrust issues. In: Gosfield A, ed. *1989 Health Law Handbook.* Philadelphia, Pa: Clark Boardman Callaghan; 1989:547–608.

Medicare/Medicaid Reimbursement

- *Applicability:* Applies to joint ventures that will be providing health care services.
- *Goal:* Maximize reimbursement opportunities.
- *Example:* Joint ownership of a SNF by a hospital and an LTC provider will disqualify the SNF from obtaining hospital-based status.

CON (See Text Discussion)

Medicare Certification (See Text Discussion)

Medicaid Certification and Admission Requirements (See Text Discussion)

State Licensure (See Text Discussion)

Corporate Practice of Medicine

- *Applicability:* Applies if the joint venture intends to employ or engage physicians as independent contractors.
- *Prohibitions:*
  1. The traditional rule is that a corporation, because of its nonpersonal nature, cannot meet the qualifications of a state medical licensure statute and therefore may not practice medicine.
  2. Under this traditional doctrine, a corporation may be deemed to be practicing medicine by hiring licensed physicians as employees.
  3. Presently, the doctrine is unenforced in many states as a practical matter and is criticized as outmoded.
  4. In many states it remains a danger, however.
- *Avoidance of the corporation practice of medicine doctrine:*
  1. Nonprofit exemptions in many states
  2. Professional corporations

3. Independent contractor status
4. Other arrangements with low risk

Employee Benefits/Pension Plans

- *Applicability:* Each participant should analyze the effect of the joint venture on its own employees and on the employee benefits and pension plans of any employees who are being shifted to the new joint venture entity.

Securities Laws

- *Applicability:* Applies if the joint venture entity is a for-profit corporation.
- *Requirements:*
  1. Unless an exemption can be found, securities laws will require registration of securities to be offered to the joint venture participants and will have reporting requirements.
  2. In most cases, registration requirements are costly and time consuming.
- *Goal:* Structure the joint venture arrangement to fall within an exemption to registration requirements under federal and state securities laws.

Liability Issues

- *Applicability:* Applies to most joint venture arrangements.
- *Issues:*
  1. Allocation of liabilities among the parties
  2. Appropriate insurance
  3. Indemnification provisions

Disclosure and Confidentiality Requirements

- *Applicability:* Disclosure and confidentiality requirements will apply to areas such as:

1. Medical records
2. Confidential information and trade secrets

Insurance Regulations

- *Applicability:* These regulations are becoming an issue for MCO models and IDSs.
- *Issues:*
  1. Whether the MCO, which operates as mediator between providers and HMOs/insurers, is required to be licensed as an HMO or an insurer because it is taking on financial risk.
  2. Whether the MCO will be regulated as a third party administrator or claims administrator.
  3. Risks become greater if the MCO begins to take on capitation risks.

Contractual Issues

- *Applicability:* All joint venture models will involve contracts.

Other Issues

16

Financial Feasibility for Subacute Providers

Allwyn J. Baptist and Jerome R. Serwa

Once it is determined that sufficient demand exists for subacute beds, the logical next step is to determine whether the establishment of a subacute unit is financially viable. This chapter describes the numerous factors that should be considered when a financial analysis is performed, explains the interrelationship among these factors, and provides examples of the financial models used to perform this analysis.

The objectives of a financial feasibility study are to translate the assumptions contained in the demand analysis into financial information and to project the revenue, expense, and cash flow streams over a period of time (typically 5 years). The focus of the financial analysis is projecting the incremental revenues and incremental expenses that the health care facility will experience by establishing the subacute unit. It should be based on stated assumptions that management believes are reasonable. This projection provides management with some basis for deciding whether to proceed with establishing the subacute unit.

As explained in previous chapters, subacute care can be provided in a variety of settings. These include hospital-based units, freestanding units, long-term care hospitals, rehabilitation

hospitals and units, or swing bed programs. The specific work steps for performing a financial feasibility analysis will vary depending on the specific setting in which subacute care is being provided. The overall approach to analyzing the financial feasibility of providing these services is essentially the same, however.

For the purposes of this chapter, a hospital-based skilled nursing facility (HB/SNF) is analyzed. During the analysis of an HB/SNF, it is important to understand that profitability is derived from two sources: HB/SNF operations and decreases in hospital costs and contractual allowances due to reduced length of stay (LOS). The terms used in this chapter are intended for the lay person and may not be consistent with terms contained in the American Institute of Certified Public Accountants' (AICPA) *Guide for Prospective Financial Statements*.[1] Any accountant compiling, examining, or performing agreed upon procedures to prospective financial statements for third party use should refer to the AICPA guide.

ASSUMPTIONS FROM DEMAND STUDY

The starting point for any financial feasibility study is the report on the demand analysis. This document should provide answers to a number of questions, such as: How many beds will the unit contain? How quickly will the unit be filled? What is the expected mix of patients on the unit? What will be the average stabilized occupancy level for the unit? What types of services will be provided on the unit? What is the price that the unit will charge for these services? Will the unit be housed in a hospital-based or freestanding setting?

The person performing the financial feasibility study should carefully review the demand analysis and extract from it all information that could affect the financial analysis. A detailed listing of assumptions derived from the demand analysis should be prepared. Sometimes these assumptions may be in the form of ranges, indicating that more than one financial scenario will need to be tested. All assumptions normally derived from the demand analysis are detailed below.

ADDITIONAL ASSUMPTIONS FROM MANAGEMENT

There are a number of additional factors that will drive incremental revenues and incremental expenses. Many of these factors are not found in the demand analysis and therefore have to be listed and reviewed with management. These include the following:

- What is the expected staffing for the unit, given the programs or services that will be provided in the unit?
- What are the staffing salary levels?
- What are the supplies that will be needed for the unit?
- Where will the unit be located, within the hospital or outside the hospital?
- What are the renovation costs for establishing the unit?
- What services will be moved from the existing space, and where will these services be transferred?
- How much space will the unit occupy?
- Will the unit be Medicare certified, and, if so, will it qualify for the 3-year exemption period under the Medicare skilled nursing unit rules?
- Will the unit be Medicaid-certified?
- What are managed care payment rates in the area?

Once answers to these questions are obtained through discussions with management, the next step is to attach dollars and cents to the various assumptions, incorporate these in a logical fashion into a computer model, and determine the results under various scenarios for the desired 5-year period. Some of the individual factors that drive a financial feasibility study are now examined in more detail.

SERVICE DEMAND STATISTICS

Most of the following factors should be contained in the demand analysis report (Table 16–1).

Number of Admissions

The number of admissions from internal sources (hospital discharges) and external sources (other hospitals and nursing facilities) should have been considered in the market study. The ramp-up period (monthly build-up) of these admissions should also be contained in the study. With this information, and through discussions with management, the projected number of admissions for the 5-year period should be determined.

Average Length of Stay

The market study should have provided a range for the estimated average length of stay (ALOS) on the subacute unit. Where there is more than one service being provided, it may be necessary to determine a weighted ALOS for the unit. As can be seen from Table 16–1, the ALOS is usually higher in the first year, when the program is getting off the ground. Thereafter, it stabilizes to within a relatively narrow range. Once again, this item needs to be discussed and agreed upon with management.

Table 16–1 Service Demand Analysis

Service Demand Statistics	Year 1*	Year 2	Year 3	Year 4	Year 5
Number of admissions	144	230	263	263	263
ALOS	35	27	25	25	25
Total patient days	5040	6210	6575	6575	6575
Occupancy percentage (assuming 20-bed unit)	70.00%	85.07%	90.07%	90.07%	90.07%
Financial payer mix					
Medicare	80.00%	75.00%	70.00%	65.00%	60.00%
Managed care	10.00%	15.00%	20.00%	25.00%	30.00%
Other	10.00%	10.00%	10.00%	10.00%	10.00%
	100.00%	100.00%	100.00%	100.00%	100.00%
Patient days by financial payer					
Medicare	4032	4658	4603	4274	3945
Managed care	504	932	1315	1644	1973
Other	504	621	658	658	658
	5040	6210	6575	6575	6575
Admissions by financial payer					
Medicare	115	173	184	171	158
Managed care	14	35	53	66	79
Other	14	23	26	26	26
	144	230	263	263	263

*360 days in year 1.

Occupancy

Occupancy is calculated based on the number of admissions multiplied by the ALOS and divided by the total available days. After the first year or two, when occupancy in the unit is building up, the average occupancy typically should stabilize in the 85% to 90% range. This assumes that the demand analysis was prepared using a sound methodology and approach.

Financial Payer Mix

The estimated number of Medicare, Medicaid, managed care, and other patients should have been identified in the market study. Many of these units start up with a heavy Medicare percentage during the early years, after which the percentage of managed care patients increases. One of the reasons is that, during the first 3 full years, plus the initial stub period, the subacute units can generally qualify for full cost reimbursement from Medicare under the exemption rules (see Chapter

4). Some of the national subacute companies are currently experiencing managed care percentages in the 40% to 50% range. In fact, their major emphasis is managed care as opposed to Medicare once they achieve stabilized occupancy in the unit. In Table 16–1, the Medicaid and other patients have been grouped together. The financial payer mix percentages have been used to derive the patient days and admissions by financial payer class in Table 16–1.

Types of Services Provided

The types of services provided on the subacute unit will drive both staffing levels and service volume levels, particularly for ancillary services. These issues are addressed later in the chapter.

DIRECT SALARY COST

The direct salary cost (Table 16–2) is derived by estimating the average number and mix of

Table 16–2 Direct Salary Cost Analysis

Direct Salary Cost	Salary per Full-Time Equivalent, Year 1	Year 1	Year 2	Year 3	Year 4	Year 5
Direct patient care						
Total patient days		5,040	6,210	6,575	6,575	6,575
Productive hours per patient day						
Registered nurse		1.74	2.12	2.00	2.00	2.00
Licensed practical nurse		1.74	1.41	1.33	1.33	1.33
Certified nurse aide		3.48	3.29	3.11	3.11	3.11
		6.96	6.82	6.44	6.44	6.44
Productivity factor		85.00%	85.00%	85.00%	85.00%	85.00%
Paid hours per patient day						
Registered nurse		2.05	2.49	2.35	2.35	2.35
Licensed practical nurse		2.05	1.66	1.56	1.56	1.56
Certified nurse aide		4.09	3.87	3.66	3.66	3.66
		8.19	8.02	7.57	7.57	7.57
Summary of staffing (full-time equivalents) and salary costs						
Staffing						
Direct patient care						
Registered nurse	$40,000	4.96	7.45	7.44	7.44	7.44
Licensed practical nurse	$26,000	4.96	4.95	4.95	4.95	4.95
Certified nurse aide	$18,000	9.92	11.56	11.57	11.57	11.57
Other staff						
Nurse manager	$50,000	1.00	1.00	1.00	1.00	1.00
Ward clerk/receptionist	$20,000	1.40	1.40	1.40	1.40	1.40
		22.24	26.36	26.36	26.36	26.36
Salary costs						
Direct patient care		$505,938	$660,013	$686,053	$713,495	$742,034
Other staff		78,000	81,120	84,365	87,739	91,249
Total		$583,938	$741,133	$770,418	$801,234	$833,283

staff on the unit during the 5-year period. The team preparing the demand and market study normally has considerable background and experience in the type of staffing on subacute units. The staffing can also be affected by the types of services that will be provided on the unit, however. Staffing issues are addressed in greater detail in Chapter 7. Based on this experience, the mix of patients expected on the unit, and discussions with management personnel, the following factors should be developed.

Direct Patient Care Hours and Staff

With the use of the detailed staffing schedule by shift that is provided by the demand analysis team and management, the direct patient care staffing levels for the unit per day should be determined. These should be broken down as average full-time equivalents (FTEs) for registered nurses (RNs), licensed practical nurses (LPNs), and certified nurse aides (CNAs). There may be other direct care staff involved, depending on the type of services being provided. The average FTEs should be translated to direct nursing hours per patient day by level of staff. Thereafter, an appropriate productivity factor should be applied to determine the total paid hours per patient day.

From the example of the RN in Table 16–2 and based on the detailed shift staffing patterns in year 2 provided by management, an average of 2.12 productive RN hours per patient day is anticipated. These direct RN hours are grossed by a productivity factor (also obtained from management) of 85% to give a total of 2.49 paid hours of RN time per patient day. These paid hours equal 7.45 RN FTEs on average for the year (2.49 paid hours per day times 6210 total patient days divided by 2080 hours per year).

The next step is to obtain the average salary cost for each direct patient care category and to multiply these by the average FTEs to determine the direct patient care salary cost for year 1. The average salary cost is inflated by an appropriate inflation factor for each year, which should be clearly stated in the assumption section, to arrive at the direct patient care salary cost for each of the subsequent years. In Table 16–2, an inflation rate of 4% has been used for salary cost.

Other Unit Staff

Under the category of other unit staff, the nurse manager and the ward clerk/receptionist typically are included. In Table 16–2, it is assumed that there will be one nurse manager and approximately 1.4 FTE ward clerks/receptionists on the unit. These data are obtained from management. Once again, multiplying these FTEs by their annual salary cost, the total salary cost for other unit staff is determined for each year.

Total Direct Hours per Patient Day

It should be noted that the total patient hours for the unit stabilize at approximately 7.58 hours after year 2. This indicates the intensity of services being provided on these units. Also, as in a typical medical-surgical unit of a hospital, the combined RN and LPN hours are usually greater than the CNA hours per patient day. Medicare has recently imposed a maximum ceiling of 9.6 hours of direct patient care per day for consideration of Medicare routine cost limit exception requests. The outcome of Table 16–2 should be the total salary cost per year for the first 5 years of operation.

INDIRECT COSTS

Employee Health and Welfare Benefits

This figure is determined for each year by applying a standard hospital-wide percentage of employee benefit cost to direct salary cost. In Table 16–3, an average of 20% has been used to determined the total employee benefit cost for each year. In actual practice, this percentage can range from a low of 15% to a high of 25%.

As a separate and later calculation, the estimated employee health and welfare cost for all indirect salaries also needs to be considered in the total equation. As can be seen in Table 16–3, indirect salary cost relating to social workers and activity therapists has been recognized, and employee benefits of 20% have been calculated on these costs. This provides the total incremental employee benefit cost for each year.

Other Indirect Costs

Other indirect costs include items such as the stationery required on the unit, nonchargeable supplies and drugs, the cost of training programs for the direct unit staff, and the like. An average cost per patient day for such items can be obtained from one of the other units in the hospital or from industry averages. In Table 16–3, a cost of $12 per patient day has been used to determine the direct nonsalary cost for each year. Once again, this figure of $12 per patient day is inflated for each subsequent year using a stated inflation percentage, which in this example is 4%.

Administration and General Cost

There are two types of administrative and general costs: the incremental cost that will be incurred by establishing the unit, and an allocated administrative and general cost, which will take place through the normal cost reporting step-down process. For this item and many of the following indirect cost items, the incremental cost that will be incurred is dealt with primarily as opposed to the allocated cost. The allocated cost concept is useful only when one is calculating Medicare or Medicaid cost report reimbursement.

In Table 16–3, a factor of 10% has been used to determine the incremental administrative and general cost. This factor represents the additional cost that may relate to additional billing and collection staff, Medicare logging staff, managed

Table 16–3 Indirect Cost Analysis

Indirect Costs	Salary per FTE	Year 1	Year 2	Year 3	Year 4	Year 5
Employee health and welfare						
Direct salary costs		$583,938	$741,133	$770,417	$801,234	$833,283
Indirect salary costs		38,500	40,040	41,642	43,307	45,040
Total salaries		622,438	781,173	812,059	844,541	878,323
Employee benefit percentage		20.00%	20.00%	20.00%	20.00%	20.00%
Total employee benefits		$124,488	$156,235	$162,412	$168,908	$175,665
Administration and general						
Direct salary costs		$583,938	$741,133	$770,417	$801,234	$833,283
Employee benefits—Direct salaries		116,788	148,227	154,083	160,247	166,657
Direct nonsalary costs	$12.00	60,480	77,501	85,338	88,752	92,302
Accumulated costs		761,206	966,861	1,009,839	1,050,233	1,092,242
Incremental cost factor		10.00%	10.00%	10.00%	10.00%	10.00%
		$76,121	$96,686	$100,984	$105,023	$109,224
Maintenance and operation of plant						
Variable cost per square foot		$6.00	$6.24	$6.49	$6.75	$7.02
Square feet		7,000	7,000	7,000	7,000	7,000
Incremental cost		$42,000	$43,680	$45,427	$47,244	$49,134
Laundry						
Patient days		5,040	6,210	6,575	6,575	6,575
Variable cost per patient day		$1.50	$1.56	$1.62	$1.69	$1.75
Incremental cost		7,560	9,688	10,667	11,094	11,538
Housekeeping						
Variable cost per square foot		$3.00	$3.12	$3.24	$3.37	$3.51
Square feet		7,000	7,000	7,000	7,000	7,000
Incremental cost		$21,000	$21,840	$22,714	$23,622	$24,567
Dietary						
Variable cost per patient day		$10.50	$10.92	$11.36	$11.81	$12.28
Patient days		5,040	6,210	6,575	6,575	6,575
Incremental cost		$52,920	$67,813	$74,671	$77,658	$80,764
Social service and activities						
Salary costs						
Social worker	$35,000	$17,500	$18,200	$18,928	$19,685	$20,473
Activity therapist	$15,000	21,000	21,840	22,714	23,622	24,567
Other costs per patient day	$1.00	5,040	6,458	7,112	7,396	7,692
		$43,540	$46,498	$48,753	$50,703	$52,731

care contracting staff, or accounting department staff. These do not usually represent FTEs and are made up of a number of partial FTEs in various of these departments. One can either come up with an actual figure if management proposes to do this or use a global percentage estimate, as has been done in the example in Table 16–3. With this factor, the incremental administrative and general cost for each of the 5 years has been determined.

Maintenance and Operation of Plant

This incremental cost is determined by utilizing two factors: the total estimated square feet of the unit as provided by management, and the variable costs per square foot for maintenance of the unit. This variable factor is usually an estimated percentage of the total direct cost per square foot for the entire hospital for maintenance and plant operations. Typically, a 40% to 50% factor is used.

Laundry

The incremental cost for providing laundry services to the unit can be determined in a variety of ways. Where the laundry service is contracted out, the incremental cost will be based on the total patient days for each year times the average pounds of laundry per patient day times the incremental cost per pound. In Table 16–3, a factor of 6 lbs per patient day times the variable cost of 25 cents per pound in year 1 has been used to calculate the incremental cost.

Housekeeping

The incremental cost for housekeeping should be based on the total square footage of the unit multiplied by the variable cost per square foot for housekeeping services. This factor is obtained through discussions with management.

Dietary

The total incremental cost for meals for the unit should be determined by multiplying patient days by the variable cost for meals per patient day. Once again, this factor should be provided by management.

Nursing Administration

There is typically no incremental cost for nursing administration for the establishment of this type of unit. There certainly will be some allocated nursing administration cost that needs to be recognized when Medicare or Medicaid cost report reimbursement is being calculated.

Medical Record Personnel

Any incremental cost for additional medical record personnel should be considered and included in Table 16–3. This will be based on how many FTEs management believes are necessary because of establishment of the subacute unit.

Social Services and Activities

There will typically be additional social services and activities personnel required for providing services to this type of unit. Table 16–3 uses an addition of 0.5 social worker and 1.4 activity therapists. Multiplying these numbers by the average annual salary for year 1 and inflating it thereafter by 4% per year yields the total incremental salaries for this cost center for each year.

ANCILLARY COST AND CHARGES

Ancillary Cost

The volume and types of ancillary services to be provided on these units should be obtained from the demand analysis consultants and management. The average ancillary cost per day for the various ancillary cost centers should be determined. In the example given in Table 16–4, these total approximately $120 per day. Once again, this is the incremental ancillary cost per day based on industry averages and management's concurrence, not the total allocated ancillary cost per day. In addition to this incremental cost, one would typically allocate a fixed cost of 20% to 30% to each of these ancillary departments to come up to the total reimbursable cost on a Medicare/Medicaid cost report. The average cost per day for each service is multiplied by the number of days for each year to arrive at the total ancillary cost in year 1. This is inflated by an appropriate factor to arrive at the total ancillary cost for years 2 to 5.

Table 16–4 Ancillary Costs and Charges Analysis

Ancillary Costs and Charges	Cost per Patient Day*	Year 1	Year 2	Year 3	Year 4	Year 5
Incremental ancillary costs						
Therapies	$48.75	$245,700	$314,847	$346,687	$360,554	$374,976
Drugs	15.00	75,600	96,876	106,673	110,940	115,377
Medical supplies, chargeable	11.25	56,700	72,657	80,005	83,205	86,533
Other	15.00	75,600	96,876	106,673	110,940	115,377
Incremental ancillary costs	$90.00	$453,600	$581,256	$640,037	$665,638	$692,264
Total ancillary costs						
Therapies	$65.00	$327,600	$419,796	$462,249	$480,739	$499,968
Drugs	20.00	100,800	129,168	142,230	147,920	153,836
Medical supplies, chargeable	15.00	75,600	96,876	106,673	110,940	115,377
Other	20.00	100,800	129,168	142,230	147,920	153,836
Total ancillary costs	$120.00	$604,800	$775,008	$853,382	$887,518	$923,018
Ancillary charges						
Physical therapy	0.6000	$546,000	$699,660	$770,415	$801,231	$833,281
Drugs	0.2500	403,200	516,672	568,922	591,678	615,346
Medical supplies, chargeable	0.4000	189,000	242,190	266,682	277,349	288,443
Other	0.5000	201,600	258,336	284,461	295,839	307,673
Total ancillary charges		$1,339,800	$1,716,858	$1,890,479	$1,966,098	$2,044,742
Charges per patient day		$265.83	$276.47	$287.53	$299.03	$310.99

*Figures for ancillary charges are cost-to-charge ratios.

Ancillary Charges

The total allocated ancillary costs for each ancillary department are grossed by the cost-to-charge ratio appearing on the Medicare cost report to develop the total ancillary charges for the unit. The total ancillary charge per patient for each year is also developed in Table 16–4. This provides a good yardstick for an overall reasonableness test of these charges.

CAPITAL COSTS

Table 16–5 presents the total additional expenditures for the 20 beds on the subacute unit estimated to be approximately $20,000 per bed. The actual cost could range from $10,000 to $40,000 per bed. This includes renovation and modifications necessary to the unit. In addition, there is an equipment cost of approximately $25,000 for the unit. These estimates are provided by manage-

ment. The total cost is then depreciated over an average 15-year life to arrive at the average depreciation cost for each year. If there is any borrowing anticipated, then the interest cost for each year should be recognized on Table 16–5.

Note once again that the incremental capital cost is different from the allocated capital cost for reimbursement purposes. This allocated cost is determined by running a cost report with appropriate statistics for the unit and is usually significantly higher for all indirect cost items than the incremental cost.

TOTAL REVENUE

The total routine revenue is determined by multiplying the routine cost per day by the total patient days for each payer category. In Table 16–6, an estimate of $200 per day has been used in year 1, and this has been inflated by an appropriate factor for subsequent years. The total an-

Table 16–5 Capital Costs Analysis

Capital Costs	Starting Costs	Year 1	Year 2	Year 3	Year 4	Year 5
Building renovation						
(20 beds at $20,000 per bed)	$400,000					
Equipment	25,000					
	$425,000					
Depreciation (15-year life)		$28,333	$28,333	$28,333	$28,333	$28,333

cillary revenue from Table 16–4 has also been distributed to the various payer classes. Combining routine ancillary revenue by payer class yields the gross revenue for each year.

It should be noted that the routine revenue may vary by type of service being provided on the subacute unit. If so, this information should be obtained from management and included for modeling purposes.

DEDUCTIONS FROM REVENUE/ CONTRACTUAL ALLOWANCES

Medicare

The total Medicare charges per patient day are obtained from Table 16–6. The total Medicare cost per patient day is derived by actually running a pro forma cost report for the latest available

Table 16–6 Routine Revenue Analysis

Routine Revenue	Year 1	Year 2	Year 3	Year 4	Year 5
Routine charge per day	$200.00	$208.00	$216.32	$224.97	$233.97
Patient days					
Medicare	4,032	4,658	4,603	4,274	3,945
Managed care	504	932	1,315	1,644	1,973
Other	504	621	658	658	658
	5,041	6,216	6,576	6,576	6,576
Routine revenue					
Medicare	$806,400	$968,760	$995,613	$961,478	$923,018
Managed care	· 100,800	193,752	284,461	369,799	461,509
Other	100,800	129,168	142,230	147,920	153,836
Total routine revenue	1,008,000	1,291,680	1,422,304	1,479,197	1,538,363
Ancillary revenue					
Medicare	1,071,840	1,287,644	1,323,335	1,277,964	1,226,845
Managed care	133,980	257,529	378,096	491,525	613,423
Other	133,980	171,686	189,048	196,610	204,474
Total ancillary revenue	1,339,800	1,716,859	1,890,479	1,966,099	2,044,742
Total revenue					
Medicare	1,878,240	2,256,404	2,318,948	2,239,441	2,149,864
Managed care	234,780	451,281	662,557	861,324	1,074,932
Other	234,780	300,854	331,278	344,529	358,311
Total revenue	$2,347,800	$3,008,539	$3,312,783	$3,445,294	$3,583,107

period and inserting therein the direct cost, square footage, and other statistics for the subacute unit. These costs should be higher than the incremental cost discussed in the previous section on indirect costs. The total routine cost should be limited after the first 3 years plus the stub exemption period by the routine cost limitation. In Table 16–7, the routine cost limitation has been recognized in year 5. If the hospital already has a skilled nursing unit, then this 3-year plus exemption may not be available, and the routine cost limitation will apply in year 1.

The difference between the Medicare charge per patient day and the Medicare cost per patient day (Medicare reimbursement per patient day) gives the Medicare contractual allowances per patient day for each year. This, multiplied by

patient days, gives the total Medicare contractual allowances for each year.

Managed Care

The total managed care revenue per patient day less the total expected per diem reimbursement for managed care times managed care days gives the managed care contractual allowance for each year on Table 16–7.

Other

Because this category may include Medicaid and self-pay, the contractual allowance has been estimated at 50% of the gross revenue.

Table 16–7 Contractual Allowances Analysis

Contractual Allowances	Year 1	Year 2	Year 3	Year 4	Year 5
Medicare					
Medicare charges per patient day	$465.83	$484.47	$503.85	$524.00	$544.96
Medicare reimbursement per patient day	396.37	398.45	400.87	416.56	319.00
Contractual allowance per patient day	$69.46	$86.02	$102.98	$107.44	$225.96
Medicare contractual allowance	$280,079	$400,637	$473,944	$459,168	$891,403
Medicare costs per patient day					
Direct costs	127.86	131.83	130.15	135.36	140.77
Indirect costs*	137.27	132.70	132.31	137.60	143.10
Subtotal—routine costs	265.13	264.53	262.46	272.96	283.87
Routine cost limitation	Not Applicable	Not Applicable	Not Applicable	Not Applicable	170.00
Routine costs (allowable)	265.13	264.52	262.46	272.96	170.00
Ancillary costs*	120.00	124.80	129.79	134.98	140.38
Capital costs*	11.24	9.13	8.62	8.62	8.62
Medicare costs per patient day	396.37	398.45	400.87	416.56	319.00
Managed care					
Total managed care revenue	234,780	451,281	662,557	861,324	1,074,932
Reimbursement					
Managed care days	504	932	1,315	1,644	1,973
Per diem rate	400	400	400	400	400
Reimbursement	201,600	372,600	526,000	657,500	789,000
Managed care contractual allowance	33,180	78,681	136,557	203,824	285,932
Other					
Total other revenue	234,780	300,854	331,278	344,529	358,311
Write-off percentage	50.00%	50.00%	50.00%	50.00%	50.00%
Uncollectible other revenue	117,390	150,427	165,639	172,265	179,155

*Includes fully allocated costs from pro forma Medicare cost report.

SUMMARY OF REVENUES AND EXPENSES FOR SUBACUTE UNIT

Total revenues by payer class, contractual allowance by payer class, and details of expenses are brought forward from the other schedules and the total expenses to produce the statement of revenues and expenses for the subacute unit (Table 16–8). The excess of revenue over expenses for each year will enable management to determine whether it is meaningful to proceed with the subacute unit. There are certainly other nonfinancial factors that could affect this decision.

OTHER FINANCIAL CONSIDERATIONS

There may be a number of other considerations that affect the financial viability of the unit, such as:

- Does the establishment of the subacute unit result in fewer patient days in the medical/surgical units of the hospital? If so, what are the corresponding cost savings and revenue losses?
- Will there be any decrease in the number of patients currently transferred to a skilled

Table 16–8 Statement of Revenues and Expenses

Revenue/Expense	Year 1	Year 2	Year 3	Year 4	Year 5
Revenue					
Total revenue					
Medicare	$1,878,240	$2,256,404	$2,318,948	$2,239,441	$2,149,864
Managed care	234,780	451,281	662,557	861,324	1,074,932
Other	234,780	300,854	331,278	344,529	358,311
	2,347,800	3,008,539	3,312,783	3,445,294	3,583,107
Contractual allowances and uncollectibles					
Medicare	280,079	400,637	473,944	459,168	891,403
Managed care	33,180	78,681	136,557	203,824	285,932
Other	117,390	150,427	165,639	172,265	179,155
	430,649	629,745	776,140	835,257	1,356,490
Net revenue					
Medicare	1,598,161	1,855,767	1,845,004	1,780,274	1,258,461
Managed care	201,600	372,600	526,000	657,500	789,000
Other	117,390	150,427	165,639	172,265	179,155
Total net revenue	1,917,151	2,378,794	2,536,643	2,610,039	2,226,616
Expenses					
Direct costs					
Salary	583,938	741,133	770,417	801,234	833,283
Other	60,480	77,501	85,338	88,752	92,302
Indirect costs					
Employee health and welfare	124,488	156,235	162,412	168,908	175,665
Administration and general	76,121	96,686	100,984	105,023	109,224
Maintenance and operation of plant	42,000	43,680	45,427	47,244	49,134
Laundry	7,560	9,688	10,667	11,094	11,538
Housekeeping	21,000	21,840	22,714	23,622	24,567
Dietary	52,920	67,813	74,671	77,658	80,764
Social service and activities	43,540	46,498	48,753	50,703	52,731
Ancillary costs	453,600	581,256	640,037	665,638	692,264
Capital costs	28,333	28,333	28,333	28,333	28,333
	1,493,980	1,870,663	1,989,753	2,068,209	2,149,805
Excess of revenues over expenses	$423,171	$508,130	$546,890	$541,828	$76,811

nursing facility owned by or related to the hospital? What are the cost savings and revenue losses associated with these transfers?

- How will the establishment of the unit affect cost allocations to other existing departments which are cost reimbursed (rehabilitation or psychiatric units, home health agency, outpatient departments, etc.) and what are the related reimbursement losses?

- Will a potential decrease in the average length of stay trigger any physician risk pool payments under capitated managed care contracts?

These considerations will vary for each situation, and should be discussed with management. The financial model should be adapted to recognize these and other factors that may affect the financial analysis of the unit.

CONCLUSION

Once an appropriate microcomputer model has been set up to prepare the financial pro formas, it is fairly easy to test different assumptions for the subacute unit. For example, the fill-up period, the patient volume, and the unit size can be varied to simulate different financial scenarios.

Once the financial feasibility analysis has been completed, an appropriate report should be prepared listing the assumptions used and including the various tables prepared during the study. The report should contain an executive summary describing the results of the financial analysis. The form of the report will vary, depending on whether it is meant for purely internal decision making, for negotiation of financing for the unit, or for other purposes.

REFERENCE

1. American Institute of Certified Public Accountants (AICPA). *Guide for Prospective Financial Statements.* New York, NY: AICPA; 1992.

17

Preopening and Start-Up Operations for Subacute Providers

Kathleen M. Griffin

The preopening and start-up operations for subacute providers are based on the results of the comprehensive market analysis, which should have provided the following information:

- potential volume of patients from each referral source
- potential payer mix of patients
- types and acuity levels of potential admissions
- managed care payment strategies
- appropriate positioning for targeted patient populations and potential referral sources
- strategies for meeting financial objectives

The steps involved in the start-up of the subacute unit or facility depend on the nature of the unit or facility and its location. If the subacute unit is to be housed in a skilled nursing facility unit within an acute hospital and created through the conversion of hospital beds to skilled nursing beds, then the start-up is conducted in two phases: licensure of the facility, and subacute program development. If, however, the subacute unit is created by changing the nature of the programs in skilled nursing beds within a freestanding nursing facility, then the

focus is subacute program development. Similarly, if an acute hospital elects to create a subacute product line and convert to a long-term care hospital exempt from Medicare's prospective payment system, the focus is programmatic rather than related to licensure unless the renovations required exceed the capital cost floor for certificate of need (CON) requirements.

This chapter provides guidelines and specific steps for the creation of a new subacute unit through either the construction of new beds or conversion of hospital beds to new skilled nursing facility beds as well as the steps to create a successful subacute operation.

LICENSURE OF NEW HOSPITAL OR SKILLED NURSING FACILITY BEDS

Creating a subacute unit or facility in newly licensed beds involves procedures to achieve state licensure as a health facility and Medicare certification. The majority of states require that a CON be obtained for the creation of newly licensed beds, whether the beds are to be located in a new facility or converted from acute hospital beds to skilled nursing beds. Certain states (eg, Indiana) provide options for conversion of limited numbers of acute hospital beds to nursing facility beds without a CON.

STEPS TO ACHIEVE LICENSURE OF FACILITY

The following discussion illustrates the licensure procedures for start-up of a subacute unit. Whether constructing new beds or converting hospital beds to skilled nursing subacute beds, the provider must be thoroughly familiar with requirements for state licensure as well as federal requirements for Medicare certification.[1]

Step 1: Identify Potential Site and Costs of Construction or Renovation

After the market assessment, the provider should have determined the number of beds for the subacute unit or facility. The federal regulations for Medicare certification should be reviewed in concert with facility licensure standards for the state. Several of the requirements for certification as a Medicare provider that may require renovations in an existing facility include the following:

- *Separate nursing station:* In a hospital-based skilled nursing subacute unit, federal regulations require that the unit be distinct from the rest of the hospital and that there be a dedicated nursing station with the support components of the nursing station available within the skilled nursing unit.

- *Compliance with life safety codes:* Over the years, building requirements for life safety code compliance have become stricter. As a result, buildings licensed as hospitals years ago may be under a waiver for certain life safety code requirements. When the license is to be modified from a hospital license to a skilled nursing facility license, however, the waiver usually becomes null and void.

- *Emergency power:* In the event that the normal electric power supply is interrupted, the emergency electric power system must supply power adequate at least for lighting all entrances and exits; equipment to maintain

the fire detection and alarm systems; and life support systems. Nursing facilities that have not provided subacute services utilizing life support equipment may have electric power systems that do not meet code requirements. The facility may have retained its license under a waiver. With the addition of ventilators, the electric system may have to be enhanced significantly for the subacute care unit.

- *Space:* The subacute skilled nursing unit within a hospital must meet the requirements for space and equipment for a skilled nursing facility even though the unit is not a freestanding facility. A patient/resident dining area and an activities/recreation area usually must be added by renovating either a patient/resident room or some alternative space. In addition, families will be visiting the subacute patients/residents frequently during the short-term stay, and an area for visiting is a necessity. Finally, if the physical therapy and occupational therapy spaces are located in another area of the hospital or nursing facility, which is inconvenient for transport of subacute patients, then a satellite therapy room often is included in the subacute unit.

- *Patient/resident rooms:* Although federal regulations require that rooms have 80 square feet per resident in a semiprivate room and 100 square feet per resident in private room, those minimum requirements typically are inadequate for a subacute care unit. Subacute patients may require a number of equipment items in the room for nursing care, respiratory therapy, or rehabilitation. As a result, the patient/resident rooms for a subacute skilled nursing unit should be at least 25% larger than required by code.

- *Nurse call system:* Certain older nursing facilities may not have an adequate nurse call system to meet federal regulations. Moreover, if a hospital has elected to utilize an older wing for the subacute skilled nursing unit, the nurse call system may need to be upgraded to comply with code and to ensure the safety of the patients.

- *Lighting:* Many nursing facilities do not have adequate lighting above the patient/resident beds to provide for the number of nursing and respiratory therapy procedures expected to be performed on the subacute patients.

In addition to the federal requirements for Medicare certification, each state has certain requirements for licensure of the facility as a skilled nursing facility. An engineer from the state health department or health facilities office can provide consultation on the physical facility renovations that would be required for compliance with the state licensure code for skilled nursing facilities.

Since 1992, subacute providers have been required to comply with requirements of the Americans with Disabilities Act (ADA). Architectural and construction firms that work with health facilities are aware of these requirements and can provide guidance about renovations to comply with the requirements of the act.

After the renovation requirements to comply with federal, state, and ADA codes have been determined, cost estimates for the renovations need to be obtained.

Step 2: Develop Financial Feasibility of the Project

The internal or external market assessment will have identified the revenue and expense items for the financial feasibility analysis, including revenues from sources other than Medicare, staffing, ancillary and support service utilization, and other operating costs. The financial feasibility analysis for a hospital-based subacute skilled nursing unit involves the following steps:

1. Identify staffing costs, ancillary and support service utilization, and other operational costs.
2. Rerun the hospital cost report on a prospective basis, identifying the hospital-

based subacute skilled nursing unit as a separate revenue/cost center.
3. Identify resulting benefits to the hospital from cost reallocation.
4. Identify renovation costs and any capital costs for equipment.
5. Determine the financial feasibility of the project.

In the case of a skilled nursing facility that is adding a subacute unit, the financial feasibility steps will include the following:

1. Identify bed need based on referral source interviews and the potential number of patients from each of the referral sources.
2. Identify staffing and operational requirements to attract patients from the targeted referral sources.
3. Project ancillary service utilization and costs related to same.
4. Estimate revenue per patient day from non-Medicare sources.
5. Rerun the nursing facility's cost report to estimate additional Medicare costs and revenues.
6. Run a revenue/expense or profit/loss projection for the subacute unit, and determine its impact on the profitability of the entire facility.
7. Assess the cash flow requirements during the start-up phase and until the Medicare exception so the routine cost limit can be obtained, if appropriate.
8. Identify remodeling and other capital equipment costs.
9. Determine the financial feasibility of the project.

Chapter 16 provides in-depth information about determining the financial feasibility of a subacute project.

Step 3: CON Application, if Necessary

Steps involved in obtaining a CON are specific to individual states. Typically, however, they include providing information from the market assessment and financial feasibility analysis; reviewing patient/resident types and census in other skilled nursing facilities in the area; submitting a detailed application; providing public notification, usually through the newspaper; responding to inquiries about the application from the CON board; and appearing at a public hearing before the CON board for approval.

SUBACUTE PROGRAM DEVELOPMENT

Program development for the subacute unit or facility should occur concurrently with the renovations. A 3-month start-up period is generally needed. The following are components of the subacute program that must be developed during the start-up phase.

Mission and Purpose

Subacute providers furnish services to a wide spectrum of patients. The care is provided in diverse inpatient settings. As a result, the subacute provider should develop a well-defined purpose and mission, focusing on the types of patients for subacute care, the scope of the subacute care to be provided, and how the subacute care program will be organized.

Organizational Structure

Typically, subacute providers are components of larger health care entities, such as acute hospitals, health care systems, or nursing facilities. The subacute provider should document a clearly defined structure that shows the authority and accountability of key personnel, their relationship to one another, and the reporting mechanism among them.

Staffing

The full range of qualified staff to provide services in the subacute setting should be defined and available. Organizational charts and staffing models by patient census are documents that should be prepared by the subacute provider. These documents allow the orderly recruitment and employment of qualified staff and appropri-

ate time for orientation of the staff to provide quality subacute services.

Typically, the subacute care program is directed by a program director with a health care background and appropriate experience with subacute patients. In addition to the managerial functions for the subacute unit or facility, the program director oversees the program's clinical integrity and patient care. The clinical staff, particularly the nursing staff, with their qualifications, philosophy of care, and competencies, form the linchpin for successful subacute care programs. Nurses with backgrounds in both acute and long-term care should be recruited to form the core team of the subacute program. The nursing staff in a subacute program provide more technical and intensive nursing procedures than those performed in a skilled nursing facility. Nurses interact extensively with the patient's family and may involve them in the treatment plan, a role that may be unfamiliar to nurses recruited from a hospital setting. Subacute care provided in licensed skilled nursing facilities must comply with the nursing facility regulations, and nursing staff must be familiar with these regulations.

The start-up plan for the subacute provider should include early employment of the program director and a clear plan for recruitment of the clinical staff team for the subacute care program. The start-up plan also should allow for orientation of clinical team members and team building before the subacute care unit opens.

Medical Staff

The most successful subacute programs have one or more "medical champions." Because subacute care is not well understood by the health care community or the public, a medical director for the subacute program who takes an active interest in defining the program, developing protocols for the various specialty programs within the subacute setting, and promoting the subacute setting to the health care community is an essential member of the subacute care team.

One of the functions of the medical director of the subacute unit or facility is to create a medical staff who, after admitting patients to the subacute setting, may follow their patients and who will be part of the interdisciplinary team that provides outcome-oriented care to the subacute patients. For the medically complex programs and postoperative programs in a subacute setting, an internist or family practice physician may be an appropriate medical director. For specialty programs, such as ventilator weaning programs or rehabilitation programs, specialty physicians such as pulmonologists, physiatrists, or neurologists are the most appropriate to serve as medical director.

Recruiting the "medical champions" and involving medical staff from the host hospital and/or referring hospitals in the development of the subacute unit are essential steps in the start-up phase to ensure commitment of the physicians to the subacute programs.

Policies, Procedures, and Systems

Before the survey for state licensure or Medicare certification, the subacute provider will want to ensure that policies, procedures, and systems that comply with federal and state requirements are in place. The *1995 Survey Protocol for Subacute Programs* of the Joint Commission on Accreditation of Healthcare Organizations[2] provides guidance on the policies and procedures that the Joint Commission considers appropriate for subacute programs. The policies and procedures in this publication reflect the requirements for Medicare certification.

During the start-up phase, policies and procedures should be developed for the following areas:

- *Patient rights and responsibilities:* Federal regulations for nursing facilities specify a number of patient/resident rights. These rights should be specified in policies and procedures. Systems should be outlined to ensure that the rights are recognized and respected within the subacute setting.
- *Admission:* Clear criteria for admissions to each of the subacute programs to be offered in a subacute setting should be developed during the start-up phase. In addition to the specific admission criteria by program, continuing stay and discharge criteria should be specific to the program. Admissions procedures must comply with federal requirements; subacute care settings should focus on paperwork simplification, however, to ensure timely admissions of subacute patients.
- *Patient assessment and evaluation:* Policies and procedures for the assessment process should involve the interdisciplinary team and should be completed within 48 hours of admission. This means that the subacute provider must have staff qualified and prepared to conduct the assessments 7 days a week.
- *Patient care:* Specific protocols that include clinical procedures and may also include critical pathways or care paths must be developed for each of the subacute programs to be offered in the setting. The policies and procedures also must provide for participation of the patient/resident and family in the development and review of the plan of care. Federal regulations require the completion of the Minimum Data Set (MDS) for each patient/resident within the first 14 days of admission. Care plans must reflect the patient/resident needs determined from the MDS. Departmental manuals may contain policies and procedures specific to the clinical disciplines in the department.
- *Continuity of care:* Discharge planning procedures and follow-up policies and procedures should be developed during the start-up phase. Policies and procedures for assessing patient satisfaction should be developed.
- *Information management and documentation:* Facilities may elect to purchase automated documentation systems. Whether these systems are automated or manual, however, policies and procedures should clearly delineate the components of the medical record, forms to be utilized, per-

sons responsible for making entries into the medical record, and the format and content of the medical record entries.

- *Plant, technology, and safety management:* Policies and procedures should be prepared to assure that there is compliance with all plant, technology, and safety regulations and that patient/resident and staff safety is optimally ensured.

- *Human resources management and leadership:* Personnel policies and practices should be delineated, and procedures for medical staff credentialing and privileging should be defined.

- *Infection control and quality assessment/improvement:* Procedures and policies that are specific to the patient types and acuities in the subacute setting should be developed to ensure that there is surveillance, prevention, and control of infection and that there are ongoing procedures for quality assessment and improvement.

Documentation System

Before opening the subacute unit, the provider should determine the documentation system and the specific forms that will be used. The forms must comply with federal and state regulations and should facilitate ease of documentation regarding the subacute patient by the interdisciplinary clinical team. Chapter 12 provides further information about automated documentation systems.

Outcome Measurement

The final step in the start-up operations involves ensuring that interdisciplinary care con- ference procedures and outcome measurement policies and procedures are in place. The orientation of the initial staff for the subacute program should involve a review of all policies and procedures. Opportunities to practice new systems should be provided so that, upon admission of the first subacute patient, the interdisciplinary clinical staff function as a team to provide patient-centered care. Chapter 10 provides additional information about outcome management.

CONCLUSION

The preopening and start-up steps for subacute providers are more extensive for those providers that must first become licensed as a health care facility. The operational preopening and start-up procedures, however, are similar for facilities with existing licenses and for facilities that have applied for a new license as a subacute provider. These include defining the mission and scope of the subacute programs; recruiting and employing appropriately qualified staff, including medical directors and staff; creating polices and procedures that comply with federal and state regulations and best serve the types of subacute patients to be admitted; orienting the staff to subacute policies, procedures, and systems and allowing them adequate time to practice the systems; carefully defining the documentation systems and determining whether a manual or automated system will be utilized; and establishing an outcome measurement system for the subacute care setting that provides for continual assessment and improvement to optimize cost-effective patient care.

REFERENCES

1. 42 CFR §405, §442, §447, §483, §488, §489, and §498.
2. Joint Commission on Accreditation of Healthcare Orga- nizations. *1995 Survey Protocol for Subacute Programs.* Oakbrook Terrace, Ill: Joint Commission; 1994.

18

Preopening Marketing Program for Subacute Providers

Kathleen M. Griffin

The preopening marketing program for a new subacute provider should include strategies to achieve name recognition and to establish a reputation for quality care in the community. Although the program director, case manager, and nurse liaison manage the preopening marketing activities, all facility staff are involved in the effort and have assignments to carry out. Ideally, preopening marketing should begin 6 months in advance of the opening of the subacute unit or facility. Active referral development activities should be initiated 3 months before opening, with a numerical goal for admissions being set the opening week. This chapter includes suggested steps for the preopening marketing and referral development activities.

MARKET ANALYSIS

The market feasibility study (see Chapter 14) should be used as a starting point. The procedures for market analysis also can be used as a means of developing name recognition for the subacute provider. The market feasibility study should have included a review of the environment and a determination of the demographics and psycho-graphics of referral sources with specific emphasis on independent case managers, health maintenance organization (HMO)/insurance case managers, physicians, discharge planners, and self-insured employers. Key components of the marketing analysis also should have been a competitive analysis and an analysis of HMO/indemnity insurance contracting in the area.

PREOPENING MARKETING PLAN

The preopening marketing plan sets an overall strategy for census development and for achieving the census and payer objectives through a mix of sales, promotion, and public relations; advertising; and other exposure strategies. The plan needs to be focused carefully on the target that will be most likely to provide the ideal kinds of referrals to the subacute provider. For example, discharge planners typically refer primarily Medicare patients. Independent case managers and HMO/insurance case managers, on the other hand, will refer managed care and commercially insured patients. Many insurers, HMOs, and preferred provider organizations (PPOs) also will work with a facility with which they do not have a contract to place individual patients when the quality of care is exceptional and the price competitive.

The preopening marketing plan should include assignments for all facility staff. At least weekly, and more often if necessary, an all-staff marketing meeting should be held to ensure that the marketing and referral development objectives are being achieved and to redirect efforts as necessary. The program director and/or case manager needs to be an organized quarterback for these efforts.

PREOPENING MARKETING BUDGET

The preopening marketing plan will require a marketing budget. The budget should include salaries of staff directly involved in preopening marketing efforts as well as the direct expenses related to marketing and referral development. Items generally included in the preopening marketing budget are shown in Exhibit 18–1.

MARKETING AND REFERRAL DEVELOPMENT

Preopening marketing involves all the activities related to creating an appropriate image of the subacute provider in the community. Although referral development technically is part of marketing, typically referral development refers specifically to one-on-one sales calls to key referral sources as well as inservice programs and presentations about the new subacute provider to potential referral sources.

REFERRAL SOURCE DATABASE/ MAILING LISTS

The database and mailing lists should consist of all targeted referral sources to which the provider intends to market the new facility. The admissions coordinator usually manages the database development and maintenance. Target referral sources include the following:

- independent case managers

Exhibit 18–1 Items for Preopening Marketing Budget

Salaries and benefits (3 to 6 months)
- Case manager
- Nurse liaison
- Admissions coordinator
Advertising—design, layout, ad space
- Yellow Pages
- Newspapers
- Health/business directories
- Radio/television ads
Collaterals—preparation and printing
- Brochures
- Stationery
- Invitations
- Press releases
- Newsletters
- Folders
Postage
Travel/Meals
- Referral development calls
- Inservices
Seminars—invitations, food, gifts
Trade shows—booth and exhibit design, purchase

- insurance, HMO, and PPO case managers, including telephonic case managers
- discharge planners
- intensive care unit nurses
- utilization review nurses
- physicians and their office staffs
- hospital chief financial officers
- rehabilitation professionals
- attorneys
- home health administrators
- the facility's own employees
- former patients/residents and their families

PREOPENING MARKETING ACTIVITIES

The preopening marketing plan and budget should reflect a variety of activities.

Direct Mail

Letters, brochures, and articles designed for targeted referral sources should be utilized in the direct mail effort. Postage-paid postcards that recipients can return for further information about the facility or its programs should be included. The fact that these individuals return postcards for more information should be recorded on the database, and appointments should be scheduled as appropriate to provide further information to those potential referral sources and to obtain referrals.

Advertising

In addition to the telephone Yellow Pages advertising and listings for the facility or unit, other types of advertising should be considered. Because efforts need to be focused on the targeted referral sources, consideration should be given to advertising in directories that will reach the targeted referral sources rather than to general health care magazine advertising. However, to inform the community and other hospitals about the opening of the facility, it may also be desirable to utilize local newspaper advertising as an awareness mechanism and as a means for interested individuals to obtain the facility's address and telephone number for further information.

Promotion and Public Relations

Promotional and public relations activities serve as excellent ways to obtain leads and to make people aware of the subacute services. Generally, these efforts do not result directly in an immediate referral. Therefore, all the marketing activities—direct mail, advertising, promotion and public relations, and direct sales for referral development—need to be planned and utilized strategically to maximize awareness before the sale and to ensure optimal closing of direct sales. Promotional and public relation strategies include at least the following:

- *Seminars:* Seminars may be held for targeted referral groups as well as for health care professionals and even the general public. The seminars can include a "hot topic" for that group as well as provide an

opportunity to promote the new subacute facility or unit as the sponsor of the seminar.

- *Meetings:* Meetings that involve breakfasts, luncheons, and/or dinners for various targeted referral sources and professionals are a means of developing the important relationships that will facilitate the referral development strategy. If possible, a construction or renovation tour of the facility should be conducted and the meeting held on site if an adequate amount of construction or renovation has been completed. Discharge planners/social workers, independent and insurance/HMO/PPO case managers, physicians, provider relations representatives from HMOs and PPOs as well as indemnity insurers, clergy, rehabilitation and nursing professionals, hospital administrators, agencies that deal with worker's compensation, rehabilitation agencies and rehabilitation professionals in private practice, chief executive officers, chief financial officers, and employee benefits managers from businesses and industries in the area should all be included.

- *Media:* Press releases should be utilized as a promotional vehicle and should be distributed to a wide variety of potential publics and referral sources. The following groups should receive a press release: the hospital association; the local chapter of health care executives; the Chamber of Commerce; consumer groups; business clubs; professional associations for nursing, physical therapy, occupational therapy, rehabilitation nursing, critical care nursing, psychology, physician specialties, and speech-language pathology; schools, churches, and civic groups; and health care facilities such as hospitals, nursing facilities, and home health agencies and companies. Efforts should be made to obtain free radio and television coverage and newspaper coverage by directly contacting the appropriate individuals in charge of talk shows, morning shows, evening shows, and health editors, science editors, and community activities editors of local area newspapers. Consideration should be given to the development of a speaker's bureau with key staff members who have expertise in particular areas. The speaker's bureau may be promoted to volunteer groups, civic clubs, the Chamber of Commerce, local area businesses and industries, and health care associations and facilities. Consideration also should be given to sponsoring a free clinic at the new subacute unit with blood pressure checks, hearing tests, and the like, which will draw in community members and give them a positive feeling about and awareness of the new facility.

• *Exhibits:* Health care and health facilities associations should be queried about local area conventions, meetings, and trade shows, and arrangements should be made to exhibit at the ones that will give the best return for the dollars and time invested.

• *Newsletters:* A preopening newsletter may be initiated and continued on a quarterly basis after the subacute unit or facility is open. The preopening newsletter can be used as a direct mail piece as well as a handout. The needs of the primary referral sources that were assessed during the market feasibility study should be addressed in the most positive fashion in the newsletter. The newsletter should utilize the facility logo and have a consistent look to create a distinct image of the subacute facility or unit in the eyes of the readers.

DIRECT REFERRAL DEVELOPMENT

Direct mail, advertising, promotion, and public relations activities are important parts of the marketing mix. For subacute care, however, obtaining referrals means relationship selling. Because of the multiplicity of the referral decision makers and referral decision influencers, it is critical that the referral development efforts be focused and that the goal be development of long-term referral relationships.

COLLATERAL MATERIALS

Any generic collateral materials on the subacute program should be supplemented with those that are developed to reflect the specific needs and interests of specific referral sources. The appearance of collateral materials needs to be professional and exciting. With the availability of desktop publishing and quick printing, attractive supplementary collateral materials can be developed and prepared in a short time. Collateral materials should be targeted to the needs, wants, and interests of the referral source for which they are intended and should reflect the kind of quality that the referral source expects in terms of care provided at the facility.

OPEN HOUSE

The open house should be viewed as a major opportunity to promote awareness of the facility and to create the appropriate image of the subacute provider in the eyes of referral sources, potential patients and families, the community, and new employees. Typically, the open house consists of a series of events scheduled during the month of opening.

The open house often can be an effective vehicle for targeting various referral sources and audiences. For example, insurance/HMO case managers and independent case managers as well as hospital administrators may appreciate, and therefore attend, an early morning breakfast meeting for the open house. Discharge planners and social workers may be interested in attending a luncheon. Critical care nurses and rehabilitation nurses may prefer an afternoon tea at 3:30 or 4:00 PM. Physicians may be attracted to an evening cocktail function or dinner.

Detailed arrangements well in advance are required for an effective open house. Dates should be scheduled early and special speakers commissioned well in advance of the actual date. Invitations, catering, parking arrangements, arrangements for tours, greeters, and the like are some of the areas for which planning is required for a successful open house or series of open houses.

Media coverage for the open houses is important. By having the governor, mayor, or other celebrity conduct a ribbon cutting, television or newspaper coverage of the event might be obtained. Newspapers and television editors also may be attracted to a special speaker. Coverage is most likely to occur when a relationship with these editors has been established before the opening of the facility. During the open house, it is wise to have an adequate amount of collateral materials available for each of the targeted groups. The open house will be the event that establishes the type and quality of the facility in the minds of the public, the community, and referral sources for years to come. Therefore, it is an important event in the preopening marketing planning.

INTERNAL MARKETING SYSTEMS

Case managers report that one of their primary criteria in utilizing a facility is the ease of referrals/admissions and the responsiveness of the facility. Therefore, a well-operating admissions system is a critical component of the overall marketing plan. The internal marketing systems begin with an effective intake and end with the follow-up of the patient after discharge. The intake system must be available to referral sources 24 hours per day and must allow for ease of admission. This means that trained employees must be available to serve as intake coordinators 24 hours per day.

Systems to track referrals, referral sources, and patients should be in place and functioning effectively before opening. There is little forgiveness by referral sources for failed intake and

admissions systems. A satisfaction survey should be developed and utilized for physicians, referral sources, and patients and families. Information from the satisfaction survey should be shared with employees. Positive remarks are reinforcing to staff. When concerns are expressed, the facility must have a well-functioning mechanism to investigate and develop/alter systems to be "customer driven."

A follow-up reporting system to referral sources, primary care physicians, payers, and others regarding patients' status during their subacute stay and at discharge should be implemented and checked for effectiveness. Finally, a system to measure and document patient outcomes should be developed. Patient outcomes are becoming an important referral criterion for case managers and discharge planners and are valuable data for provider relations personnel for HMOs, PPOs, and insurers. Good patient outcome data can be persuasive in obtaining favorable contracts with these payers.

CONCLUSION

The preopening marketing program for subacute providers is an important key to the future success of the facility or unit. A cogent plan, a realistic budget, and a series of diversified start-up marketing activities should be components of a preopening marketing program. The internal systems for admissions, tracking, and reporting are equally important in ensuring that marketing program results meet the subacute provider's expectations.

19

Managed Care Contracting for Subacute Providers

Michael H. Cook, Laurel L. Fleming, and Ellen P. Pesch

In an environment where health care expenditures are closely scrutinized to reduce costs, managed care is playing an increasingly important role. Although managed care organizations (MCOs) initially focused on reducing the cost of providing hospital and physician services by monitoring the use of the services and negotiating discounts with the providers of such services, MCOs now are looking at additional ways to reduce health care costs. These include arranging for patients to be treated in less expensive environments, where appropriate, and negotiating discounts or other reduced fee arrangements with such step-down providers.

The types of step-down providers that are used by MCOs as an alternative to inpatient hospitalization include not only home health providers but also nursing facilities that provide subacute care (SAFs). Many MCOs, however, which are used to negotiating and contracting with physicians and hospitals, are familiar with neither the operations of SAFs nor the regulatory environment in which they operate, and frequently attempt to use a standard form agreement drafted for a hospital to contract with an SAF. Such an agreement may not be appropriate for an SAF and in many instances will require substantial

modification before use. This chapter identifies the typical operational and legal concerns that arise in the context of MCO contracting with SAFs and contractual terms that should at least be addressed or considered in the process.

THE MANAGED CARE ENVIRONMENT

The concept of managed care encompasses a variety of mechanisms, plans, or processes that are structured to focus on the price of services, the site at which they are delivered, and their utilization. Health maintenance organizations (HMOs) and preferred provider organizations (PPOs) are traditional vehicles for managed care. HMOs are entities that provide a package of specified benefits to their members (the term frequently used by HMOs to describe the individuals who are entitled to receive health care benefits under the HMO plan) on a prepaid per capita or prepaid aggregate fixed sum basis. Because HMOs undertake risk for the provision of care to members, they often are regulated by state insurance departments. HMO members typically are required to obtain all nonemergency care from designated participating providers and may be required to make copayments each time they seek care, in an effort to control their behavior in seeking health care services.

Unlike HMOs, PPOs do not undertake to provide care to individuals. Instead, PPOs provide a network of designated participating providers that have agreed to provide their services at discounted rates. Although individuals participating in PPO arrangements are not required to receive services from the designated participating providers for their care to be reimbursed, they are provided with incentives to utilize such participating providers. The incentives usually include lower copayments, higher reimbursement percentages, and no claim forms filing because the participating providers usually prepare the claim forms on behalf of the patient. PPOs typically are used in conjunction with a traditional indemnity insurance plan or by self-funded employer plans.

In addition to HMO and PPO arrangements, payers of health care, including indemnity insurers, self-funded employer plans, and the state and federal governments, are increasingly integrating various levels of managed care elements into their programs to deliver or reimburse for the delivery of health care. An SAF may find itself participating in a managed care arrangement by directly contracting with an HMO, PPO, or other such payer. Alternatively, it may do so through its affiliation with other providers that offer an integrated system to provide a continuum of health care to payers. Such integrated systems include physician–hospital organizations, independent physician associations, and other multiprovider systems. All references in this chapter to MCOs refer collectively to HMOs, PPOs, and other payers and systems of providers with which an SAF contracts within the context of a managed care arrangement.

The most important concept for SAFs to understand in the contracting process is that MCOs, as entities responsible for the payment of care, have a tremendous incentive to restrain what they pay for that care. As such, a key strategy for these entities is to minimize the number of days that patients spend in the acute care setting and to encourage movement to a lower-cost setting consistent with achieving positive patient care outcomes.

SAFs become attractive in this process because they often have a lower cost structure than acute care hospitals, especially in the area of capital costs, and therefore can undercut the prices for certain services that traditionally have been provided in hospitals. Thus, MCOs have a strong incentive to enter into arrangements with SAFs that have the capacity to provide care for patients, such as those who are ventilator dependent, have suffered head trauma, require wound care, require cardiac telemetry, require intravenous therapy, or require intensive rehabilitation. With the increasing incentives to utilize these facilities, this list can only grow.

CONTRACT TERMS

Because SAFs are different from traditional MCO providers such as hospitals, the SAF management should carefully review the written contract proposed by the MCO before executing it. The contract should clearly identify the responsibilities and duties of each party in the relationship, and the relationship should be structured to avoid any unnecessary risk, to apportion any risk that cannot be avoided, and to manage the risk that is apportioned.

To identify both parties' duties appropriately, the MCO contract should address various operational issues, such as admissions, transfers, discharges, services, utilization review, quality management, payment, marketing, referrals, exclusivity, and inspection and record keeping, as well as legal issues, including term and termination, insurance, indemnification, coordination of benefits (COB), compliance with laws and policies, amendments, and bankruptcy. In this regard, it is important to keep in mind the SAF's present operations and the regulatory environment under which it operates. If an MCO arrangement is overly burdensome or jeopardizes the provider's licensure, the value of entering into the arrangement is clearly questionable. Because most MCOs are not familiar with contracting or working with SAFs, however, it may be necessary to educate the MCO as to the SAF's operations and regulatory requirements. It is critical that both parties have a mutual understanding of how their arrangement will operate to minimize future disputes and liabilities. An overview of key operational and legal managed care contracting issues follows.

Solvency of the MCO

The fiscal solvency of an MCO should be of critical importance to an SAF. Under many, if not all, state laws, a provider that is treating a member may be under a duty to care for that patient in the event of the fiscal insolvency of the MCO and may have no recourse against the patient for the cost of covered services provided during the stay other than co-insurance and deductible amounts.[1] The provider also may be unable to terminate its contract with the MCO in the event of insolvency and may find itself with an ongoing obligation to provide services.[2] For this reason, it is critical to know one's partner in advance. Information about an MCO's financial status may be available through such sources as the office of the state insurance commissioner or, in some instances, newspaper articles or trade publications.

In this regard, it also is important for an SAF to monitor the contract during its operation. For example, the contract might require the MCO to provide financial data on a periodic basis. Chronically late payments might signify financial problems. Again, trade periodicals can serve as an important source of information.

Additionally, the contract should address the issue of insolvency, generally through termination clauses. For example, the contract might provide for the SAF to have the right to terminate in the event that the MCO files for protection under the bankruptcy laws, if the state takes action to require an increase in reserves that is not generally required of all MCOs, or if the MCO receives a request from state officials for a corrective action plan. Finally, the contract might provide for termination without cause to offer the option for an SAF to withdraw from the arrangement in the event that it discovers warning signals that do not rise to official action but raise a level of concern that outweighs the benefit of the contract.

Definitions

MCO contracts may provide important definitions that often are overlooked by providers. For example, SAF providers should pay particular attention to any definition of covered services. Many MCO agreements incorporate the MCO's entire schedule of benefits in the covered services definition, thereby potentially extending the SAF's obligations beyond its intent or capacity to provide services. The covered services definition should be limited to those services that the SAF is actually able and willing to provide, or, depending upon how the contract is structured, a separate definition (eg, subacute services) should be included that specifically identifies covered services that the SAF is willing and able to provide at that price. The services can be itemized within the definition (often in a separate exhibit), or the definition simply can refer to those services that the SAF customarily provides to other patients and that are within the scope of its license. The SAF should avoid overly broad definitions that could obligate it to provide services that it does not offer.

The definition of medical necessity also requires special attention. A determination of medical necessity is one of the key factors in obtaining payment from an MCO. Thus its definition should not be too narrow. A reasonable and typical definition is as follows: Medically necessary or medical necessity means services or supplies that, under the terms and conditions of the contract, are determined to be:

- appropriate and necessary for the symptoms, diagnosis, or treatment of the medical condition of members; and
- provided for the diagnosis or direct care and treatment of the medical condition of members within standards of medical practice in the community; and
- not primarily for the convenience of the member, the member's physician, or another provider; and
- the most appropriate supply or level of service or supplies that can safely be provided.

As discussed later in this chapter, it is important to ascertain which party will be making determinations of medical necessity, the processes to be followed, and the effect of providing care in the absence of medical necessity approval.

All defined terms within the contract should be used consistently and capitalized or otherwise identified to ensure that the reader will know to refer to the definitional section to clarify meaning and content.

Admissions

MCOs often require that admission to any participating provider be based on an order by a participating physician who contracts with, or is employed by, the MCO. The contract between the MCO and SAF should therefore specify the procedures by which such admission will take place. Specifically, how much advance notice will be given before an admission? Which party will determine the unit (if the SAF offers more than one) into which the patient initially will be admitted? Which party will make the transfer arrangements? What records will the SAF receive with the patient?

The contract also should address the manner in which the SAF will verify the patient's eligibility and ideally should provide that once eligibility is verified there cannot be a retroactive denial of coverage. In short, there should be a mechanism for preauthorization upon which the SAF is entitled to rely.

In addition, the contract should identify when, if ever, the SAF has the right to refuse admission of a patient or what happens if the SAF has no beds available. The contract also should provide that any patients will be admitted in accordance with the SAF's normal and customary admissions policies and criteria, including those that require the patient to execute any required resident agreements. In this regard, although the SAF will be receiving payment from the MCO, federal and most state laws require that facilities such as SAFs have a separate resident agreement with each patient. In doing so, the SAF should utilize a separate contract or addendum specifically reflecting the unique relationship among the MCO, patient, and facility. Among other things, such a contract or addendum should specify any bed hold policies and services that are covered by the contract.

Transfers and Discharges

For new admissions who are being transferred to the SAF from another facility, the contract should set forth the specific responsibilities of the transferor and transferee. The contract also should address transfers from the SAF to another facility as well as transfers between units in a multiple-unit SAF due to changes in the patient's condition. Bed hold policies and expectations should also be addressed. These transfer provisions are extremely important in the SAF setting because many facilities offer only a limited type of service, and when a patient falls outside the range of such services it is necessary and appropriate to transfer the patient to another, more appropriate setting.

Discharges from an SAF are different from those generally experienced by MCOs in the hospital setting. Of course, the SAF should retain the authority to discharge a patient in certain circumstances, such as to protect the health and safety of other patients or in the event of failure of the MCO to pay for the patient's care. Federal and many state laws place additional restrictions on a nursing facility's ability to discharge residents involuntarily, however.[3] Moreover, these laws also allow nursing facility residents to appeal transfers and discharges.[4] Thus it is critical that SAFs consider the impact of these provisions in structuring any agreement.

For example, it is not inconceivable that an MCO's utilization review process might conclude that a patient should be discharged from the facility but federal or state law prohibits the discharge within the time frames established by the MCO. The parties should address the issue of whether the MCO is required to pay for the care that the patient receives during the period subsequent to the date on which the MCO seeks discharge as well as which party bears the expense of defending against any patient appeals. Also, to the extent that the MCO does not bear the responsibility of payment, and to the extent permitted by state law, the SAF may wish to structure its admission agreement with the patient to provide for payment by the patient.

Services

As discussed above, the contract with the MCO should clearly set forth the services that the SAF is expected to provide and should address ordinary nursing services, extraordinary nursing services, rehabilitative therapies, and other specialized services. Furthermore, when an SAF offers a variety of units to treat different categories of patients, the contract should specify which units are included in the contract and which services each specific unit will provide. In addition, the contract should address the provision of supplies, medication, and private or semiprivate rooms. If the SAF subcontracts for the provision of any of its services, such as physical therapy, then the issues of the subcontractor's payment, malpractice insurance, and indemnifications, if any, also should be addressed in the contract.

Utilization Review

Most MCOs monitor the level of care and its appropriateness for each particular patient through a process called utilization review to ensure that patients only receive care that is necessary and appropriate. Such review includes a determination of the appropriate level of services or supplies that can safely be provided. Utilization review is an integral function in all successful MCOs and can include prospective reviews of care (precertification or preauthorization), concurrent reviews (the appropriateness of continued care), and retrospective reviews.

MCO utilization review programs and procedures should be reviewed carefully before any contract is executed. Such procedures should be incorporated into the contract by specific reference and ideally should not be subject to change unilaterally by the MCO. Rather, wherever possible these procedures should be subject to prior notification and approval by the SAF. Alterna-

tively, the SAF should be permitted to terminate the contract within a relatively short time period in the event that unilateral amendments are unacceptable, and the SAF should not be required to abide by an amended procedure during any notification period required before termination.

MCO utilization review programs should be examined for their adherence to certain minimum specifications, including:

- whether utilization review policies and procedures are followed on a regular basis
- whether utilization review personnel are properly qualified (eg, nurse reviewers should be licensed and trained with minimum experience requirements)
- whether physician reviewers practice in the area they review
- whether the utilization management entity complies with applicable certification groups and, if required by law, whether utilization review entities are licensed or certified in their respective states
- whether the procedures include discussion with the attending physician before a denial is rendered
- whether emergency admissions are exempt from preadmission review
- whether the basis of denials and protocols followed are consistently documented
- whether denials can be appealed by the patient and provider
- whether medical criteria are based upon local practice standards

Furthermore, where MCOs engage in concurrent utilization review, SAFs may wish to require the MCO to continue payments during any periods when state or federal law would prohibit the transfer or discharge of the patient even though the MCO's concurrent review concludes that transfer or discharge is appropriate. There should not be any retrospective reviews of precertified or preauthorized services, and, to the extent that an MCO participating physician has ordered certain care, such care rendered by the SAF in response to the physician's orders should not be subject to further determinations of medical necessity. Additionally, in the event that the MCO makes an administrative error in either the eligibility or the utilization review process, the contract should provide that the SAF will be paid by the MCO notwithstanding any such error.

In considering a case where a patient was discharged from a hospital based solely on a payer's utilization review determination, at least one court has held that a provider that complies with a payer's limitations without protest, when medical judgment dictates otherwise, cannot avoid ultimate responsibility for the patient's care.[5] Thus the contract should contain a utilization review appeal mechanism that allows the SAF to appeal any adverse utilization review decisions made by the MCO. The contract also should specify which party is responsible for notifying patients of any denials made under the MCO's utilization review program.

Another case has held that the MCO can be held liable for its utilization review decisions where the decisions proximately cause injury to a patient.[6] Therefore, language should be included in the contract that specifically states that the MCO is responsible for the design and implementation of any utilization review programs and that the MCO will indemnify the SAF for any loss incurred by the SAF as a result of such programs. MCOs should not be allowed to shift to the SAF all responsibility for medical decisions relating to termination of treatment resulting from the utilization review program. In this regard, any exculpation clauses identifying the SAF as being solely responsible for all health care provided should be avoided.

Quality Management

Because many MCOs will require SAFs to comply with certain quality management procedures within the MCO program, the MCO's quality management procedures should be reviewed against the SAF's own quality management program to ensure that they are consistent with, or will not cause any problematic conflict with, the SAF's own programs. As with utilization review procedures, quality management procedures should be incorporated into the contract by specific reference and should not be subject to amendment by the MCO without prior notification and approval by the SAF. Alternatively, the SAF should be allowed to terminate the contract in the event that unilateral amendments are unacceptable.

Payment

Payment issues, both the amounts and the processes for obtaining payment, are critical to any negotiations between an MCO and an SAF. As a general matter, the contract should address the manner in which claims are to be submitted by the SAF to the MCO, including the format of the claims, any time limits on the submission of claims, and the address to which they should be sent. The contract also should specify the claim turnaround time and include penalties in the event that the MCO fails to remit payment within the specified time.

Generally, MCOs make payment to acute care hospitals after patient discharge. Because it is not atypical that a patient will spend relatively long periods of time in the SAF, however, a provision should be included for periodic interim payments from the MCO for such patients. Furthermore, if the payment mechanism is case mix sensitive or is based upon the unit to which a patient is admitted, the SAF may wish to consider requiring periodic repricing based on changes in the patient's condition.

MCOs utilize a variety of payment methodologies to compensate their participating providers. General descriptions of the various methodologies are as follows:

- *Fee for service:* Payment under this type of arrangement is usually limited to the lesser of the provider's billed charges or the usual, customary, and reasonable amount as determined by the MCO.
- *Discounted fee for service:* Under this type of arrangement, the provider typically

agrees to provide services at a discounted percentage of its standard charges or the usual, customary, and reasonable amount.

- *Per diem:* Under this type of arrangement, the provider will receive a certain fixed payment amount per day of service provided to an MCO enrollee. It is important to identify clearly which services are included in the per diem arrangement and which are compensated outside the per diem. Also, providers should consider including a stop-loss threshold that provides a specific dollar amount set in advance such that, if charges exceed that amount, reimbursement by the MCO will be calculated pursuant to another method, such as fee for service or discounted fee for service. In the area of subacute care, the parties may wish to vary payment by case mix utilizing indices such as Reference Utilization Groupings III (RUGs III) or mechanisms developed by the parties.

- *Per case:* A per case payment method typically constitutes a prospective payment amount that is paid per patient based on case mix. With any kind of per case payment arrangement, the SAF should consider outlier and stop-loss protection.

- *Capitation:* Under a capitation arrangement, a provider receives a fixed payment per member per month for which the provider is obligated to provide specified services to a specified member population. At the time of this writing, we are unaware of any instance in which an SAF is paid on a true capitation basis. We contemplate that such arrangements may be developed in the future, however. If this occurs, it will be important to specify which services are included in the capitation services and which members are included in the population that the provider will be required to serve. Also, as with the per diem or per case payment arrangements, SAFs should consider stop-loss protection when they are compensated on a capitated basis.

- *Risk pools:* Risk pool type arrangements require the provider to share the risk of financial losses, which serves as an incentive for the provider to utilize services appropriately.

The contract also should specify payment obligations of the patients, such as copayments, deductibles, and/or noncovered services. Ideally, the SAF should retain the right to bill and collect such amounts as well as any amounts that the MCO fails to pay for covered care to the extent permitted under state law. Under many state laws, however, payments made by an HMO are considered payment in full, and providers are prohibited from billing patients for covered services regardless of whether the HMO actually made payment.

Relationships with Participating Providers

The contract between the MCO and the SAF should clearly specify the manner in which the SAF will coordinate with other participating providers of the MCO in the provision of health care services. For example, the SAF may prefer to have the patient treated by a physician with whom it already is affiliated rather than by the physicians of the MCO, with whom it may not be familiar. The SAF may have no choice in this matter, however, because the contract may require the SAF to coordinate with the MCO participating physicians for patient care. Accordingly, the MCO periodically should provide the SAF with a listing of all participating providers and should notify the SAF of any additions or deletions in a timely fashion. Moreover, all MCO participating physicians should agree to abide by the SAF's policies and procedures, and the contract should address the procedure to be followed in the event that an MCO participating physician does not comply with facility policies or applicable state or federal law. The contract also should address those situations in which the SAF must transfer the patient to a hospital. Except in emergency situations, such transfers may need to be made to other MCO participating facilities.

Federal law requires that SAFs allow a patient to have a physician of his or her choice. A patient selecting a managed care plan that provides a closed panel of providers, however, arguably constitutes the patient exercising his or her choice of provider.

Inspection Rights and Record-Keeping Requirements

If the MCO contract permits the MCO to inspect the SAF premises, there should be a provision limiting when such inspections can occur and potentially requiring that a minimum advance notice be given to the SAF. If the contract specifies that the MCO is entitled to copies of SAF records, the contract also should specify which party is responsible for the costs associated with such copies. Furthermore, provisions allowing MCOs access to patient records should state that such access will be permitted only to the extent allowed by state and federal law.

Exclusivity

SAFs should be cautious of any type of MCO contract that requires exclusivity on the part of either party. Such exclusivity arrangements may give rise to antitrust issues and should be reviewed by legal counsel before execution.

Marketing

The contract should address when either party is permitted to use the other's name and/or logo for marketing purposes. Preferably, the contract should provide that the advance consent of the SAF is required if the MCO is to use the SAF's name and/or logo for any purpose other than inclusion in the participating provider listing.

Reimbursement

An increasing percentage of contracts between MCOs and SAFs provide for payment from the MCO on a fixed price per diem in some form.

Especially for SAFs that provide care for patients who require extensive rehabilitation, vendors of therapy services to nursing facilities have been developing mechanisms to share risk with SAFs. These mechanisms generally take the form of offering therapy services on a fixed price per day. Additionally, because of the extreme pressure to deliver care in the most efficient manner under these contracts, independent vendors of therapy services and facilities are examining innovative mechanisms for delivering therapy services, including a mix of licensed and unlicensed staff and the delivery of these services to more than one patient at a time.

Where care of this nature is delivered in facilities that are certified under the Medicare program, it does not fit neatly into the cost reporting mechanisms that exist. This occurs because Medicare allocates the cost of therapy services among various payers based on a charge per unit of care actually delivered that is consistent among payer services, rather than on a fixed price per day, and because Medicare historically has not been presented with circumstances where more than one patient at a time has received therapy services in nursing facilities. Apart from other possible legal concerns, these arrangements raise a number of issues with respect to the Medicare and Medicaid requirements for certification and in the manner in which services are billed and costs are allowed under, and are allocated to, the Medicare program. These issues arise even where the arrangements do not involve Medicare (or Medicaid) patients if the facility in which the care is delivered is certified under the public programs.

The authors believe that at least some of these arrangements can be structured to comply with the applicable laws in a manner that would allocate costs fairly to the various payers. Because these relationships are unique, however, SAFs should consult knowledgeable counsel and reimbursement consultants, as well as their fiscal intermediaries and potentially the Health Care Financing Administration, before entering into these arrangements to ensure that any arrangements are structured to prevent or minimize the likelihood of creating unintended reimbursement consequences and to ensure that they do not run afoul of other federal and state requirements.

SAFs also should be especially cognizant of Medicare, and potentially Medicaid, implications of vendor agreements that provide different prices for managed care patients for items or supplies that are billed through the cost report where these arrangements are not on a fixed price per diem but instead provide for discounts on an item-by-item basis for managed care patients. These types of arrangements may raise serious issues that should be examined by counsel and reimbursement consultants in advance. Finally, the contract between the MCO and the SAF should address the extent to which the SAF will be permitted to utilize outside providers (eg, therapists) without MCO interference.

Term and Termination

The term of the contract should be specifically set out, including the date upon which the SAF is expected to commence services. Many MCO contracts contain "evergreen clauses," or automatic renewal provisions, which generally are acceptable so long as the SAF has the right to terminate the agreement without cause and so long as the rates are not subject to automatic renewal. Where contracts contain these clauses, the SAF has less leverage to negotiate with the MCO to change the rates that are initially established. When the rates are nonrenewable, however, the MCO is forced to discuss rates with the SAF on an annual or other periodic basis, and the SAF is in a better negotiating position.

The SAF should review carefully the termination provisions to determine whether they are reciprocal and whether termination is permitted with and without cause. For terminations with cause, the contract should define clearly what constitutes cause (eg, material breach of the contract) and should specify whether termination for cause is immediate or whether there is a cure period.

In this regard, SAFs should ensure that for cause provisions are not worded so broadly that

they bring within their ambit insignificant deficiency citations in a licensure or certification survey without the opportunity to cure. The contract also should address what happens to patients in the SAF at the time of a termination. MCO contracts typically require the SAF to continue to provide services to patients in the SAF at the time of a termination, and state and/or federal law may restrict an SAF's ability to discharge the patient upon termination of the MCO contract. Thus the contract should require the MCO to remain responsible for payment, at a specified rate, for the services provided to the patients in the facility at the time of termination until such patients are discharged or transferred.

Insurance and Indemnification

Both the SAF and the MCO should be required to carry general liability and professional liability insurance coverage. The actual amounts and types of coverage should be specified in the contract, and the contract should not contain open-ended language such as "in amounts or with companies approved by MCO." Additionally, the contract should require the parties to provide evidence of coverage to each other as well as notification to the other party in the event of a material change in coverage.

If the MCO contract contains indemnification language, it should be reviewed with extreme care. Many typical indemnification provisions contain elements that arguably are unfair to providers, and many expose the providers to potential liabilities that might far exceed any benefit to them. It is important to consult legal counsel when such a provision is encountered. It may be advantageous to avoid including indemnification provisions in a contract (other than those necessary to protect the SAF from MCO utilization review). If an indemnification provision is included, SAFs may wish to limit the scope of the provision.

An SAF should not agree to indemnification without receiving reciprocal indemnification obligations from the MCO. When negotiating an indemnification provision, SAFs should be aware that many insurance policies may not cover contractually assumed obligations such as indemnification, and an SAF that agrees to such a provision may be jeopardizing its assets.

Coordination of Benefits

An SAF should be aware of any obligations it has under COB provisions with the MCO. The party responsible for obtaining COB payments and the party financially at risk should be specified in the contract, and the party at risk should be entitled to any COB payments. Where the MCO performs the COB, SAFs may wish to negotiate the right to retain any payments due from third parties other than the MCO that exceed the amount that the MCO is obligated to pay to the SAFs up to the SAF's full charges. It is certainly reasonable for the MCO to shoulder most of the COB burden because most MCOs are much better equipped to pursue COB recoveries than SAFs.

Compliance with Applicable Laws

If the contract contains a provision requiring compliance with all applicable laws, it should specify what constitutes an adverse regulatory action that would result in cancellation of the contract as well as any cure periods to remedy such adverse action.

Policies and Procedures

Any MCO policies and procedures referenced in the contract should be thoroughly reviewed by the SAF before the contract is executed. Also, any MCO policies with which the SAF will be expected to comply should be specifically referenced in the contract to limit the MCO's ability to change such policies unilaterally.

Amendments

The best case scenario is to require that any modification or amendment to the contract be in writing and signed by both parties. This approach may be unrealistic in the current contracting environment, however. At a minimum,

the SAF should require that the MCO provide advance written notice of any amendment to the MCO policies, procedures, or contract and allow the SAF to terminate the contract before the effective date of the amendment if it is unacceptable to the SAF.

Miscellaneous

The contract should specify that the parties are independent contractors and that there are no third party beneficiaries to the contract. SAFs may consider the inclusion of an arbitration provision in the contract in the event of a dispute over the contract. If so, the SAF should consult with legal counsel to ensure that language is drafted that adequately protects the SAF. Additionally, the contract should specifically address procedures to be followed in the event of the bankruptcy of either party.

CONCLUSION

Today's health care environment presents opportunities for nursing facilities that can provide subacute care to enter into arrangements with MCOs that are mutually beneficial. Because of the novelty of these arrangements, however, coupled with the lack of historical familiarity of MCOs with nursing facilities and vice versa, it is critical for SAFs to understand the importance of the contractual arrangements among MCOs, their member patients, and SAFs.

In today's competitive MCO contracting environment, it may well be impossible for SAFs to negotiate the inclusion of all the recommended items addressed in this chapter. SAFs at least should be cognizant of potential areas in which the contract language may affect their rights and obligations, however, and should make an informed business decision as to whether the potential benefits of proceeding with the MCO arrangement outweigh the potential risks. Furthermore, the passage of comprehensive health reform as well as the evolution of MCO arrangements and subacute care undoubtedly will affect future arrangements between providers and MCOs.

REFERENCES

1. See, for example, Utah Code Ann §31A-8-407 (1994); Fla Stat Ann §641.315 (West Suppl 1994); 215 ILCS 125/2-8 (Smith Hurd 1993) (formerly Ill Ann Stat ch 111 1/2 §1407.1).

2. 11 USC §365(a).

3. 42 USC §1395i-3(c)(2) and 1396r(c)(2), 42 CFR §483.12.

4. 42 USC §1395i-3(c)(2) and 1396r(2), 42 CFR §483.200.

5. *Wickline v State*, 183 Cal App 3d 1064, 228 Cal Rptr 661 (Cal App 2d Dist 1986).

6. *Wilson v Blue Cross of S Cal*, 222 Cal App 3d 660, 271 Cal Rptr 876 (2d Dist 1990).

Part IV

Health Care Reform and
the Subacute Industry

20

Impact of Health Care Reform Legislation on the Market for Subacute Care

Valerie S. Wilbur and Michael H. Cook

Health care reform was the leading domestic issue on the congressional agenda during the 103rd Congress. Motivated in large part by President Clinton's campaign promise to make health care a number 1 priority, Congress introduced scores of health reform bills in 1993 and 1994. Congressional health committees spent months analyzing and debating key aspects of the health care reform legislation, from the organizational structure of financing and delivery systems to funding of new health care benefits. Despite the intense effort mounted by both the administration and Congress, however, Congress was unable to achieve consensus on health care reform or to enact legislation before adjournment of the 103rd Congress.

The two most critical factors driving the health care reform debate include the need to expand access to health care coverage to the uninsured and to contain the dramatic escalation of health care spending. Although the United States is credited with the most sophisticated health care system in the world, 38.9 million Americans had no health insurance coverage in 1992. This represented more than 17% of the population younger than 65 years. Another 40 million Americans were insured by policies that would not protect them against serious illness.[1] Furthermore, the amount of national resources that the United States devotes to health care services and the annual growth rates in spending far exceed those of any other developed country.

As a percentage of the nation's gross domestic product, US health care spending grew from 5.9% in 1965 to 14.3% in 1993.[1] In 1994, the United States will spend almost $1 trillion on health care. If current trends continue, this number is projected to rise to approximately $1.65 trillion by the end of the century.[1] A large percentage of these costs is financed by the federal government. Federal expenditures for health care in 1994 will reach $318 billion and now consume about 21% of gross federal outlays.[2] If unchecked, health care spending is projected to account for 28% of the federal budget in another decade.[3] These growth rates have serious implications for the government's ability effectively to address other important social needs, such as adequate housing, education, and crime prevention.

To address the twin problems of inadequate health care coverage and rapidly escalating health care costs, Congress proposed a number of measures. Some called for comprehensive reform of the health care financing and delivery system and rely heavily on government regulations, such as employer mandates and global budgets, to increase access and reduce spending growth. Others took a more incremental approach and attempted to contain costs through insurance system reforms and private market incentives to spur competition among providers and payers. Regardless of the size and shape of the various proposals, however, all included several elements common to the managed competition model underlying President Clinton's Health Security Act legislation. Many of the strategies and goals embodied by this model are consistent with the philosophy underlying subacute care and represent important opportunities for this emerging industry.

Managed competition is a managed care model, conceived by the Jackson Hole Group, that envisions a combination of regulatory measures and private market incentives to contain health care costs. Regulation would be used to level the playing field among health care purchasers through standard benefit packages, guaranteed access to coverage, and community-rated premiums. Health care providers would compete for subscribers by managing care in terms of quality, efficiency, and price rather than by avoiding high health care risks. Efficiencies would be achieved by reducing unnecessary treatment, minimizing the use of expensive medical technologies and services, and vertically integrating care across all providers and health care settings. Such practices increasingly are being employed by today's managed health care systems as a way to contain costs and increase market share. This is occurring through both pressure from payers, and the bonding of providers and practitioners through various models of integrated delivery systems and networks.

Subacute care services represent a growing specialty niche in the health care market that is fast becoming an integral component of managed care. It was a $1 billion industry in 1993, and growth estimates by the end of the century range from $10 billion to $30 billion.[4] This level of care has evolved to fill a treatment gap for individuals who no longer require medically necessary acute care services delivered in a hospital setting but whose health care needs are too extensive or complex to be delivered at home. By substituting lower-cost postacute care services for care traditionally provided in the hospital, this model could result in substantial cost savings to public and private payers alike. Cost savings as high as $3 billion annually have been projected by the American Health Care Association.[5]

Although the subacute care market represents the potential for tremendous cost savings to the health care system, a number of regulatory barriers have impeded the development of this market to some degree. For example, the elimination of return on equity for proprietary providers and the $150 million cap on tax exempt bonds for nonprofit providers limit access to the capital needed to establish subacute care programs. The freeze on Medicare routine cost limits for skilled nursing facility payments imposed by the Omnibus Budget Reconciliation Act (OBRA) of 1993 and Medicare limits on payment for certain therapeutic services delivered in skilled nursing facilities pose additional barriers to reimbursement for subacute care services. Administrative lags of 1 to 2 years in obtaining exceptions or exemptions from Medicare payment rules have caused substantial cash flow issues for subacute providers in the past, although recent regulatory action by the Health Care Financing Administration (HCFA) holds the promise of substantially shortening the time frame for relief.[6] (See discussion on Routine Cost Limits.) Despite these and other regulatory barriers, however, creative providers have been able to work within the regulatory system in many instances to create a win–win situation.

The health care reform legislation introduced during the 103rd Congress included both opportunities and potential barriers to the development of the subacute market. Opportunities relate to the compatibility of the subacute care model with many of the components of the managed competition legislation. Clearly, the goals of increased access to appropriate services, cost containment, and integrated service delivery are common to both. Furthermore, some of the most critical components of the subacute care model, such as a comprehensive program of care and an interdisciplinary team approach, would be fostered through the structure of the delivery system envisioned under managed competition.

Legislation introduced by Senator Orrin Hatch[7] devoted an entire section of the bill to removing current regulatory barriers to subacute care. For example, the bill would have equalized physician payments for comparable services provided in hospitals and nursing facilities, regardless of setting. It also would have required Medicare to reimburse skilled nursing facilities for respiratory therapy services as an ancillary service whether or not the respiratory therapist is employed by a hospital with which the facility has a transfer agreement.

Other components of the health care reform legislation could have exacerbated existing regulatory barriers. For example, a significant share of the savings for financing low-income subsidies came from cuts in Medicare and Medicaid spending ranging from approximately $60 billion to $500 billion over 10 years. Many of these savings would have been achieved by decreasing provider payments through cuts in existing Medicare reimbursement levels for inpatient and outpatient capital-related costs, a reduction in Medicare routine cost limits for skilled nursing facility and home health care services, a reduction or elimination of disproportionate share payments under Medicare and Medicaid, and other measures. Although subacute care clearly represents a significant opportunity to reduce costs throughout the entire delivery system (including Medicare) in a more rational fashion than simply ratcheting down provider payments, certain measures for achieving Medicare savings, such as routine cost limit reductions, are at odds with the provision of subacute care services.

Whether health care reform legislation turns out to be an asset or liability to the subacute care market depends in part on the approach taken by Congress and the administration to address health care cost containment. If Congress continues to look for short-term responses (eg, rate caps or payment cuts) to a long-term problem, the resulting legislation is more likely to impede than promote the development of this market. A more rational approach that addresses the systemic problems in health care delivery, however, will include incentives to treat patients at the lowest level of care that is medically acceptable. Under any system of this nature, providers of subacute care should benefit substantially, as should the entire system.

It is not a fait accompli that major health care reform legislation will be enacted in the 104th Congress. In fact, lessons learned in the past 18 months regarding the genuine complexity of developing a bipartisan agreement on health care reform and the change in the leadership and balance of power in Congress are likely to result in a much more conservative approach to health care reform. Furthermore, the ostensible commitment to deficit reduction and the fundamental change in attitudes toward government represented by the newly elected Republican Congress will probably limit the scope of health care legislation introduced in 1995.

Pressures to contain health care spending and to increase access, however, will not recede. In the absence of a comprehensive health care reform bill, incremental measures that can be integrated into OBRA of 1995 are likely to be introduced. Ongoing attention to deficit reduction is sure to result in proposals to cut Medicare and Medicaid expenditures, among other programs. Such measures will intensify the pressure to identify less costly delivery modes, such as the subacute care market, and may provide opportunities to eliminate legislative and regulatory barriers to the development of this market.

HEALTH CARE REFORM PROPOSALS IN THE 103RD CONGRESS

Health care reform proposals included provisions that could either eliminate or exacerbate regulatory barriers to entering the subacute market. Many proposals would have reduced health care spending by restructuring the delivery system and incorporating incentives to substitute lower-cost care for traditional services. Others would simply have slashed provider payment rates to reduce system costs. Subacute care clearly offers a cost-effective alternative to hospital services for certain medically complex patients. To manage this care more effectively in a lower level setting, however, regulations regarding reimbursement and payment levels would need to be more flexible.

Subacute care has evolved as a solution to address the need for more appropriate and less costly transitional care for certain patients who traditionally would have received care in the acute setting. After the implementation of Medicare's Prospective Payment System (PPS), there was a shortage of postacute care services. Hospitals responded to PPS cost containment pressures through earlier discharges and encountered severe placement problems. Furthermore, they incurred significant financial losses by absorbing the costs of administratively necessary days (ANDs) not covered under diagnosis-related groups (DRGs) while awaiting patient placement in skilled nursing facilities and other postacute settings.

During the first 9 years of PPS, the update factor increased payment rates by a cumulative 32%, but cumulative operating costs per discharge actually increased by 106%.[8] Annual costs of $25 million for ANDs were reported in Michigan,[8] costs of $35 million for 300 patients awaiting posthospital placement were reported in Washington, DC,[8] and California's costs for ANDs nearly doubled between fiscal years 1985–86 and 1986–87.[9] Many of these losses were passed on by hospitals to private insurance companies. For example, in 1990, although Medicare covered 90% of hospital costs, private insurance accounted for 128% of these costs.[8]

Difficulties in placing transitional care patients are largely the result of inadequate payments. Medicaid reimbursement rates in most states for extensive care patients in skilled nursing facilities have created tremendous disincentives to accepting such patients, as have the substantial cash flow shortages that facilities have experienced under Medicare while they await the processing of their Medicare routine cost limit

exceptions. Average nursing facility rates do not cover the costs of the more highly trained staff, sophisticated equipment, and intensive services required by subacute patients.

These same forces to shorten hospital lengths of stay, however, coupled with an increased emphasis on care and cost containment, have provided an opportunity for sophisticated nursing facilities to provide a more rational use of capital. For example, nursing facilities that can provide care to ventilator-dependent patients, survivors of head trauma, certain patients needing cardiac telemetry care, and those needing intensive rehabilitation have been able to increase revenues while reducing costs to the system by undercutting the costs of treating these patients at the acute care level. By developing specialty units, these facilities have enhanced the level and quality of patient care.

The managed competition model could substantially decrease placement problems in numerous ways. First, the fundamental orientation of this model is to reduce costs by changing the basic delivery structure and pathways of care. Subacute care can provide a less costly pathway for medically complex patients without compromising patient needs or quality of care. Second, this model provides subacute providers with the vehicle to affiliate with larger networks of providers. The capacity problems related to the provision of a comprehensive program of complex medical services would be alleviated through affiliations with vertically integrated systems of care. Such affiliations could provide prospective subacute care providers with the range of medical and clinical specialties needed to deliver more complex care. These affiliations also would create an entire network of referral sources for providers entering the subacute care market.

Framework for Managed Competition

All major health care reform legislation introduced during the 103rd Congress was based on the managed competition model underlying President Clinton's Health Security Act. According to Alain Enthoven,[10] this model is a prescription for health care reform that requires health care plans to compete by managing care in terms of quality, efficiency, and price rather than by avoiding high health care risks.

The managed competition model uses rules for competition designed to reward (with more subscribers and revenues) health plans that do the best job of improving quality, cutting cost, and satisfying patients. Furthermore, unlike models such as preferred provider organizations and independent practice associations, managed competition occurs at the level of integrated financing and delivery plans (ie, at the system level, not at the individual provider level). The goal is to divide the providers in each community into competing economic units and to use market forces to motivate them to develop efficient delivery systems.

Key elements of managed competition proposals include a standard benefit package, health alliances or purchasing cooperatives, health plans, and community rating of health insurance premiums. Each of the major health care reform proposals contained some version of these elements. All plans would have been required to offer a standard package of health care benefits, including preventive, diagnostic, rehabilitative, and major medical coverage. Standard packages are intended to level the playing field among plans so that consumers can compare prices among basic packages of benefits and insurers cannot exclude certain services from high-risk populations. Furthermore, standard benefit packages would be adjusted over time based on patient outcomes research. Services deemed ineffective relative to cost and quality would be eliminated over time.

The standard benefit packages in the original health care reform bills universally included a 100-day extended care benefit. This benefit would have been available for all covered individuals receiving care in a skilled nursing facility or rehabilitation facility. The second- and third-generation versions of these bills delegated authority for the composition of the benefit package to the Secretary of Health and Human Services or a national advisory board.

The extended care benefit could have a favorable impact on subacute care providers in two ways. First, because the benefit would no longer be limited to Medicare beneficiaries, it could be used to finance care for individuals of all ages who require a variety of subacute care services. Second, a 1991 study by Kilgore and colleagues[11] found that, overall, the subacute program was significantly more cost effective in terms of functional gains made per dollar of expenditures. If this evidence continues to be supported, more extensive benefits for subacute care could be added to the standard benefit package over time on the basis of the patient outcomes research mentioned above. This factor, coupled with the incentive inherent in the managed competition model to move patients to the lowest level of care that is medically acceptable, almost certainly would inure to the benefit of cost-effective providers of subacute care. Indeed, even in the absence of a specific extended care benefit, there would be a substantial incentive for health plans to contract for these services for patients who otherwise would require more expensive hospitalization.

All proposals also included some form of health alliance or purchasing cooperative. These purchasing groups are central to the insurance reforms contained in the legislation, such as the elimination of underwriting procedures to screen out health care risk. By pooling large numbers of subscribers under a single entity, adverse selection would be minimized. The health plans formed under managed competition represent a partnership between insurers and networks of providers that would be required to offer the full array of services mandated under the standard benefit package to all subscribers regardless of health status.

As discussed below, subacute care providers would be attractive to both the health alliances and the health plans because of their ability to offer high-quality, lower-cost care. These features would allow plans to be financially competitive, meet quality standards, and produce consumer satisfaction. Similarly, the alliances and health plans would provide subacute providers with key opportunities to increase their market share.

Although all health care reform proposals included standard benefit packages, health care alliances, and health plans, the structures varied considerably. For example, the Health Security Act had a generous standard benefit package, mandated health care alliances and prohibited any underwriting. Other proposals, such as those introduced by the Republican leadership, contained a less generous benefit package and provided for voluntary alliances, and some plans allowed limited underwriting. Most proposals also included a variety of additional cost-containment mechanisms such as administrative simplification, malpractice reform, and strengthening of fraud and abuse statutes.

The second generation of health care reform proposals introduced by certain members of Congress significantly modified the regulatory structure of the initial proposals. For example, almost all the later bills moved from mandatory health care alliances to voluntary alliances and from single-area purchasing cooperatives to multiple cooperatives in one region. Later proposals also gave states additional flexibility in structuring health care networks. Legislation introduced by members of bipartisan groups focused primarily on insurance reforms, subsidies for low-income individuals, and some of the least controversial elements of earlier legislation (eg, malpractice reform and fraud and abuse provisions).

Impact of Managed Competition on Subacute Care Providers

The managed competition model represents another step in the long evolution of managed health care plans, which are designed to control costs by reducing fragmentation among health care financing and delivery systems and by identifying the lowest-cost care denominator that can meet patients' needs without sacrificing quality of care. The integrated delivery networks envisioned under managed competition would control costs by restructuring fundamentally the

manner in which care is delivered. According to Sokolov, former medical director at Southern California Edison (SCE), "You get far more value from truly managing care than from getting discounted services. And managing care in a more precise way is what integrated networks are all about."[12(p28)] By way of example, Sokolov indicated that, of the $20 million in savings achieved by SCE over a 3-year period, 50% came from carefully managing the catastrophic illnesses of less than 5% of the patients.

An integrated delivery system has the potential to enhance entry into the subacute care market. The medical complexity of patient care requires traditional skilled nursing facilities to undertake a number of operational adjustments, such as the employment of more professional and more highly trained nursing staff with experience in caring for patients with more acute conditions, changes to the physical design of the facility, and greater contact with physicians.[13]

The provision of subacute care requires a far more complex array of professional staff and services in meeting patients' needs. The interdisciplinary approach to providing care requires different staffing patterns and more licensed professionals, such as registered nurses, rehabilitation specialists, and other clinical disciplines. Additionally, one or more physician specialists to serve as program directors of the various subacute specialties offered and more frequent visits by patients' physicians are essential.[13] Access to the wide range of medical specialists is enhanced for subacute care providers that participate in an integrated delivery system. Depending on the scope of integration, virtually all resources needed could be obtained through this network.

The development of integrated networks that either take risk or contract with cost-conscious payer networks seeking to minimize costs increases the types of incentives inherent in the Medicare hospital PPS (ie, treating patients at the lowest level of care that is medically acceptable). Such incentives increase the attractiveness of nursing facilities and other "downstream" providers that can treat medically and physically complex patients who otherwise would be treated in more costly acute care settings.

Subacute providers can benefit from integrated delivery systems in two ways. First, they can obtain referrals through contracts with health plans or networks of providers that establish these plans. Second, they can become full partners in the plan or network by taking a portion of the insurance risk, not only through accepting payments on a per case or per diem basis but by becoming a partner in a network that, in essence, has taken over the role as the insurer.

Medicare Cost Containment Measures

The majority of public expenditures for health care are paid by the Medicare and Medicaid programs. Growth in these programs is responsible for a major share of federal health care spending and contributes to the growing national deficit. Medicare expenditures in 1991 reached almost $120 billion. These costs are estimated to grow to approximately $191 billion in 1995 and $328 billion by the year 2000. This would represent a 71% increase by the end of the decade.[14]

The administration and Congress planned to finance health care reform, in part, by redirecting existing dollars toward subsidies for low-income individuals. Medicare was one program targeted for spending reductions that could be used to expand coverage to the uninsured. Reductions in Medicare funding over a 10-year period under various reform proposals ranged from about $63 billion under the Rowland-Bilirakis bill[15] to approximately $467 under the Gephardt legislation.[16] The two principal strategies for achieving Medicare savings included reducing provider payments and imposing regional spending limits on health care services. Either savings method would have created tremendous pressure on providers to lower service delivery costs. A significant percentage of Medicare dollars currently is spent on inpatient hospital care. Because subacute facilities can provide medically complex services at a significant savings over hospital costs for certain patients, such facilities should provide a promising vehicle for slowing the growth in Medicare expenditures.

Reductions in Medicare Payment Rates

Most health care reform bills introduced during the 103rd Congress included the following methods of reducing Medicare payment rates:

- reductions in the update factor to the hospital market basket index of 1% to 2%
- reductions in inpatient capital payments for both PPS-exempt hospitals and those subject to PPS rates
- reductions in the Medicare fee schedule conversion factor for physicians of 3% for specialty services
- reductions to disproportionate share payments by 50% (some bills would phase out such payments)
- a reduction in routine cost limits for skilled nursing facilities from 112% to 100% of the mean per diem costs

According to estimates developed by the American Hospital Association, Medicare reductions would have affected hospitals disproportionately.[17] For example, under the Mitchell bill, which projected Medicare reductions of almost $294 billion over 10 years, the hospital share would have been about 45%.[18] Hospitals' share of the Mainstream Coalition's proposed 10-year reductions of $248 billion would have been about 54%.[19]

Medicare Part C: Savings through Regional Expenditure Limits

Members of the House adopted the global budget provisions included in the Health Security Act to achieve savings through regional spending limits. Representative Gephardt introduced legislation establishing a new Medicare Part C to provide a standard package of benefits for all individuals not covered under a private plan (eg, low-income, seasonal, and temporarily employed individuals; employees working for firms smaller than a specified size; and current Medicare beneficiaries).[16] Savings would be achieved through the establishment of national health expenditure estimates for public and private programs. A federal fall-back cost-containment system would be imposed in states failing to comply with private sector spending estimates. Additional savings would have been achieved through mechanisms such as reductions in indirect medical education and disproportionate share adjustments.

The Secretary of Health and Human Services would establish national health expenditure estimates in 1995 for Medicare and private plans as well as baseline growth estimates. Spending estimates would be established on a per capita basis and allocated to various classes of services. Target growth rates would be set to reduce Medicare spending by two percentage points in 1996 and one point annually thereafter until the growth rate was slowed to the 5-year average per capita rate of growth in the gross domestic product. For services currently paid on a cost-related basis, rate of growth limits would be imposed until prospective payment methodologies could be developed, with implementation occurring no later than January 1, 1997.

Impact of Medicare Rate Controls on the Subacute Care Market

Any measures reducing the overall payments to hospitals will increase the viability of providing subacute care in nursing facilities or satellite facilities. Because of lower capital expenses, nursing facilities are able to offer profitable, cost-efficient care for patients who traditionally are "financial losers" in the hospital setting, all at considerable savings to third party payers.[20] This savings will be especially attractive to integrated delivery systems because it will enable them to compete for patients more effectively.

The reduction in capital reimbursement for PPS exempt and nonexempt hospitals is likely to encourage new building and/or expansion in organizations that are not subject to the capital limits. This could make skilled nursing facilities more attractive to investors where certificate of need laws do not impede bringing additional beds on line. In addition, nonprofit facilities could benefit under a proposal in two of the health care reform bills that would have lifted the $150 million bond cap on tax exempt organizations. The elimination of this cap also would solve a problem experienced by organizations engaging in affiliations. Such affiliations can be complicated or thwarted by this cap in cases where the combined debt of two or more organizations exceeds the cap under the newly established corporation.

The establishment of regional expenditure limits included in the Medicare Part C proposal would create systemwide incentives to reduce costs. Moreover, because spending estimates would be allocated to specific classes of services, hospitals would be under intense pressure to reduce costs or face rate caps under the fallback proposal. Access to nursing facilities that can provide subacute care would provide hospitals with a mechanism to reduce costs and maintain their ability to devise their own cost-saving strategies.

Routine Cost Limits

One provision included in the health care reform legislation could have adversely affected the provision of subacute care, at least with respect to Medicare patients. Routine cost limits for skilled nursing facilities were frozen for 2 years under OBRA 1993. Many of the health care reform bills would have exacerbated this situation by actually reducing the limits. Nursing facilities that already are at or above their cost limits could have experienced severe hardships under these provisions, depending on the manner in which the HCFA implements the reduction or freeze.

Skilled nursing facilities that exceed their cost limits currently can apply to the HCFA for exceptions and exemptions under a number of categories, such as a new provider exemption or an atypical services exception. As more facilities have filed for exceptions, however, the lag time between filing and receiving approval has greatly increased because the HCFA has not been afforded additional staff to cope with the increasing volume. Facilities that have had legitimate grounds for exceptions often have experienced long and severe cash flow shortages because of the delay. The reduction in the limits that is imposed under many plans may serve to exacerbate the cash flow shortage that nursing facility providers or subacute providers experience by decreasing the funds that such facilities receive before the exception process.

The HCFA has responded to these frustrations by issuing a formal revision to the process under Chapter 25 of the *Provider Reimbursement Manual*. Chapter 25 revisions provide formal guidance and streamline the process for ruling upon exception requests. First, they shift much of the responsibility for reviewing requests to fiscal intermediaries. Moreover, under the new procedures intermediaries are required to make recommendations to the HCFA within 90 days of receiving a final request, and the intermediary's recommendation becomes the final decision if the HCFA does not act upon the recommended decision within 90 days. Additionally, intermediaries now have the authority to grant interim requests without HCFA approval, and they must do so within 90 days. These changes have the potential to reduce cash flow shortages in the long run. In the short term, however, the HCFA may simply be shifting substantial responsibilities to intermediaries, many of which have limited or no experience in the area.

Even more critical may be the manner in which such reductions affect the exception process. The HCFA construes the freeze on the cost limits to reduce the amount of any exception to account for the freeze. Thus facilities that justify exception requests do not receive the amount by which they exceed the limit but rather the amount by which they would have exceeded the limit in the absence of the freeze. In other words, they can never receive their true costs during the freeze period irrespective of the validity of their request. If the HCFA were somehow to have interpreted the reduction in the routine cost limits also to limit exception amounts in a similar manner, the lowering of the limits might have affected not only the timing of payment that providers receive but also the ultimate amount of payment after the exception process.

Quality of Care for Life Act

Legislation introduced by Senator Hatch in 1994[7] addressed a number of regulatory barriers to subacute care, including a specific statutory remedy to the problems created by the lag in ap-

proving exceptions to routine cost limits. This legislation would have required the Secretary of Health and Human Services to establish an expedited atypical exceptions process for skilled nursing facilities by January 1, 1996. Under this process, skilled nursing facilities would have been granted interim exceptions within 90 days of submission of an exception request accompanied by data and documentation determined by regulation. This provision would have provided for recovery of any overpayments or reimbursement of any underpayments made during the exception period.

The Hatch bill[7] also would have eliminated additional regulatory barriers to adequate reimbursement. Under current HCFA interpretations, facilities that provide ventilator care can only be reimbursed for respiratory therapists as an ancillary service if the therapists are employees of a hospital with which the facility has a transfer agreement. If the therapist is not a hospital employee but is under the direct supervision of the nursing department, the cost of the therapist is covered as a routine service and is subject to the cost limits. As noted earlier, the Hatch legislation would have required Medicare to reimburse skilled nursing facilities for respiratory therapy as an ancillary service that is not subject to these limits regardless of whether the therapist is a hospital employee. The legislation also addressed nursing facilities' historical problems with physician absenteeism. It would have required payments to physicians for visits to patients of similar acuity levels to be the same for hospitals and skilled nursing facilities regardless of the site of service.

Finally, the Hatch bill would have required the Secretary of Health and Human Services to review the provision of subacute care in skilled nursing facilities and to determine which hospital DRGs are appropriate for these facilities to treat. Unlike the hospital-based PPS system, however, copayments would have been established to recognize the cost-sharing responsibilities that beneficiaries typically face under the first-day hospital deductible and skilled nursing facility copayments for day 21 and beyond.

The Secretary of Health and Human Services would have published a list of applicable DRGs with appropriate hospitalization periods and copayments and would have required the rebasing of Medicare payments for such groups to reflect the lower cost of such care provided in skilled nursing facilities. This provision would have provided legislative recognition that skilled nursing facilities are legitimate providers of subacute care services.

CONCLUSION

Any meaningful program of health care reform should encourage the provision of subacute care in nursing facilities and other facilities with lower capital intensity than the acute care setting. Most important, it should encourage accurate pricing for health care that is related to the intensity of care necessary to treat the patient. This should occur because virtually any health care reform measure should encourage changes in utilization patterns for all patients that result in placing the patient in the lowest and most cost-efficient level of care that is medically appropriate to

the patient's treatment needs. These goals are consistent with the managed competition proposals introduced in the 103rd Congress, which attempted to achieve cost savings with incentives to identify more cost-effective delivery methods.

Subacute care providers that can respond to these incentives should flourish. How much of the original managed competition model will be salvaged in the health care reform proposals introduced in the 104th Congress remains to be seen. Given the change in congressional leadership, comprehensive systems reform is not likely. The intense focus on deficit reduction in 1995, however, will maintain pressure on Congress to reduce federal health care expenditures. To the extent that Congress does not stifle the development of subacute care through draconian reductions in payment levels to skilled nursing facilities and other satellite providers, this emerging market represents a promising vehicle for reducing overall system costs. Furthermore, it represents a far more rational approach to the efficient delivery of health care than rate caps, which do not address the root of the problem.

REFERENCES

1. Starr P. *The Logic of Health Care Reform.* New York, NY; 1994.
2. Committee for a Responsible Federal Budget. *The Economy, The Budget, and Health Care Reform.* Health Care Reform Project. Phase II: Comprehensive Reform Proposals. Washington, DC; 1991.
3. Peterson PG. *Facing Up: How to Rescue the Economy from Crushing Debt & Restore the American Dream.* New York, NY: Simon & Schuster; 1993:118.
4. Burns J. Tis the reason to be jolly: Subacute care feeds need to diversify. *Mod Healthcare.* Dec. 13, 1993; 34–38.
5. Hartwell R. Subacute care: The LTC link. *Provider.* March 1994; 21–22.
6. *Provider Reimbursement Manual,* HIM-15 Transmittal No. 378; July 1994.
7. Quality of Care for Life Act. S. 2205, 103rd Congress, 2d Session. Senator Orrin Hatch.
8. Altman S and Young D. A decade of Medicare's prospective, payment system: Sources or failure? *The Journal of American Health Policy.* 1993; 3, (2) 11–19.
9. US General Accounting Office. *Long-Term Care Case Management: State Experiences and Implications for Federal Policy.* Report to Hon. Ron Wyden, House of Representatives, April 1993, GAO/HRD 93-52.
10. Enthoven AC. Managed competition in health care financing and delivery: History, theory and practice. Robert Wood Johnson Foundation Workshop: Rethinking Competition in the Health Care System: Emerging New Models; Jan 13, 1993.
11. American Health Care Association. *Background: Nursing Facility Subacute Care: The Quality and Cost-Efficient Alternative to Hospital Care.* Washington, DC; 1994.
12. Findlay S. Networks of care, may serve as a model for health reform. *Business & Health.* 1993; 27–31.
13. American Health Care Association. *Subacute Care: Medical and Rehabilitation Definition and Guide to Business Development.* Washington, DC; 1994.
14. Health Insurance Association of American. *Source Book of Health Insurance Data.* Washington, DC; 1993.
15. H.R. 5228, 103rd Cong. 2d Session, Rowland.
16. H.R. 3600, 103rd Cong. 2d Session, Gephardt.

17. American Hospital Association. Internal working document. Washington, DC; 1994.

18. S. 1957, 103rd Cong. 2d Session, Mitchell.

19. Mainstream Coalition Proposal—not introduced, 103rd Cong. 2d Session.

20. Cook M. Tremendous opportunities, pitfalls await subacute care providers. *The Brown University Long-Term Care Quality Newsletter.* 5 (17), Sept. 15, 1993.

21

State Health Care Reform and Its Impact on the Subacute Care Industry

Jonathan L. Rue

As the nation focuses its attention on the national health care reform debate, and as the prospects for achieving comprehensive national reform remain uncertain at best, states have been considering and are continuing to consider and implement their own initiatives. Indeed, virtually every state at least evaluated some type of health care reform plan during 1993.[1] States are seeking to improve health care access or coverage to all state residents and at the same time to control rising state expenditures for health care. Key states at the forefront of health care reform include Florida, Hawaii, Oregon, Arizona, Maryland, Washington, Kentucky, Minnesota, and Vermont. Many other states, such as Tennessee, have taken more moderate steps to reform their systems, including modification of state Medicaid programs.

States have considered and adopted several approaches to health care reform. These include managed competition, single payer plans, and even rationing. The reform initiatives are a result of key policy considerations and concerns relating to health care. The concerns include escalating health care costs, lack of access to care, high percentages of uninsured individuals, and medical malpractice.

This chapter examines the policy issues leading to state health care reform initiatives and the policy responses and alternatives considered by various states. State health care reform initiatives that have been adopted by key states are summarized. Finally, the chapter examines the impact of state health care reform initiatives on subacute care providers.

CENTRAL POLICY ISSUES LEADING TO STATE HEALTH CARE REFORM INITIATIVES

During the 1980s, health care expenditures in the United States increased rapidly, accounting for approximately 12.3% of the gross domestic product (GDP) by 1990. It is estimated that, without intervention, US health care costs in the year 2000 may exceed $1.7 trillion, or 18.0% of the GDP. Nationwide, health care costs to employers increased by 46.3% between 1988 and 1990.[2]

Consistent with escalating costs nationwide, many states have experienced skyrocketing costs. For instance, in Florida, as is shown in Figure 21–1, per capita health care expenditures for Florida's residents increased by 152% during the 1980s (from $962 to $2427).[2] In 1990, Florida

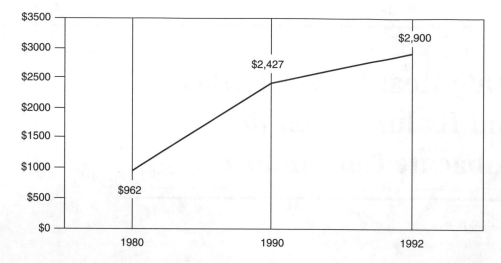

Figure 21–1 Florida per capita health care costs, 1980, 1990, and 1992. *Source:* Data from *A Blueprint for Health Security: Interim Florida Health Plan* by the Florida Agency for Health Care Administration, pp. E-1, 14, December 1992.

spent $31.4 billion on health care. Without intervention, Florida's state health care bill has been projected to increase to $90 billion by the year 2000, almost tripling in 10 years.[2] In addition, in 1991 the average Florida family spent $3392 on health care, which amounted to approximately 12% of the average family income. By the year 2000, absent changes in the health care delivery system, the average family's health spending is projected to more than double, to an average of $8235.[2] Many factors contribute to the increase in health care costs. Key among them are administrative inefficiencies, heavy demands by the consuming patient for the best care that the health care system can offer, inappropriate use of too many health care services, excess capacity in the form of underused health care facilities, medical technology, an aging population, physician utilization patterns, the insurance system, malpractice litigation, and waste and fraud.[2]

The large number of uninsured Americans has also been a major problem that severely affects the health care system. This problem has been described as an epidemic of uninsurance. Approximately 37 million Americans lack health care insurance coverage.[2] These people include

the working uninsured (often small business employees or the self-employed), people who are unable to obtain insurance because of preexisting medical conditions, and low-income families. In 1993, 46% of all US families had members who either lacked insurance or were underinsured for health care purposes.[3] Millions more Americans would be uninsured if Medicaid spending had not grown dramatically in the past 3 to 4 years.[4]

An increase in the uninsured population has occurred in most parts of the nation, with the biggest increases occurring in New England, the east/north central states (Ohio, Indiana, Illinois, Michigan, and Wisconsin), the South Atlantic region (Delaware, Maryland, the District of Columbia, Virginia, West Virginia, North Carolina, South Carolina, Georgia, and Florida), and the west/south central states (Arkansas, Louisiana, Oklahoma, and Texas).[4] In 1991 alone, 1 million Americans lost private health insurance.[4]

States such as Florida have an extremely large percentage of uninsured patients. Approximately 2.5 million Floridians (one in five) are uninsured. Seventy-five percent of these are workers or their dependents. Almost one third of the uninsured are children.[2] Other states with large percentages of uninsured residents include Texas (22.1%), New Mexico (21.5%), Louisiana (20.7%), Mississippi (18.9%), and California (18.7%).[4] Such high percentages of uninsured residents lead to problems in accessing the health care system. In addition, cost shifting, whereby health care providers set their rates and fees to insured and paying patients at a level that covers losses on nonpaying patients, results from the uninsured patient problem.

OVERVIEW OF POLICY RESPONSES AND AVAILABLE ALTERNATIVES

States have considered several different approaches to health care reform. Some 21 states have evaluated a Canadian type single-payer plan, but none has actually implemented this type of program. In Vermont, Maryland, and New York a single payer model has been considered. Approximately half the states have considered some type of managed competition. Washington, Minnesota, and Florida have enacted this type of program. Several states have evaluated a plan that combines managed competition and tax-based financing.[1]

As part of the debate on health care reform, most states have established, as a matter of policy, certain principles to guide them in enacting health care reform measures. For example, in conjunction with the state's health care reform initiatives, Vermont policymakers have delineated as part of the state health plan certain guiding principles for reform that were derived from extensive discussions among Vermont Healthcare Authority Board members, the Vermont Health Policy Council, and the public. Exhibit 21-1 summarizes these guiding principles, which typify the principles of reform being discussed in many states.[5]

The former White House Health Care Task Force, in considering national health care reform, examined various successful model reform programs implemented by states, cities, and companies around the country. The task force noted that the successful health care reform programs had several crucial characteristics in common, including

Exhibit 21-1 Vermont's Guiding Principles for Health Care Reform

- There should be both universal access to health services and equity in the financing of health care.
- Priority will be given to services that are appropriate, effective, and valuable.
- Health promotion, preventive health services, and health protection are priorities.
- Services that ensure that every person receives care, comfort, and support in the face of terminal illness, functional decline, and death are a priority.
- Because financial resources are limited, priority should be given to appropriate and effective health services from which the greatest good for the greatest number of people can be derived.
- Services that help Vermonters stay in the most independent, least restrictive environments of their choice for as long as possible or help them return to such environments as early as possible are a priority.
- Individuals bear significant responsibility, to the best of their capacity, for the maintenance of their own health and for appropriate use of the health care system. To enable individuals to fulfill this obligation, the system and the professionals who work within it should value and maximize each individual's knowledge, skill, and unique capacity.
- Freedom of choice for consumers regarding providers and services is important and desirable and should be balanced against other priorities within the health care system.

Source: Reprinted from *Health Resource Management Plan 1993–1996* by the Vermont Health Care Authority, pp. 8–11, April 1993.

cluding choice of physicians, market-based reform, a comprehensive package of benefits with control of costs, and elimination of administrative waste.[6]

In June 1993, the Maryland Health Resources Planning Commission published the results of a survey of health care reform measures actually implemented or being considered in the 50 states and Washington, DC. The results of that survey indicated that the common goal of the states was to increase access to health care by more residents while controlling the costs and improving the quality of health care. Reform measures were undertaken in the areas of coverage, benefits, cost containment, financing, and quality management.[7] The Maryland survey of states revealed 23 states (46%) that reported initiatives designed to provide health care benefits to all residents of the state. The method of achieving universal coverage varied from state to state. Some states adopted a managed competition model; others proposed a single-payer system. Several states worked to cover the entire population through incremental reform that improved access to health care for certain groups in the state.[7]

In terms of covered benefits, the survey indicated that there was a strong emphasis on primary care and prevention, including prenatal care, well-child care, and recommended cancer screening and immunizations. Acute care benefits generally included emergency care and inpatient hospitalization. Thirty-three states (66%) provided such acute care benefits. Fifteen states (30%) specified long-term care benefits, sometimes with conditions such as limited numbers of home health visits or a limited number of days in a nursing facility per year. Many reform measures provided for the establishment of a basic package with a minimum level of benefits. As a condition of doing business in a state, insurance carriers were often required to offer a basic health care plan to qualified small employers with a provision for more generous benefits at an additional charge.[7]

With respect to cost containment, benefit plans based on managed care represented the primary cost control relied upon by 24 states (48%). States have enrolled more Medicaid recipients in managed care programs, and managed care was listed among the cost containment features in most basic insurance plans. Managed care arrangements included health maintenance organizations (HMOs), preferred provider organizations (PPOs), and traditional indemnity coverage with utilization controls.[7] As part of their cost control measures, 21 states (42%) focused attention on reducing administrative costs through electronic billing and payment of claims using standardized forms. Fourteen states (28%) developed strategies based on global budgeting or statewide health care expenditure goals. Utiliza-

tion review was adopted by 13 states (26%) as a way to control costs by encouraging the appropriate utilization of services.[7]

Certificate of need (CON) reform was included by 12 states (24%) that strengthened or reinstituted CON jurisdiction over major medical equipment, new services, or capital expenditures above a specified amount. Other reforms, such as setting providers' rates and limiting referrals of patients to facilities in which referring physicians have a financial interest, received increased attention from some states.[7]

As a way to finance health care by making insurance more available, 26 states (52%) enacted insurance reform. To encourage small businesses to offer coverage to their employees, the reforms eliminated or limited certain insurance rating and underwriting practices. Most states limited the use of preexisting condition exclusions, required carriers to offer basic plans and to set rates within prescribed limits, guaranteed companies the opportunity to renew their policies, and prohibited carriers from writing new policies in a market for a specified period after canceling business in the state. Some states required health insurers to use community rating when setting premiums for groups of a certain size; others provided for modified community rating that allowed specific risk factors to be factored into rates.[7]

In 23 states (46%), reforms were financed in part from the redistribution of public funds. The money that states spend currently, combined with additional federal funds for health-related programs, was to be restructured to fill gaps in the coverage of low-income persons through publicly subsidized private insurance. Twenty states (40%) also relied on the creation of pooled funds to make insurance more available. Revenue sources for financing pools included premiums from enrollees, assessments on insurers, and subsidies by the state.[7] Nineteen states (38%) identified a requirement for federal waivers to implement reform plans that do not comply with existing federal laws. For example, waivers from the federal government were required to integrate federal funds (Medicare and Medicaid) into a single-payer system and to extend employer mandates that address employee benefits.[7] Revenues from levying taxes were included by 13 states (26%). Reforms were to be paid for in part by taxes on cigarettes, alcohol, insurance premiums, and providers.[7]

In terms of reform initiatives addressing the quality of health care, 19 states (38%) emphasized data collection, analysis, and dissemination measures. State-mandated information measures were designed to provide information about prices for comparative purposes, to support research on the outcomes of treatment, and to give consumers and providers objective data upon which to base their decisions. In addition, 16 states (32%) utilized practice guidelines. Practice parameters were based on outcomes research in an attempt to ensure that only appropriate services were provided and that generally accepted standards for quality were met.[7]

Initiatives related to malpractice reform were also included by 13 states (26%). Efforts were aimed at changing the professional liability system to address the avoidance of high-risk specialties, such as obstetrics, and the use of defensive medicine practices by providers that lead to overutilization of services. Some states incorporated the required establishment of uniform practice guidelines as a feature of tort reform, allowing providers that follow clinical guidelines to use their compliance as a defense in malpractice litigation. Finally, some states sought to resolve disputes concerning malpractice through arbitration.[7]

The survey found several common themes in the states' initiatives, which are set forth in Exhibit 21–2. For a listing of the states implementing health care reform and the issues addressed by these states, see Appendix 21A.

OVERVIEW OF TYPES OF STATE HEALTH CARE REFORM PROPOSALS

The primary strategies for health care reform that have been either implemented or considered by states include managed competition, managed competition with global budgets, single-payer/global budget systems, play or pay, and ration-

Exhibit 21–2 Themes from State Health Care Reform Measures

- There are gaps in coverage that should be corrected either universally, by guaranteeing health care insurance for all residents, or incrementally, by focusing on particular underserved populations.
- There should be a minimum set of benefits available to all residents emphasizing prevention and primary care services and including a basic set of acute and long-term care services with the option to purchase supplemental benefits.
- The costs of health care should be controlled by increasing enrollment in managed care plans, setting ceilings for total health care spending, reducing administrative inefficiencies, and encouraging the appropriate distribution and use of services.
- The financing of health care should include some new sources of revenue (eg, taxes on items found to contribute to poor health) along with existing government funds that are redistributed as needed and employer and individual contributions.
- The quality of health care should be improved by instituting better systems of information, evaluation, and arbitration and by making providers and consumers more informed.

Source: Reprinted from *Survey of Health Care Reform: 50 States and Washington, D.C.* by the Maryland Health Resources Planning Commission, p. 6, July 1993.

ing. In addition, as noted in the Maryland survey of states, other incremental reform measures have been enacted or considered (Figure 21–2). A summary of the key components of each approach to health care reform follows.

Managed Competition

Pure managed competition proposals have been advocated by several key authorities, including Elwood, Enthoven, Etheredge, and other members of the Jackson Hole group (a group of health policy experts who began meeting several years ago in Jackson Hole, Wyoming); the Conservative Democratic Forum; certain progressive policy institutes; the Health Insurance Association of America; the National Governors' Association; and some members of the US House and Senate. The Jackson Hole group described the

Figure 21–2 Approaches to health care reform.

concept as "the use of allowable tools to structure cost-conscious consumer choice among health plans in the pursuit of equity and efficiency in health care financing and delivery."[8(p.28)] Managed competition also has been described as a strategy designed to reward with more subscribers those health care financing and delivery plans that offer high-quality care at relatively low costs.[9] Although the Jackson Hole group has proposed the managed competition model as a model for national health care reform, states such as Florida have adopted the model, at least in part, for implementation at the state level. When fully implemented, the managed competition proposal envisions the components set forth in Exhibit 21–3.[10]

Managed Competition with Global Budgets

This approach combines the elements of managed competition and regulatory global budgeting that would set an overall budget for health care expenditures.

Single-Payer/Global Budget Systems

A single-payer system is one in which all covered health care services are insured and paid for by a single insurer. Health insurance is financed through a combination of employee contributions, employer taxes, and other taxes and funding. Other variations to this approach include an all-payer system, in which services are covered and paid for by multiple insurers but all payers adopt the same payment methods and rates. The single payer model typically involves global budget features.[2]

Play or Pay

This approach establishes universal coverage by building in a system of employer-sponsored health insurance. The approach relies on a play-or-pay incentive, under which employers can either provide the standard, mandated, minimum benefit package by purchasing insurance or pay a

Exhibit 21–3 Key Components of Managed Competition

- Most health care services are delivered through accountable health plans (AHPs) competing on the basis of cost and quality. These organizations are similar to managed health plans, deliver a uniform set of health benefits, and are publicly accountable for their health outcomes.
- Small employers and individuals must purchase coverage through health insurance purchasing cooperatives (HIPCs). HIPCs arrange for consumers to obtain coverage from competing AHPs. Medicare and Medicaid coverage will also eventually be purchased through HIPCs.
- The federal tax exclusion for health benefits is limited to AHP enrollees and is capped at the price of the lowest cost AHP in the HIPC service area.
- Three private sector boards propose standards to a Security Exchange Commission-like, independent, nongovernment agency that approves standards and registers AHPs and HIPCs.
- Employers are required to provide full-time workers with the equivalent of AHP coverage. Coverage is purchased or a payroll tax is paid for all other employees (eg, part-time or low-income employees). There is no public insurance carrier for those paying a payroll tax. All payroll tax–based coverage is provided through AHPs by way of HIPCs. Individuals with adequate incomes are required to purchase health care through an HIPC from an AHP.

Source: Jackson Hole group.

---

payroll tax to a public plan for their employees' coverage.[11] Play or pay is viewed as a hybrid of a nationalized health system (like the Canadian system) and the current private health care system in the United States.[12]

Rationing

The rationing approach is best exemplified by Oregon's health care reform initiative. That approach is based on three central ethical commitments that the methodology seeks to serve[13]:

1. It is more equitable to assure everyone basic health care than to offer a larger collection of benefits to some of the poor

while excluding others from anything but emergency care.
2. The explicit, publicly accountable choice is better than the hidden rationing that now occurs.
3. Health care priorities should combine authentic community values with expert technical judgments about health services.

The Oregon approach is based on a prioritized list of health services that is to serve as a guide for the Oregon legislature in making Medicaid budget decisions. The list is also used to guide benefit package choices for private insurance plans that are to be made available to small businesses and to persons unable to obtain insurance in the private insurance market.[13]

Other Approaches

Other approaches to health care reform include medical savings accounts, tax vouchers, and limited health insurance reform measures. The medical savings account idea involves encouraging individuals to save for their own medical costs with pretax dollars.[14] The tax vouchers approach generally involves allowing deductions, credits, or vouchers to individuals to assist them primarily with the purchase of health insurance and secondarily with the direct purchase of health services.[15] Limited health insurance reform measures often involve small market insurance reform to facilitate the purchase of affordable insurance. Insurance reform measures also often address the problem of exclusions for preexisting conditions and other issues that affect individuals' ability to obtain affordable insurance. Some states also have implemented requirements that all insurance plans meet or exceed certain basic benefit standards.[2] The issue of reform of the long-term care system also has been debated and addressed by at least some states. Reforms have included ideas such as the promotion of home and community-based alternatives to nursing facilities and expansion of Medicaid service coverage to include long-term health care benefits.

SUMMARY OF KEY STATE HEALTH CARE REFORM INITIATIVES

Arizona

Arizona Health Care Cost Containment System for Medicaid

In 1982, Arizona implemented the Arizona Health Care Cost Containment System (AH-CCCS), a managed competition model for its Medicaid recipients (Figure 21–3). The plan was based on the concept that Medicaid recipients will be covered by HMO type provider networks.[16] Arizona is the only state to run its Medicaid program entirely on the basis of managed care plans.[17]

AHCCCS was initially approved by the Health Care Financing Administration (HCFA) as a 3-year demonstration project. HCFA subsequently granted the program several extensions to continue operating and receiving federal funds under demonstration status. The state of Arizona has given the program permanent status.[18]

The plan basically works as an HMO. Under the terms of the plan, each patient is enrolled in a health plan that contracts with the state to deliver care to patients. The health plans must bid competitively for AHCCCS contracts, which are generally awarded for 2-year periods. Contracted health plans receive a fixed capitation payment regardless of the number or type of services provided and thus have an incentive to control utilization and costs.[18] Health plans can negotiate discounts from hospital rates in return for referring patients to particular hospitals. Most of Arizona's counties have at least two participating plans, and the larger counties typically have six or seven plans.[19] Provider payment is also capitated. The capitation rates are generally higher than those for commercial health plan patients under the theory that the Medicaid population tends to be sicker. Recipients are responsible for a minimum copayment, usually $1, for covered services.[19]

Under the terms of the plan, beneficiaries receive all services available through a traditional Medicaid program except full mental health services for adults. Services covered by the plan are reflected in Exhibit 21–4.

Arizona Long-Term Care System

In 1987, the Arizona legislature approved expansion of Medicaid service coverage to include long-term care. The Arizona Long-Term Care System (ALTCS) is a program of institutional and home health care services for the indigent elderly, physically disabled, and developmentally disabled residents of the state (see Figure 21–3).[18] The long-term care services are delivered and financed through a system that incorporates the major elements of the current AHCCCS program. The long-term care system uses a prepaid capitated approach, with its incentive to control the risk of the volume and cost of services, thereby providing an alternative to the escalating long-term care costs that have been noted in other states. The long-term care program

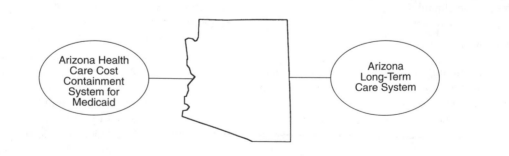

Figure 21–3 Arizona health care reform.

Exhibit 21–4 Services Covered by AHCCCS

Outpatient health services
Laboratory and medical services
Pharmacy services
Medical supplies and equipment
Inpatient hospital services
Emergency services
A children's program called Early and Periodic Screening, Diagnosis and Treatment
Podiatry services
Home health care services
Medically necessary kidney, cornea and bone transplants and immunosuppressant medications; medically necessary heart transplants, liver transplants, and bone marrow transplants
Mental health services for children younger than 18 years, mental health services for adults who are seriously mentally ill

Source: Data from Overview. *The Arizona Health Care Cost Containment System: Arizona's Health Care Program for the Indigent,* pp. 17–18, September 1993.

provides a continuum of services that focuses on less intensive and less expensive services and settings (Exhibit 21–5).

Acute and long-term care services are bundled; that is, anyone eligible for ALTCS will also be eligible for all other medical services available through AHCCCS. To be eligible for the long-term care system, individuals must meet certain income level and other eligibility requirements. Generally, the gross income limit is set at 300% of the Social Security income benefit rate for an individual. Only those individuals who are at risk of institutionalization may enter ALTCS.[18]

Other Legislation

In addition to AHCCCS for Medicaid, the Arizona Legislature recently passed other health care reform legislation. Senate Bill 1109, which became effective July 1, 1994, creates accountable health plans (AHPs) for small employers. Under the new legislation, insurers (as a condition to doing business in the state) will offer a basic health benefit plan to small employers. Small employers qualify if they have not provided health benefits to employees for 90 days and employ at least 25 but not more than 40 workers. Plans must provide basic health benefit coverage to each small employer without regard to health status or claims experience. There are certain exceptions if an insurer can show that its ability to serve previously enrolled groups and individuals would be impaired. Insurers cannot exclude an eligible employee, spouse, or dependent.[20]

The new legislation also requires that a nine-member health benefit plan committee appointed by the governor develop a basic health benefit plan. The basic health benefits that must be provided include inpatient/outpatient hospital services, physician services, diagnostic services, and preventive care (including prenatal and well-baby care). The committee is to recommend benefits and cost-sharing levels, exclusions, limitations, and the licensed health care providers who would be eligible for reimbursement under the basic health benefit plan. The committee also is to consider affordability, social and financial factors, deductibles, and provider cost effectiveness in developing the basic health benefit plan.[20]

Hawaii

Hawaii took innovative steps to reform its health care system long ago. Hawaii is the only state in the country that mandates that its employers must provide health care benefits to eligible employees. There are three basic components to

Exhibit 21–5 Services Covered by ALTCS

Skilled nursing facilities
Intermediate care facilities
Intermediate care facilities for the mentally retarded
Home and community-based services
Acute medical services
Mental health services for those older than 65 years

Source: Data from Overview. *The Arizona Health Care Cost Containment System: Arizona's Health Care Program for the Indigent,* p. 31, September 1993.

the health care delivery system in Hawaii (Figure 21–4). Medicaid covers those at the poverty level. Hawaii's Prepaid Healthcare Act covers almost all employees and many dependents through employer- or union-sponsored health insurance. The State Health Insurance Program (SHIP) provides coverage for the "gap group": the self-employed, seasonal workers, part-time workers, students, and dependents not covered by an employer. In addition to these three basic components, Hawaii has enacted certain insurance reforms, including voluntary modified community rating measures. Through this approach, Hawaii has been able to obtain virtually universal coverage for its residents.[21]

Hawaii's Prepaid Healthcare Act

Hawaii's Prepaid Healthcare Act was enacted in 1974 and became effective on January 1, 1975. The act mandates that employers provide health care benefits to eligible employees. Hawaii obtained an exemption from the Employee Retirement Income Security Act (ERISA) of 1974, which enabled it to include the employer mandate aspect of its reform measures.[16]

The act requires coverage for any employee who works 20 hours or more per week for a month or longer. Although dependents need not be covered, most dependents are covered because insurance companies typically offer family coverage for competitive reasons and because

the state is heavily unionized. Employers must pay at least half the premium to provide the coverage. Employee contributions are limited to 1.5% of their gross monthly wages. Businesses that do not comply with the law can be fined, held liable for the health bill for their workers, or even shut down.[21] The mandated benefit package must include coverage for hospitalization, surgery, primary medical care, maternity, and laboratory and radiology services.[21] The two dominant medical plans in the state are offered by the Hawaii Medical Services Association, the state's Blue Cross/Blue Shield Plan, its largest health insurer, and Kaiser Permanente's Foundation Health Plan.[21]

Hawaii's SHIP

The SHIP was enacted in 1990 to cover the "gap group" not covered by the Prepaid Healthcare Act or the state's Medicaid program. Under the SHIP, the state subsidizes health insurance for eligible individuals. Private insurance companies provide the coverage, and private providers provide the care.[21]

SHIP benefits focus on prevention and primary care. The benefit package covers health appraisals, related tests, prenatal care, well-child care, immunizations, and the treatment of accidental injuries. Physician visits are limited to 12 per year. Hospitalization is limited to 5 days. Elective surgery and some tertiary care services

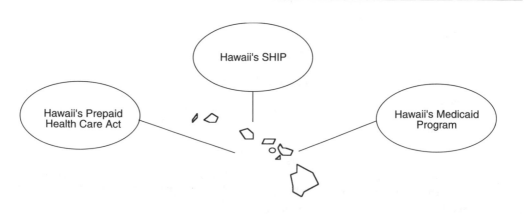

Figure 21–4 Hawaii health care reform.

are excluded.[21] SHIP benefits are limited to Hawaii residents with incomes of less than 300% of the federal poverty level who are not covered by health insurance. SHIP premiums are shared. Enrollees pay part of the premium according to their income level and a $5 copayment at the time of visit. The state pays the remainder of the cost.[21]

Medicaid

Finally, Hawaii provides coverage to low income residents through its Medicaid program. To be eligible, individuals must earn less than 62.5% of the poverty level, have limited assets, or belong to certain federal categories such as pregnant women and infants.[21]

Maryland

In April 1993, Maryland passed groundbreaking health care reform legislation, House Bill 1359: Health Care and Insurance Reform. The legislation was designed to address the dual problems of access to health insurance coverage and costs. The major components of the bill are shown in Figure 21–5.

Small Employer Group Market Reform

Effective July 1, 1994, insurers doing business in Maryland must follow certain guidelines in offering insurance to employers with 2 to 50 employees that want to offer health insurance coverage to their employees. These guidelines include requirements such as guaranty of issuance of policies, guarantees of renewal of policies, consumer protection measures such as notification of cancellation, limitations on preexisting conditions, guidelines for adjusted community rates for a health benefit plan, and comprehensive standard health benefits.[22] The bill permits employers to offer health insurance to their employees without contributing to these benefits.[22]

General Health Insurance Market Reforms

In addition to the small group insurance market reforms, the bill contains general health insurance market reform provisions that are designed to ensure access to health insurance coverage for residents of Maryland. Under these provisions, if one of two conditions is met, insurers would be required to issue comprehensive standard health benefit plan coverage to any individual or group that wants to purchase insurance. The two conditions relate to the amendment of the federal ERISA law to allow states to control employee health benefit plans and the percentage of the population younger than 65 years that is in

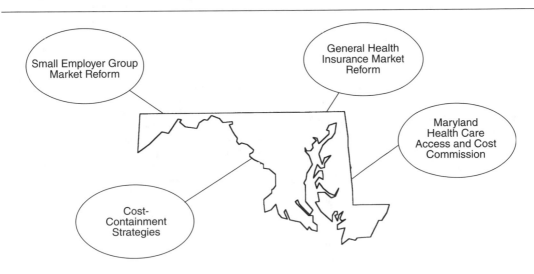

Figure 21–5 Maryland health care reform.

the fully insured market or covered by an employer that would be willing to leave self-insurance to join a community insurance pool.[23] In the event that either of these triggers is met, then the general health insurance market reforms would be implemented.

Maryland Health Care Access and Cost Commission

The new legislation establishes a seven-member Health Care Access and Cost Commission to formulate a comprehensive standard health benefit plan, to establish a health care database, to develop a standardized system for processing claims, to establish performance measurements for HMOs, to foster the development of practice parameters, and to implement a payment system that will serve as a framework for the determination of appropriate prices for health care services.[22] The Maryland legislation also extends the state's existing rate-control system for hospitals to physicians and insurance companies. The commission is to establish annual adjustment goals for the cost of health care services. If spending exceeds these goals, the commission, through voluntary and cooperative arrangements with practitioners, may make an effort to bring spending into compliance with its goals. If these efforts prove to be unsuccessful, the commission may then adjust allowable prices for services. Thus the commission may actually set the price for health care services only under extraordinary conditions.[22]

Cost-Containment Strategies

In terms of cost-containment strategies, the bill is designed to reduce insurance costs and to encourage administrative efficiencies in the delivery of quality health care. The bill requires more detailed reporting by insurers and HMOs to the insurance commissioner. In addition, the bill provides an electronic claims clearinghouse to decrease administrative costs. Health care practitioners are encouraged to control costs voluntarily by utilizing clinical resource management systems that allow them to analyze their charges and utilization of services in comparison with

their peers. Practice parameters will also be developed for medical specialties with the assistance of a committee of the commission.[22]

In December 1993, pursuant to the reform legislation, the commission proposed a standard benefits package that must be offered to small employers in the state (Exhibit 21–6). Additional benefits can be offered but must be packaged and priced separately. The commission recommended that the package be made available through four delivery systems: indemnity plans, PPOs, point-of-service plans, and HMOs.[23]

Minnesota

Minnesota's major effort to reform its health care delivery and financing system occurred with the passage of the 1993 MinnesotaCare Act. The legislation was the result of intense study and debate by the Minnesota Health Care Commission, an independent 25-member commission representing consumers, employers, labor unions,

Exhibit 21–6 Standard Benefits To Be Offered to Small Employers

All medical services provided by a licensed health care practitioner and unlimited inpatient hospitalization, including emergency department treatment, ambulance charges, and hospital outpatient services and surgery (hospice and home health care as alternatives to otherwise covered hospital services would be included, as would 100 days in a skilled nursing facility)
Heart, bone marrow, and other transplants
Pregnancy and maternity services
Limited (25 days annually) inpatient coverage for psychiatric and substance abuse care
Unlimited outpatient mental health visits
Outpatient diagnostic services, certain preventive services, and nutritional services for certain illnesses
Short-term rehabilitation for a maximum of 60 days per condition per year
Durable medical equipment coverage
Prescription drugs after a $150 deductible.

Source: Data from *Health Law Reporter*, vol. 2, pp. 1657–1658, Bureau of National Affairs, December 1993.

providers, health insurers, and other major stakeholders that was charged with the responsibility to develop a comprehensive health care cost containment plan to slow the rate of growth of public and private health care costs in Minnesota by at least 10% each year for the next 5 years. The act basically restructures Minnesota's health care system by creating large medical networks, called integrated service networks (ISNs), and limiting their spending. The other major component of Minnesota's plan is called the regulated all-payer option (RAPO)[24] (Figure 21–6).

The ISN Concept

ISNs represent a new form of health care delivery designed to provide a complete array of services to all enrollees for a fixed, predetermined price. ISNs work under a fixed budget and thus have strong incentives to contain costs and to deliver timely, cost-effective preventive and primary care with the most efficient mix of providers.[24]

ISNs arrange and deliver full health care services for a fixed price and compete based on their costs and quality of services. They are formed by health care providers, HMOs, insurance companies, employers, or other organizations. ISNs may be established as separate nonprofit corporations or cooperatives under state law. ISNs offer services ranging from routine primary and preventive care to inpatient hospital care. Health care providers would not be required to participate in ISNs. Those not participating, however, would be subject to more direct regulation.[24]

ISNs are required to provide a full array of appropriate and necessary services. Five standard benefit plans must be offered. These will vary only according to cost-sharing options. ISNs are required to provide services within a reasonable geographic distance for enrollees. ISNs also are subject to certain financial solvency requirements, including net worth and reserve requirements for ISNs sponsored by providers.[24]

The act also provides for annual limits on the growth of health care costs. The annual limits on the rate of growth in health care spending are set at the urban consumer price index (CPI) plus 6.5% in 1994, CPI plus 5.3% in 1995, CPI plus

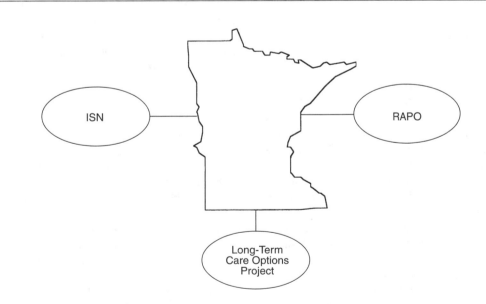

Figure 21–6 Minnesota health care reform.

4.3% in 1996, CPI plus 3.4% in 1997, and CPI plus 2.6% in 1998.[25]

RAPO

The ISN system is a voluntary system in which providers are not forced to participate. RAPO is to provide an alternative to ISNs for those who prefer to participate in a fee-for-service system. The RAPO concept will involve rule making to regulate insurers and providers that do not participate in ISNs. One of the primary goals in the development of the RAPO concept is the establishment of the fees that will be paid to providers. Other initial goals include reduction of administrative costs and burdens by including an all-payer option and a uniform, standard system of billing and utilization review. The longer-term goals of RAPO include the establishment of a uniform reimbursement system, reimbursement and utilization controls, and quality standards and monitoring. The RAPO concept will also strive to ensure that the annual rate of growth and the costs for services not provided within an ISN remain under the state's growth limits on health care.[24]

Long-Term Care Options Project

The Minnesota Department of Human Services also is separately pursuing the development of a Long-Term Care Options Project (LTCOP), which involves the provision of long-term care services through managed care organizations (see Figure 21–6). LTCOP would complement reform legislation by contracting with ISNs and other provider networks. The population targeted for the project includes elderly individuals living in either institutional or noninstitutional settings.[26] LTCOP's financing method relies on capitated payments to managed care organizations, which would incorporate both Medicare and Medicaid funds. Enrollees would receive the full range of services covered under Medicare and Medicaid, including home and community-based services. Uniform capitation rates would be determined by historical cost experiences of the various recipient groups, with adjustments.[26]

Florida

Florida's centerpiece of health care reform is the Healthcare and Insurance Reform Act of 1993. The act constitutes a series of reforms and programs enacted by the Florida legislature in 1993 in an effort to provide more Floridians, especially small businesses and their employees, with affordable insurance. The new law also provides for a program called MedAccess, which will allow individuals to purchase state-sponsored health insurance coverage. Finally, the new law establishes a Medicaid buy-in program that may allow individuals to purchase insurance coverage through the state-run Medicaid program[27] (Figure 21–7).

Managed Competition through Community Health Purchasing Alliances and AHPs

Florida's reform effort is based on the principle of managed competition. The new law divides the state into 11 geographic regions and calls for the establishment of a community health purchasing alliance (CHPA) in each of these regions. The CHPAs serve as clearinghouses for information about health care services in each region.[27] CHPA membership is available to small businesses that have 50 or fewer employees as well as to state employees, Medicaid and MedAccess program participants, and ultimately Medicaid buy-in enrollees.[28] Small employers are not required to purchase coverage through alliances, nor are employers required to contribute to the purchase of insurance for their employees; the system is totally voluntary.

For a health plan to offer coverage through the CHPAs, it must be formally designated as an AHP. An AHP may be formed by providers joining together with insurers approved by the Florida Department of Insurance. Indemnity insurers, preferred provider networks, exclusive provider organizations, and HMOs all may apply for AHP designation.[27] AHPs will respond to requests for proposals from CHPAs for basic and standard plans and specialized extras that CHPA members may wish to offer employees. The main

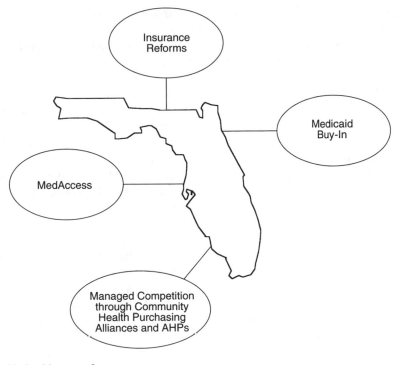

Figure 21–7 Florida health care reform.

incentive for small employers to join a CHPA is that they will have access to comparative information about these plans through the CHPA. Thus, rather than facing a confusing array of health insurance contracts, each with different terms and conditions, CHPA members will have that information condensed so that they will be in a position to make informed choices in purchasing their coverage.[27]

The Florida Agency for Health Care Administration will be responsible for regulating the process through administrative rule making. The rules will determine and define aspects of the program, including what information will be gathered from AHPs and CHPAs, how it will be presented to CHPA members, and the ways in which AHP providers will respond to complaints from purchasers.[27]

MedAccess

Florida's MedAccess program is designed to allow individuals who have been uninsured for a 12-month period to buy coverage from a state-operated insurance program. The program is designed to cover the "gap group" of Floridians who cannot afford more comprehensive coverage but who earn too much to qualify for the Medicaid program. Financial eligibility is capped at 250% of the federal poverty level. Annual covered benefits include such services as 12 physician office visits, 10 hospital inpatient days, $1,000 of hospital outpatient services, and annual check-ups. A maximum lifetime benefit cap of $500,000 will apply. Providers will be reimbursed according to Medicaid reimbursement rates.[27]

Medicaid Buy-In

The Medicaid buy-in program also targets those who earn too much to qualify for Medicaid or are categorically ineligible for Medicaid. The program will subsidize premiums of those individuals desiring to buy into the Medicaid program. Individuals or their employers would be required to pay a portion of the costs of their coverage based on a sliding scale related to income. To implement this program, Florida was required to obtain a waiver from the federal government.[27] That waiver was granted in September 1994.[29] Further legislation is needed, however, to enact the waiver and its requirements.

Insurance Reforms

Florida's health care reform package also includes insurance reform measures. These include requirements such as guarantee-issue health insurance for small businesses, limitations on pre-existing conditions, limitations on experience rating, and restrictions on dropping small business groups from insurance based on their claims experience.[27]

Oregon

The State of Oregon has implemented one of the boldest and most controversial health care reform plans. The plan contains both rationing and play-or-pay components. It is a result of a series of laws passed by the Oregon legislature from 1989 to 1993. These laws are collectively known as the Oregon Health Plan.

The goals of the Oregon Health Plan include universal access to health care services for all residents. This is achieved through the three major aspects of the plan: Medicaid expansion, mandated employment-based coverage, and a high-risk insurance pool[30] (Figure 21–8). The plan also defines a basic benefit package that critically evaluates the relative effectiveness of medical services. The basic benefit package requires the public to set priorities to guide health care funding decisions and explicitly links basic benefits to effectiveness. The plan also reforms the small group health insurance market.[30]

The plan includes major cost-containment provisions. These provisions are designed to reduce cost shifting among health care providers, to emphasize managed care delivery, to emphasize primary and preventive care and early intervention, and to evaluate critically the use of medical services and technology. Cost-containment goals are also served by certain aspects of the plan that do not pay for ineffective care.[30]

Medicaid Expansion

The Oregon plan mandates that all individuals below the poverty line ($991 per month for a family of three) will be covered by Medicaid and will be guaranteed a basic benefit package based on a prioritized list of health care services. This expansion was contingent on receiving a waiver of federal law from HCFA, which the state received on March 19, 1993.[31] The expanded program added 120,000 persons to the approximately 250,000 persons already on Medicaid in Oregon.[30]

Coverage under the Medicaid plan is determined according to a priority-based ranking of 696 health services. These services are ranked based on factors that include medical effectiveness of a particular treatment and the cost and social value of the treatment. The plan's extended benefit package includes 565 of the total 696 health services that are ranked. Funding for those 565 services has been approved for 1993 to 1995.[30] The package covers all major diseases of women and children and provides services such as dental, hospice, prescription drugs, most transplants, and routine physicals. The benefit package stresses preventive services such as maternity and newborn care and immunizations. The benefit package does not pay to treat conditions that are deemed to improve on their own, conditions where home treatments are effective, and conditions where treatment is generally ineffective, such as aggressive medical treatment for advanced cancer. Examples of the conditions for which treatment is ensured under the package are shown in Exhibit 21–7.

The priority list to define the basic benefit package has been developed over time. In February 1991, the Oregon Health Services commission ranked medical services from the most important to the least important to the entire population. The categories were ranked by the Commission as essential, very important, and valuable to certain individuals. The commission then recommended that the state legislature fund all essential and as many very important services as it could afford.[30] The Oregon legislature used the priority list to define the basic benefit

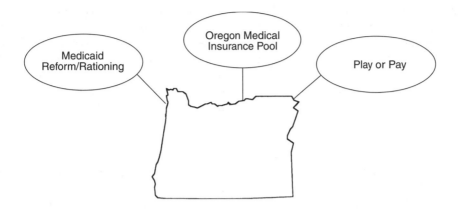

Figure 21–8 Oregon health care reform.

package by funding services to a certain point based on the money available for health care. The process provided accountability by making it clear which programs are funded at the expense of other programs. All the participants in the Medicaid plan are guaranteed in the standard benefit package.

To coordinate treatment and reduce costs, the majority of Medicaid patients will be treated within managed care plans. Where managed care is not available, Medicaid will pay individual physicians a fee for service. The managed care plan gives Medicaid patients a family practitio-

ner to coordinate care and help contain the cost of care. Practitioners in managed care plans are reimbursed at reasonable rates to cover their costs. The plan will be studied as a 5-year demonstration project. HCFA will monitor and oversee the project.[30]

Oregon Medical Insurance Pool

The second major aspect of the Oregon Health Plan is known as the Oregon Medical Insurance Pool. This plan involves a high-risk insurance pool that covers approximately 28,000 persons

Exhibit 21–7 Conditions Covered under Standard Benefit Package

Pneumonia	Ulcers
Appendicitis	Kidney stones
Broken bones	Bone marrow transplant for certain leukemias
Burns	Glaucoma
Head injuries	Ear infection
Rheumatic fever	Liver transplants, except for liver cancer
Asthma	Spinal deformities
Diabetes	Shoulder repairs
Epilepsy	Heart bypass
Cancers such as breast, skin, stomach, other treatable cancers	AZT and treatment for opportunistic infections associated with human immunodeficiency virus infection
Chest pain due to heart disease	

Source: Data from *The Oregon Health Plan* by the Oregon Department of Human Resources Office of Medical Assistance Program, p. 27, August 1993.

who cannot obtain insurance because of preexisting medical problems. The Oregon legislature created the pool as a nonprofit entity in 1987. It became a funded state agency in 1989 and began offering coverage in July 1990.[30]

The high-risk pool provides coverage to those denied health insurance, those with restrictive riders on existing policies, or those who have to pay charges well above standard premiums because of certain serious preexisting conditions such as heart disease, cancer, and diabetes. The pool is currently supported entirely by assessments on Oregon's health insurance carriers and the premiums paid by enrollees. Premiums are set at 150% of the industry standard for Oregon.[30]

Employer-Mandated Health Insurance

The third major aspect of the Oregon Health Plan is a provision requiring employers to cover all permanent employees (those working 17.5 hours or more per week) and their dependents by July 1, 1995 or to pay into a special state insurance fund that will offer coverage to those employees (ie, a play-or-pay plan). The employer mandate was needed to cover the 300,000 uninsured people in the state who would not be covered by the expanded Medicaid plan and the Oregon Medical Insurance Pool. There are two conditions that could preempt this employer mandate: the failure to implement the Medicaid plan described above, or the voluntary enrollment of 150,000 previously noncovered workers in health benefit programs. In addition, to go into effect the employer mandate must be approved by Congress for an exemption from the ERISA laws.[30]

Tennessee: TennCare

Tennessee's health care reform initiative, known as TennCare, became effective January 1, 1994 (Figure 21–9). The plan authorized the state to apply for a Medicaid waiver to abolish Medicaid for acute care services and replace it with TennCare while continuing to obtain matching funds from the federal government. The waiver was granted by the US Department of Health and Human Services on November 18, 1993.[32] The project is a 5-year demonstration project involving the delivery of health care services to Medicaid recipients, uninsured residents of the state, and certain uninsurable residents through managed care organizations. The plan combines such concepts as global budgeting, a standard benefit package, the pooling of purchasing power, managed care, incentives for preventive care, elimination of certain welfare incentives, cost sharing, quality control, and the elimination of distinctions in coverage based on socioeconomic factors.[33] The plan will shift 1 million Medicaid patients along with approximately 500,000 uninsured individuals into private managed care plans.[34]

TennCare coverage will provide access to hospitals for all program beneficiaries and will include additional services such as prenatal care and childhood immunization coverage. Medicaid qualified individuals will pay no premium, deductible, or copayment. Uninsured individuals between 100% and 200% of the federal poverty guideline will pay a premium, deductible, and copayment on a sliding scale based on family income. Those individuals above the 200% federal poverty guideline will pay the full premium, deductible, and copayment.[35] Enrollment in TennCare will be capped at 1.3 million individuals in the project's first year and 1.5 million individuals in subsequent years.[32]

All TennCare enrollees will be served through capitated managed care plans, including HMOs and PPOs. Enrollment and delivery of care will be organized through 12 community health agency areas, which will operate under global budgets.[32] Each managed care organization will offer a standard benefits package, which will include inpatient and outpatient care, ancillary services, medical supplies, and prescription drugs. The benefits are more generous than those offered under the state's Medicaid program. Long-term care, however, will not be offered under the program. Instead, long-term care will continue to be reimbursed under the Medicaid program.[32]

TennCare participants will choose from managed health care provider networks that will in-

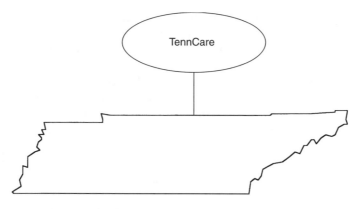

Figure 21–9 Tennessee health care reform.

clude the present Blue Cross–administered network for state employees, selected HMOs and PPOs presently operating in Tennessee, and other qualifying plans. Tennessee will negotiate contracts with these networks in an effort to acquire the most cost-effective and quality medical care available for TennCare participants.[36]

Each community area will be rated separately, and each TennCare plan within each community will be given a per capita spending target. Initial per capita spending targets and provider reimbursement will be based on the actual medical care costs plus a management fee, with the final spending target being based on the final number of participants in each TennCare plan.[36] Forecasters have estimated that reimbursement rates will actually be 20% to 50% less than the state's traditional Medicaid payments.[32] Each TennCare plan within a community exceeding its target expenditure would be required to prorate the targeted reimbursement to providers. TennCare plans also will be permitted to distribute any savings among its providers so long as final reimbursement does not exceed 105% of the provider's negotiated rate. After TennCare stabilizes, full capitation rates will be paid each month (with no discount for anything other than charity care), with the annual capitation being based on the lowest cost network meeting TennCare quality standards within each respective community.[36]

Central to the project is a detailed quality of care monitoring plan. TennCare's structure includes significant financial incentives for health plans to maintain quality of care. AHPs will compete for enrollment based on quality of service. Furthermore, the state may withhold a portion of the capitated payments pending regular quality reviews by auditors. All communities in the state will have access to TennCare, thereby increasing the availability of health care services to residents across the state.[33]

Vermont: Act 160

The Vermont legislature passed a major health care reform bill in 1992. Commonly referred to as Act 160, the law commits the state to ensuring that all Vermont residents can get health coverage regardless of their ability to pay, controlling the costs of health care with the creation of an overall health care budget for the state, and unifying the government oversight of health care planning, cost containment, and hospital budget review under one agency: the new Vermont Health Care Authority.[37] The law requires that the Vermont Health Care Authority design two different plans for providing residents with access. One plan would create a single-payer system to handle all health claims. The other plan would set up a system of regulating multiple payers. Both plans must provide for a uniform set of health benefits (Figure 21–10).

The single-payer model is required to include at least the elements listed in Exhibit 21–8.[38] Under the multiple-payer system, the state government would be responsible for regulating the multiple entities that would provide benefits, including regulations for enrollment, changes in premium rates, payment rates to providers, and aggregate health expenditures. The design of this second system is required to include at least the elements set forth in Exhibit 21–9. Under either model, all residents of Vermont, including employed persons, dependents of employed persons, and those not in the workforce, would receive health care coverage. In this way, the state seeks to achieve universal coverage. The state anticipates applications for federal waivers to allow persons qualifying for coverage under the Medicare or Medicaid program to participate in the universal access program that is eventually adopted.[38]

In September 1993, the Vermont Health Care Authority unveiled its plan for implementing Act 160. In accordance with the act, the plan includes the specified models for universal access. In addition to federal Medicare/Medicaid waivers, the state will need an exemption from the federal ERISA laws to implement the plan.[39] The plan calls for a new system of integrated systems of care (ISCs), which would be networks of health care providers and facilities managed and financed through a single administrative structure. Each ISC would be governed by a board of directors consisting of system participants, providers, administrators, and facility representatives.[39] Preventive, routine, emergency, and catastrophic care would be covered through the ISCs. Covered services would include hospital, medical, ambulatory, hospice, home and skilled nursing facility (SNF), mental health, alcohol and substance abuse, vision, and emergency department care; routine dental care for children; and emergency dental care for adults. The program

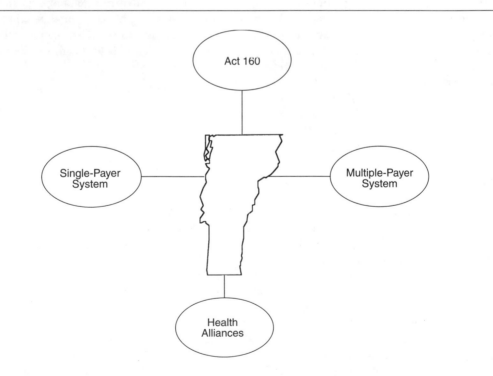

Figure 21–10 Vermont health care reform.

Exhibit 21–8 Elements of Single-Payer Model

Universal coverage for all Vermont residents

A single administrative entity to make payments
(either governmental or private)

Portability of coverage regardless of job status

Uniform benefits from a single source

A broad-based public financing mechanism
(revenues can come from employers, employees,
and/or public sources)

Provider expenditures capped and hospitals subject
to a global budget

Control of capital expenditures

A binding cap on overall expenditures

Accountability in policymaking for the entire
system to reside with state government

Source: Data from *Single-Payer and Multiple-Payer
Plans: Putting the Pieces Together* by the State of Vermont
Health Care Authority, pp. 1–2, June 1993.

---

would emphasize preventive care and the guidance of a primary care provider within the ISC.[39]

Under the Vermont Health Care Authority's proposal for the single-payer model, care for the entire covered population of approximately 450,000 would be financed by a payroll tax. A single health care purchasing trust would be set up to administer the single-payer model. ISCs would be developed on a regional or geographic basis, and state payments to the ISCs would be at a risk-adjusted annual capitation rate.[39] Under the proposal for the multipayer model, individuals would pay a portion of their premium through their employer or obtain coverage on their own. Full-time employees would pay 20% of premium costs for themselves and 50% for dependents. The state would subsidize expenses for low income individuals and small businesses. Under the multipayer model, residents would purchase a health plan through the health care purchasing trust or through purchasing alliances (see Figure 21–10). Strict rules would force insurers to hold costs down.[39]

Although Vermont has made progress in meeting its goals of universal access, its reform efforts have not been completed. The 1994 legislature was unable to agree on a comprehensive reform

bill utilizing either of the models under consideration.[40]

Washington

The state of Washington enacted major health care reform legislation in 1993. The new law, known as the Washington Health Services Act of 1993, incorporates employer mandates and managed competition (Figure 21–11). Universal coverage is targeted for 1999.[40] Under the new law, all Washington residents will have health insurance coverage for a uniform benefits package designed by the newly created Washington Health Services Commission (HSC) and approved by the state legislature. No one will be denied coverage because of employment, economic status, or a preexisting health problem.

Exhibit 21–9 Elements of Multiple-Payer System

Compulsory and universal health insurance, which
may be based on employment, region of
residence, or other basis

Claims processed by multiple insurers

Portability of coverage regardless of job status

Uniform benefits for all Vermont residents available
from a variety of payers, public or private
(services not included in the uniform benefits
package may be purchased from insurers)

Financing to come from employers/employees/
public sources, with revenues being collected and
disbursed by insurers

Uniform reimbursement for hospitals and
physicians, regardless of reimbursement
mechanism or payer, through either negotiation
or regulation

Control of capital expenditures

A binding cap on overall expenditures

State government responsibility for rating the
multiple insurers as to enrollment, premium
costs, provider payments, and total expenditures
(accountability for operating within the set
parameters lies with the insurers)

Source: Data from *Single-Payer and Multiple-Payer
Plans: Putting the Pieces Together* by the State of Vermont
Health Care Authority, pp. 2–3, June 1993.

Figure 21–11 Washington health care reform.

The universal access will be phased in over 6 years starting in 1993.[41]

The uniform benefits package will be offered through certified health plans. The package will emphasize preventive and primary care and will include the health services listed in Exhibit 21–10. Long-term care is targeted for inclusion in the package by July 1999. Employers and individuals may buy supplemental or additional health benefits not included in the uniform benefits package.[41]

The certified health plans can be existing insurance companies and health plans or new organizations that bring together hospitals, physicians, and other providers. Certified health plans must offer the uniform benefits package to all residents within the plan's geographic area. The plans must offer the package at or below the maximum premium set by the HSC. The plans will be managed care systems that integrate care and financing using a variety of methods. They must allow every category of licensed health provider to deliver services in the package as long as conditions are met. Plans must provide coverage on a prepaid community-rated basis to spread the risk of paying for illnesses over many people. Certified health plans may not deny, cancel, or refuse to renew coverage because of health status. Residents will be able to change jobs without losing coverage.[41]

All residents of Washington State are required to enroll in a certified plan for at least a uniform benefits package by July 1, 1999. On a phased-in basis, employers will be required to offer full-time employees and their dependents the uniform benefits package from a choice of at least three certified health plans, including the lowest-priced ones in the area. Employers will be required to pay at least half the premium of the lowest-priced package for full-time employees and their dependents, and a maximum premium cap is established for the uniform benefits package. For part-time employees, the employer's share of the premium will be prorated. In lieu of sponsoring coverage for its employees and their dependents through direct contract with certified health plans, an employer may combine the employer contribution with the employee's contribution and enroll in the basic health plan or a health insurance purchasing cooperative.[41] The state will need an exemption from the ERISA laws to implement the employer mandate.

The state will provide health insurance coverage through Medicaid and the basic health plan for more than 195,000 low-income adults and children. To be eligible, individuals must live in households with annual incomes of less than twice the federal poverty level.[41] Financing for the health care reform initiative in Washington will come in part from additional taxes. The new

Exhibit 21–10 Uniform Benefits Package

Primary and specialty health services
Inpatient and outpatient hospital services
Prescription drugs
Reproductive services
Maternity and well-child care
Case-managed chemical dependency, mental health,
    short-term SNF, home health, and hospice services

law will add a new tax on beer, liquor, and cigarettes and other tobacco products. In addition, a new business and occupation tax on hospitals will be imposed. Effective in January 1994, HMOs, health service contractors, and certified health plans were also required to pay the 2% premium tax paid by other insurers.[41] The new legislation also contains cost control elements. The uniform benefits package will be offered only by certified health plans that agree to comply with certain conditions regarding premium limits, package design, enrollment, portability, and health data reporting. Balance billing is not permitted.[41]

To permit employers and individuals to strengthen their purchasing power, the insurance commissioner is also charged with authorizing the creation of four health insurance purchasing cooperatives with no less than 150,000 members in distinct geographic regions to receive benefits on a group basis from certified health plans.[41] To promote managed competition, the lowest priced uniform benefits package is to be determined by the HSC on a regional basis. Although employers are required to pay no more than 50% of the cost of the lowest priced plan available in their market, they can choose to pay more.

Kentucky

Kentucky closed its 1994 legislative session with passage of House Bill 250, a broad plan to reform its health care system. Under the new law, the Kentucky Health Purchasing Alliance, an insurance purchasing cooperative covering approximately a quarter of the state's residents, will be created (Figure 21–12). Participation will be voluntary for individuals and employers with 100 or fewer employees. Participation will be mandatory for all state employees and Medicaid recipients.[42]

The health purchasing alliance will contract with AHPs to offer services to alliance members. The alliance will be able to negotiate with health plans to obtain the lowest possible price for its enrollees. It also will collect and distribute premiums on a risk-adjusted basis.[40] The bill also establishes a five-member health policy board that would oversee operations of the health purchasing alliance, data collection, benefit plans, and other aspects of the new system.[42] The law also seeks to expand access through the creation of a Medicaid buy-in program, allowing persons with incomes of less than 200% of the federal poverty level to purchase health services from Medicaid providers at the Medicaid rate.[40]

To fund its reforms, Kentucky has instituted a tax on providers. Hospitals are taxed at the rate of 2.5% of their gross revenues, and physicians, SNFs, home health agencies, and HMOs are taxed at the rate of 2.0%.[40] Other Medicaid provisions in the new law augment Kentucky's existing statewide Medicaid managed care system, which is based on a fee-for-service primary care case management system. New provisions in the law also supplement the Kentucky Medicaid access and cost containment demonstration project, which expands coverage to all Kentuckians whose incomes are less than 100% of the federal poverty level. Kentucky has successfully obtained a waiver from the federal government to expand its Medicaid program.[40]

OTHER STATE HEALTH CARE REFORM MEASURES UNDER CONSIDERATION

There are also many other states currently engaged in discussion of numerous proposals for state health care reform. Virtually every state in the country has been moving forward with health care reform initiatives since 1992, and the issue was a major topic of debate and legislation during 1994 legislative sessions.

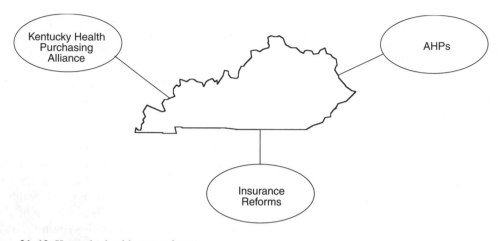

Figure 21–12 Kentucky health care reform.

The Idaho legislature, for example, has considered several health care reform measures, including ones that would broaden access to individual health care insurance.[40] Iowa has considered a bill designed to prepare the state for federal health care reform. The bill would not ensure universal coverage or mandate employers to pay for health care, but it would make a number of changes in the state's system, including the establishment of community health management information systems, AHPs, health insurance purchasing cooperatives, and insurance reform.[40] Furthermore, in early 1994 the Arizona Senate passed legislation that would permit individuals to establish medical savings accounts to pay eligible medical expenses not otherwise covered by the holder's medical coverage. The accounts would be trusts, and the money in them, including interest accrued, would not be included in Arizona gross personal income unless it were withdrawn and used for purposes other than medical expenses.[40]

Even states that have passed comprehensive health care reform continue to modify their health care delivery systems. For example, the governor of Hawaii recently has urged the state legislature to reform the Hawaiian health care system by creating a statewide health care alliance and providing financial relief for employers that currently are required by state law to provide health care coverage for employees working more than 20 hours each week. The governor maintains that an alliance would help the state control health care costs. The governor also seeks to reduce employer contributions by asking workers to make larger contributions.[43]

STATE MEASURES TARGETING LONG-TERM CARE AND SUBACUTE CARE

To date, long-term care has not been addressed in the vast majority of health care reform proposals being considered by the states. Vermont is one of the few exceptions to that general statement. In response to provisions contained in Vermont's Act 160, Vermont's Health Care Authority has proposed a social insurance financing model to support long-term care benefits on an as-needed basis. Under the proposal, residents of Vermont would contribute 0.7% of their annual adjusted gross incomes to a trust fund that would pay for long-term care services when they are needed. The plan relies on continued Medicaid coverage for long-term care for low-income persons. The plan will not pay for all the long-term care services that an individual may need. Instead, the goal of the program is to make the catastrophic cost of long-term care more manageable for the majority of individuals needing those services.[44]

Other states have examined other measures to reform the long-term care delivery system. Some states, such as Virginia, have examined measures designed to allow individuals to receive long-term care in as homelike a setting as possible. Virginia has done this through the creation of a category of facilities called adult care residences in which four or more adults are cared for in a primarily residential setting.[44] Florida has enacted a law that is designed to allow adult congregate living facilities to offer services needed by residents with functional impairments.[43] States such as Montana, Wyoming, and Georgia have enacted legislation that allows residential care providers to offer a broader range of services to their residents. As an example, Montana allows personal care homes to obtain skilled nursing services for residents under certain circumstances.[44] Finally, states such as California are experimenting with managed care concepts in the delivery of long-term care services to the elderly and non–severely impaired individuals.[44]

Even less attention has been paid in the comprehensive health care reform debate to the specific topic of subacute care. States are just now focusing on the appropriate definition of subacute care and the regulation of the facilities providing that care. Some states, however, have taken the initiative in examining subacute providers and services. For example, Illinois has proceeded with a 13-site comprehensive medical rehabilitation demonstration project. The project will include hospital- and nursing facility–based programs to determine the most appropriate setting for subacute care. The sites are expected to include 7 hospital-based and 6 nursing facility–based participants.[45] In addition, several state Medicaid programs have established coverage criteria and a special payment rate for a subacute care benefit in nursing facilities. These states include California, Wisconsin, Arizona, and Vermont.[46]

IMPACT OF STATE HEALTH CARE REFORM INITIATIVES ON SUBACUTE CARE PROVIDERS

The major comprehensive state health care reform efforts to date have not directly addressed the issue of subacute care. As a result, a great deal of uncertainty surrounds the question of what effect health care reform may have on the emerging subacute care industry.

In response to that uncertainty, subacute care providers clearly will need to advocate for reform packages to include explicitly the role of subacute care providers in a reformed setting. Advocates will need to insist, for example, that subacute care be included in standard benefit packages that are under consideration or being implemented by many states. These advocacy efforts may become more effective as the subacute industry clarifies the scope and definition of subacute care and as regulatory standards, such as national accreditation standards, are developed to provide guidelines for the industry. In the short term, subacute providers should continue to push for piecemeal state health care reform efforts. These include such measures as a separate Medicaid reimbursement category for subacute care, such as that enacted in Virginia. Providers may also want to push for funding of demonstration projects examining the most appropriate setting for subacute care, such as that undertaken in Illinois.

Because health care reform initiatives are so new in many states, it is unclear what direct impact they will have on the subacute market. Nevertheless, the incentives resulting from state health care reform clearly will significantly affect subacute care providers, at least indirectly. Subacute care appears to be well positioned to respond to the implications of reform, including the emphasis on managed care, the development of integrated systems offering an entire continuum of care in one system, the focus on cost containment and appropriate low-cost settings, the shifting of health care services to nonhospital settings, and the importance of quality care and outcome data to support quality claims by providers (Figure 21–13). The observation that subacute care is in step with reform incentives is one reason why most investment firms have a favorable view of subacute care.

Health care reform initiatives at the state level have contributed to the tremendous growth in the managed care industry. Tennessee, for example, has experienced a recent growth in the presence

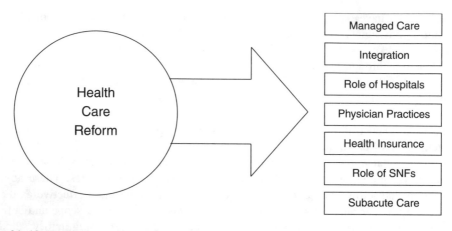

Figure 21–13 Implications of health care reform.

of managed care organizations after approval of its TennCare plan. With that influx of managed care organizations, hospitals have looked at SNF beds with the idea of decreasing acute care utilization and caring for patients needing less than acute care in a SNF setting. As a result, Tennessee has considered the development of criteria and standards for long-term care hospitals and is studying criteria and standards for subacute providers (Penny L. Personal communication. September 15, 1994). Because Tennessee hospitals have reported receiving less than their costs of providing care under the TennCare program, those hospitals have focused their attention on finding the least costly setting.

The growth in managed care and the assumption of the risk of capitated payments by providers under many state health care reform proposals will probably fuel the growth of the subacute industry. Such a conclusion is supported by the fact that managed care was the driving force behind the subacute industry during the early 1990s. The cost effectiveness of subacute programs has been well documented. For example, a 1991 study by Kilgore[47] found a 37% lower cost for individuals in subacute facilities than in inpatient facilities. That study concluded that the subacute program was significantly more cost effective in terms of functional gains made per dollar of expenditures. Other data demonstrate that up-

graded SNFs can provide subacute care at an average of two thirds of the cost now charged by hospitals. This could result in a savings of billions of dollars per year to the government and private sector.[47] Because of the lower costs, both providers and purchasers of health care will look to subacute care as the least costly setting for treatment and as a way to reduce lengths of inpatient hospital stays. These concerns will point toward further development of subacute care units to which patients may be transferred from hospital inpatient units.

Health care reform also complements the trend toward nonhospital settings for health care services. For example, the Arizona health care reform proposal includes flexibility on the part of health care policymakers to recommend various licensed health care providers who would be eligible for reimbursement under basic health benefit plans. This policy allows for consideration of all appropriate licensed health care providers to provide the care covered under the basic health benefit plan. Minnesota's concept of the ISN includes strong incentives to contain costs and to deliver high-quality care with the most efficient mix of providers. Thus, although subacute care has not been addressed directly in the reform plans to date, the provisions will complement the trend toward consideration of providing care in nonhospital settings. Cost, however, will not be the only consideration in a managed care environment. Subacute care providers in hospital, SNF, and other settings will need to develop quality of care data to substantiate their claims that they are in a position to provide less costly and high-quality care.

Health care reform initiatives have also resulted in an explosion of collaborative efforts among acute care hospitals, long-term specialty hospitals, freestanding nursing facilities, physicians, and other health care providers. Mergers and other affiliation strategies are at an all time high. Subacute providers must develop strategies to affiliate with these networks. This is particularly true in an era of reform in which joint venture opportunities and other affiliation strategies have proliferated. These efforts will point toward the development of subacute care facilities or units as a way to provide the full continuum of care in a lower-cost setting sought by managed care organizations and other insurers. The future success of subacute care will depend, to a large extent, on the ability of subacute providers to affiliate with and become an essential component of integrated delivery systems.

In addition to creating opportunities for collaboration between the long-term care and the hospital industries, the restructuring of the health care industry as a result of state health care reform will create conflicts. Hospitals and SNFs, for example, will compete for patients. These facilities will debate issues such as the appropriate site of care, reimbursement, and regulatory issues. In addition, SNFs will compete with home health care providers at a time when policy-makers, insurers, and patients emphasize the desire to provide care at the community level and even within homes. In essence, subacute providers will need to develop strategies for survival and success in a highly competitive market.

Key issues that must be addressed and monitored at the state level by subacute care providers include: sufficient reimbursement for subacute care, barriers that affect subacute care such as CON and licensure issues, and long-term care reform. In addition, the development of quality of care and cost of care data will be critical.

CONCLUSION

States are continuing to move forward with their own health care reform initiatives. Those initiatives have included proposals based on various approaches to health care reform. Those states that have adopted health care reform proposals will serve as models for other states and the nation as a whole. State health care reform initiatives to date have not addressed directly the role of subacute care providers. As a result, subacute care providers will need to monitor closely the impact of state health care reform plans on the subacute industry. They will also need to define their role clearly in an era of health care reform, including the inclusion of their services in comprehensive benefit packages and the inclusion of their sites as appropriate sites of care. To accomplish this, subacute care providers will need to convince policymakers that they are both cost efficient and capable of providing high-quality care in new settings.

REFERENCES

1. KPMG Peat Marwick. State Healthcare Reform Initiatives. *Update: Healthcare.* Feb. 1994: 9.
2. Agency for Health Care Administration (AHCA). *A Blueprint for Health Security, Interim Florida Health Plan.* Tallahassee, Fla: AHCA; 1992.
3. Families USA Foundation. *Half of Us: Families Priced Out of Health Protection.* Washington, DC: Families USA Foundation; 1993.
4. Himmelstein D, Woolhandler S, Lewontin J, Tang T, and Wolfe S. The growing epidemic of uninsurance: New data on the health insurance coverage of Americans. *Cent Nat Health Program Stud.* 1992: 1–6.
5. Vermont Health Care Authority. *Health Resource Management Plan 1993–1996.* Montpelier, Vt: Vermont Health Care Authority; 1993.
6. White House Health Care Task Force. *Health Care Talking Points.* Washington, DC: Congress of the United States House of Representatives; 1993.

7. Maryland Health Resources Planning Commission. *Summary—Survey of Health Care Reform: 50 States and Washington, DC.* Baltimore, Md: Maryland Health Resources Planning Commission; 1993.

8. Enthoven A. Managed competition: An agenda for action. *Health Affairs.* Summer 1988: 25–47.

9. Enthoven A, and Kronick R. Universal health insurance through incentives reform. *JAMA.* 1991; 265: 2532–2536.

10. The Jackson Hole Group. *The 21st Century American Health System: Managed Competition.* Teton Village, Wyo: The Jackson Hole Group; unpublished.

11. Pettey S, and McGillan P. Long-term care legislative and regulatory update. Presented at the National Health Lawyers Association 1992 Conference on Long-Term Care and the Law; February 12–14, 1992. Las Vegas, Nev.

12. Davidoff D, and Pyenson B. *Actuarial Issues in Play-or-Pay. Research Report.* New York, NY: Milliman & Robertson; 1992.

13. Garland M. Rationing in public. Oregon's priority-setting methodology. In: Strosberg M, Wiener J, Baker R, and Fein I, eds. *Rationing America's Medical Care. The Oregon Plan and Beyond.* Washington, DC: Brookings Institution; 1992:37.

14. Bureau of National Affairs. Senate passes bill to permit medical savings account. *Health Law Rep.* March 3, 1994;3:277–278.

15. Office of Technology Assessment. *An Inconsistent Picture: A Compilation of Analyses of Economic Impacts of Competing Approaches to Health Care Reform by Experts and Stakeholders.* Washington, DC: Government Printing Office; 1993. Office of Technology Assessment Rep No OTA-H-540.

16. Shapiro J. Real health care fixes. *US News & World Rep.* August 26–September 2, 1991: 35, 37.

17. Eckholm E. Late starter in Medicaid, Arizona shows the way. *New York Times.* August 7, 1991: A1, A6.

18. Arizona Health Care Cost Containment System (AHCCCS). *Overview. The Arizona Health Care Cost Containment System: Arizona's Health Care Program for the Indigent.* Phoenix, Ariz: AHCCCS; 1993.

19. Azevedo D. No kidding—There's a state where doctors like Medicaid. *Med Econ* December 21, 1992: 126, 130.

20. Arizona State Senate Staff. *Final Revised Fact Sheet for SB 1109.* Phoenix, Ariz: Arizona State Senate; 1993.

21. Sybinsky P. Briefing on Hawaii's health care center. Presented at the First Annual Convention of the International Subacute Healthcare Association, March 2–4, 1994; Atlanta, Ga.

22. Maryland House of Delegates, Committee on Economic Matters. *House Bill 1359. Health Care and Insurance Reform.* Annapolis, Md: Maryland House of Delegates; 1993.

23. Bureau of National Affairs. State commission proposes package of benefits to be offered to small plans. *Health Law Rep.* December 16, 1993;2:1657–1658.

24. Minnesota Department of Health. Report from the Commissioner of Health to the Legislature and the Governor. Implementation Plan and Recommendations for Integrated Service Network (ISNs) and a Regulated All-Payer Option (RAPO). Minneapolis, Minn: Minnesota Department of Health; 1994.

25. Minnesota Hospital Association. *1993 MinnesotaCare Act.* Minneapolis, Minn: Minnesota Hospital Association; 1993.

26. Clark W, and Rhodes R. State reforms in long-term care: Budgets, waivers, and state initiatives as catalysts. *Long-Term Home Health Care.* 1994;13:17,22.

27. Association of Voluntary Hospitals of Florida. *CHPAs: Florida's Prescription for Health Care Reform.* Tallahassee, Fla: Association of Voluntary Hospitals of Florida; 1993.

28. Agency for Health Care Administration (AHCA). *The Florida Health Security Plan, Healthy Homes 1994.* Tallahassee, Fla: AHCA; 1993.

29. Association of Voluntary Hospitals of Florida. *Legislative pulse.* Tallahassee, Fla: Association of Voluntary Hospitals of Florida; 1994.

30. Oregon Department of Human Resources, Office of Medical Assistance Program. *The Oregon Health Plan.* Salem, Ore: Oregon Department of Human Resources; 1993.

31. Bureau of National Affairs. HHS approves Oregon's Medicaid waiver request with conditions. *Health Law Rep.* March 25, 1993;2:355–356.

32. Roeder K. Tennessee's "TennCare" program approved, aims to restructure delivery of Medicaid services. *GA Hosp Today.* 1994;38:3.

33. State of Tennessee. *TennCare: A New Direction in Health Care, Application for Medicaid Waiver to US Department of Health and Human Services.* Nashville, Tenn: State of Tennessee; 1993.

34. National Health Lawyers Association. Tennessee wins approval for Medicaid overhaul. *Health Lawyers News Rep.* 1993;21:3.

35. Bureau of National Affairs. Managed care Medicaid program goes into effect in Tennessee. *Health Law Rep.* January 13, 1994;3:49.

36. Office of Governor Ned McWherter. *A New Direction in Health Care—TennCare.* Nashville, Tenn: Office of Governor Ned McWherter;1993.

37. Vermont Health Care Authority. *Act 160—Vermont's Plan for Health Reform: What It Means for You.* Montpelier, Vt: Vermont Health Care Authority;1993.

38. Vermont Health Care Authority. *Single-Payer and Multiple-Payer Plans: Putting the Pieces Together.* Montpelier, Vt: Vermont Health Care Authority;1993.

39. Bureau of National Affairs. Blueprint to provide universal access unveiled by state health care authority. *Health Law Rep.* September 30, 1993;2:1305–1306.

40. Ladenheim K, Lipson L, Markus A. *Health Care Reform: 50 State Profiles.* Washington, DC: Intergovernmental Health Policy Project, The George Washington University; 1994:50.

41. Committee for Affordable Health Care. *Straight Talk about Washington's Health Care Reform Law.* Seattle, Wash: Committee for Affordable Health Care;1994.

42. Ernst & Young. *State Health Care Reform. Not Waiting for Washington.* Washington, DC: Ernst & Young;1994.

43. For the record. *Mod Healthcare.* February 7, 1994:14–26.

44. Folkemer D. *Long-Term Care: An Overview of 1993 State Legislature Activity.* Washington, DC: Intergovernmental Health Policy Project, The George Washington University;1994.

45. 210 Illinois Compiled Statutes §3/1 (1992).

46. American Health Care Association (AHCA). *State Subacute Care Developments.* Washington, DC: AHCA; 1993.

47. Willging P. Medicare program changes and reductions in skilled nursing facilities' routine cost limits under the health security act. *Testimony before the US House Committee on Ways and Means Subcommittee on Health.* Washington, DC: 103rd Congress, first session; November 23,1993.

Appendix 21A

Survey of Health Care Reform by States: Summary

COVERAGE

Universal	Small Group	Children	Uninsured	Medicaid	Pregnant Women	Rural or Underserved	Elderly	High Risk
Alaska	Alaska	Alaska	Arizona	Arizona	Alaska	Alaska	Connecticut (also disabled)	Alaska
Arizona (except Medicare and Medicaid)	Arizona	Arizona	Connecticut	Arkansas	Arizona	Arizona	Indiana	Indiana
California	California	Arkansas	Florida	District of Columbia	Connecticut	Florida	Maryland	Minnesota
Colorado (<65)	Colorado	Colorado	Georgia	Florida	Indiana	Massachusetts	New Hampshire	Oregon
Delaware	Connecticut	Connecticut	Indiana	Indiana	Kansas	Minnesota	North Carolina (also blind, disabled)	West Virginia
Florida	Florida	Delaware	Iowa	Maine	Maine	Nebraska	West Virginia	
Hawaii	Iowa	Florida	Kansas (uninsurable)	Maryland	Maryland	North Carolina	Wisconsin (also disabled)	
Idaho	Kansas	Illinois	Louisiana	Minnesota	Minnesota	North Dakota		
Kentucky	Louisiana	Indiana	Massachusetts	Mississippi	New Hampshire	Pennsylvania		
Louisiana	Maryland	Kansas	Minnesota	Montana	Oklahoma	South Dakota		
Maine	Massachusetts	Louisiana	Mississippi (uninsurable)	New Jersey	Rhode Island	Texas		
Maryland	Minnesota	Maine	Nebraska	Rhode Island	South Carolina			
Massachusetts	Montana	Maryland	New Jersey	South Carolina	Texas			
Minnesota	Nebraska	Massachusetts	New York	Tennessee	West Virginia			
Missouri	Nevada	Michigan	Oklahoma (uninsurable)	Washington				
Montana	New York	Minnesota	South Carolina	West Virginia				
New Jersey	North Carolina	New Hampshire	Tennessee	Wyoming				
New Mexico	Ohio	New Jersey	Texas (underinsured)					
North Carolina	Oklahoma	New York	Utah					
Texas	Oregon	North Carolina	West Virginia (uninsurable)					
Vermont	South Dakota	Oklahoma						
Washington	Tennessee	Pennsylvania						
West Virginia	Texas	Rhode Island						
	Virginia	South Carolina						
		Texas						
		West Virginia						

BENEFITS

Prevention	Primary Care	Acute Care	Long-Term Care	Catastrophic
Alaska	Alaska	Alaska	Alaska	Arizona
Arizona	Arizona	Arizona	Delaware	Indiana (critical care, Medicaid only)
Arkansas	Arkansas	Arkansas	Florida (home health, SNF: 100 days)	Kentucky
California	California	California	Idaho (home health)	Missouri
Connecticut	Connecticut	Connecticut	Indiana	Nebraska
Delaware	Delaware	Delaware	Kentucky	Nevada
District of Columbia	District of Columbia	Florida	Missouri	Oklahoma
Florida	Florida	Georgia	Nevada	Oregon
Georgia	Georgia	Hawaii	New Hampshire	
Hawaii	Hawaii	Idaho	Oklahoma	
Idaho	Idaho	Illinois	Oregon	
Illinois	Illinois	Indiana	Texas (home health, rehabilitation, hospice, long-term care)	
Indiana	Indiana	Iowa	Vermont	
Iowa	Iowa	Kansas	Washington	
Kansas	Kansas	Kentucky	West Virginia	
Kentucky	Kentucky	Louisiana		
Louisiana	Louisiana	Maine		
Maine	Maine	Massachusetts		
Massachusetts	Massachusetts	Michigan		
Michigan	Michigan	Minnesota		
Minnesota	Minnesota	Mississippi		
Missouri	Mississippi	Missouri		
Nebraska	Missouri	Nebraska		
Nevada	Montana	Nevada		
New Hampshire	Nebraska	New York		
New Jersey	Nevada	North Carolina		
New York	New Hampshire	Oklahoma		
North Carolina	New Jersey	Oregon		
Oklahoma	New Mexico	Pennsylvania		
Oregon	New York	South Carolina		
Pennsylvania	North Carolina	Texas		
South Carolina	Oklahoma	Washington		
Texas	Oregon	West Virginia		
Vermont	Pennsylvania			
Washington	South Carolina			
West Virginia	Tennessee			
	Texas			
	Vermont			
	Washington			
	West Virginia			

continues

Source: Data from *Survey of Health Care Reform: 50 States and Washington, D.C.* by the Maryland Health Resources Planning Commission, July 1993.

Appendix 21A continued

COST CONTAINMENT

Standardized Forms	Managed Care	Utilization Review	Global Budgeting/ Expenditure Targets	Insurance Reform	CON	Other
Alaska	Alaska	Alaska	Alaska (expenditure limits)	Alaska	Alaska	Arizona (capitated total)
Arizona	Arizona	Arizona	Idaho (expenditure limits as needed)	Arizona	District of Columbia	California (overall budget, competition)
Arkansas	Arkansas	Arkansas	Kentucky (expenditure targets, global budgeting)	California	Maine	Delaware (competition)
California	California	Connecticut	Minnesota	Colorado	Nebraska	Florida (price controls, volume discounting)
Colorado	Connecticut	Kansas	Missouri	Connecticut	New Hampshire	Indiana (volume discounts)
Connecticut	Delaware	Maryland	Montana (global budget, expenditure caps)	Delaware	North Carolina	Iowa (Medicaid reduction)
Georgia	District of Columbia	Nebraska	Nebraska	Florida	Pennsylvania	Louisiana (limits on referrals)
Kentucky	Florida	North Carolina	Nevada	Georgia	South Carolina	Maine (competitive bids, limit on administrative costs)
Louisiana	Georgia	Oklahoma	New Mexico	Hawaii	Tennessee	Maryland (physician fee schedules, referrals)
Maine	Hawaii	Oregon	North Carolina	Kansas	Virginia	Massachusetts (facility conversion)
Maryland	Illinois	South Dakota	Tennessee (spending targets)	Louisiana	West Virginia	Minnesota (major medical equipment, limits on provider payments, limits on referrals, competition, all-payer system, technology controls)
Minnesota	Indiana	Tennessee	Texas (expenditure limits)	Massachusetts	Wisconsin	Mississippi (reduction in bad debt, charity care costs)
Nebraska	Louisiana	Texas	Vermont (global budgeting)	Minnesota		Missouri (disclosure of costs, rate setting)
Nevada	Massachusetts		West Virginia	Nebraska		Nebraska (indexing, rate setting)
North Carolina	Minnesota			New Jersey		Nevada (hospital rate setting)
Oklahoma	Nebraska			New York		New Jersey (market forces, diagnosis-related group limits)
South Dakota	Nevada			Ohio		New York (reduction in bad debt, charity care costs)
Tennessee	New Jersey			Oklahoma		North Carolina (managed competition)
Texas	North Carolina			Oregon		North Dakota (rate setting)
Virginia	Oklahoma			South Dakota		Ohio (limits on referrals)
Washington	Pennsylvania			Tennessee		South Dakota (moratorium, single survey, generic drugs)
	South Dakota			Vermont		Tennessee (limits on referrals, reduced competition)
	Tennessee			Washington		Texas (limit on administrative costs, negotiation of uniform rates, limits on referrals)
	West Virginia					West Virginia (rate setting, standards for referrals)
						Wisconsin (alternative care)

FINANCING

Redistribution of Public Funds	Insurance Reform	Pools	Taxes	Waivers	Savings	Other
Alaska	Alaska	Alaska	Alaska	Alaska	Alaska	Arizona (tax credits)
Arizona	Arizona	California	Colorado	Arkansas	Indiana	California (HIPCs)
Connecticut	California	Colorado	Delaware	Colorado	Kentucky	Maine (revision of tax plans)
Delaware	Connecticut	Connecticut	Florida	Connecticut	Louisiana	Oklahoma (user fees, medical trusts)
District of Columbia	Delaware	Florida	Idaho	Florida	Minnesota	Texas (charity care by hospitals)
Florida	Florida	Idaho	Illinois	Hawaii	Nebraska	Virginia (trust fund)
Illinois	Georgia	Indiana	Kentucky	Indiana	Oregon	Robert Wood Johnson Foundation grant:
Indiana	Hawaii	Iowa	Minnesota	Kentucky	West Virginia	Arkansas
Kansas	Iowa	Kansas	Missouri	Minnesota		Colorado
Massachusetts	Kansas	Massachusetts	Nebraska	Mississippi		Florida
Missouri	Louisiana	Mississippi	Nevada	Nebraska		Iowa
Montana	Maine	Montana	North Carolina	Nevada		Minnesota
Nevada	Maryland	Nevada	Washington	New Mexico		New Mexico
North Carolina	Massachusetts	New York		North Carolina		New York
North Dakota	Minnesota	North Carolina		Oregon		North Dakota
Oklahoma	Missouri	Oklahoma		South Carolina		Oklahoma
Oregon	Nebraska	Oregon		Tennessee		Oregon
Pennsylvania	Nevada	Tennessee		Texas		Vermont
South Carolina	New Jersey	Utah		West Virginia		Washington
South Dakota	New Mexico	Vermont				
Texas	New York					
Utah	North Carolina					
West Virginia	North Dakota					
	Ohio					
	Oklahoma					
	Oregon					
	Pennsylvania					
	Rhode Island					
	South Dakota					
	Tennessee					
	Texas					
	Vermont					
	Washington					
	West Virginia					
	Wisconsin					
	Wyoming					

continues

Source: Data from *Survey of Health Care Reform: 50 States and Washington, D.C.,* by the Maryland Health Resources Planning Commission, July 1993.

Appendix 21A continued

QUALITY ASSURANCE

Practice Guidelines	Data	Malpractice Reform
Arizona	Arizona	Alaska
Arkansas	California	Arizona
Connecticut	District of Columbia	Delaware
Delaware	Florida	Indiana
Florida	Indiana	Kentucky
Idaho	Kentucky	Maine
Indiana	Maine	Minnesota
Kentucky	Minnesota	Nebraska
Maine	Missouri	Nevada
Minnesota	Nebraska	Oklahoma
Nebraska	Nevada	Texas
Nevada	North Carolina	Vermont
North Carolina	Ohio	West Virginia
Oregon	Oklahoma	
Texas	South Dakota	
West Virginia	Texas	
	Vermont	
	Virginia	
	West Virginia	

Source: Data from *Survey of Health Care Reform: 50 States and Washington, D.C.,* by the Maryland Health Resources Planning Commission, July 1993.

Index

Note: Tables are designated by a "t," exhibits by an "E," and appendices by an "A." Figures are italicized.

About the Author/Editor

Kathleen M. Griffin, PhD, is President and Chief Executive Officer (CEO) of Griffin Management, Inc., in Scottsdale, Arizona, a full service consulting firm specializing in implementation of provider and integrated networks, managed care, subacute care, and rehabilitation. Griffin Management, Inc., has conducted market assessments and situational audits for numerous health care institutions and systems, and has assisted them in developing the essential components of their integrated systems to prepare operations for managed care contracting and capitation. Prior to founding the firm in 1992, Dr Griffin was President and CEO of American Transitional Hospitals, Inc., where she created the nation's first transitional hospital as well as the model for subacute care units in nursing facilities and hospitals. Prior positions include President and Chief Operating Officer, Rebound, Inc., Henderson, Tennessee; Executive Vice President/CEO of the American College of Health Care Administrators; and Deputy Executive Director of the American Speech-Language-Hearing Association in Washington, DC.

Dr Griffin is the author of numerous articles in professional publications on the subacute industry, managed care, rehabilitation, and health care system integration. She has been quoted frequently in such publications as *Hospitals and Health Networks*, *Modern Healthcare*, *Provider*, *Contemporary Long-Term Care*, *Hospital Purchasing News*, and *Continuing Care*.

In 1993, Dr Griffin founded the International Subacute Healthcare Association, the national trade association for the subacute industry, which includes providers, payers, and suppliers to the industry. Currently, she serves as Past Chairman of the Board and is a member of the Executive Committee.

Dr Griffin received her PhD from the University of Oregon; MA from Stanford University; and BS from the University of Wisconsin–Madison. She continued her graduate studies in finance, marketing, and management through courses offered by the Wharton School of Business, University of Maryland, and US Department of Agriculture Graduate School.